Share Attack

Share Attack

80 great tips
to survive and thrive
as a trader

Malcolm Stacey

Hh

HARRIMAN HOUSE LTD

18 College Street

Petersfield

Hampshire

GU31 4AD

GREAT BRITAIN

Tel: +44 (0)1730 233870

Email: contact@harriman-house.com

Website: www.harriman-house.com

First published in Great Britain in 2015

Copyright © Malcolm Stacey

Paperback ISBN: 9780857194190

eBook ISBN: 9780857194961

British Library Cataloguing in Publication Data

A CIP catalogue record for this book can be obtained from the British Library.

 Harriman House

*For Jo, Eleri, Robin
and Jack*

Disclaimer

This book is intended for those interested in trading in the stock market. You should be aware that shares can go up or down in value. You may not get back what you put in.

Not everyone succeeds with shares and no one can promise to make you successful. The author and the publisher accept no legal responsibilities for the contents of this work.

This is not a definitive exposition of share trading. You are strongly advised to seek professional advice before trading. Conditions in financial markets forever fluctuate and evolve, and what worked in the past is not guaranteed to work in the future.

About the Author

Malcolm Stacey was for 30 years among the BBC's most experienced investigative reporters, specialising in business. He produced and reported for Roger Cook's *Checkpoint* and *You and Yours*. After reinventing himself as a private share trader, he has written two previous books on making big money from shares. He has continued to follow his own tips and hints, gleaned from some of the top financial minds in the country – including well-known City luminaries he met in the course of making 8,000 television and radio programmes.

Malcolm is also an experienced tutor, having presented BBC Schools TV and worked with the Broadcasting Corporation's training department.

Preface

Many books about shares pursue just one system, one strategy, one method. There may be variations to the grand plan, but it is still only a single methodology.

Relax. You won't be burdened with following a single master blueprint in this book. I don't think that's the best way, because if you follow just one method, you won't have the opportunity to pick 'n' mix from hundreds of other brilliant wheezes.

While working in financial investigative departments of the BBC, I chatted to hundreds of politicians, tycoons and entrepreneurs with experience and influence in the financial world. From them I collected a cornucopia of imaginative ways to win with shares.

Since leaving the corporation to make a new career as an armchair share trader, I have test-driven many of these tips, seeking to find out which of them are the most successful. Many are included in this book for the first time. I also include a number of my earlier ideas, which have been brought bang up to date. Within these pages you'll find a number of potent ways to milk the share market. Putting them together could make you rich.

Whether you're a complete beginner or already an experienced trader, you'll find hundreds of useful tricks and techniques. You'll also hopefully be entertained along the way, as I share some humorous anecdotes from down the years.

This book is divided into two main parts. In the first, I will put you in the right frame of mind to trade shares successfully. I'll then move on to reveal 60 of my favourite systems for making big money from shares. You'll learn what to do and when to do it. And more importantly how to avoid costly mistakes.

Your thrilling journey to trading success begins here.

Contents

Introduction

GO ON. YOU KNOW YOU WANT TO. SO JUST ADMIT it.

You'd love to make loads more money buying and selling shares. If you already own a few shares, you yearn to hold more. And if you already trade shares, you'd like to chuck in the day job and trade full-time.

You ache to hold a phone in each hand at parties and shout into one "Sell Black Stuff Oil!" and yell into the other "Buy Ice Cream Holdings!" Then turn to fellow guests and casually announce: "I've just made five thousand pounds."

You crave a halt to the dreary commute to work. You'd rather slob around the house in old clothes. You want to break off from a bit of light trading now and then to swing in a hammock, smell the honeysuckle, study Proust, learn Walloon, or watch more telly.

You need to be rid of the boss on your back, the boredom of being nice to colleagues you don't like, the clock-watching and the stressful avoidance of work. Above all, you hanker after real wealth. To be well and truly rolling in it.

Freedom to go your own way and plenty of legal tender to do it with. How does that sound? Marvellous? Enchanting? Ravishing?

But is it that easy? Yes!

I've been trading shares since my blind date with Boadicea. And I can tell you that being old isn't much fun. For some bizarre reason God plucks hair from our heads and sticks it in our ears. Still, longevity has a great advantage in the golden game of share trading. It's called experience.

When I first took an interest in shares it was the eighties, and you couldn't trade except through a broker. And this stuffy bunch wouldn't even look at you unless you were already rich. Furthermore, they usually chose the bunnies you invested in. And you couldn't really dig in and out of the markets anyway, because long phone calls and longer expenses were involved.

Then in October 1986 Big Bang came to the City. From that point anyone could dabble in shares in his or her own right. That's when I began buying shares. I have not let my old peepers stray off the markets since.

So unlike most writers on shares, I have hangar-loads of hard-knock, bashed-on-the-head, climbing the walls experience. I'll share it all with you in this book.

Journey to the Centre of the Earth's Wealth

WHY YOU SHOULD SHIFT SHARES

YOU DON'T BELIEVE TRADING SHARES CAN MAKE you rich? That only happens in trashy novels? No.

Do you know how many share trades are made in the world? The answer is a mind-wrenching two million every second! Thomson Reuters, the financial information people, tells us that ten years ago it was only 20,000 trades a second. So share trading is becoming more popular all the time. If it were not profitable, would this massive gold rush continue?

People who've invested a few thousand in one company *have* become millionaires. Sometimes a lot wealthier than that. The world's richest man, the USA's Warren Buffett, did it all with shares. They say he's sitting on 66 billion dollars. It's thought he makes 37 million greenbacks a day. Yes, every day.

My personal best was Overnet Data Ltd., a small British company which became a 200-bagger. That means the share grew in value by 200 times. Golly! And the story behind its change of fortune is the sort of event in Shareland which can transform your life just as much as any big pools win.

Overnet Data was not doing particularly well as an internet company. But a totally different kind of enterprise coveted a listing on the London Stock Exchange. So it bought out Overnet Data as a cheap and easy way to join the club. The invader was FuturaGene. Their business was modifying seeds to produce more food in deserts or salty land.

The City warmed to this useful venture and the shares rocketed. Sadly, I did not invest in this dream firm when the share was at its cheapest and – being a nervous soul – I sold out before it reached its high point. I only invested £300… but I realised a gain of £23,000. If I'd put £10,000 in at the lowest point, I would have pocketed two million pounds!

Very few shares yield such a fabled return. But some companies do, like Microsoft, Apple, Google, Facebook and Twitter. They all began as tiny operations.

Taking an example from September 2013, shares in Sable Mining, which operates on the borders of Guinea and Liberia, rose nearly 300% in a very short space of time. See the chart below. So big windfalls can and do happen.

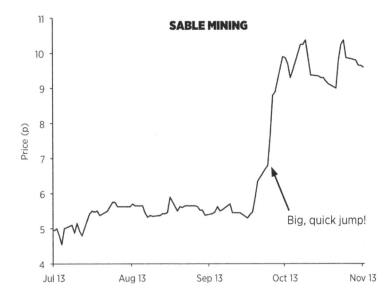

The shares of Sable Mining have since fallen back, but my point was to illustrate to you what's possible with share trading. It's really the best place to put your money if you want big returns over the long term.

Ok, you're not a fool. You know this book cannot guarantee instant wealth. Disaster might strike. We may be bowled out by a truculent asteroid the size of Mars. A global economic disaster could plunge all shares into a dark hole. There might be a third world war. Or you could just choose the wrong shares at the worst possible time.

But the truth is that eye-watering disaster is uncommon and often equities recover anyway. So if you have cash sitting around, you ought to be putting it to work in the stock market, or shifting shares as I like to put it.

CHALLENGE EXPERT ADVICE

You've decided to trade in shares. Good move. Your next step will be to look for guidance on how to be successful. One thing's for sure, you won't be short of experts willing to share their views. But you need to watch out, as a lot of what they say tends towards the asinine.

For instance, some commentators give you stunning hints, such as: "Always know when to sell your shares." Really? And when is that, then? It's the most difficult decision in share trading and it deserves proper answers.

I've even seen: "Only buy shares which have a good chance of returning capital growth." By capital growth they mean "the share price will go up." Fine – only buy shares which will rise. Suits me. But how do you do that exactly? Keep reading.

Another gobbet of naff advice they give on financial websites is "Match your trading style to your lifestyle." Well, apart from my loathing of that depressing expression "lifestyle," what's that all about? My mode of living requires buckets of money. While my trading style will be the best available to make the most dosh from my shares.

My trading style will also adapt as companies and the financial markets change. My trading style will therefore have nothing to do with whether I enjoy making jam, playing poker, weaving floral tapestries or going to bed early. So there!

I don't let articles, speeches, blogs or anything else said or written about shares sway me, unless the arguments are top-notch. Economists are notorious for reaching widely different conclusions on the same set of facts. When ASOS, the online fashion outlet, had a warehouse fire, a writer I really respect said "sell the shares." He believed customers would go elsewhere while the firm was off the air. Conversely, another pundit said "buy the shares," because the stock would be insured.

If you had read only one contributor you would have either grabbed the shares or sold them, depending on who you'd read. But I was aware of the views of both authors and decided that their arguments cancelled each other out. So I decided that the company was of no interest to me.

Don't get me wrong, you've got to read all you can on a share before you buy it. Just don't take the first 'expert' view you find, as the next person could say the opposite.

YOU NEEDN'T BE A FINANCIAL PRODIGY

When I was just beginning life as a private share trader, I bought a highly-praised book to help me out. It was chock-full of technical terms and formulas. At that early stage in my career, I didn't understand much of it. I'm not sure I'm entirely clear about the contents now.

The author of this most learned and technical work later confided to journalists that his personal portfolio wasn't performing much better than average.

Why wasn't I surprised?

The jargon, the complicated sums, the equations and the drawing of pretty patterns on graphs… it's all a bit much. It confuses the issue and I wonder if it is really worth the effort? The truth is you don't need to master all manner of arcane techniques to be a share trader, so don't be put off for that reason.

THE SEDUCTION OF SHARES

You will never be bored with shares, but you mustn't become addicted. Just stay very enthusiastic. Maybe you'll return to your computer every hour or so. You may even grow to dislike bank holidays, with no London markets open to get your juices going.

But if you value your time, or are stuck at work anyway, there's no need to hover over your screen like a jittery hummingbird. My guests are often surprised that I'm not at my trading station (a tatty Victorian armchair with a battered laptop) all day long.

It's not necessary to spend all day staring at price movements. In fact, you need only check your shares once in the morning and just once more near the afternoon's market close. Except maybe when there's a frenzy of action over a particular share. If you are driven to review your holdings every hour or so, that's when overtrading and mistakes creep in. Keep calm, be disciplined and enjoy shares.

WHY SHARE PRICES EBB AND FLOW

Allow me to explain why share prices fluctuate. It's simple. Prices climb when more traders want to buy 'em than sell 'em. It's our old friend supply and demand. When demand falls, so do prices and vice versa. (Occasionally a share price will stumble when there are more buyers on the day than sellers. This is because of various minor, but complicated, forces which needn't trouble us here.)

Once you understand that supply and demand is at work, you will see how the big secret of making money is to see further into the future than all the other traders. You are really locked in a tussle with rivals.

RISE OF THE MACHINES

Don't underestimate your opponents, especially the pros. Some of them use advanced computer software to carry out their trading automatically. They're called *black boxes*. Investment strategies, algorithms and formulae are woven into them. When a share price changes, these beasts buy or sell automatically. The trades are almost instant and there can be many black boxes working at the same time.

It's even been calculated that a fraction of a second's advantage can inject an extra 100 million dollars a year into some hedge funds. Robert Harris wrote a cracking thriller called *The Fear Index* about the use of similar machines and the dramatic effect they have on the way shares charge up and down.

But never fear. As we'll see, investing strategies are not always reliable. And being human, you have so much more flexibility than a silly old machine. For example, once the computers start selling for a fairly trivial reason, they trigger more mechanical monkeys. We get a rapid downward spiral in a particular share price. This makes the shares extremely cheap and this creates a buying opportunity at a bargain price.

RISK IT FOR A BISCUIT

There is a rather inconvenient component to share shifting to be discussed now. It's the concept of risk. I can already feel you twitching. The word should not scare you. We'll discuss some fine ways of reducing it later, but first I have to tell you that you can't expect to make big money without it.

In fact, the more you're prepared to risk, the yummier your profits will be. Take a look at the following chart. Here you can see the historic returns of three asset classes – cash, bonds and shares – after inflation is taken into account over a period of 41 years. Cash is often considered to be risk free and look at the returns it's delivered – very poor over the long term. In the middle we have bonds, with moderate risk, delivering medium returns. And then come shares. The riskiest investment of the three, but over the long term their average returns of 5.1% a year outstrip all other assets.

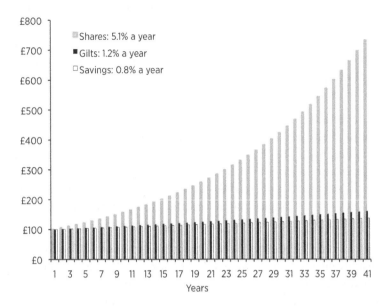

KEEP FANTASY PORTFOLIOS A FANTASY

Many 'experts' on share trading urge newbies to start with a fantasy portfolio.

This is how it works: you pick a few shares, but don't actually put any money down. Then you're supposed to monitor your share choices over the next six months to see how they go. The idea is to give you a bit of trading experience before you take the plunge with your real money.

Most brokers offer you these imaginary portfolio facilities. Their websites will still add up your gains or losses in the usual way, it's just that if your shares do energise, you won't see any improvement in your bank account.

Well, I can't see the point of fantasy portfolios. For one thing, there is no imperative to research the shares you fancy in any depth. While if your shares do well, you'll be lulled into a false sense of security. When the time comes to put in some real money, you might not look hard enough before you leap.

Also, without putting your money where your mouth is, you'll not reap the benefit of any beginner's luck. You might scoff at this concept, but I've seen starters do extremely well in their first few months. I began by doubling my money in two weeks back in the days when share certificates were in Latin. I've no proof that investors do well with their initial few trades, but I'm convinced it happens.

It might be related to the confidence of youth. When we first start out on life's rocky road, we expect to win, so we do. A self-fulfilling prophesy, you see. New traders might also be more alert than experienced dealers, who've become jaded. Or perhaps a newbie to the stock exchange is more fearful – because he or she is trading with the unknown. This might bring more effort and performance-boosting adrenalin into the task of choosing your first shares.

Any road up, beginner's luck exists. But if we're not playing for real, that joyous advantage is wasted. If your fake portfolio is showing you a winning profit of £2,000 and you can't get your hands on it because it was never actually there, how will you feel? Pretty deprived, I would think. And if your fantasy bag is displaying a nasty loss, what then? You might be put off for life, which would be a pity.

Lastly, are you really prepared not to earn anything from your investments for months on end? I say the best thing is to get straight to it. So without further ado, let's get down to it.

Getting Down to It

You'll need some cash to get started

YOU WILL NEED SOME READY CASH. THIS MUST BE your own dosh. Don't even think of borrowing money to do shares.

Mark me well, if you can't afford to lose it all, wait until you can. If you don't have the readies ready, save up. Go without a holiday abroad, a new wide-screen telly, a conservatory, new suit or a bigger car. Buy your clothes from charity shops. I still do. Where else can you buy £400 shoes for a fiver like the ones I'm wearing now?

The only time I borrowed money to buy shares ended in disaster. The overall market was flying and my bank, RBS, was happy to make £20,000 available for any new opportunities that came up. The only snag is that I had to lodge many of my existing shares with the bank as security. Of course, the market fell like a conker in September the minute I did that. And I couldn't get hold of my shares in time to sell them as the bear market took an even stronger hold.

Only trade with your own money, and money you can afford to lose!

Choosing a broker

IT'S NOT POSSIBLE TO CONTACT A PERSON WITH shares to sell or to find a buyer for yours directly, so you need to go via a broker. You could plump for an advisory broker, one who tells you what companies to buy into and when to sell the shares. But if you do that, you don't need this book, because you will lose the complete freedom to pick and choose yourself. How's that for tedium!

So pick an execution-only, internet broker. A quick Google will turn up loads of them. There's Barclays, Halifax, Hargreaves Lansdown, etc., etc. I'll tell you the one I use. It's called Traders Own (www.tradersown.co.uk) and you earn a share in the company each time you buy or sell. At the moment this is not much of an incentive, but it could be more lucrative later on if Traders Own, which is presently a modest setup, suddenly takes off.

It's easy to set up an account with an internet broker, but check the terms and conditions carefully before you do.

Look for brokers who do not levy management charges. Also avoid those with inactivity fees. Yes, it's pretty awful, but some brokers charge extra if you stop trading for a while. They take the cash from your account. You don't want that. Also check that the broker is registered with the FCA (Financial Conduct Authority), Britain's financial governing body. Just because it says so on their website, it doesn't necessarily mean it's true.

I also advise finding a broker who does not charge extra if you phone in with your trade rather than entering it online. There are some occasions when your connection will be down or you don't have your mobile handy to buy or sell your shares online.

And one more thing, I have found one or two brokers keep you waiting till the park bench dries before they answer the phone. They're obviously being miserly

with staff. Such a firm should be treated with the contempt with which it treats its customers – and avoided. You should try a broker out by making an exploratory call before you set up an account. The last thing you want when trying to sell a share fast is to be kept hanging about. It's bad for blood pressure, but worse for your pocket.

Traders Own does not have management or activity fees and it has always answered my phone calls with the speed of light, even at busy periods. Some other brokers I've tried have fallen down on all these counts.

A suggestion for your first trades

ONCE YOU'VE CHOSEN A BROKER AND SET-UP AN account, with a couple of clicks you'll have transferred your cash into your account. Why not start with £1000?

Next, my suggestion for your first trades would be to split your starting cash between three shares. Perhaps put £300 each into two companies of your choice and £400 into a third firm.

The first three hopefuls I bought in this way were Southern Television, Marks & Spencer and HBSC. Marks & Sparks rose by 50%, but it took a number of years. The bank rose consistently by about four times, until it was hit by the big 2008 credit crunch. And the television company was soon involved in a takeover story which turned my £300 into £5000. I told you beginners can be lucky.

The speed at which shares can be bought might rattle you a bit. It's very swift. Once you have clicked to buy a share, the website will give you a countdown, allowing time to change your mind. If you don't confirm the trade with another click during these 10 or 20 seconds, the sale is aborted.

The countdown is more useful than you might think. I've occasionally drawn back at this very advanced stage. It's funny how late some alarm bells can ring.

Don't let 'em get you in the spread

YOU BUY SHARES AT A LITTLE BIT DEARER THAN the sell price – to give the middlemen a commission. This gap between buy and sell prices is known as the spread.

Owing to the spread, you will immediately see a loss in the profit-and-loss column when you first buy a share. This is a skin-prickly time. You automatically think the shares have lost value in a flash. You'll believe you've made a monumental mistake and you're already on the road to ruin. But this isn't so.

The share values shown in your account have simply been adjusted for the initial costs of purchase – the spread, the broker's cut and the stamp duty. If you've bought well, following the lessons in this book, this early 'loss' will soon be ironed out.

The gap can be negligible in the case of huge companies with household names, such as banks or oil giants. The table below gives some examples of tiny spreads.

Company	Spread
Marks & Spencer (retail)	0.02%
BT (communications)	0.02%
HSBC (banking)	0.03%
GlaxoSmithKline (pharmaceuticals)	0.03%
Lloyds Group (banking)	0.03%
Barclays (banking)	0.04%
BP (oil)	0.05%
RBS (banking)	0.05%
Royal Dutch Shell (oil)	0.05%

Yet the spread can be horrendous, especially for some penny share outfits. Here are some companies whose spreads make them unattractive, because you would need a massive share leap just to clear your buying costs and leave you at break-even. This list is just a snapshot I gathered at the time of writing, as spreads can change dramatically on a daily basis.

Company	Spread
Cambria Africa (equity investment)	63%
Regal Petroleum (oil)	58%
Helius Energy (energy)	57%
Pires (real estate investment)	50%
Resource Holdings (media)	37%
Physiomics (healthcare equipment)	30%
TXO (oil producer)	28%
Forte Energy (oil)	28%

The maximum spread I would be prepared to pay is 5% – any more than this and you are carrying a significant loss before you even start.

Is it gambling?

LET'S CONSIDER THIS PHILOSOPHICAL QUESTION, which might be troubling you a little:

Is share trading gambling?

Certainly not!

When you first dip into shares, you'll be irritated by friends and neighbours who accuse you of feckless gambling. But buying shares because you've found good reasons to do so is not making a common wager.

The overriding reason why investment is more respectable than gambling is that we do not pick shares with a pin. We don't arbitrarily choose red or black. We don't select a horse just because it's won a few races in the past. We research our company first, we sound out other traders, we monitor the share price. We do a fistful of other checks.

There are also many more reasons why share trading is not gambling – and is much safer to boot. With horse racing, for example, you cannot ring up your bookie and say "Golden Boy isn't doing too well so far in the 2.30 at Epsom. So can I have most of my money back, please?" No, you are lumbered with a dud nag till the bitter end. With shares, you can call a halt to the race. You can limit your loss by pulling out if the share starts to decay.

Another difference to gambling is that shareholders are not in competition with their brokers. Whereas a bookmaker hopes you lose, the broker wants your share to make you money so that you will sell at the right time and buy different shares, so endowing him with more commission.

Yes, there are some share traders who do gamble. They do not research properly and deliberately take an arbitrary chance on shares which could go either way. Heed my tips and strategies and there's no need to be one of those twits.

I'm not saying that we don't take risks when we trade. There's no getting away from that. But we are cool, responsible, informed and cautious – we don't gamble.

Greed and fear

THERE ARE TWO MIGHTY BUT CONFLICTING FORCES in Shareworld – greed and fear. Greed makes us buy equities and hang on to them. Fear prompts us to sell them. Neither instinct is very attractive, is it? It's not how you'd wish to be remembered, I'm sure. No one would want the epitaph: "She was always greedy and scared to death."

It's because greed and fear make share trading seem sleazy that financial writers rarely mention the two instincts by name. They prefer gentle jargon, like "opportunities" and "corrections". But they're still talking about greed and fear. You need to accept that these two terrifying forces are at the heart of share-picking. Choose to be led by the right emotion at the right time and you will succeed.

THE GREED BREED

We hear about a marvellous company. We're told that the shares will double in less than a month. We don't do any research or make any checks, but we froth at the mouth in anticipation and buy the shares in a hurry.

A former BBC business correspondent I once worked with rang to tell me that his City contacts were convinced that the Bradford & Bingley bank would soon release startlingly good figures. I immediately thought, "These people are at the coalface; they must know something we don't."

I rushed through a large order. Yes, we all know what happened to the Bradford & Bingley now. This little leap in the dark cost me £30,000 and it's an example of negative avarice at work. Not good. But we can still employ greed, the positive kind, by investigating the company properly when you hear a piece of news like this.

Later on, we'll look at scores of ways you can control your initial greed and find shares with a rosy future. But at this early stage we should just note that failing to curb our cruder greedy instincts is to court disaster.

FOILING THE FEAR FACTOR

FEAR STALKS THE SQUARE MILE. IT SUCKS MONEY out of your portfolio like a Dyson in a power surge. We see a share shudder down. We panic and sell it. An hour or so later it is back to its old value and may even have improved since our hurried sale. It was fear which cost me a small fortune with my shares in ASOS.

ASOS began life under the name As Seen on Screen, one of the first companies to sell fashion online. We all buy groovy gear on the net these days, but like Apple and Facebook, ASOS was a pioneer in a little-known field of business which went on to revolutionise the world. I think I paid 5p a share in April 2003. But when the share reached ten times what I paid for it two years later, to the month, I woke up in a cold sweat. My subconscious mind was telling me that this was too good to be true. At crack of dawn, I sold the lot. Big mistake!

I'd let fear block the very reasonable view that the company was making healthy profits and the shares still had a long way to go. They certainly did keep rising, peaking at a marvellous £70.07p each in February 2014 – see the following chart.

Why should I have kept the shares? Because companies which increase their share prices ten-fold might be on the cusp of even more spectacular success. Examples are Microsoft, Apple, Gillette, Google and eBay.

When assailed by cold fear that all the money we've made on a share could be in peril, we should first Google all the latest opinions from City analysts. If the share is currently falling, we should check if they give good reasons for this. If there is no respectable cause, or the reason seems spurious, we have two choices and neither of them is to sell. One is to do nothing, the second is to buy more shares while they seem cheap. More on that later.

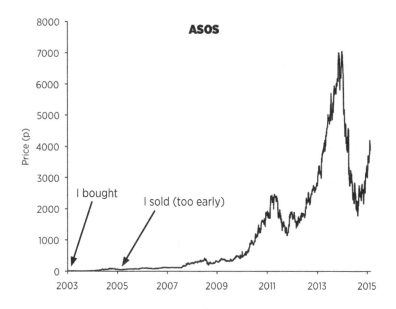

Pop goes the psychology

THERE ARE SOME CITY FOLK WHO'LL TELL YOU THAT success in shares comes from studying the figures. Profit and loss, debt, sales numbers, order books, new contracts, dividends and all that baloney. They make you think qualifications in accountancy are required before you start to trade.

Well, I don't knock those things. I'm sure that taking all those factors into account will not do your trading any harm. But the *fundamentals* as these technicalities are known, are not the most important area of front-room share trading. This golden game is mostly about psychology.

So now I've got you worried, again. Well, let me quickly say that I am talking about pop psychology here – not the serious stuff. I suppose another expression for it might be common sense.

Why do we need this pop psychology? Well, we have to second-guess which way the price of a share is going. If we believe it will move down, we need to drop it. If we take the opposite view, we need to buy. If we don't know what to do, we should follow the Yorkshire Directive:

"When in doubt, do now't."

I'm not a soothsayer. I doubt you are. There is only one other way open to us. We need to work out how other people are likely to treat the situation: how will they think? It doesn't matter what we believe, it's what all the other traders are considering. Where will they shove that share price next? It's not the market that goes up or down. It's the people who populate the market who make it move.

Here are a few ways in which simple psychological analysis can help you buy at an opportune moment:

- **Sell when the sun is out**. That surprised you. It certainly raises a laugh from the stuffier end of the share fraternity. But it works for me. A spell of good weather brings out optimism in traders. It secretly nudges them to buy, so share prices often rise with the sun. And when prices are high, it's selling time. It follows that really dreary weather works the opposite way: a good time to buy.

- **Sell in the run-up to Christmas**. Traders get carried away with festive jollity and feel happier in December. All those office parties fuel the fun. So prices are perky and it's a good time to cash in. You can always buy back the same shares cheaper in January if a hangover sets in.

- You might want to be trading in **overtime during a big sporting event**. If England was to win the World Cup, or a British player triumphs at Wimbledon, shares will rise. No doubt about that. Wait a day till the rises ease back, then sell. And when England are booted out of a competition, you could do a spot of bargain buying.

- **After a bank holiday**, shares sometimes take off. This is due to the fact that the boring period when the markets are closed builds up a wall of gelt behind a kind of dam. Trading which has been held up for a day or two causes a previously pent-up rush of tenners to hit the market hard – and prices soar. Selling is recommended.

How much to trade – safely

IF YOU ARE A NEWBIE TO SHARE SHIFTING – AND
even if you aren't – the biggest worry you face is how much money
you should trade. Let me help you.

Putting up more than you can afford to lose is barmy. We have to
believe that if we lost the whole of our share pot, it would not make
any difference to our lives. We might have to do without an exotic
holiday in the year, but that should be the extent of our guilt, pain
and suffering.

It's worth repeating here that an added cushion to your sense of
security is that very few companies go bust altogether. And for you to
lose the lot, all your choices would have to go belly up. This is about
as likely as being struck by lightning in the Albert Hall.

You're probably not a millionaire, though let's hope you become one.
So I suggest you start small. Then, if you're successful, you'll have
more pounds to play with. It's a lovely feeling, by the way, to speculate
with slews of cash you didn't have when you first started.

If I were on a modest salary, I would not begin with more than
£2,000. And many an ecstatic trader who became wealthy in later
years began with less than that. If you are strapped for funds, you
could just try buying into one company for a few hundred quid. Then
top up with a little more as you save up and have more cash available.

KEEP SOME CASH BACK

Nearly all the money I have for trading is in shares. But even in the
most promising markets, I always retain a bit in cash. We all need
money to live on and if I didn't hold some readies, I would have to
sell shares now and then to give me some cash. By holding a few

pounds in reserve, I am never forced into a sale I don't want to make at a time that isn't right.

It can take all my self-control to avoid spending my remaining cash on shares, especially when I have a few hot tips to try out. But it must be done.

There are those who say you should never plough more than half your total wealth into shares. You wouldn't expect me to agree. I am far too much in love with the golden game. But if you are a more cautious soul, this could be a sound approach for you.

THE 10% IMPERATIVE

It's stupid to leave more than a tenth of your money in any one share. If a company hits the rocks, you need to feel that you still have at least 90% of your mazuma intact. After all, it's fairly easy to come to terms with a 10% loss. You realise that a subsequent rally of just a few percent in your other holdings will make the setback seem pretty insignificant. And of course, any one of your other shares could really hit the big time, making a 10% dip for one of your babies rather trivial.

But if you had say 50% of your money in a share which went supernova, how would you feel then? It would take a lot of sweaty wheeling and trading to bring you back to an even footing.

WATCH THE PROPORTIONS

If you make some good share choices, you may soon find that you have more than 10% of your share wealth in one firm. You might end up with more than a tenth of your lolly in quite a few outfits. This is why.

You start out with a portfolio of £5000 and you like the look of Ice Cream Holdings (ICH), so you put £500 into it. That's the maximum

10% of your portfolio that you'll allow yourself in any one company. There's a very hot summer while a hostile takeover bid looms. The share price rattles up by four times. You now have £2000 worth of shares in ICH. This is more than 10% of your portfolio's value; depending on how your other shares have done, it could be 40% of your portfolio, or more. A red light comes on.

You're now stuck with a dilemma. Two of your fundamental rules contradict each other. You know you should stick with your winning share, but you've pledged that you'll not invest more than a tenth of your assets in one business.

If I were you, I would trim your holding to less than 10% of your share pot in this scenario. After all, a fourfold rise is unusual and might not last. You should take some of the profit while you can, and rebalance your portfolio.

The folly of dumping too many eggs in one basket is illustrated by the big howler I made with BG. This company is not British Gas, which is actually Centrica. Confusing isn't it?

BG and British Gas were one company when British Gas was privatised in 1986. Remember the "Tell Sid" campaign? As the years rolled by the company was split into various parts – BG, National Grid and Centrica, each time giving us new shares in the new brand.

As it seemed a reliable investment, I never paid it the same attention as the rest of my bag. Till one day I realised I was sitting on a bonanza that was a third of the valuation of my entire share collection. As the share kept rising, I broke my own rule and didn't rebalance the holding to 10%.

What a mistake. BG fell mightily when reserves were not as high as expected in 2013 and again when the price of crude was halved in 2014. If I had pruned my BG shares to just 10% of my portfolio, I would now be a lot richer. There's a chart of BG below and you can see the price drops I am referring to.

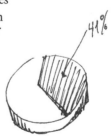

So, when one of your holdings exceeds a tenth of your total portfolio, peddle some shares quickly, before things get out of hand.

Now say after me, please – "No more than 10% in any one company!" And never forget it.

Be a chirpy contrarian

MOO! THERE IS A HERD MENTALITY IN SHARE trading. It's strong and it's everywhere. It's why the stock market puts on a spurt and then continues to rise, or when it falls a few points, it picks up speed and continues in that direction. Nobody likes to take the opposite path once the ball is rolling. Like teenagers, traders don't want to seem different.

It was because I spotted on the net that Lloyds Bank was one of Britain's most bought shares of the week, that I invested £20,000 in it on a whim. Some new banking revelation hit the news later in the week and I lost £2000. It was purely the herd mentality that made me take the risk.

When buying shares in companies to hold over a few months or more, it's an unwise policy to follow everyone else. Traders who make decisions against the majority view are known as *contrarians*. It's an ugly word, isn't it? Still, the richest investor in the world, Warren Buffett, is one of the club.

You need an element of contrarian philosophy to make better gains than average. The big idea is to look for shares which have fallen too low because the herd instinct has driven too many people to sell. You can now buy these shares, then wait for common sense to return and the price to scurry back to its true level.

Shares can drop out of favour for all sorts of reasons. But one of the strongest happens when a few traders sell on a hint of discouraging news about a firm. Other traders follow like sheep. The fall gathers momentum. When the bloodbath is over, the shares are too cheap.

How do we measure cheapness?

A low price-to-earnings ratio (P/E) is a promising start. A high dividend in comparison to shares priced at a similar level is another guide. You'll find more info about these, and other measures of cheapness, elsewhere in the book.

Picking growers

THE WORD YOU NEED TO LOOK FOR MOST IN Shareland is *growth*. If a company is expanding its profits year after year, good. If it's increasing its customers and orders as time rolls by, excellent. If debt is reduced year after year, be happy. If the dividends keep swelling, even better. These are the shining stars of Shareland. Buy, top up or hold the shares.

But it's not quite as simple as that. Look again at those "improved" sales figures. Were they grown under normal circumstances? Or was the figure swelled artificially by a one-off deal, while the company's overall sales were actually quite terrible? They might have flogged a factory or a lucrative arm of the business. Or was there some other windfall, like a winning court case? The company's actual sales might be well down on last year, but abnormal circumstances have made the firm seem much more profitable than it is.

An ideal vehicle for an investor's aspiration is the gilded company which grows its profits year after year, steadily and reliably. Sometimes the upward pace is slow, but that doesn't matter. As long as the gains are consistently better each time, you can't go far wrong. It means customers want more and more of the goods or services on offer. The firm knows what it's doing, does it well and keeps on doing it. Sadly these magic companies are hard to find.

A few companies which have consistently and substantially boosted profits for the last four years are shown in the table below.

Company	Average annual rise in operating profit (£m)	Total rise 2010-2014 (£m)
BT (communications)	383	1132
Reed Elsevier (publishing)	205	818
easyJet (airline)	94	377
Ashtead (tool hire)	82	337
ITV (media)	72	287
Next (retail)	66	256
Whitbread (hospitality)	43	133
Signet (jeweller)	36	142
Photo-Me (photographic)	5	20
S&U (financial services)	4	14

The chart below shows the share price performance of the top three companies from the table in the four-year period, compared to the FTSE All-Share index. As you can see, a pattern of profit growth led these companies to outperform the index in the period.

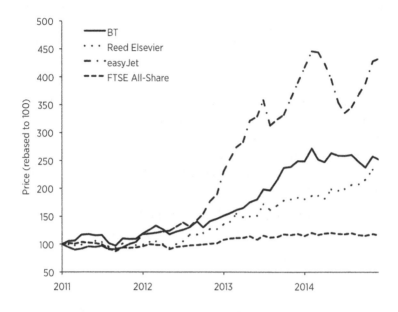

If annual profits suddenly take a dip, beware. Nothing lasts forever. It could well mean that the company's glittering years of growth have run their course. The product may be coming to the end of its long and happy life. It could be time to steel yourself and drop the shares.

But first check the company's latest report. Is there a good reason for the dive in profit? This might be the takeover of another really promising firm which has yet to bear fruit. Or was a mountain of cash spent on another factory which will be hugely useful in expanding the business in the future? Or has it been a warm winter, which depressed the sale of oil or hot-water bottles?

Recently, I was very tempted to sell my shares in Diageo, the international drinks colossus. I'd held them for 25 years, before they were born of a merger between Guinness and Metropolitan. They had produced an interim report showing flat profits, which is not a good sign for a leading firm. Yet the shares rose 4% on the day. How's that for a good selling opportunity for a company which seemed to be slowing down?

I was about to tap the 'Sell' button but it clicked in my mind that the pound was now worth 1.35 euro, when six months ago it was more like 1.15. So no wonder profits were flat for a company that does nearly all its business abroad. Being able to withstand a huge currency movement is a sign of a very strong company. I kept the shares.

If you come to believe the reason for a disappointment is a hiccup rather than a trend, you should not sell. You might even buy more of the shares, which will now have a more reasonable price tag because of that profit dip. But if you can't find a blindingly obvious and easily reversible reason for shrinking profits, I would sell out and find another biscuit to bake.

Remember that companies which grow profits, year after year, are probably the most important driver in your glorious quest to become rich.

The number one investing rule

IF I WERE TO PUT INTO ONE SENTENCE MY paramount plan for making big money from shares, what would it be? There's no hesitation. None at all. Ready for this? Emblazon it in your conscious. Tattoo it on your tum. Write it down, roll up the paper and stick it in your nose. Not literally, perhaps. It's this:

"Ride the Winners and Ditch the Losers."

If you find a share is showing a profit on your buying price, you may be tempted to cash it in. You would almost certainly do this if you were playing roulette. But shares are different. With equities, if red comes up, it will probably keep coming up. A rising share price is a sign of health, not a piece of good luck. It can be assumed that the burgeoning price will continue. At least for some days. Probably a few more months or years. This is not always the case, but in Shareland we can only talk about probabilities, never certainties.

Also, statistics show that shares which have risen steadily in recent months go on to do better than shares which have been a let-down over the same period. So it seems that winning shares build up a momentum which enables them to defy gravity. Long after the news which started the ball rolling, they are still motoring on. It also appears that shares which are slow to start, even in a bull market, never really do get going. And surprisingly, the *momentum effect*, as this tendency is known, has little to do with the true worth of companies.

So to sell a share while you are winning could be to kill the goose that lays 24 carat eggs. I mean, how will you feel if a share you abandoned goes on to double or treble its price in the next week? Also, you might take your peremptory profits and sink them into a company which turns out to be a weak imitation of your original choice. No, to hang on to the share in the reasonable hope of another dollop of northerly action is the better course.

THE TOP SLICING GAMBIT

You could *top slice* a winning share. When you think your climbing shares are ready to take a rest you could sell enough shares to cream off the profit. You leave just enough invested in the company to account for your original stake.

Or you could sell enough shares to reclaim your original investment. As the share price will have risen heartily since your purchase, you will now be left with a wedge of shares you didn't pay for. In share parlance, you can now enjoy a free ride.

Top slicing like this enables you to hold on to your winning holding at the same time as ensuring your stake in this company doesn't exceed 10% of your portfolio (which, as you'll remember, is another of my golden rules).

What to look for in a company

HERE ARE A FEW THINGS TO LOOK FOR WHEN seeking out winning shares. You can find all you need to know about a company by Googling it to see what people have been saying, or by looking at the shareholder pages on the firm's official website. Or try the truly helpful ADVFN.com.

1. **Profits are currently greater than spending.** There are plenty of firms which can't stop hurling money about. They use shareholder cash to fuel the habit. For example, I'm wary of companies which make frequent announcements about the appointment of new senior staff. They make a great play of how these recruits are better than sliced bread. There is often a press statement from a big cheese saying how lucky they are to recruit this genius. Such announcements are intended to encourage us to buy more shares, because they claim the new brains will kick the company into the stratosphere. But I always ask: who's going to pay this monumental new salary? And if the original management needs new help, then there must be something inadequate about them. Sometimes, firms which keep appointing 'whiz kids' are not actually making any dosh at all – but are merely hoping to. Avoid big spenders and find firms which are already making galloping gains with their existing staff.

2. **Search out companies whose profits keep on growing.** I discuss this in detail under 'Picking growers'.

3. **Debt is low and assets are high.** I regard debt as the opposite of profit. Eventually it has to be paid back to the lender, leaving less for shareholders. High debt is also a sign of profligate managers. And you never, ever want that. Just like ordinary folk, if you're weighed down with debts you cannot save and prosper. While assets are the opposite of debt. For example, if a company owns a couple of swish factories and a fleet of new lorries, they can be sold off when the business plan is changed. Such tasty assets will bump up the share price, if a takeover looms.

4. **The number of shares bought on a daily basis is larger than average (this is called high volume).** Such strong activity usually hikes the share price. There are several free websites, like LSE (www.lse.co.uk), which show you the number and value of shares being traded. And obviously, if the number of sales outweigh purchases, eventually the share price will suffer. Sell before it does.

5. **The company is always publishing updates and reports.** Managers would keep a low profile if the firm was struggling. They won't crow about developments and changes unless the news is good. A lot of published stuff means the bosses are proud of themselves, which, unless they are barking mad, is probably justified.

Free expert help

HIRING PROFESSIONALS TO CHOOSE YOUR SHARES is expensive. Here's how to pick top investors' brains without it costing you a thing. You'll have heard of mutual funds, unit trusts and the like. Investors in these funds hand over their money to professional fund managers, who pool the money together and invest in shares which the fund managers think will do very well for their clients.

These managers and their teams of researchers put a lot of hard graft into these choices. The pressure to get it right is immense. It always is when you play with other people's money. But these boffins are not just making personal choices. They also rely on some pricey software to do some very fine analysis. In other words, if these funds can't get it right, nobody can.

And the great thing is, you can borrow their ideas without paying for the privilege. Do a search on the internet for the most successful share funds. Then rummage around to find lists of the companies they're invested in. Make a few notes and pay particular attention to names that come up again and again.

Which companies' names are common denominators? Make a short list. Think about it for a few days, then buy into the ones you fancy.

Here's a list I made by following this exact process; you'll recognise some household names:

- AstraZeneca
- BT Group
- Roche Holdings
- GlaxoSmithKline
- Lloyds Banking Group
- HSBC Holdings
- Royal Dutch Shell
- Diageo
- National Grid
- Vodafone
- Prudential
- BP

You can trust to your instinct at this stage. No further research is necessary because you've already tapped into the expertise of some of the best operators in the business. You can't beat their experience, their resources or their contacts. They don't earn their whacking salaries and bonuses for nowt.

By looking for companies which appear most in a range of fund portfolios, you are ruling out the possibility of eccentric choices. If most fund managers like the same share, it really says something.

The only thing to watch out for is that the story for some companies may have taken a turn for the worse since the lists were compiled. And funds do of course modify their holdings now and again. A recently decimated share price will give you a warning sign about a company whose fortunes could be changing – tread carefully if this is the case.

This little system enables you to avoid the steep management charges that clients of these firms have to bear. Also, by making the final choices yourself, you have nobody to blame for any losses but yourself. I always find, for some reason, that this is a comfort.

The magic PE

I'VE PROMISED NOT TO BURDEN YOU WITH formulae, ratios, spreadsheets, list of figures and all the other paraphernalia of technical share selection. But there is one technical-sounding indicator which is really very simple to understand. And for me, it's one of the very best ways of assessing the true value of a company.

We are talking here about the price-to-earnings ratio or PE of a company. This magic number is the value of a firm, divided by its annual earnings. Plainly put, the lower the number, the cheaper the share in relation to the company's money-making skill.

If a share has a low number, for example 6, then they are not asking you to pay much for the share. If it is 50, say, then it is pretty pricey. Consequently, before you buy any share, do a quick search for its PE ratio. If it is more than 30 you need to think a bit more carefully before you plough ahead.

So any share with a high PE figure is out of bounds?

Not necessarily. And here's why. The price-to-earnings ratio is a number from the past – it's based on historic data – and you may be looking at a share with a glamorous future.

I know of one technology company with a huge PE ratio of around 66 at the time of writing. Based in Cambridge, it's called ARM Holdings and it makes microchips. ARM turns hefty profits now – but nothing like the huge sums it will garner in the future. You see, ARM's microchips are so special that nearly all the world's techno companies rely on them.

The giant Apple Corporation use them in their iPads – and you know how popular they are. Sixty billion ARM chips have been sold, but that is nothing compared to how many more will be produced for an exploding market for mobile gadgets and computers. The currently high price-to-earnings ratio is due to the share buying fraternity knowing the tide of profits has only just started. And the bigger the gains, the faster that high PE ratio will crash to more normal levels. So in this case, a price-to-earnings ratio which is roughly three times more than normal is almost a bargain.

You might do even better if you find a company with a much more modest PE but which also faces shimmering prospects further down the line. Sometimes the City has simply failed to spot future potential.

I believe this to be the case with Inmarsat, with a PE of 20. This British gem boldly goes where no one has gone before, developing satellites for communication and navigation. You may recognise them for their high-profile scanning of the seas for the missing Malaysian Airlines flight MH370 in 2014. The average PE figure doesn't reflect the huge payback that their phalanx of satellites will deliver in the future.

Some traders believe that a high PE ratio is better than a low one because a hefty price for shares indicates a company of diamond quality. They see this as a company that can only grow, because people increasingly want what it supplies. It may also have management who're at the top of their tree and profits and dividends which are likely to climb like a monkey up a pole. Everyone wants a share in the company so its PE is higher than most. So the story goes.

Well, maybe. But a tall PE also shows me that the company may have peaked, that I am probably paying for shares at their most expensive, or that the shares have been overbought. None of those possibilities fill me with hope that the share price will double, which is normally what I hope for.

Yes, a high PE is sometimes justified. There are some brilliant firms in the world which deserve a walloping PE. But I still prefer my shares to display a low PE before I buy them. Then if the enchanted number soars after my purchase, well, that's a great bonus. A low PE gives room for a company's share price to grow.

Here are some of my favourite firms with low PEs:

- Vodafone: 5
- United Utilities: 9
- Wood Group: 10
- National Grid: 13
- BT: 18
- easyJet: 16

There could, however, be a warning on the way for shares with a tiny PE. It could show that few investors are willing to pay much for the shares. Companies with low PE ratios are not always well regarded. Some say they're riskier and slow growing. You might think you see a bargain when the company prospects are really rather poor. On the whole, though, I'm more inclined to invest in a company with a low PE than a high one.

Having a peek at PE ratios is a spiffing way to assess whether it is a good time to buy shares in general. If most PE ratios are higher than normal in the market, then it might be time to sell your shares and go to cash, till they calm down again.

Good timing

LIKE EVERYTHING IN LIFE, BUYING SHARES DEPENDS on good timing. If we buy shares at the exact time when the price is at its very lowest and sell when the price is at its all-time peak, well, wouldn't that be nice? But, like a royal flush, it has never happened to me. No, not in all the zillions of trades I have made. The aim, though, is still to get as near to this ideal as we can.

The correct policy is to buy on the dip and sell on the pinnacle. You wait for a share to reach the kind of low which makes you feel "Wow, this can't get any lower." Then you sidle in. When your new share reaches a level which makes you say "Crikey, this is an amazing jump," you flog it. Sounds simple doesn't it?

But when a share drops, how do we know it won't fall further? And when a share motivates, when do we know when it will stop? We can never be sure. We just have to discipline ourselves not to expect too much and to set our buy and sell targets at a reasonable level.

I believe the correct time to buy shares is when the market is undergoing a longish set-back. One or two days of falling is not enough to establish a significant bear run. But if you'd bought shares in 2008, the time of the big credit crunch, they would be worth thousands of lovely lolly a few years down the road.

Yet when times are bad, poor old traders are much more likely to sell buckets of shares than to buy them. I don't know why this should be. You wouldn't be interested in a sofa unless there's a sale in the store. Well, I wouldn't. Yet loads of traders will only shell out for shares when prices are nudging new record highs.

Instead, they should sell their shares when everyone else is buying – when shares are flirting with new high points.

Shares which hit new highs always come down. It might happen the moment the record is breached or it may be months down the road. But it happens. Otherwise, all shares would be way overvalued. Overvalued in all other walks of life means overpriced, and so it does with shares too.

My easy way to value a company

THERE ARE ALL MANNER OF ABSTRUSE FORMULAE available to help you deduce the value of a company. These cyphers are usually referred to by their initials. We have PEG, EPS, NAV, and so on. It's a matter of dividing or multiplying one thing, the share price, say, by something else, such as the company's earnings. Or estimating a company's expected growth and dividing it by another estimate. Or doing some clever sums with dividends, sales, asset value, growth and all sorts of other gubbins. Nothing is absolutely certain to work, so I don't trouble myself with this kind of maths. Life's too short.

There is one sum I do, though. It's part of the method used by Warren Buffett. I take a company's total number of shares in issue and multiply it by the share price. This gives the market's valuation of the company.

Now, how to use this figure. A useful thing to do is to value the company completely differently – by the profit and loss and debt on the balance sheet, taken with future prospects. If you work this out and find that this valuation, which is more to do with reality than the stock exchange value, is higher than the market's current value, then you're contemplating a bargain. You should buy these shares.

By way of example, Compass is a catering giant on a huge worldwide scale. Annual profit is £1208m. It has debt of £297m. It's future prospects (this will be your own informed view) is that the population is growing like stink and all will need feeding. This share is a go-er. Debt is only a quarter of annual profit and the market is wide open.

Another illustration is United Utilities, which supplies water and sewage to 7 million folk in northwest England. Profit is £1704m. Borrowing is £211m. So debt is only a fifth of annual profits, but the future may include Ofwat price-capping and climate change causing drought or flooding. So not a bad investment, but it depends on your personal view of what might happen down the road. (It's one of the joys of armchair share-shifting that we can exercise our imaginations in this way.)

OK, you want to know how to find a company's operating profit, its debt and to tease out an idea of future prospects. I use a broker's website called London South East. It goes by the initials LSE, so it's often confused with the London Stock Exchange and the London School of Economics. But apart from this minor branding issue, they do run a detailed, informative and largely free website. Just enter the name of your company in 'search' and punch the 'fundamentals' button. It's all there. You can also summon up the latest share price, charts and a bulletin board.

Yes, there will be some entries that make little sense to anyone who is not an accountant, but not many. Reading a balance sheet is easy-peasy. I'm sure we can all understand the words 'profit',' loss' and 'borrowing' and they're the important bits.

To return to Warren Buffett's favourite method, if the market valuation is higher than the company's real value, then you should avoid the company. Or if you already hold shares, expunge.

You may have spotted a fly in the ointment. The onus is on you to set the *real* value. You're probably not an accountant, so how can you trust your valuation? Study the firm's official website. Does it look like a vibrant, growing company to you? Search the web for City analysts' views of the firm – do they think it's going places?

Then finally apply your own intuition. If you're still of a mind to buy, wait for a dip in the price and then give it a go. Be comforted that the drop in price will make the firm even more undervalued by the market.

If all of the above information about valuing a company has given you a headache, here's a bit of encouragement. I've listened rather carefully to Mr Buffett the Bountiful talk about the way he determines the true value of a firm. He says he buys the shares if he likes the look of a company after inspecting the fundamentals and reading the company report. It's seems to me that there's as much instinct as science involved in his decision-making.

Three layers of the trading cake

USE A CAREFULLY DEFINED TIMELINE TO BUY A share after reading an article praising a company to high heaven.

I do not immediately log into my account and hit the buy button. Others will have read the article too, and they'll have acted quicker than you. You're never the first to act. So that share's price will already have moved on.

When the upward action dries up, a gaggle of profit-takers will be on their sell buttons. The price will come down again. I wait until this dribble down has stopped and the price begins to twitch up again. This is the prime time to pounce on shares.

To begin with, I only lay out a third of the cash I wish to invest into the chosen company. Then I wait another week. By now, the initial excitement will have waned somewhat, so in goes the second tier of my stake. Then, when another week has gone by, the final third of my investment in this company is swapped for shares.

The purpose of investing in this three-stage fashion is that if the price falls after I make my initial investment, my second tranche will be invested at a lower, and better, price. If the price falls again before the third week, my third instalment is invested at an ever lower price. These price falls average down the price I have paid for the shares, making it easier for me to turn a profit when the price rises.

Checking your choices

HERE ARE A FEW CHECKS YOU CAN DO WHEN YOU are weighing up whether to weigh in on a company's shares:

- Google the company you fancy to find its official website. Check all its nuts and bolts (known in the business as the 'fundamentals'). Does it look slick and professional? Would you buy this company's products?

- Compare the company's latest sales data with that from a year before. If it's a FTSE 100 whale, you need to see an increase of at least 4%. If it's a tiddler, the annual improvement should be more than 12%. If this hasn't happened, leave the shares for somebody else. It's not a good enough performer for you.

- Has the company been buying back its own shares on the open market? This is a good sign. After all, why would a company use its money to buy back its own shares, rather than increase its dividends, say, or use the money to expand? The probable answer is that it feels its shares are underpriced – and the company ought to know.

- Monitor the number of shares a company has in issue (known as the number of shares outstanding). If the number decreases, earnings per share will pick up and the shares will become more valuable. But if the hill of shares grows, there's less profit per share and dividends will suffer, together with the share price. You can find out the number of shares a company has in issue by making an internet search.

The importance of earnings

THERE ARE MANY COMPANIES THAT HAVE NOT made any money, yet. That's right; they're earning nothing at all.

How do they keep going? They're living on shareholders' money, loans, director stakes and other results of handing round a sticky begging bowl.

They tend to be explorers for oils, metals or minerals. Or researchers into early medical cures and treatments. Or developers of magical software which they hope will transform Silicon Valley.

Sadly, the earth isn't keen to give up its secrets and the explorers go to the wrong places. "Promising oil fields" are notorious for coming up dry. Occasionally, the drillers are embroiled in legal quarrels with tetchy governments.

Medical treatments require licences. Sometimes what is discovered doesn't pass muster and all that research money goes to waste. Technological endeavours come to nothing when a different firm develops something far better.

All in all, taking a punt on a company that has no current earnings is too big a risk to take. It's best to avoid investing in companies with no revenue.

Beware the competition

BEFORE YOU BUY A COMPANY'S SHARES, LOOK AT other companies that are doing exactly the same thing. Are the rival firms bigger? Are they more popular with people you know, or in media coverage? Are their products cheaper?

Competition is a powerful company destroyer. Remember how Beta tapes were wiped out by VHS? Look at how Google and eBay decked the competition in the early internet days. They were bigger. And in mass global markets, size matters. Google has turned a strong market share into an almost total market share. Same with eBay.

Yonks ago, I lost a lot of money in an online auction company called Scoot. It just couldn't compete with eBay and went bust. Not many companies have lost me every last penny of my investment and I like to think I can act quickly in the early days of a decline to prevent this from happening. But this firm went bang so fast, there was no time.

Tough competition can do that to a firm. Don't invest into a market that is both young and competitive, unless you're sure you're picking the market leader.

Companies which corner the market

I LOVE NICHE COMPANIES; THEIR SHARES CAN REALLY soar. I've known the shares of such firms rise by 500% in a year. They could be the golden chicks in your nest.

A nice niche company is one with a small setup that is hardly noticeable, except that it provides an important service. More accurately, they are small firms which make something important and are among the only ones doing it. Or at least, they do it better and cheaper than anyone else.

They're usually experts, or suppliers of a unique and vital component or service. Expertise is a precious thing in Shareland. Hence it's common for them to be a valuable supplier to large companies. And they tend to become even more indispensable with time.

Niche companies sometimes have a vital geographical advantage. They operate in a confined area. They could be the only ones doing what they do for hundreds of miles. Perhaps they're the only company of this kind in an entire country. This means they can set their prices high.

These companies are not easy to find. But if you read news stories about changes in well-known companies, you'll often discover one or two of their suppliers you knew nothing about. Bring up their websites and see if there's anything you like.

An example of a firm which I consider a fine niche operator is Zytronic, which has factories in Blaydon-on-Tyne (home of the famous races). They are engineers of touch technology, making important bits of display kiosks, ticket machines and hole-in-the-wall dispensers. I bought in April 2014 when shares were priced at 216p. Ten months later they were 307p, an improvement of about 43%. The chart below shows this performance.

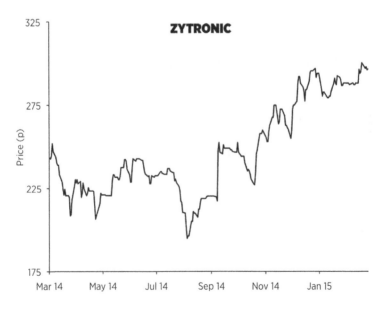

True, they've not moved higher since, but when a share doesn't lose too much ground over six months, say, I usually hang on in there. That's because a non-rising share is much more encouraging than a slow faller. And I find that an inactive share often puts on a later spurt, as if water has been collecting behind a dam.

Another service company which has brought me tidy bonanzas over the years is Aggreko. It hires out portable electricity generators, which may not sound scintillating, but such is demand that it is in the FTSE 100 and worth about £4bn. Aggreko lit up the 2012 Olympic Games, for example.

Another company that supplies other companies is Ashtead, a share that has ballooned in price by 11 times for me. Another Footsie favourite, it hires diggers, forklift trucks, ladders and other stuff to the building industry.

Spiders in company websites

THE FIRST PLACE TO LOOK IF YOU'RE DRAWN TO A share is the company's official website, but be very critical of what you read. Remember it's written by wily press relations officers. They're appealing to customers of the company as well as shareholders.

The good thing is that spin doctors can't muck about with hard facts. Not unless they've gone completely to the dark side. Look out for any data that doesn't seem quite right. It might be the high mountain of debt. It could be dwindling profits in recent years. It could be none of these things – just an ethereal feeling of desperation that comes across in the wording.

Or you might not warm to the board of directors very much, just by looking at their pictures. They may seem stuffy, lethargic, past their best or a bit shifty. A spry company needs a spry board. Have they got one? Some people believe that an unprepossessing bunch of characters on a board is a trivial reason not to buy shares. Let them believe what they want. I stick to my belief that a tired-looking and miserable board is not the best guardian of my money.

Necessity versus luxury

FOR ALL THE HUGE DIVERSITY OF PRODUCTS AND services sold by businesses, we can, for the purpose of share-picking, divide them into just two categories – luxuries and necessities.

Luxury goods are non-essential and therefore the companies that supply them are vulnerable when the financial roof falls in. Whereas firms which produce indispensable goods and do indispensable things will always trundle on, less affected by recessions and slumps.

Shares which, like cockroaches, can survive in horrid conditions include purveyors of food, energy, medicines, water and alcohol. In the luxury camp are cars, travel, holidays, clothes, chocolates, toys, cinemas and… well, everything that is not essential to everyday living. In between are oil, builders, film-making and anything we could do without at a pinch, but generally hate to do so.

If you want to keep risk as low as possible you should invest in the providers of essentials. These companies are known as defensive shares, because they defend your investment against economic downturns. They share the added advantage of usually paying healthy and consistent dividends. Shares in luxury goods and services will rise faster in good times.

If the market is generally on an upward track you need more luxury firms in your bag. If it ain't – and you fear the worst – the more defensive shares you embrace the better.

Don't grab the cutlery

A FAMOUS INVESTMENT SAYING IS "NEVER CATCH A falling knife." Too true! If someone drops a chiv in our house, we let it fall on the floor.

The plan is not to entertain a share which is falling fast. Don't grab the shares because they are suddenly cheap. You will cut your fingers if you do. A share which is on the back-step is giving you a warning. The warning is: things are bad now, but you ain't seen nothing yet.

You can always do a bit of bargain snaffling after the blade has stopped dropping. Or better still, after it's already bounced off the kitchen floor a bit. But only if others are saying that the share deserves a better price. And even then – be careful. It's been shown many times that it's better to invest in rising shares than take a chance on falling shares making a recovery.

Buying FTSE 100 shares

THE BIGGEST, AND SOME SAY THE BEST, PUBLIC companies in Britain are in the FTSE 100 index (Footsie). When you see all its illustrious members written down, the list seems longer than you'd expect. So even if you decide to invest only in Footsie firms, the choice is generous.

So what's the big attraction?

Well, companies have to pass stringent tests to be admitted to this elite group. Principally, they are the country's highest capitalisation companies – i.e. loadsa money. For this reason of size, Footsie companies are perceived to be safer than all other shares.

ARE FOOTSIE GIANTS REALLY SAFER?

The main disadvantage of Footsie picking is that a big oil tanker is clumsier than a racing yacht. These companies lumber along, not putting on much value. Whoever heard of a Footsie member increasing 200% in a week? Yet this has happened to quite a few of my penny shares – up to 600% in fact, in the case of Tadpole Technology.

Another thing is that even Footsie companies are not always safe. British Energy was in the Grand Order of Footsie, but it still caused real pain to many investors, including myself.

All my big losses have been due to underperforming shares in the big index. My other nasty Footsie failures include RBS, Lloyds Group, Bradford & Bingley and Northern Rock. Quite a list isn't it? And all of them household names. I'm ashamed to say that I put money into most of these pesky firms solely because I thought they were substantial and safe.

Naturally, I no longer consider Footsie shares as an automatic safe-haven. But at the same time, I still reckon that larger firms with fat share prices are likely to be sounder than penny share firms. They are protected by their brand, economies of scale, reputation and customer loyalty. So I would advise you to spread the risk by holding the same value in Footsie shares as you do in medium or small firms. Half and half is about right.

You must watch all your shares, including Footsie mammoths, for signs of weakness. Run some fast checks and then, if things seem bleak, or even mildly bleak, give your shares the bum's rush. Trading exclusively in Footsie firms is not wrong, but remember that they're not immortal. Treat them with as much caution as your penny shares.

TAPPING ON THE FOOTSIE WINDOW

An alternative strategy to investing in Footsie shares is to find companies which are on the outside now, but which are pushing up against the doors in the hope of joining this elite band. Here's why.

There are some funds which have to buy stakes in every enterprise that comes inside the Footsie circle. There are also City institutions which stick to the same rule.

So once a new company is enrolled in the Footsie, there's instantly an army of captive customers for its shares. Consequently, the share price bustles higher on admittance to the club. Actually, the price can begin to rise just before entry, as there is always speculation about which lucky firms are going to win a coveted place.

So the job for share shifters is to take a position on who will get in and who won't, then buy shares in our choice. It clearly depends on how much we rate our chosen candidate. But it's worth having a go because the share price of a Footsie winner can really motor.

Another advantage of Footsie shares is that they attract some disproportionate attention in the press. Smaller firms, with fewer shareholders, hardly get a mention. But the behemoths are always in the news. Sometimes, the publicity is damaging – as in the case of BP when it was involved in that messy Gulf of Mexico oil leak. But on balance, the heightened publicity of a Footsie company bolsters its share price.

When to sell

TAKING PROFITS ON YOUR WINNERS

YOU CAN'T MAKE A PROFIT UNTIL YOU SELL A share. If you buy equities to hold forever, you might as well burn the money in the first place. It will never be yours again. All shares should be peddled sooner or later.

Also, it's obvious that the best time to sell your shares is when prices are high. Only chumps dump equities at the point at which they get the least money for them.

The bottom of the market is the best place to buy shares, but if you never sell shares, you probably won't have the resources handy to snaffle promising new shares at their cheapest.

The ideal then is to do what the professionals do. Sell shares when the Footsie scintillates. Then save the money for the next time the market goes into reverse and shares become inexpensive again, as they surely will.

My next piece of advice may sound like a contradiction to the imperative to cream off profits. But the landscape for the successful trader is one of balance. And as well as cashing in profits you must also be prepared to cut your losses early.

WHY YOU MUST SELL LOSING SHARES

You may be surprised to learn that picking winning shares is not the best way to make hay while the sun shines. An even stronger key to success is to limit your losses. You can sometimes let the profitable puppies take care of themselves.

Many is the time I've become hopelessly excited about a few big winners. But I've taken no notice of the shares which are not cutting it. When I add up the total value of my portfolio, I'm shocked to discover that I've mislaid quite a bag of lolly.

Unless we recognise when a share is going into a long-term decline, we will shed money.

WHEN THE MARKET TELLS YOU SOMETHING

Here's a handy hint.

You always have to assume that a share which topples more than 10% from its most recent highest price is going to keep falling. This won't always be true and some shares recover from disaster, but you'll make more money ditching losing shares than you will hanging on to them.

When a share falls and the rest of the market doesn't, there is a hard reason for it. Something is going wrong. In the ordinary world, when projects go pear-shaped, you know how difficult it is to turn them around. The best thing to do is to call it a day and start again. It's the same with shares.

PICKING THE RIGHT TIME TO SHED A SHARE

We need to go back in time, here. When you first buy shares you should set a price at which you will sell for a profit. Then when it reaches that point you could sell. I say *could*, because if the price is still rising fast, you might want to move your selling notch a bit higher. If, however, the share seems to be stuck, or it is rising so little now that it is hardly noticeable, you should honour your original limit by calling time.

Another wizard way to decide when a share should be kicked out of your bag is to ask a simple question: would you buy the same shares today? Would you cheerfully nab it with the same confidence you had in the company when you first bought the shares? If the answer is no, I would first do some instant Googling to see if anything good is about to happen. Is there a new big cheese on the board, a thumping great order perhaps, or a beneficial change in the law? If nothing like that is cooking in the kitchen, it could be time to let go.

Just to be on the safe side, you might take a final peek at the last set of profits. Were they up or down on the year before? If they were strong and the outgoings were down, well, you might want to hang on in there. If not – if the data show a decay or slowing growth – I would opt for a sell. You can use the proceeds to find a new share which is only just starting out on an illustrious period of growth.

Delicious dividends

DON'T UNDERESTIMATE THE BOON OF DIVIDENDS. They are the equivalent of interest paid by banks and building societies. Yet they're much more lucrative. Some big companies pay divis of up to 10% per year. Compare that to your bank's savings account!

Dividends still keep coming in, two to four times per year, however downtrodden the markets. Even when the company's share price shudders, the dividends are slow to change. In fact, when the price dives, you can often buy more shares for the same loot and so increase your regular dividend haul.

Some people ask their brokers to reinvest their divis – which means they use the dividends to buy more shares in the same company. I don't, because I regard them as the cornerstone of my income. I'm rarely forced to sell shares for ready money because the dividends keep my bank account topped up.

It's worth pointing out that if you do reinvest the divis, you'll find that most of your overall gain from shares over time can be put down to your recycled dividends. That's right, divis can be more useful to your asset pile than your shares' rising prices. It really depends on whether you'll need your half-yearly handouts to pay the bills.

You need to be aware that there's an element of having your cake and eating it in the fascinating subject of dividends. Some economists say that if the dividend keeps rising, it depresses the share price, as you can't have both capital growth and booming dividends. They point out that some companies use resources they could pay in dividends to buy back shares instead. This accelerates the price, as fewer shares in issue means a better price for their holders.

WHERE TO FIND THE DIVIS

To scoop the really juicy handouts you need to look at the 100 members of the Footsie club. You'll be able to find lists of the most generous payers by making a Google search. Some of the most open-handed and consistent dividend suppliers are enterprises which provide the bare necessities of life. Medicines, food, electricity, oil, booze and that sort of thing. They maintain a decent dividend for long periods because they peddle what nobody can do without. Some examples of high divi companies are shown in the table below.

Company	Dividend
William Morrison Supermarkets	6.75%
Royal Dutch Shell	6.34%
J Sainsbury	6.24%
Scottish and Southern Energy	5.59%
HSBC Holdings	5.43%
Friends Life Group	4.92%
GlaxoSmithKline	4.87%

The Royal Insurance Company (now called RSA), which I've been with for donkey's years, has a poor record on share prices – they've hardly moved – but the dividends were the biggest in my bag for a long time. I say 'were' because, following some accounting difficulties in Ireland, they've recently dropped the dividend altogether. Never mind, it will return.

NO DIVIS FOR PENNY SHARES

You don't normally scoop any dividends at all with penny share outfits. They are also thin on the ground in growing companies. With truly ambitious ventures, any money going spare is lavished on expansion, research and development rather than returning it to shareholders through dividends.

DIVIDENDS AS A GUIDE TO THE FUTURE

It's easy to probe into the success or failure of a company over its recent past – we study the annual report. But signals about the future are very hard to pin down, yet it is the times ahead, not the past, that share shufflers like us should be really concerned about. Successful share-picking includes the art of seeing what will happen a year or two down the road. Sometimes even further. The dividends a company pays twice a year are one way of seeing into the future. Here's how.

You can consult dividend records to see if the share price is likely to rise steadily in the future. If a firm increases its dividends year after year this is a reliable indicator that the share price will ascend too, as it shows management has confidence that profits are growing year after year. In fact, a regular handout which is raised at every opportunity is perhaps the best of all signals that your shares are going to put on weight year after year. But be careful with a firm which suddenly hikes its dividend when its profits are static or falling. Bosses have been known to fire up divis to give an impression the company is thriving just to attract new buyers, when in reality, the enterprise is running on air.

Dividends will be cut if the company is having a hard time of it now – if profits are down, expenditure is up and debts are growing. The incredible shrinking divi can signal the management's lack of confidence to stay on course. Directors fear the worst – and they're the ones with first-hand knowledge. It could be a sign for you to exit, stage left.

Let's also consider another explanation for a reduced dividend. It might be that the money is needed to snaffle another company. That new firm may have incredibly useful assets. Or the cut in dividends might be required to pay for the development of a thrilling new product.

You can probably find out whether the dividend is being reduced for positive or negative reasons by looking up recent press cuttings on the company. If there's no such news, I would sell any firm that trims its divi. Not out of spite, you understand, but out of real fear for its future. A company will almost certainly slash a dividend if it expects profits will stagger.

THE BIG CASH BACK

Fortune Oil, a Chinese oil producer listed on the London Stock Exchange, has been one of my more enduring share holdings. On the face of it, they've not made me much dosh over the years. I suppose that the share price has roughly doubled. Not very good in ten years, is it?

But they splurged out a special dividend one day. And it was a walloper. I didn't even bother to look up where all this lovely dosheroo came from. It's only a penny share, after all, and the share price itself was withering on the vine. I could have easily found out, but as my grandpappy used to say: "Never look a gift horse in the gob."

Now, this kind of cash back bonanza isn't uncommon. It happens when a company doesn't really know what to do with the cash they're building up. They don't fancy launching a takeover because they're wary of expansion. They don't think there's enough new business available to fill the new space. Instead, they believe quite rightly that the dough should be used to sweeten the shareholders. There's nothing like a band of ebullient shareholders to keep the share price in the clouds.

One way canny managers choose to jolly along their share fraternity is to use some of their money glut to buy back a block of their own shares on the open market. Then these extra shares are discombobulated. It sounds rather drastic, but not for share shovellers like us. The fewer shares out there, the fewer sharers there are in the profits. And you know what that means – higher share prices and juicier dividends.

But it's even better when the head honchos decide to hand some of the spare loot directly to the shareholders via a dividend. This not only puts pounds in our pockets, but it accelerates the share price instantly as word whizzes round the Square Mile that the firm has money to burn.

Somehow, such a free gift of mazuma seems too good to be true. It can come out of the blue, too. So, before you sell a share which seems to be slow at putting on weight, see if you can discover whether it has dispensed big money in the past. You might feel like keeping the share until it happens again.

DIVIDEND PLAY

Now comes one of the best money-makers in the game. There's a top way to bag more dividends than average. It involves buying shares on the day before the company goes ex-dividend. Over the years, I have made a lot of money out of exploiting ex-dividend dates.

For example, if you buy the Candy Floss Group on 23 November and the ex-dividend date is on the 24th, then you will be awarded the six-monthly pay-out. You will still win it even if you sell the shares on the 24th, because you owned them the day before. It seems a bit unfair on the poor saps who've held the shares for six months patiently waiting for a few quid, but there we are.

There is a slight snagerooni, though. Legions of chancers try this dodge and so the value of the share can retreat rather a lot when the ex-dividend date arrives. This has been known to cancel out the dividend gain. As this is a complete nuisance, I can give you a couple of ways to get around it.

Shares tend to rise in value in the ten days before the dividend, as traders anticipate the payout. So if you buy twelve days before, say, you will benefit from the rises up to the ex-dividend day. Then on ex-div day, you can sell the shares, hopefully still at a profit, while also trousering the six-monthly bonus after less than a couple of weeks of share ownership.

One of my favourite divi plays is HSBC, or Honkers Bonkers as I prefer to call it. As this is one of the few companies that pays a dividend four times a year, rather than the usual two, it makes things easier. The pay-out is nearly 5% a year, which is good for a bank, and the spread between buying and selling is very low at only 0.03%.

Another other way around the annoying price drop when shares go ex-dividend is to hang on in there for another fortnight after the 'ex' date. In this pink period, as it's known, it's common for shares to rise again to the level they were before the dividend drop. I guess traders became used to the old price level and move to reinstate it. If you can pull this off, you get the dividend without enduring a dip in the share price.

THE FREE SCRIP SHOW

Another way of rewarding shareholders by shaving the cash pile is for the board to launch a scrip issue. Here, money is taken from the company's pot to buy new shares which are then sloshed out to the shareholders. The more shares you hold, the more new shares come your way. Hurrah!

Overenthusiastic research and development

BEWARE OF COMPANIES WHICH SPEND TOO MUCH on research and development (R&D) of new widgets and thingamies. While this is considered laudable for the world at large, it can be risky for shareholders. Some of these experiments – because that's all they are – come to nothing.

R&D costs an arm, a leg and a set of teeth. It often requires expensive boffins in the top league, an army of extra employees, pricey specialist equipment, purpose-made buildings and so on. And if the final gubbins doesn't work, it's all up the spout. There's no extra profit at all, because there's nothing to sell. Disaster and a bombed-out share price could be the only result.

Your stop-loss system

SENSIBLE HOME TRADERS USE A STOP-LOSS SYSTEM. The one I recommend is 10%. If a share drops by more than 10% of the price you bought it for, then sell. If the share has risen substantially since you bought it, dispose of it when it loses more than 10% of the highest price it reached while in your care. This way you'll keep most of the profit.

You should always sell at a 10% loss. There should be no reprieves. But we are only talking here about shares with a high or mid-range price. Really cheap shares – penny shares – can easily fall 10% or more, even when they are set to make a killing in the near future. This is because their very cheapness makes their price sensitive to only a few sales.

Take a company like Feedback PLC, a medical diagnostics minnow, which is worth only £3m. It has comparatively few shares in existence. If only a few of these shares are sold, for any reason, the price could come down by half a penny. It doesn't sound much, but the share is only worth 2p, so you lose 25%. If the same number of shares were sold in a giant like BT, the share price would be unchanged.

So, it's unwise to sell a cheap share after a 10% drop without there being a very good rationale for the fall. Instead, it's best to wait and see what happens. If the share continues to fall, Google the company and read up on it. You might see some dire news that worries you. Then you should sell. But for some very low-price shares, I have often sat tight on a 60% loss, say. Then I've enjoyed a rapid rise to double my purchase price – and sometimes beyond that.

My ITV shares are a case in point. I bought them for around 100p in mid-2005. By February 2009 they were about 23p each. Now, in early 2015, they're around 270p. The chart below shows the price performance of ITV since I purchased.

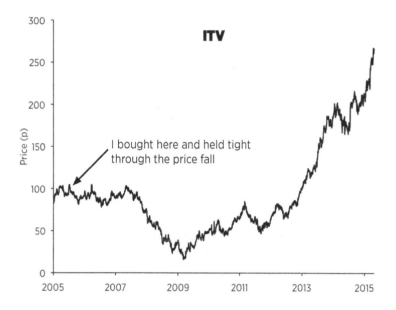

Another example is Photo-Me, a company which allows you to take selfies from their kiosks in shopping centres. I bought them for around 100p in 2004. The price fell to 10p in 2009. But as I write this in 2015 they're at 148p. The following chart shows Photo-Me's price history since I purchased the shares.

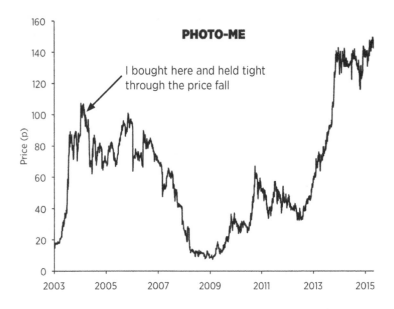

I held tight on these ITV and Photo-Me shares when the price made these drops of more than 10% because I trusted my initial analysis that led me to buy the shares in the first place. In the absence of any new, negative news, there was no reason for me to sell, so I held on and waited for the rise.

AUTOMATIC STOP LOSSES

It's possible with most internet brokers to set an automatic stop price when you buy the share. At the same time as the purchase, you electronically set a figure at which you want to sell if the share price drops. In theory, this prevents you forfeiting more than you're prepared to lose should the share flounder.

I never use these automatic stop losses. For one thing, they don't always kick in at the set price. And brokers often won't guarantee they work, unless you pay some extra money for the privilege. Stop-loss systems can be clunky if the drop is sudden and everyone wants to sell at the same time.

There is another reason why I don't favour automatic stop losses. A share can suddenly dip a long way down and then shoot straight back up again when some sort of error or misjudgement is almost instantly rectified. If the share totters, even for a micro-second, below your stop loss, it will be sold. Gone forever. Meanwhile, the share could have shot back up to its previous value or even higher a short while later. You are out in the cold – no longer the owner of a promising share. And that's just because an unfeeling sod of a robot dumped your shares.

This fate befell me with some BG shares I bought as a side investment to my main tranche. I set an automatic stop of £10 when the market price was about £12. For some reason the share suddenly lurched down, a bit like an air pocket affects a plane. Then financial computers panicked, if a machine can panic, and the price dropped below £10. This all happened in a short space of time before the previous share price was resumed. But too late! My shares had been sold automatically at a loss of about £2,000.

The wonder of the steady riser

MY FAVOURITE TYPE OF SHARES ARE THE SLOW, steady risers (SSRs). There are seldom any dramatic leaps forward. They fall a bit when all shares drop. They rise a shade on moribund days. They improve a little more than most when the overall market is buoyant. People like what they do. The number of customers grows, the sales flourish and debts dribble away.

They are often rather boring. One of my SSRs is a Cheltenham engineering firm, producing systems and gear for steam-using companies, including (yawn) steam pipe-sizing tools. It's called Spirax Sarco. Another of my steady risers is Footsie firm Ashtead, which hires out machines and tools to the building trade. Nothing sexy about either firm. But everyone likes and needs what they do. I don't even check their progress much, because I just know that share price will climb ever so slowly in the right direction. I just know it. The chart below shows the progress of Spirax Sarco and Ashtead since 2000, compared to that of the FTSE All-Share index.

Happily, the sluggish progress of slow, steady risers ploughs on month by month, year after year. You suddenly find the few hundred quid you put in has gradually become thousands. Excellent. But perhaps I should be more on my guard. Like hot, passionate love, it won't last forever.

One day, your faithful ship will hit choppy waters. It won't be fatal, but there will come a set of annual figures which will disappoint. They may not be too bad in themselves, but if they reflect a worse showing than last year, the share price will stall. Typically, the price will stagger even further in the next few days, as financial writers pore over the results and publish more of their doubts. Companies in my portfolio that have enjoyed regular and dramatic price rises over many years, and then have suddenly experienced poor periods, include HSBC, Tesco, BG, BP and Diageo. They are now back on course and I'm glad I kept them.

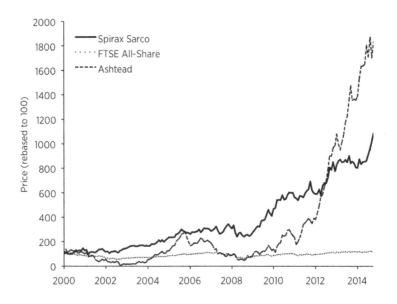

But quite often a firm which was a darling of the Square Mile will never recover from the knock. It may be because something of a bubble has been burst. Everyone was so used to the company's seamless progression, they forgot to monitor the fundamentals. There may have been lurking signs that the share was overvalued for some years, but further progress was taken for granted and niggling shortcomings were overlooked.

I would not pull out of an old favourite on one poor set of results – unless they were something quite atrocious. But I would keep a sharp eye on the share price. If it falls by more than 10%, that would be time to say goodbye.

Recovery shares

THE MOST PROMISING COMPANIES CAN SPRING A leak. The shares can plummet in an instant. They can carry on foundering, as more and more traders jump ship. Yet I have made more money out of companies which have recovered from disaster than almost any other branch of the share dealer's art.

One of my earliest forays concerned a company called Southern Television. Its share price crashed when it lost its franchise to broadcast. A terminal happenstance, you might think. But the company held on with a share price of a few pence. I read in my Sunday paper that Southern still had a stock of shoes, of all things. But then I discovered it also owned a library of old TV comedy shows. Soon afterwards a takeover battle began, presumably with this visual horde in mind, and I made a quick and easy £5,000.

Suppose you are selling holiday cottage rentals in Britain. You have a terrible summer, followed by even more rain in the following year. On top of that, there's a general recession going on. Profits will spiral and so will the share price. The shares are suffering and nobody feels like supporting them.

But we know the best time to buy a share is when it's depressed, except where there is a good reason for its decline. So we check the net for recent press reports and publicity. We discover that bad weather is mostly to blame and we also remember that the holiday industry is a luxury business – always the first to suffer when hard times close in.

We also discover that the company has not recently lost any of its previously outperforming managers, the number of foreign holidays is decreasing and that the recession's days are numbered. Growth is returning to the economy. We also note that long-range forecasts say the next number will be a scorcher.

Can you see how evidence can be built up from a range of widely different sources?

It's now odds on that this company, which you've already ascertained was once a high-flyer, is going to recover. As it does so, the City, which was so hard on it when ill-fortune struck, will forgive, forget and come cringing back to re-buy the shares. That means the share price will soon rally. We should snatch the shares now, while they're cheap.

The important thing is to find compelling reasons why a firm can or should recover its poise. Look for new products, efficiency savings, better marketing, whizzy new managers, or the retention of previously performing managers – all the usual trappings of success.

How to be disloyal

THE THREE MUSKETEERS WOULD HAVE MADE rubbish share traders. Too much loyalty. "All for one and one for all" doesn't work well in the City.

Some of the biggest foul-ups I've made trading shares were caused by falling in love with a company. Loyalty may be a virtue in human relationships, but it's an unwanted vice in Shareland.

We buy shares in a rising star. It does very well for us. We double our money in a few months. Over a few years, we may have a very significant rise. You need to divest before your paper profits turn black, curl up and vanish into smoke.

This happened to me with a new technology firm called Tadpole Technology. Up 600% it went one week. How could I ditch it after that? But I should have, as it hit the skids big time. All my considerable profits gone!

What kept me in, even as the fundamentals weakened, is old-fashioned loyalty. The company did well for me. How can I abandon it, just because the share price was on the slide?

Well, it could have been done very easily, actually. A company does not have feelings. Even with the smallest set-up, it's unlikely that anybody in the firm will even know you have sold. They won't even know who you are. They don't study the list of minor investors. So if a firm you have previously made deep profits from looks like entering a decline, cash in and look for another candidate for your attention. Find one which is at the start, not the end, of something big.

One way of stopping false allegiances getting in the way of a welcome profit is to set a target when buying a share. As an example, you could fix your high point at £5. As soon as this price is reached, even if you're convinced that the share could now go on to bigger things, force yourself to divest. If you never break this rule you'll be very glad in four out of five cases.

Following the Footsie leader

USED TO THINK THAT TO MAKE THE BIG TIME IN Shareworld, I must not follow the crowd. I must plough my own furrow, preferably in the opposite direction to everyone else. To me this meant buying shares which no one else was buying and selling what the world and his wife were buying. This can work in certain circumstances, but on the whole it is dangerous. It's a bit like the overly proud mother watching an army parade. "Look! Everybody is out of step, except my Johnny!" Going against the trend may be liberating, but it's rarely profitable.

There's a popular saying in the City, "All boats rise with the tide." If the Footsie improves by more than 30 points on the day, for example, I've found it's nearly always the case that at least nine out of ten shares are trundling the same happy way. Do not sell into an upwardly mobile market. A rising Footsie is a bit like a tanker: hard to turn round. It can go into reverse, of course, but generally a Footsie which starts the day on the up, keeps on going up. The ascent may get a bit shaky in the middle of the session, only to put on an even stronger spurt in the last few minutes.

When shares are all sashaying upwards, obviously it means there's some industrial-scale buying going on. So I often start purchasing early in the day and ride the upward trend. If the Footsie is still striding north just before the closing bell, I will hold the shares.

However, I will be extra pally with the 'sell' button at the start of the next session. At the first sign of Footsie weakness, I will be out. Daily leaps on day one are so often followed by early, and quite dramatic, dips on day two.

You should be aware that big traders cannot go on buying for ever. They can only make profits if shares tumble now and again. Then they can buy the same shares more cheaply in anticipation of the next rise.

This is why a good day for shares is often followed by a poor one. My theory is that Footsie fluctuations are not so much triggered by world events – as the journos and pundits would have us believe – but by the need to sell equities and snatch them back at cut-rates shortly afterwards.

FOLLOW THE AMERICAN WAY

The Dow Jones indicator of top American shares is even more fixed in its daily ways. When New York opens in Britain's early afternoon (2.30pm), the Footsie has already given us an idea of how US shares will move. If the Footsie is rising at lunchtime, the Dow will often perk up on opening. This is because the UK and US stock markets are highly correlated. The following chart showing the price performance of the FTSE 100 and S&P 500 from early 2014 illustrates this situation – you can see how the two indices mirror each other closely on a day-to-day basis.

Crazy, isn't it? Why should American employment figures affect the pennies taken by Tesco in Barnsley? But it's always been that way. The Dow Jones has more affect on the direction of UK shares than the British economy. The Colonists win again.

I've found – though it's certainly not always the case – that the Dow is even more likely than the Footsie to keep going the same way it begins the day. There are variations, but the trend once set as up, continues up. Once again, you should not sell UK shares when the Dow begins the day in a rising mood. Your price should move even higher as the US trading day progresses.

The seven-hour American session still has four and a half hours to go when the London Stock Exchange closes at 4.30pm. But if you want a pretty reliable idea of how your shares will fare the next day, you need to chart the Dow's progress on the ADVFN website. If it closes on a high, expect your UK shares to surge in the morning. But if the Dow tanks at the close, brace yourself for the opposite effect.

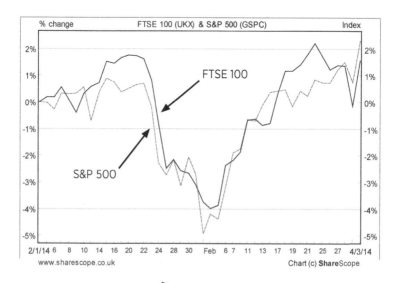

And yet I would still not rush to sell on a dreary overnight Dow, as shares will be marked down in London before you can react. And two times out of three, UK shares depressed by a dodgy overnight Dow will slowly recover anyway, as the day moves on.

To sum up: include the Dow's progress in your daily watch list, even during the UK evening, as it will have a strong influence on your share prices.

The trend of individual shares

THE TIME-HONOURED ADVICE TO FOLLOW THE trend applies to case-by-case shares as well as to the broad market.

If Halcyon Humbugs Limited has been building on its share price all week, there's a good chance it will continue to rise over the next five days, too. The trend is up and trends can last.

How does this phenomenon work?

Well, there will have been a jolly bit of news to set the price going. But then more punters notice that the success train is moving and they clamber on. The money from extra passengers bumps up the price even more, so attracting even more opportunists. By now the bulletin boards are buzzing and more grasping aspirants join the party. The upward trend rattles on and on, while the initial reason for the share boost is forgotten.

Too good to last? Too right! Sooner or later, some bright sparks notice that the share price has become pretty toppy. It's known in the City as being *overbought*. There is now a trickle of wiser investors leaving the train. This causes a small paring of the price, as supply exceeds demand again. Even more subscribers are spooked and the trickle soon becomes an undignified exodus. The upward impetus is over, but you made money because you followed the trend – till it ran out.

The other side of the coin is when a company's shares fall prey to a downward trend. Some small thing alarms the market and the price quivers. This is noticed over the next few days and the equivalent of a run on the bank sets in. The share falls day after day.

There are two strategies available here. You can follow the downtrend closely over a period of days and wait for it to stop. Then you go *bottom-fishing*: that is you buy the share once the panic is over. You wait for reason to prevail again, as indicated by a recovering share price.

Or, if you can spot the downtrend soon enough, you can sell your holding early. Then when the action has burnt itself out, you can spend the same money and buy heaps more of the same shares back again. Then wait for the correcting rise and maybe sell at the top of the heap again. That's the way I would play it.

Channel hopping

A RELATED STRATEGY TO KEEPING YOUR EYE ON trends is watching out for a share's highest and lowest points. Find a basic chart for your share's progress over two or three years. You will easily come across a free one on ADVFN. Note the highest price the share reached. Then search out the lowest point. Draw a horizontal line through both blips. You now have a crude channel. With a risky, but a potentially highly profitable share, this tunnel will be quite wide. More reliable shares, but possibly more boring, will have a narrower passage.

Keep watching the situation. If your company breaks out of the channel, rising above it, well, this is quite an event. It's like the Great Escape. Having been held down for a period of years, your prisoner has now tunnelled out (the difficult bit) and is running for freedom (easier). A break-out often means that a share's price races higher. Be ready with the old selling button though, as the price can turn around and head back towards the channel quite quickly.

But if your share is not sent back to its usual channel within a week or so, it could be worth topping up. See if you can find out the reason for the excitement. If it's a humongous new order or a hard takeover offer, then the share isn't likely to berth in its old channel for long. But if the reason is less tangible, or downright missing, don't load up any more shares and consider a sale.

PROMOTION TO ANOTHER LEAGUE

If a share breaks upward out of its previous comfortable channel and stays outside it for a couple of months or more, you can enjoy a shudder of relief. The chances are that it will now stay in this more desirable bracket. This is good because it removes the stress of wondering if you should sell and take profits. Just allow your share a few more months to settle down in its new home.

Stick-in-the-muds

IF A SHARE LANGUISHES IN YOUR PORTFOLIO without losing value, you might breathe more easily. You may be tempted to leave it there.

But a share which is stuck in the mud is not earning money. Yes, it might attract a dividend twice a year. But there are many more companies out there which are growing in capital value, while also paying juicy handouts. A lazy share is not worth having. You need to find a company which is improving daily. Even on the worst of bad share days, there are some prices which are bobbing along like red robins. Sell your weakling and haul yourself on to the next gravy train.

Sometimes, I even prefer falling shares to stick-in-the-muds. At least you know something is happening, even if it's a setback. Fallers can easily become risers when the selling peters out. Once a share becomes cheap, there are always new buyers who pile in and revitalise it. Unless of course it is in very deep disgrace and can't be revived.

I always ditch idle shares. It's as bad as having a block of flats with no tenants. It's an affront. An obscenity. If nothing has happened to one of my shares for a couple of months, it's toast.

The golden triangle

THIS IS A SECURITY MEASURE I CALL THE GOLDEN triangle. It's a way of cutting down the risks when buying a share. Always look for three independent angles before clicking on the buy button. You need the share to be recommended from a trio of different sources before you go ahead. It could be a tip from a mate, a newspaper article, or some genuine excitement on bulletin boards. Yes, this will slow down your buying process, but it never hurt anyone to look for deep holes on the other side before you jump the wall.

Have no regrets

THERE ARE SOME SHARE-PICKERS I KNOW WHO KICK themselves over and over again because of a mistake they made in the past. Like the time they sold a losing share which went on to triple its price. Then there was the occasion they failed to secure an oil equity which became a ten bagger (up 1000%). Or the gold share that fell down a mineshaft only a week after they firmly decided to sell, but didn't.

These pestiferous incidents happen rather a lot. We can't blame ourselves. We acted as the market indicated at the time. But the market is wayward: it changes fast. We never know where it will go because we are not Mystic Meg.

The errors we make are all part of the game. So don't kick yourself over what might have been. Just eagerly look forward to reaping the financial jollies of your next bumper trade.

Once I sell a share, I refuse to look at the price of that share ever again. Or at least, until I've good reason to believe the share will pick itself up further down the road. When I sold my shares in Anite, a computer service company, I went to great lengths not to notice its share price. Sometimes, this meant covering its name on my laptop screen with a finger. How sad is that? But I could not bear to see that I might have lost money by selling too early. I discovered later that the share had indeed risen to three times my selling price, but had since dropped back down to its old level. So that's all right, then.

It's a bit like checking your usual lottery numbers after you forgot to buy the ticket one week. Unless you want to risk dying of grief if the numbers came up, you do not check the results. Or if you do, you're asking for trouble.

No, a sold share is a forgotten share as far as I'm concerned. The affair is over.

An unbreakable high point

A S A KEEN WATCHER OF SHARES FOR 40 YEARS, I'VE noticed that for every company there is a level of price which investors will not pay. This is the share's zenith. Or near high point. Because when the price approaches this magic marker, the price always tumbles into retreat. This is a useful phenomenon, as it gives us a ready-made exit point.

When a share comes close to a perky high point that the chart shows it has crept up on a few times in the past before retreating, you can choose this time to sell. If it falls back quite a way after this latest attempt on the record, you should buy back the shares and wait until the next time.

Fortune Oil, a Chinese firm on the UK stock market, has been an example of such a company for me. However much it squares up for the jump, it is never able to leap far above 14p.

The chart below shows Fortune's price since 2000 – you can see it has approached and then retreated from the 12p-14p area a few times.

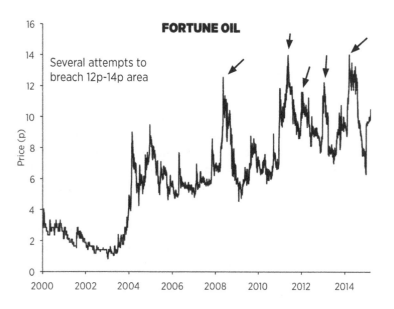

Let's get sentimental

FINANCIAL SENTIMENT IS HOW ALL THE MILLIONS of traders across the world are feeling. We divide these outlooks into two camps – optimistic and pessimistic.

To add to the complexity of the 'sentiment' calculation, we also have to separate these two perceptions into daily fluctuations and the longer term.

It's not the fundamentals of a share which drive it to success or failure in the short-to-medium term. It is sentiment. We have to consider how people are feeling now and how that will affect shares. The nuts and bolts of a company will be the deciding factor in the end. But not here and now. In the cruel present, it's what others in the market think.

There are many who buy their shares and then sit astride them forever. To them, sentiment doesn't matter. It will send shares up or down now, but in the end it's a company's actual performance and profits that will count. However, I'm not a long-term trader. This would bore me to distraction.

When the Footsie is at an all-time peak, we say sentiment is perky. And I bet a pound to a walnut shell that it will go even higher, because positive sentiment feeds on itself. Yet positive sentiment never lasts. Like Lady Luck, it's fickle. The slightest waver and the whole thing collapses faster than a dynamited factory chimney. And like a tall chimney, sentiment takes much longer to build up than it does to demolish.

Never mind, if we ride positive sentiment and are ready with the sell button when sentiment wobbles – evidenced by a drop in the share price – we can make money. It's also possible to judge sentiment even earlier – if not quite as reliably – by reading share blogs. If the majority of contributors are moaning and groaning about the market or an individual company, then we might judge that a prevailing rosy sentiment is about to shed its petals.

But negative sentiment can also be useful to share pickers like us. Take the case of Tesco. At their peak, the shares were riding at around 350p. Then profits wavered and an investigation was launched into accounting methods. The shares dived to a nadir of 170p, as the chart below shows.

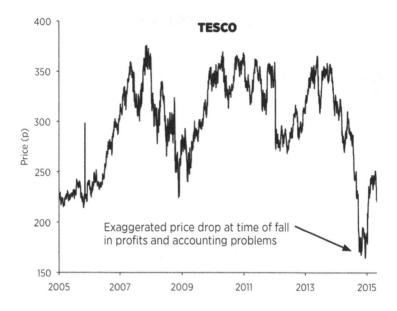

TESCO

Exaggerated price drop at time of fall in profits and accounting problems

I knew the crash was not down to the balance sheet. An accountant would have marked the shares down by a few pence. It was a wave of negative feeling in the market, which often follows a profit warning and an accounting scare. This woeful feeling made the shares seem much less desirable than they were. I had no worries about my large Tesco holding and indeed as sentiment returned, the shares are presently trading at 260p. I expect them to get back to where they were at their peak, so I'm holding on.

Read all you can

PEOPLE WHO THINK THEY ARE WELL UP ON THE subject of share trading are kidding themselves. They don't know it all. You will never know it all. Nobody will. The most experienced City *expert* learns something new every day. I know I do.

Making money from shares is not like learning to swim or riding a bike. Once you know how to do those things, that's it. You can. But with sharecraft, we forget stuff, we learn new tips, we unlearn what no longer works.

Not only do we have to keep our eyes and ears open to new info about shares, we also need to continually remind ourselves of the rudiments of share trading. So keep checking the internet, always read the newspapers and listen to the financial news. Aim to pick up something useful every hour, every day or every week.

It's also good practice to keep up with general news. Information about the latest wars, food shortages, politics, crime, shopping habits, fashion, charities, health and lifestyle are all useful to share-pickers like us. We need to know the trends to know which companies will prosper in the near and far future.

Good news bulls and bad news bears

BEWARE OF SUNNY WRITE-UPS

IT'S VERY EASY FOR A SHARE TO BE PUT IN A ROSY light. But sometimes they should have a skull and cross bones label put on them instead.

I'm not suggesting that the writer – be it a financial analyst or a journalist – is acting dishonestly by building up a company that doesn't deserve it. But an exposition of the splendid advantages of a share is totally misleading if a few snags are left out. When considering the worth of a share tip, there are always some drawbacks, no matter how promising the company.

For instance, an article may say that an oil company is producing much more of the black stuff than had been predicted. That would be a good reason to invest. Except that the writer fails to mention that there is a war going on with a neighbouring country. Rifle shots are ricocheting all over the canyons. Nor is there a reliable means of bringing the oil out and selling it on.

Or you might read that gold is being produced in lorry loads from a new mine in Africa. But the writer forgets that the world market for gold is losing its sheen. The good news is completely wiped out by the bad and the share price collapses.

Take articles that praise companies with a pinch of salt. Strive to pick holes in the arguments. Look for the vested interest. Be aware that many drawbacks are not brought up.

BEWARE OF GLOOMY WRITE-UPS

Equally, you'll see poisonous write-ups which castigate good companies unfairly. A journalist can make a saintly firm seem like the worst wretch on earth by listing all its faults, without mentioning any virtues at all.

You have to realise that there are share shorters out there, who make their money when shares fall. (This is not the way of an optimist like me, so I can give you no advice on shorting shares.) So writers think they provide a worthwhile service by disparaging a firm. Which is fair enough. Also, armchair dealers like us need to know if a company is likely to fail, so that we can pull out in time. But it is all too easy to knock a company by listing its dodgy points, if that list fails to reflect all the good bits.

Looking too hard at past errors can blind a writer to a firm's exciting potential yet to come. As an old trader, I think an outfit's future is much more important than its past.

Nearly all knocking pieces about a company look at its past failings. Or they say the latest figures are worse than the year before. Well maybe, but mistakes have been mulled over, remedial steps taken and economies made. Or if they haven't, they soon will be.

So I would never say disregard critical pieces on a company. I would rather read a knocking article than a laudatory one, any day. When I notice that positive aspects have been left out or glossed over, I try to find out what exactly has been forgotten. Then I compare the dodgy bits, as highlighted by the writer, with the more positive stuff I've teased from other sources.

Directors must have a stake

YOU WOULD EXPECT THE MANDARINS IN A company to have invested some of their private loot in their own venture. But you'd be surprised how many don't. Can they really expect us to leave them in charge of our money when they're not risking any of theirs?

Directors who haven't the confidence in their operation to invest their own coin will have share options instead of shares. In other words, they've not invested in their own firm. If they had reason to believe that the company will have a rising share price and dividends, isn't it likely they would have shelled out for some shares?

Similarly, check to see if directors of the company have bought or sold large chunks of shares recently. This is a strong signal for you to do likewise. Ask yourself: would the boss of a company dump shares if she thought that the company was going to bring in more profits than the year before? Similarly, would they be buying up shares if they didn't have cofidence in the future of the company?

Take a look at the chart of Dawson Geophysical below. Marked on the chart are occasions of director buying during the financial crisis and then the point at which the directors sold shares once the price had recovered. You can see how directors' knowledge of what is going on inside a company enables them to make informed decisions about the future share price. And you can observe and follow their actions to make a profit yourself.

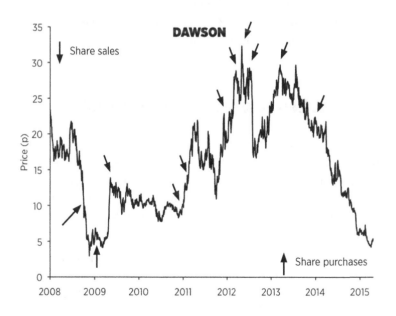

The most likely reason for a sale by one or more of the directors is that they've seen – from an insider's point of view – that things aren't going well. They're disposing of some shares before the price goes on a slimming campaign.

There is, though, the possibility that a selling director wants to raise money for personal reasons. To buy a yacht, say, or to snaffle a stake in another company. Or maybe there are school bills or a divorce to pay for. For all these reasons and a zillion more, it's best not to put too much emphasis on one director selling, especially if some of the others are buying more shares. But if a few of them are disposing, well, I would get rid of all mine, too. You can find lists of director sales on the internet – just do a search.

Just one more point on director sales. It's been known for the directors of firms in trouble to buy a few shares just to inspire false confidence among existing and future shareholders. If the purchase doesn't amount to much, treat the information as worthless.

Another worrying sign is when directors release news of their purchases in gradual bursts of publicity, rather than all at the same time. This is just a way of encouraging punters by making director dealings seem bigger than they actually are.

When fewer shares are traded

THE NUMBER OF SHARES BOUGHT AND SOLD IN A company is known as the volume. You should be able to find the number of daily trades on your broker's website. A drop in daily volumes compared to the average is a bad sign. It could mean City slickers are losing interest in the firm.

However, the level of trading can be affected by other components, too. It might be a time of year when the trading floor is much quieter. Coming up to Christmas, for example. Or between Boxing Day and New Year. Similarly, July and August have low volumes, as many traders take their summer hols. The Tuesday after bank holidays is traditionally short on trades as well, as dealers extend their weekends.

Or there may be big developments in another sector, which would divert buying away from your shares. A poor day's trading could also simply be a one-off glitch.

You need to monitor a company's trading volumes over a week or two to get a true idea of what's going on. But if there's definitely a sustained fall-off in interest, you might think of kicking the holding out of your bag.

LOW VOLUMES ON BREAK-OUTS

One of your share prices suddenly strides forward. Should you sell and secure the profit? Or should you hang on in the hope of grabbing more gains?

Check the number of shares traded on the day. If the number of deals is only marginally larger than usual, the higher share price might not have long to live.

The pros and cons of penny shares

WHAT ARE PENNY SHARES, ANYWAY?

SHARES WHICH COST LESS THAN £1 ARE KNOWN AS penny shares.

They are issued usually by small companies without much capital behind them. But don't look down on them for that. It's worth noting that nearly all big companies were penny share outfits once. They grew out of it. And growth is one of the City's happiest words. If your company has it, it means the price of its shares will rise. No question.

But sometimes long-established giant firms can hit bad times and their share values fall beneath £1. Included in this list is Lloyds Bank.

Its rival, RBS, the former Royal Bank of Scotland, in which I have lost at least £20,000, also found itself in this ignominious position. So it divided the total number of shares. This caused the value to automatically shoot up to over £3 each. The trouble was all the shareholders now held far fewer shares, so we didn't make anything out of this manoeuvre. In my book, RBS still has penny shares.

PENNY REWARDS

The cheapies have many benefits over more expensive shares, so I would advise holding at least a few of them: a fifth of your portfolio, say. As well as their more important attributes, they really are good fun.

For a start, serious researchers have found that over many years, companies which begin life by offering cheap shares do better for investors than outfits which begin with more expensive shares. More generally, tiny companies with cut-price shares earn us more money than big ones.

Here are some other reasons to trade penny shares:

1. You get buckets of shares for your money.
2. They only have to rise a penny or two, to make you a whacking profit.
3. Penny shares have done better than the blue chips for the last 80 years.
4. Small companies, more likely to issue penny shares, are the first to recover when good times return.
5. Nearly all companies are small to start with. Among the current list could be the next Google, eBay or Facebook. Imagine how much you would make if you were to invest in a future blockbuster when it's a penny share. You'd be a multi-millionaire, without question.

However, the reason you should not hold more than a fifth of your portfolio in the cheapos is that there are a few drawbacks.

Because the shares are only worth a few pennies, the spread between buy and sell price is usually high. If you buy shares in a Footsie giant, the spread can be almost non-existent. With a penny share, the difference between the buy and sell price might only be a penny, say. But, as the share is worth very little in the first place, that spread could equate to anything from 10% to 70%. For example, Ferrum Crescent is an AIM-listed iron mining company in South Africa. The selling price is 0.4p, but the buying cost is 0.6p. This means that you need to see a rise of 50% just to break even.

Another drawback is that because the price of a penny share is already near the floor, it doesn't take much for a struggler to end up with no value whatsoever. And because the bottom is so close, you may not have time to dump the shares before it's too late. In my experience, only a limited number of penny shares have imploded altogether, but it's worth being aware of the risk.

It can take some months, and in extreme cases years, for penny shares to move either up or down. They require patience, during which time you almost certainly won't get a dividend. But when they do start to motor, hang on to your hat! It wouldn't be unusual for your babies to go up 20% each day. I've had penny shares that have risen 600% in a week.

When the Footsie rises, investors will often sell penny shares and turn to the giants instead. Such sales cut the value of penny shares, of course. So while shares in the top 100 British companies soar, the penny market will go the other way. What happens is that traders decide "Why should I take the extra risk of trading penny shares, when I can enjoy price rises among companies which are more secure and safer?" So when the Footsie rises day after day, don't buy any penny shares.

Most penny share companies are respectable. But if petty crooks are going to operate in Shareland, this is the area they'll choose. One reason is that newspapers don't put minnows under the microscope.

In fact, the financial pages rarely mention them at all. Regulation is also lighter at this end of the market.

The lack of press coverage makes penny shares harder to research. Though there are one or two websites, such as ShareProphets (Shareprophets.com) and Docs Layman's Chatter (Docslaymanschatter.blogspot.co.uk), that put penny shares through the mill.

HOW TO MAKE EVEN MORE MONEY WITH PENNY SHARES

One characteristic of penny share companies is that there is less news to affect them than bigger outfits. Therefore, their price can stay static for many months. Actually, it's worse than that. If no developments come, neither good nor bad, the share price will slowly erode. It's depressing.

So why entertain the cheapos at all?

Well, the lack of activity and gradual decay is more than made up for when the share finally reacts to an event. One day, it will shoot forward like a starving terrier after a fat rabbit. The action can be so dramatic that your share will double or treble in a few days. (I'm emphasising this previously-mentioned point again because it's important.)

All right, it may not be common, but penny shares have rocket motors when they finally launch. Medium-sized companies cannot hold a candle to such value-adding power. And as for Footsie lumps – I've never known one rise by more than 50% in a week. And if a jumbo rises more than half its value in a year, well, it's quite a rarity.

Even so, it's best only to consider investing in a cheapie if it has already started to put on value. Then you are buying into a rising share. Involving yourself in a share when it's stagnant means you're tapping into a fallow period which might last for months. This isn't productive.

In my experience, a penny share starts rising on good news of its own – not happy sentiment in the market as a whole. This is another reason to consider the pennies. They can ascend when the Footsie and the rest of the market is in decline. I often make real money on a bad day for shares because I keep a chunky stable of penny shares.

DRIP FEEDING YOUR INVESTMENT

The wise way to play penny shares is to decide exactly how much money you would like to put into each company. But then only inject a third of this amount into the firm at first. See how it goes. If the share continues to froth up after you joined, then you can shove another third of your money in.

After all, you are already showing a profit so you still won't lose, even if the share begins to backpedal. But if it keeps on going, you can add the final 33% of the stake. Now you really stand to make a killing.

When the share really begins to look as though it is falling back to its starting point, you should sell and lock in what profit remains.

SHELL FISHING

When a penny share outfit deteriorates so much that it almost stops trading altogether, it becomes a *shell company*. This, believe it or not, can be a fine old time for its shareholders. Shell companies are very attractive to unlisted companies which are not members of the stock exchange but who would dearly like to be.

The application process for exchange membership is expensive. To save on costs, a company can buy a firm already registered with the exchange. Then it backs into this company, perhaps changing the name to its own a bit later on.

The rescuer does not have to pay much for the target because it is now doing very little and its share price is derisory. But when the deal is struck, the battered investors in the penny firm can suddenly find themselves hooting with joy as the share price rockets on the merry news.

So one strategy you might try is to buy into a firm whose share is almost worthless, but which stands a good chance of being snapped up by a stock market aspirant. Obviously you take a wide chance here, but backing into companies is something which is often done at immense advantage to shareholders, so it's not a bad idea.

You can either buy a likely target on spec or you can search for a company where takeover rumours are already underway. In the latter case, you won't get the shares as cheaply, but there's more chance of a merger actually taking place.

* * *

So there we are – advantages and disadvantages of penny shares. If you choose your dormice with as much care as you do your Footsie elephants, you should do well out of them. And when one penny share does really well – increasing by 1000%, say – it will easily make up for all your penny dreadfuls that disappoint.

When swing's the thing

IOFTEN WEAR THE DARK CLOAK OF A *MOMENTUM trader*. Another term for it is a *swing trader*, which I prefer as it sounds more intriguing. This roughly means that I look for hot shares and leap on board. When they cool off, I jump back on the pavement. The whole process can take only two to four days, though sometimes it morphs into a few weeks.

Hot shares are ones that are moving up. It's nice to know why they are accelerating and the reasons can be easily found if you search for them (on Google for instance). But it is not vital to know why they trip the light fantastic. It's the actual momentum, or movement, that interests me. Not the intrinsic value of the shares.

Only armchair share shovers like us can really operate properly as swing traders. Banks, hedge funds, trusts, pension funds and insurance companies deal in much bigger blocks of shares, making it hard for them to move in and out of markets with the required speed. It's just one of the exciting advantages we have over the professionals.

YOU DON'T HAVE TO BE A SWING TRADER

It's fair to say that some brainy City types look down on my activities as a momentum trader. It's not quite right in their eyes. You should accumulate your shares with dignity, caution and insight. You should consider all the fundamentals of a company, assessing its value in relation to the share price. You must check whether debt is being repaid or added to. All these things must be taken into calm consideration.

They argue that you should not attempt to time the market, but buy the shares as soon as you've completed your homework. And then you should settle down to hold the shares for life, living on the dividends or re-investing them. Oh hum.

There's nothing wrong with that approach. In fact some very well-heeled people have done exactly that. It especially suits investors who would rather do other things than monitor their shares all the time. But these people are *investors* – whereas I am a trader.

I must admit there's a risky element to momentum trading. There is also more energy, graft and time required. But don't fret. You don't have to be in the club. There are many occasions I buy shares for the longer haul. Sometimes, I latch on to a fast-rising share, fully intending to ditch it soon, but then circumstances get in the way and I hold on to it for longer.

This is what happened when I bought shares in ITV to hold for what I thought was only going to be a day or two. The credit crunch chose to bite at around this period. And one of the first things ditched by companies in trouble is the advertising budget. The shares tumbled like a 20-stone passenger in a floorless lift.

So fast, I was left holding the baby and the bathwater. Luckily for me, hit shows like *X Factor* and *Downton Abbey* came along and the shares, over a distressing period of years, slowly crawled back up to leave me in profit.

So, there are risks involved in short-term trading and you may prefer to hold for the longer term. Nevertheless, let's look at how momentum trading could earn you some faster dough.

MAKING MONEY FROM SWING TRADES

You notice that the price of The Candy Floss Group has shuffled up from 30p to 31p. This doesn't seem much, But it's roughly 3% – enough to be picked up by the financial websites – so it's easy to find the share and identify it as having instant potential. The next day, it puts on another 1p. That's 6% in two days. Not at all bad. I might well buy the shares at this point.

By now the original catalyst which set the share off may be wearing thin. But the share will still maintain progress because buyers are jumping on the rocket hoping it will go to Mars. So the share can keep on rising for a few more days, perhaps even a week.

When the price stops elevating and stays level for two days on the trot, I will sell the entire holding and look for another hot share. Of course, it may start advancing again after a pause. But it's not worth the risk of holding out for more, because it will be already obvious to you that shares which make a mighty leap soon run out of puff. They do it nearly every time. If you're greedy and hang in for more, you could find yourself back to square one and sometimes in an even worse position than that.

BE THE FASTEST TRADER IN THE WEST

You have to be nippy to be a successful momentum trader. If you're slow with the buy button you could find yourself paying too much. Find out the share's low point of the week. If the price has already risen appreciably in the last few days, you're probably too late. Look for another share nearer the start of its high jump.

Even if you decide to do some swing trading, remember that a rising price should not be your only guide. You really do need to find out why the shares are in the ascendancy. It'll take only a few seconds on Google. If you find a good reason then it's ok to buy. But if the cause of the price increase is misbegotten or temporary, move on.

Don't touch these companies

THERE ARE SOME TYPES OF COMPANIES I SUGGEST you generally avoid. I'll run through these now.

MANAGEMENT BENEFIT SCHEMES

There are some companies which seem only to exist to enrich their founders and directors. They're supposed to have the usual duty to their shareholders, but instead they snaffle our money and mostly use it to pay themselves high salaries and bonuses. The salaries seem to toddle up every year, as the sales come down, while the expenses and debts rocket.

The oil is never found. It's not economical to take the gold out. The purchase of other companies doesn't pay off. A challenging economic outlook. There are all sorts of excuses made. And guess what? Every so often the beggar's bowl comes out. This is when you're invited to subscribe to another rights issue or an open offer, so they can continue to pay their big cheeses ever-growing salaries.

One way I have for identifying these useless enterprises is to note when their company reports are released. It can be on a bank holiday, Christmas Eve or during a general election. Any old date will do, as long as it's on a day when we'll all be busy doing other things and are likely to miss the bad news. They hope we won't notice that their overblown incomes have gone up yet again. It seems rather childish of them, doesn't it, but it seems to work.

Nobody should mind if a firm with an honourable management doesn't do too well. That's life. We can sell and choose another more promising venture, or, if the runes are right, spin them another chance. But when they keep on rising their personal pay-outs in the face of ever-worsening results, well, the shares should be dropped like a boyfriend with an axe fetish.

OIL EXPLORERS

I am a fan of oil production companies. When oil prices rise, so does the share price. Nice. But I am not a supporter of oil exploration outfits that haven't yet found what they're looking for.

It's quite common for a bunch of people to set up a company, collect shareholders' money, pay themselves decent remuneration – and then not actually find any of the black stuff. The search goes on, of course, and the share price will rise and fall on various expectations, false dawns and disappointments. But all too often, the share price just fizzles away as hope fades. It amazes me how long some of these annoying companies can survive without uncovering a smear of the ebony nectar.

Desire Petroleum has been a sore in my portfolio for over ten years now. They're looking for oil in the Falkland Islands, which is becoming, for me, the elephant's graveyard of oil investment. I lost interest in reading their undesirable reports long ago. Maybe they have found something now, but if they have, it's yet to be reflected in the share price. In the early days, I kept topping up my holding. No longer. They've now been taken over by Falklands Oil and Gas, but I've still not struck loads of money from this remote region.

My wariness of oil explorers increases if they turn out to be looking for it in inaccessible places. Even if they find oil, they might have extreme difficulty getting it out for sale, especially if bullets start to fly.

There are a few companies who hire out drilling equipment and engineering know-how to oil explorers. That way they can turn scrumptious profits even when black gold isn't forthcoming. They could be a better option. I bought shares in Wood Group, which is one such company, and felt a lot safer in their hands than any oil explorer.

NOT-SO-SUPER MARKETS

The big food chains used to be a reasonable investment, especially in bear markets. The argument was that we all have to eat. Therefore nosh will always be the last thing we do without when cash is sparse.

But that was before the discount foreign supermarkets like Lidl, Aldi and Netto began to encroach on the sector. Now if these newcomers are not always cheaper, they certainly appear to be. They achieve it with clean-cut, wide aisles and no-frills presentation.

They also leave stuff out in rustic boxes and they price everything very clearly in big numbers on the shelves. This gives the illusion of everything being cheap because it looks as though no money is spent on marketing and writing prices in large characters shows they're obviously proud of their discounts.

But even without that cunning foreign competition, Tesco, Sainsbury's, Morrisons et al would still find it hard to grow profits. World food sources are under pressure, so wholesale prices rocket. This position will worsen as the general wealth of families across the globe increases and they have more money to buy more food.

There are always price wars being waged in the supermarket world. And the tighter profit margins become, the less profit goes to the company, so the share price and dividends suffer. We must expect this cut-throat battle to become bloodier year by year.

One thing that did attract me to supermarket shares – and I've held masses of them in my time – is the frequent possibility of a takeover, especially for Morrisons and Sainsbury's. But though Sainsbury's once had to see off a bid from the east – an annoying episode which mislead

me into doubling my shareholding for nothing – nobody seems to want to enter the store merger arena these days. I guess it's price competition again.

I have an admission to make. I still have small stakes in all the big British supermarkets, even though I'm suggesting they should be avoided. Sadly, the reason I hold these shares might be due to my misguided loyalty to British companies in the face of foreign competition. I've often warned about the sheer stupidity of misplaced loyalty, so please don't make the same mistake as me.

FOOTBALL CLUBS

Only one football club has ever graced my portfolio. Sorry, that should be *dis*graced my portfolio. That was Millwall and it was, thankfully, many moons ago. The club was opening a swanky new stadium at the time and hopes were high that this would put the club, with its large local following, in the country's elite top ten. Fat chance! I still have the vexing certificates somewhere in the darkest corner of my forbidding attic. But I don't care if they never turn up again, because they're worthless.

The trouble with football shares is that the owners burn the money to buy new players. Many of these overpaid stars cease to shine the moment they join their new club. The club slides into ever-increasing debt.

Yes, fans do buy the shares out of loyalty. But they usually hold so few that the cost of administration outweighs the benefit to the club. And when a club does badly, down goes the share price. Just one poor match slashes the share price and ruins your weekend.

Buying football shares is a gamble. And as I've tried to explain, trading shares is not a gamble but a business deal. So avoid soccer shares and enjoy the game for its own sake.

PACKAGE TOUR OPERATORS

Yes, there are substantial package holiday firms which still pull in armies of customers. But those members of the older population, who are not happy with home computers and mobile devices, will become fewer as years roll on.

Most of us who are computer savvy have already learned the advantages of booking holidays for ourselves. Even small hotels in really out-of-the-way places are no longer beyond our reach, and we can hop between airlines and rail companies for the best deals. We can organise our own coach tours and car transfers, too.

So what real future do package tour operators have? Not enough to make me want to risk my lucre with them, that's for sure.

MOVIE MAKERS

Every so often you'll have an email from a film company. They take your name from share registers, or your broker will be in cahoots with them. They'll invite you to invest in their latest picture. This is tempting. Sounds glamorous, doesn't it, to be part of show business? Makes you feel like a grand producer. Especially when they list an impressive array of stars who have parts. They usually trumpet the director's latest hit, too. See, you're feeling part of the celebrity club already.

But I would bring the curtain down on such glittering offers. Big stars will tell you that not all their films are box office miracles. Quite a few lose money. Some don't even get a proper release. The cinema-going public is fickle, critics are merciless and big screen tickets are extortionately priced. And films cost a truckload of money to make. Just looking at the endless credits at the end of each production gives you a good inkling of that. If nobody goes to see the film, the loss is eye-watering.

Don't join the queue. Stay away.

COMPUTER/TECHNOLOGY COMPANIES

I don't rule these out entirely. The computer and mobile device industries are still in nappies. Goodness knows where they will have taken us in ten years' time. Some giants will make a killing if they can market the right product at the right time. And there are a few outfits which currently look unassailable in our technological world.

But it only takes one competitor to raise a better idea and that's the end of your bloated share price. I've noticed that only a few firms rise to the top in this research and development jungle. Others seem rather good at survival, but that's about all. Their share prices sometimes lurch forward on a nugget of good news – a hefty new order, say, or a brilliant invention – but the excitement rarely lasts.

I've wasted an awful lot of money on techno firms which promised the earth, yet failed to deliver. I can only think of one player in the field – ARM Holdings, Apple's favourite chip designer – which has doubled my money. I've broken even with around a dozen firms, but the rest have left me out of pocket.

Around the turn of the century, lots of people, many new to shares, made a killing on technological shares. We called it The New Economy then. But it was an airy bubble. The firms had no earnings to sustain their optimistic share prices. Some of us staggered clear in time. But many people saw all their gains – which gave them so much to crow about at dinner parties – vanish before their eyes. We veterans of the new economy bubble have been wary of techno firms ever since.

FOREIGN SHARES

Nearly all Footsie companies do most of their business in other countries. Some mining companies don't do any business here in the UK at all. But buying shares in these companies with foreign earnings is as far as your foreign ambitions should take you. Only invest in companies you know well and can easily keep track of. This puts out of court foreign firms which operate solely in other places.

It's easier than ever to invest in non-British companies. Most internet brokers will do the deals for you at the drop of a hat. The same brokers can suck you into foreign trades by carrying only news of American firms, for example, on their homepages. I know some popular brokers in Britain who feature many mini articles on American companies but never mention really important updates on the UK economy.

But for you, British shares should be your only interest. I've tried investing in overseas outfits, but I just can't get to grips with their current trends. Yes, you can study their recent history, but that gives you no feeling for how things are going now and in how they'll go in the future.

Supposing I bought shares in an American supermarket. I could not see how many customers were in my local store. I could not check if the produce they sell is cheap or appealing. I could not take a view on how well they're coping with local competition from their rivals. I would be at sea.

It's hard enough to keep track of Blighty's shifting sands of shares. Do you really want to add the progress of America, Germany, France, Italy, Russia, China, Korea, India, Brazil and anywhere else to your work list? Stick to the home country and you'll have a better chance of getting rich.

You need to keep your share trading as simple as possible. It's better to know a lot about a little (by sticking to British companies) than to know a little about a lot (loads of foreign firms). I just don't think you should burden yourself with a business set-up you know next to nothing about. It shouts disaster.

Take advantage of reporting day

ABOUT TWICE A YEAR, A COMPANY REPORTS ITS latest accounts to shareholders and anyone else who's interested. Many do it every three months. It's how shareholders can check current sales compare to last year – are they up or down? Are expenses being pruned? Is debt being cut or is it ballooning? Are there spanking new orders littering the horizon? Are dividends to be hiked?

These are the most important bits of a company report. They are the nuggets picked over by the media. Though only large companies ever make the news in the bulletins.

Now a funny thing happens to share prices on reporting day. The share price will usually drop. If the figures are worse than expected the price will plummet like a lead-lined brick. But even when the figures are bouncy, the share price will often suffer. Why should this be?

If you look back at the share price over the previous week, you will find that it has probably been ticking up. When the announcement comes, the expectations which caused this improvement have come to pass. Many investors now reclaim their money so they can try out another company approaching its reporting day. These punters are following a very old saying in Shareland:

"Buy on the rumour and sell on the fact."

If the City expects a company's latest figures to be better than last year's – based on anything from blind optimism, vague intuition or a raft of positive announcements by the company over the last few months – traders have been snapping up the shares. Once everybody knows the results, there is no reasonable chance of the shares putting

on more value, so selling becomes a better idea. This does not apply to longer-term investors, so thankfully, the share doesn't tank altogether.

Once the price has fallen on reporting day, there can be a bounce-back over the next few sessions. This is because investors who were not involved in the pre-reporting ploy may now regard the share as a bargain, especially if they were secretly impressed by the company numbers all the time.

You might be able to make quite a bag of money by buying shares three or four days after a company's reporting setback. This might apply more to larger companies where the share price has – before the latest drop – seemed pretty stable.

READING COMPANY REPORTS

The chairperson and chief executive will comment on the latest accounts at the time of release. They will, of course, be tempted to put a shiny gloss on everything, just to maintain the share price.

But wise managers do not do over-egg the pudding. If they do and the truth comes out later, as is inevitable, the share price will be murdered. No, better bosses always tell the truth – especially about future prospects.

This is one reason why I tend to trust company reports, at least enough to read them carefully. If the content is optimistic, that's a buy signal. If the world "challenging" appears too much, I shun the shares. If it sounds as if the management is content to continue as they always have done, that is complacency. Avoid.

We should also note that company reports are not independent and thus are biased. But you can find plenty of unfettered reports in the press on the day after the accounts are published. Many of them are free on the net. These unbiased articles will be more critical. And if they're not, this is something to take note of and could be a buying signal for the shares.

How often to trade

THERE WAS A TIME WHEN TRADING SHARES WAS expensive. The broker spoke to you personally and charged a hefty commission. The spreads were even wider than today. On top of that, you had to cough up for a long-distance phone call. They were dear in those days and you could be left waiting a long time for your broker to stop chatting with another client.

Buying and selling has become quicker and cheaper. You click a button and it's done. No waiting. No boring chat or phone charges. Stamp duty is no longer applied to AIM shares. The spreads on some bigger shares are almost non-existent. And broker commissions have been slashed.

But we still have an issue with spreads. These, as I've said, are especially punishing for cheaper shares. So if you do a lot of in-and-out trading, the costs can mount up. Having said that, you can only beat the average – and be rich – if you wheel and deal with some alacrity. So you need to do quite a few trades a month and hang the expense.

There are some brokers who offer big discounts if you trade frequently. So if you plan to do that, you might want to change your account for one with better terms.

There is a real danger, though, that over-trading will eat into your profits. The practice can also rob you of gains if a back-pedalling share suddenly splutters into life. You might find yourself in the no man's land between sell and buy at exactly the wrong time.

I limit myself to ten trades a week. Even using the cheapest broker I can find, Traders Own, this still costs me £80 a week (£4,000 a year). Obviously, if a plethora of juicy opportunities present themselves I will trade more, but ten a week is about right. And if I go over ten trade ceiling, I scale back my trades the following week.

By sticking to a maximum ten trades I also have to think a bit harder about making a buy or sell move. And a bit of extra consideration never does any harm. I like to think that the ten trade limit has stopped me buying shares which were not actually that good. And it has prevented my selling many a company far too early.

Shareholders versus pros and hacks

I SHARED A PANEL AT THE UK INVESTMENT SHOW WITH a professional trader who plays with other people's money. Terrible pressure, as you can imagine. But this chap was a trader par excellence. A solid gold pedigree of trading for the banking world before he went independent. The view he expressed forcibly on the stage was that amateurs cannot beat the professionals at the gilded game.

He has the latest software, the fastest computers, the very best of previous experience. All of this enables him to make snap decisions, reverse them and then put them back into play. But I disagree that he's always better placed to make a profit than we are. And here's why:

1. We do not have the pressure of trading with clients' money. We can follow our own inner feelings and not search for tangible reasons. We're allowed to tap into our subconscious because we don't have to explain every decision we make.

2. We don't have to seek another's permission to trade.

3. Machines can never think better than humans because they can't think at all.

Don't always trust the news

I REMEMBER THE DAY THE BBC SAID THAT EVENTS IN Ukraine had affected the BP share price. Well, they did – by a couple of pence. But, as the shares were around £5 each at the time, that was hardly a massive drop. Less than 1%. The next day, my BP shares rose to a level higher than the fall – and guess what? The BBC didn't find time to mention the return to the status quo.

I don't blame the BBC. They learned a long time ago, as all journalists know, that nobody is interested in positive news.

It's always the same for a minor disaster on the stock market. The financial slots on the bulletins gloat with the bad news – "Billions wiped off the stock market," that kind of thing. But they don't mention it so often when a boost of similar value in size takes place.

A similar thing happens when the bulletins highlight a company's disappointing trading results. The breakfast bulletin mentions a big loss for the Seaside Rock Group. So we bury our head in the pillow. But when we check the share price while munching our cornflakes we find that the price has leapt. The reason usually is that the City had anticipated shocking results for weeks, so the news when it comes out wasn't as bad as thought.

The moral is: never let the news grind you down.

Can I turn professional?

THIS IS A DIFFICULT ONE. THE FIRST QUESTION YOU need to ask yourself is: Do I really want to give up my job? Will you miss the blokes, the girls, the office politics, gossip, the chat about last night's telly, the walk into work and the Christmas party?

Next, can you get by without the salary? Remember that your full-time share trading may trickle off to a poor start. Count up your pennies. If the market dips, could you survive for six months without an income? Do you have the confidence in your own ability/luck to make a fist of it?

How would you cope with being at home all day? Would you get bored, develop cabin fever, be tempted to stay in bed until noon, watch too much telly, put on weight? Will your partner accuse you of getting under their feet?

You should also consider whether your job will still be open to you if you make a mess of home trading. Or at least will it be easy to get a similar berth?

The clincher in my case, about 20 years ago, was realising that nearly every day my shares were making more money than I was. I reasoned that if I devoted even more time to it, my mistakes would be fewer and my victories stronger – and that would make even more mazuma.

Luckily, that indeed turned out to be the case.

Tasty targets

BROKERS AND OTHER FINANCIAL WRITERS USUALLY set a target price which they think a share they're tipping will reach. You might think that this spot is at the far reaches of the likely range and, in fact, is rather fanciful. But not in my experience. I find that share prophets usually set their targets too low.

A cynical view is that a lowish target is easier to reach and so the target-setters can crow about their success later on. Maybe, but what does this mean for cunning share shakers like us? Well, once the target is reached we are expected to sell. But if we accept the premise that targets are set too low, we should be rebellious and hold out for more.

Shares really can take on the characteristics of a stick thrust into a candyfloss machine. A gentle escalation is more common in Shareland than a gusher, but once a share really breaks out, it will often pile on bulk very rapidly. The reason is obvious – the more people spot the rise, the more it grows as they pile in for some of the action. Sadly, such bubbles can quickly burst and you need to be on constant call if you want to dabble in this practice.

So let me take you through the target game. Shares in the Iced Lolly Corporation are tipped by the *Financial Times* and *The Economist*. The share is currently £2 but they both think it will rise to £2.80. In a couple of months that target is reached. Don't sell. Just monitor the share a little more carefully. While the momentum which propelled it beyond the £2.80 level continues, do nothing. Once the action stops get ready and at the first dip, however tiny, jump clear.

If, after that, the share bumps quite a long way down – and the fundamental reasons which first caused the broker to recommend it still hold – you can gather back more shares at the lower price. Then set your sites on the target again.

Riding the cycle path

THERE'S AN INVISIBLE FORCE WHICH MOVES SHARES up and down. I'm talking about the cyclical effect. Sometimes its boost to shares comes late and sometimes it's early. This makes it an unreliable tool in the short term, but I've found it pretty dependable over time.

The main cycle seems to me to come around every seven years or so. It can make shares enter a three-and-a-half year decline and then begin a three-and-a-half year journey back again.

The origin of this interesting cycle harks back to the Stone Age. It's all about harvests, really. In the mists of time you had three bad years and three or four bumper ones. In the poor periods, doubtless caused by droughts, the worth of hard-to-grow grain went up and in the better years it came down.

Some say the droughts may have been first caused by high and low energy sunspots working on oats, wheat and barley. In any event, there's been some kind of knock-on event over the centuries, causing boom and bust years for agriculture which have filtered through to all parts of the economy – including shares.

More prosaically, the share cycle may be caused by the effects of fear and greed. After seven years of lust for money, we become fearful of a collapse. Dealers pull out and their panic begins another seven years in which the Footsie is below its earlier record. The good news is that each rise outstrips the decline, so that over the years new record highs are set for share prices.

Fine, but how can we benefit from these cycles?

Well, it gives us a rough idea of when a well-established bear market is likely to bellow into a bull market. Or it makes us believe that at the beginning of a bull market we have three or four years of rising share prices to look forward to. Or it tells us when it might be an idea to sell more shares and bank some profit.

Do bear in mind that share cycles do not operate by stopwatch. Far from it. They can be a year out, sometimes even more. The thought of a positive cycle waiting in the wings can, however, give you some comfort if all your shares take a powder.

Use your eyes

THERE ARE TWO SMALL SHOPS IN YOUR TOWN. THEY both sell old-fashioned sweets. One has a bright, clean window, with an interesting display of artefacts from the fifties. The other has a dingy shop front with dusty bottles of drab-looking small unidentified objects. One establishment is always full, the other is mostly empty. Which shop is the busy one? No need to answer.

You can boost your share awareness by looking around you. You may squat at the far end of Britain, but you can still pick up an advantage that dealers in the Smoke might miss. Just keep your eyes and ears fully receptive as you go about daily life. The evidence is all around you. Not just in stores but in pubs, hotels, cafes, cinemas, gyms, train stations and so on. You know where you spend your money and where you don't.

Which chain stores are light and airy, colourful, and fun to enter? Which ones are depressing? When you go into a chain store, check the tills. Are there plenty of people handing over their cards and cash at the counters? Is the store reduced to staging lots of sales to get rid of old stock? If the first is true, buy the shares. If sales notices prevail, avoid this company. When driving, see if any listed companies have lorries or vans with new number plates. If they have, it's a sure sign that they're doing well.

The Woolworths in my small Welsh town was not its usual vibrant self. The shelves seemed sparse, new lines were not in evidence, they kept reducing prices, held sales at unlikely times and the staff seemed depressed. I sold my shares. Six months later, the company went belly up.

Are your friends, relatives and workmates wearing a certain brand of clothes, using the same vacuum cleaners, buying identical computers? If they are, bearing in mind that everyone in Britain shops like sheep, the sales will be replicated all over the place and profits will boom. Buy shares in these companies. I know someone who bought a load of shares in Argos because he regularly saw queues outside their stores before opening. He made a killing.

What about the place where you work? You'll have a strong idea how things are going. Is it worth buying the shares? And if your firm is doing well, isn't it likely that rivals in the same game are also coining it in? Is this a share-snaffling opportunity for all firms in the same lucrative game? If it is, tell your boss that you're buying shares in his company – he might be nicer to you.

A spanking example of a firm which shines above its rivals is Wetherspoons, a thriving chain of family pubs which are very often full. Why? They set up in old and interesting buildings, which they don't spoil by modernisation or musak, their staff are helpful and cheerful and the meals are simple, but very, very cheap. Any visiting share trader immediately knows Wetherspoons' 700 pubs are going to dominate our town centres for a very long time.

The boon of profit-taking

YOU'LL OFTEN SEE THE TERMS *PROFIT-TAKING* OR *profit-takers*. It's usually part of a report that says a company's share prices are down. It's referring to the opportunistic selling of shares.

Some traders ask "Why refer to 'profit-taking' when you mean 'selling shares'?"

But profit-taking is slightly different. It means disposing of shares solely because they have risen strongly, perhaps within a few days. Such selling is done without taking into consideration the true worth of the company or that the share might keep on going north. It is turning a paper profit into a real one.

Profit-taking makes it so hard for shares and indexes to break previous records. When a company, the Footsie or another important index approaches its all-time high, profit-takers move in, selling away, and the price falls back.

WHEN PROFIT-TAKERS ARE AT LARGE

Profit-taking can be strongest towards the end of the Friday session. They are smarter-than-average traders capitalising on the Footsie's weekly progress. But it won't happen if there's been no improvement in share prices that week.

Profit-takers may also zoom in on an individual company which has seen a big jump in its share price over a few days. A common touchstone is the day a company reports its annual progress. Even when the figures look promising for the future, profit-takers will choose this day to cash in. Those who want to hold their shares are their victims, but usually not for long. A company targeted by profit-taking often recovers its old share price within a week or so.

EXPLOITING PROFIT-TAKING BY OTHERS

You can make money out of profit-taking without actually doing it. When the profit takers move in, the share price falls.

It's not fallen because of anything the company has done. Or even what the market has done (excluding the profit grab). Therefore, you could assume that the shares are now worth more than the new share price. You'd be right – it's buying time. And as profit-takers can really decimate the price, you could find a really good bargain.

Hang-ups you need to overcome

DON'T BUY IN HASTE

WE LOSE PATIENCE WHEN BUYING A SHARE. WE like the look of a company and we chomp at the bit. This is especially true if we have a wodge of cash in our trading account. We know we won't earn much interest in there and it seems like a waste. It's the equivalent of money burning a hole in our pocket.

So we attack the 'buy' button and the cash turns to shares in an instant. But we could have waited a few days and perhaps bought the shares cheaper.

A year ago at the time of writing, I found myself with £10,000 after selling shares in Marks & Spencer. I'd held them for years, during which time the share had moved upward with the speed of an arthritic sloth in treacle, with a few nasty tumbles along the way. I unwisely rushed to divide the resulting cash between five new hopefuls. My only criteria was that they had risen strongly in the last few days. How daft is that?

One choice was the City of London Investment Group. I thought they put money into London property which was booming. Wrong!

Instead they're world investors who happen to be based in London. A bit more care would have shown me this. Even so, luckily I am up 25% with this firm.

Hurried choice number two was Zytronic. They make touch sensors for electronic gadgets. I'm up 25% here too.

But Totally, a firm which attracts NHS contracts for physiotherapy projects, is down 50%. Gallimore, a builder, is off 10%, and Biome, a biodegradable plastics firm is shy 10%. I can only blame these losses on my loss of patience.

We should always carry out some basic checks before we buy. We should look at the price-to-earnings ratio to see if it's too high. We should check that profits are increasing year-on-year and that debt is steadily eroding. But with all the companies mentioned above, in my haste I did not bother and now I am vulnerable.

The way to overcome a rush like this is to imagine that you are handing over a pile of £10 notes to your broker. For a modest purchase of £500-worth of shares that would be 50 tenners. You wouldn't really enjoy handing over so much hard cash to a bookie, would you?

But that is exactly what you do when you click 'buy'. It may not seem like you've parted in seconds with 500 pound coins, but I'm afraid you have. It's always worth a hard long look before you let go of your cash.

THE RELUCTANCE TO SELL

For all sorts of reasons, we don't fancy parting with our shares, whether they are winners or losers. It's odd, because we rarely mind flogging other valuable possessions, like cars, homes or yachts. Failure to sell shares at the right time is my own biggest weakness.

Now, if a share has made a lot of money and the success story continues, we should not dispose of it. But if the price has increased hugely, and you feel, after weighing it up carefully, that the party must be nearly over, then you need to cash in. You really do!

But can we do it? Not without a lot of difficulty. It's human nature to expect a good thing to continue to be a good thing. We wait a day or two, just in case the share puts on a few more pennies. But it falls a mite, instead. So we hang on for a few more sessions, hoping for a happy return of the price we saw earlier.

Instead, the value dwindles a little more. So we decide to hold out until a *more normal* share price returns. But it never does. If we continue with thinking like this, we could end up with all of our profit eroded.

Everyone will tell you that it's hard to overcome the disinclination to sell shares, however strong the imperative. For one thing, selling a failure hurts your pride. You bought the shares after doing what you were supposed to do. By selling at a loss you admit you made a mess of things. It's not how you wish to be remembered – as a dunce with shares. You may feel you are a quitter, not something to be proud off.

All those self-perceptions are barmy. Everyone in Share Town gets it wrong. They do it constantly. It's impossible to be right every time and it's hard to win most of the time. The best operators are still proved wrong in four out of ten trades. But it would be unwise of you not to correct the situation. This is done by selling the shares.

Even the characters in the sitcom *Gavin and Stacey* understood the necessity of selling shares. In one episode, one of the cast wonders what to do about some shares that are fast losing value. She's on a phone call with a friend who advises her to "wait until Tokyo opens." This is precisely the kind of procrastination that I'm warning you about. Another character in the show has different, better advice: "Sell now and take the hit."

A wonderfully useful expression that: "Take the hit." Instead of hinting at failure, it reflects the courage of selling and putting up with your loss heroically. That's what you should do all the time – take the hit on the chin. It stops small losses becoming nasty ones. And it leaves you with the bulk of your money to put into a better bet.

There is a very common perception that your shares will rise the moment you sell them. Sadly, we have all had this happen to us. It's a pretty unpleasant feeling, possibly one of the worst for share shifters. To deal with this pesky notion that a sold share is bound to soar, there is another stock market adage that should help:

"Always leave some profit for the next trader."

It's the chivalric notion that even if you think there may be some mileage left in your shares, you should still sell, thus passing this bounty on to the next buyer. Yes, there are still some ladies and gentlemen in the City.

Don't be dejected about a falling Footsie

WHEN THE FOOTSIE FALLS, NEARLY ALL SHARES GO the same sorry way. If the top 100 British companies can't maintain their prices, then of course all shares are under attack. So on a day that the Footsie falls, the vast majority of our shares fall back and we're down in the dumps.

I know it will happen to you, because I still find myself in a murderous mood when the Footsie stumbles. However, this unhappiness is unjustified. It's a waste of time. A tottering Footsie means nothing in the end. It's only when one of your shares falls while the rest go up that any concern is justified.

When all shares stumble at the same time, it's nothing to do with your individual choices. It is a general setback, caused by the market and not the share.

The right time of day

IGNORING THE FIRST HOUR

WE'VE LOOKED AT TIMING ALREADY. WE'VE considered when to sell a share and when to buy one. We were talking about circumstances governing single companies then. But there is another kind of more general timing to consider – it's finding the best periods within the daily trading session to do our deals.

I never buy or sell shares in the first hour of the session. This often chaotic period is known in the City as *amateur hour*. It's welcome because it gives professional traders like me an extra hour in bed.

When the doors open, shares take a while to settle down. A share which begins with a gain on yesterday can instantly show an early loss as the big traders get their bearings. This can be because shares in the US, still trading when the British Stock Exchange closes, can flummox UK dealers who've gone home to an evening's telly. Also, the Asian markets are trading overnight UK time and London traders have to digest this too.

First thing, the big traders don't know whether to follow the Dow Jones lead, be it up or down, or ignore it. Same with the Eastern markets. It's only when they get the measure of what fellow traders are up to that they finally take up positions.

There are a few traders who jump in during the first hour. They hope to take advantage of overnight news. Don't be one of them. Too risky. Wait for the shares to settle. There may be a leap after you buy (or a fall after you sell) but even if there is, it will often revert to par by the day's end.

SELLING SHARES AGAINST THE CLOCK

If the Footsie has seen a price increase by the second hour, it is not the best time to sell shares. When the big index starts the day well it often continues to rise throughout the session. Therefore, for the most profits, the best time to dispose of your shares is towards the end of the trading day, say around 4pm. If you leave it later than this, you run the risk of hitting an end-of-the-day sell-off, born of the rising Footsie. In other words, profit-takers take the stage.

If shares are generally down by the second hour, you may want to put your sale off till tomorrow. But if you can't wait, perhaps because the share rang alarm bells yesterday and these are still gonging furiously today, it's wise to sell straightaway. When the Footsie begins the session in slow falling mode it often picks up speed on its downward trajectory.

One reason for the Footsie worsening during the day is that somebody has got wind of how the American market is likely to perform later on and these early hints are gloomy. This pessimistic feeling could well strengthen during the daily session as more dark clouds rumble in from across the Atlantic.

When the market is moving down, the longer you leave the sale the less money you will make. However, if you're buying, the end of the session is obviously better on down days, as shares get cheaper as the clock moves on.

Now let's look at some other optimum times to buy and sell shares.

For obvious reasons, there is often a lull in the markets around lunchtime. Many, though not all, dealers are having a munch. This can be a tasty time to buy. Shares which have been rising all morning take a break too and prices can dip between noon and 2pm. They may well resume their upward trend in the afternoon, in which case you could turn an early profit.

The very end of the session is not a good time to buy or sell. For one thing, your computer might crash, your server could stick or your doorbell might ring, leaving you crying in fury as you can't complete a vital trade.

I once planned to buy into Signet, the high street jewellery giant. The Dow was rising fast in the late afternoon and as Signet has many stores in the US, I expected the shares to soar on the London exchange the next day. With three minutes to market close, my laptop seized up. By the time I had booted up my mainframe spare, the curtain had come down. Signet took off as expected the next day, so this bungle cost me £2,000.

Bottom-fishing

THIS STRATEGY APPEALS TO ME BECAUSE I'M A natural bargain hunter. And that's what bottom-fishing is. We look for shares which have had a hard time and are now down in the dumps. It's rare for firms to disappear in a puff of smoke. The hardest hit companies can survive for years. You would think that, given the time they can exist in this miserable limbo, they would find the means of recovery, if only to a modest degree. Well, some of them do – and going out of our way to exploit this situation is known as bottom-fishing.

How do we find these companies?

Looking at the bulletin boards on financial websites is one way. There are plenty of share twiddlers like us who've bought shares which have hit the skids. They often post messages on the boards in the hope of persuading the rest of us to buy their bombed-out shares, so reviving the price a bit.

If you see a message extolling the virtues of a share with a really eviscerated share price, have a look at the company website and check out press reports on Google. The chances are that you will read some alarming stuff about the company that will put you off for eternity. But if you feel there is life in the old dog yet, you might want to risk a few quid. Don't spend too much on bottom fish – just buy a few shares to see how things go. Then top up if your choice begins to pick up speed later.

Clem Chambers, head man at the internet's fountain of City wisdom, ADVFN, automatically invests in any company whose share price is decimated by more than 50% in one day. It's a reasonable strategy, but I would not do this myself if there was a good reason for the fall.

Why might companies come back to life? Perhaps management learns from its mistakes. The global economy changes. Things hurl back into fashion. Maybe a white knight (big private investor) comes along and injects bags of cash. Perhaps another firm, a much more dynamic one, backs into the ailing firm, to pick up its stock exchange listing on the cheap. In fact, all kinds of changes can kick-start the share price again.

The noble art of bottom-fishing should not be confined to small companies. The mighty Legal & General insurance company suffered the ignominy of its share price crumbling from over 100p before the credit crunch to 19p at the height of the crisis. In those difficult days, nobody wanted to invest in financial companies in case of further upset. This proved wise in the case of the big British banks, whose shares have not recovered to this day. But in the case of L&G, I should have acted sooner. In the event, I bought at 70p and the shares are now up more than 300% on that price, as the chart below shows. So bottom fishing, even if you wait till the bottom is cleared, can be very worthwhile indeed.

LEGAL & GENERAL

I bought here

Another advantage of bottom-fishing is that the share price cannot fall much further. You can still lose the lot, of course, if your choice eventually goes bust, but complete disaster is a rarity.

You need just a little more care in selecting likely risers from the river bed than you would picking a healthier company. Don't rush it.

It must also be acknowledged that shares which seem to be at the lowest ebb, and have bumped along at that level for some time, can sometimes lurch even lower. This brings them close to vanishing altogether. So be warned that bottom fishing can have serious risks.

If you go ahead and buy a bottom fish, be prepared to settle down for rather a long wait. The share will not lose much value now – it's already on the bottom – but that rally you hope for may take some time to emerge.

Reading annual reports – the easy way

BE WARY OF FAT ONES

OCCASIONALLY, AN ANNUAL REPORT THE SIZE OF *War and Peace* will drop through the letterbox – or more likely these days, you'll be invited to plough through it online.

You might think a hefty report points to a company where lots of profitable stuff is going on. That the management is punctilious. They want to bring all the company information to you because they're proud of what they've achieved.

But I'm more encouraged if an annual report is slim. For one thing, it indicates that the bosses are not blasé about spending money. Thick reports take a lot of preparation because they have to be right. Lawyers and accountants are not cheap. A long report can also be used to bury embarrassing facts, such as a big hike for the bosses' pay or undeserved bonuses.

Reports which contain disturbing figures can begin with many pages about peripheral matters which don't affect the share price. Like health and safety considerations. Or a wordy exploration of company efforts towards bettering the environment. All very laudable, I'm sure, but I can't help feeling that they hope we'll all stop reading the report long before we reach dreadful facts about cancelled orders, rocketing expenses, paltry profits and exploding debt.

So skim through until you find the very few pages that talk about hard cash. With less-than-promising companies, these are more likely to be found at the end.

You might also read the chairman's annual report, but cynically. Of course, he or she is going to highlight the best bits and downplay the damage. This text will have been rewritten many times, usually with the help of crafty press relations staff. Try to spot the important bits that have been left out and then imagine how harmful those omissions are going to be.

The chief executive will also put in his or her pennyworth. Read this with the gimlet-eyed suspicion of a revengeful tax collector with gout. Visualise what has carefully not been said.

LATE RESULTS

Well-managed firms are ahead of the game on annual reports. If they've brought them out on the same date for six years on the trot, that says something positive for the operation. But if the annual report appears late one year, I often sell the shares.

This is because I believe that if there are perky tidings to be relayed, the management will get it out there as soon as possible. Whereas the opposite motive applies to disappointing news. If a company has a skeleton or two in the cupboard, something it would rather not be known, like desperate sales data, it will put off the news as long as possible. Delays means the company can maintain an unmerited share price for a while longer.

Data feed

GROW MAN, GROW

ONE OF THE BEST SIGNS OF HOW SHARE PRICES ARE likely to motor in the near future is the Gross Domestic Product – or GDP. It should really stand for Gosh! Difficult and Perplexing. This is because the final figure contains so many disparate factors and is rather vague to boot.

Britain's growth is worked out by adding up all the country's consumer spending on stuff and services. To this is added all government spending and the entirety of the country's outlay on capital. Then we add the value of every export, minus all our imports.

I wouldn't like to work all this lot out, would you? It's because of the sheer complexity of such a task that some economists think the figure is likely to be inaccurate. For example, when the country was said to be in negative growth in 2013, many firms reported that they were doing rather well. This was supported by official figures showing falling unemployment.

Another criticism of GDP is that it doesn't take into account the black economy, which includes car boot sales, charity shops, other second-hand transactions, naughty trading in cash to escape VAT, unregistered workers and so on.

Despite all of these problems, on days when growth is reported to be sturdier than expected, your share prices will often rocket. I've also found that the announcement of healthy growth figures has the capacity to keep share prices bubbling up for weeks and even months. It's the kind of news that makes everyone in the Square Mile more confident. And confidence is a strong driver of share prices – much more important than how well firms are actually doing.

THE JOB LOTTERY

Unemployment figures are not as relevant to share prices as national growth, but they do exert some influence. You can bet on the figure by buying shares before the next jobs announcement if you feel that unemployment will be down. But that is more like gambling than trading.

If employment does turn down, you'll have to act very quickly on the announcement to take advantage of rising share prices. I've discovered that, though an increased number of people in work will boost their spending and so add to company profits, the effect of employment figures on share prices is limited to one or two days only, unlike the more lasting affect of positive GDP data.

PROPERTY VERSUS SHARES

We used to believe that rising property prices were bad for shares, because they encouraged investors to buy bricks and mortar instead. But now higher house costs are seen as an improvement in people's wealth and therefore a reason to expect companies to make more money. So now if house prices rise you should buy shares rather than sell.

Don't be tempted to switch out of equities into buying property when shares are shaky and house prices are on a roll. Shares are a better investment than bricks – and not just because of the money.

Do you really want to be painting, decorating and repairing a house you don't even live in? Do you need to be thrashing around on Christmas Eve trying to find a plumber because your tenant broke the toilet? What if you end up with tenants from hell? What if they won't pay their rent? Are you happy to leave your money tied up where you can't get at it, without waiting for months or years before you find a buyer?

The only time I bought a house to rent put me in touch with an exotic and frightening world. Though I had some exemplary tenants, I also met some of the other tenants' interesting visitors. They included anxious relatives, bailiffs, policemen, government investigators, VAT officials and tax collectors. It was like being part of a soap opera.

With shares, there is no hands-on hassle. When you get fed up with your shares, you just click a button and they're off your hands. Not quite as secure as property, I grant you, but much less trouble.

Have I the right to hold you?

WHEN RIGHTS ISSUES ARE RIGHT

EVERY SO OFTEN, ONE OF THE COMPANIES IN YOUR collection will need more cash. It might be that the bosses want to expand, cut down their debt or take over a rival.

One way of doing it is to issue more shares. This is known as a rights issue. Sounds like an easy way to make a fast buck, doesn't it? But there are strict rules about making new shares, mainly to protect existing shareholders. They would otherwise run the risk of their holding being diluted. Obviously, the more shares that are out there, the less they are going to be worth.

One of the rules is that the new shares should be offered to the current shareholders first. To entice them to buy, the new equities are offered cheaper than the current price on the open market.

The stumbling block is that as soon as the discounted price for new shares is announced, the price drops for ordinary shares on offer through the stock exchange. This is a bummer if you hold the shares but can't afford to buy any more, or simply if you don't want any more.

But hold on. Your rights to buy the new shares can be sold, which would give you some extra dosh. This can be done through your broker in the usual way. If you don't take up the offer, all is not lost. The firm will return you some cash by way of compensation for the reduced share price when the rights issue rigmarole is wound up.

Should you buy the new shares? In most cases, I would say yes. It depends on the price of the new issue compared to the price the existing shares are trading at. If there is a reasonable difference, it's worth buying the new offering. You are getting the new shares cheap and have a chance to sell at a profit later on.

A reasonable difference would be anything over 5%, as there's no spread or commission for accepting the new shares. But the variance is often much more than that. I've known new shares to be 50% less than the old ones. With discounts in that league, it's definitely worth gobbling up the new shares you are offered.

And here's another benefit. If you haven't got the readies, you can sell some of your old shares on the market to raise the cash to buy the new ones. Once you've been offered the right to buy new shares, they can't be taken back just because you are sneaky enough to sell some of your present holding to pay for new ones.

Occasionally overoptimistic managers set the price of the new shares in a rights issue too high. The market reacts by cutting the price of the old shares. When the cost of the new issue to existing shareholders is higher than the price anybody could obtain on the stock exchange, the whole operation is in big trouble. Only a twit would buy the more costly rights shares. So it could be that the costs of launching the rights issue – always an expensive procedure – will go down the drain.

For this reason, a wise board of directors will set the price of the rights issue at a low level. Too high and the whole exercise could crumble, with only accountants and lawyers feeling happy as they will still get their fees.

READY, STEADY, GO

It's important when thinking of taking up rights shares to wait till the last minute. Otherwise you risk the possibility of the ordinary shares falling to a value below the new issue. In which case, you ought to buy on the open market, or better still, walk away from the whole shooting match.

It may not have been the organisers' intention, but I have made mountains of loot out of rights issues. For one thing, I've found that shares depressed by a rights issue nearly always rise after a few months to their original higher price. This means that I got some new shares a lot cheaper than they were really worth. Nor did I have to fork out a spread, stamp duty or commission (none of these apply on rights issue purchases). Lovely jubbly!

Hi ho, hi ho, it's IPO we go

PRIVATE FIRMS WHICH TAKE THE HUGE STEP OF deciding they'd like to be traded on the stock exchange will launch an IPO – initial public offering. This means they will have real-life, living, talking shareholders for the first time. They are really selling part of the company, something that appeals to the directors as it puts loads of cash in their pockets.

The government launches IPOs to sell nationalised companies to the institutions, such as hedge funds, insurance companies, pension pots and banks, as well as to the public. In these sales, there is pressure in Whitehall to set the price of the new shares low. If they pitch too high, nobody wants to buy the equities and the project becomes as popular as dynamite in the toaster. It's because of this earnest desire to keep the share price down that government IPOs are nearly always worth supporting.

For example, when Royal Mail was privatised, everyone partied because the asking price was too low. You can see in the following chart how the price rose after the shares were listed in October 2013.

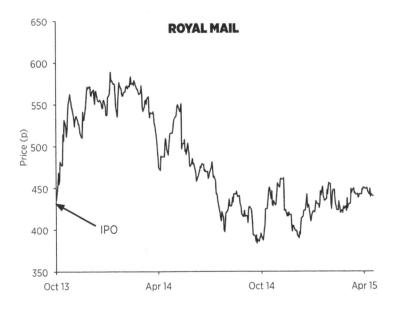

ROYAL MAIL

But things can go wrong. In 1987, British Petroleum was partly owned by the government. They offered the shares to the public at £3.30. But then Black Monday struck. Financial markets in Blighty dropped by a massive 20%. I bought my new shares too early. I should have waited, then grabbed shares much cheaper on the open market in the ordinary way. Nobody else bought the new issue and banks and other financial set-ups who underwrote the whole sorry exercise had to stump up for a large bill. I recall that, by jumping too quickly, I lost £2,000.

The lesson is clear. Don't subscribe for IPO shares until the last minute. Or you risk the price on the ordinary market moving against you.

THE GREAT STAG PARTY

The best way to make fast, easy money out of a government IPO is to try a bit of stagging. This is the nifty practice of offering in advance to buy new shares which are being toted in the IPO, only to dump them in an instant.

Let's return to the Royal Mail spectacular. The government decided to sell new shares to City institutions (hedge funds, insurance companies, trust funds, pensioner purveyors and so on) and to the public. Everybody who bought these underpriced babies suddenly found themselves with zappy profits. I sold mine straightaway. The shares rose a bit after that. This made me a bit miserable – until the price fell back.

Public offerings are a licence to make money. But history warns us that you sometimes need to sell them rather quickly. Those who held onto Railtrack and British Energy, after successful public offerings, were burned badly when both outfits came to grief later on. On the other hand, those who subscribed for British Gas and British Telecom made a killing as the shares took off and stayed in the pink.

I didn't subscribe for Railtrack after reading that no railway anywhere in the world has ever made a profit. Facts like this stick in your mind and have prevented me from investing in any railway operators since – much to my benefit.

But I invested one of my largest ever single cash mountains in British Energy, expecting nuclear fuel to wage war on carbon pollution. I woke up one morning to find my investments had gone bang – though thankfully not the power stations. The benighted enterprise didn't go bust entirely and I was able to buy more shares on the dips. In the end I managed to claw back three-quarters of my stake. Plus I earned a bit extra by talking to the media about the debacle.

On the whole, public offerings by the government have really done well and future ones are worth a look.

CARRY ON PRIVATES

So far I've talked about Whitehall share offers, but private firms often give it a whirl, too. You need to treat these affairs more cautiously than the government ventures.

You have to ask yourself: why would any firm want to give over so much control by flogging shares to people it doesn't know? Why should it make itself vulnerable to hostile takeovers later on? Perhaps it's trying to bring down an onerous burden of debt. Fine, but would a promising firm be in that mess in the first place?

Is it that the company needs a taller cash pile? Well, that doesn't sound like they're expecting to make big profits, does it? Maybe it's just a spiffing wheeze for the bosses to line their own pockets. But doesn't this suggest a lack of faith in their company to continue making money from its traditional business?

If you suspect any of this might be happening – and, to be fair, it is sometimes acknowledged in the prospectus – then you might want to stay clear.

However, there are some better reasons for a previously unlisted company to want to sell shares. It might, for example, need hard cash to acquire a new company to dispose of troublesome competition. This is a more encouraging motive. Or they may plan to launch thrilling ventures in fast-developing countries.

Before companies go public, they have to prepare a detailed prospectus. These are as heavy as bricks. I ought to advise you to study them carefully before you decide to buy the shares. But let's be practical, they're mostly unreadable.

Let other, more pedantic minds study the fine print. Then check Google to see if enough punters are buying the shares and whether experienced City pundits believe the shares are worth a whirl. My own experience of private IPOs is that the share price can drop soon afterwards and sometimes even on the first day of normal trading in the stock market. One common reason is that greedy boards of directors set the asking price too high in relation to the firm's real value and then sell for a profit when trading in the shares begins. This hardly ever happens to government-led share sales.

Perks and freebies

SOME SHARES CARRY EXTRA PERKS AND USEFUL gifts. Share buyers can bag cheaper hotel rooms, travel, theme park entry, jewellery, books, clothing and all sorts of other discounted stuff.

Some of these perks can be generous. Just by holding 317 shares in Merlin Entertainment you can have 40% off two adult passes to their theme parks or the same discount for one family pass.

At the time of writing, you need 64 shares in Whitbread PLC to snaffle a sheet of vouchers with various discounts off Premier Inn, Costa, Beefeater and Brewer's Fayre. While holders of more than 5000 shares in Newbury Racecourse are sent a badge entitling entry in the member's enclosure for every race day.

Some stores, like Signet, who own H. Samuel and Ernest Jones jewellers, will send you a plastic card which you can waft about to get money off. In Signet's case it's 10%.

For some firms, it doesn't matter how few shares you have. Owners of just one share in Moss Bros get 20% off every sale, Greene King give you a fifth off your food and drinks bill for just 100 shares and Johnson Services allow holders of one share to get £5 off dry cleaning bills. Others insist that you have a fairly big holding. Telecom Plus require a holding of 1500 shares before you're given 10% off.

Carnival, the cruise company, give you a free amount to spend on board, depending on the destinations and length of the sailing. Just 100 shares needed here. Groupe Eurotunnel gives a big 30% off for six journeys a year.

These days, only your broker has tangible proof that you own shares so you may have to ask for some sort of confirmation that you can use at reception desks and cash tills. But you might find it worth the effort – 35% off the price of a book published by Bloomsbury is, after all, not bad going for holding just one share.

However, never buy shares for the sole reason that shareholders are entitled to a few bargains. The size of the perk has nothing to do with how the company performs now or in the future. And do not be seduced into holding a share with lacklustre price performance just because you're used to the discounts.

I once enjoyed big family mark-downs on hotel rooms with a well-known chain, called Queen's Moat. My cheap rooms lasted for years. But the firm suddenly went into a rapid decline. I only just checked out before it gave up the ghost. I don't think my total of discounted rooms made up for my thumping loss. Without that enticing discount I would have bid farewell to the shares years earlier.

Cut them off

BOILER ROOM BOUNDERS

ONCE YOU START TRADING SHARES, YOU MAY notice a slight change in your popularity. You'll take a few more phone calls from awfully nice people. They'll call you by your first name. You'd almost think they've been your dear chum for years. You've just temporarily forgotten them, that's all.

The normal introduction is "How are you today?" And that's as far as they get with me. I hang up fast.

If you allow these charmers to keep talking, your attention will eventually be drawn to some *amazing* shares. They'll cheerfully predict that the price of these wonder shares will triple in a few days, though that is only the start of their golden future.

Why, you wonder, if these shares are so marvellous, doesn't the firm stop wasting time ringing up total strangers and get on with buying up all available shares for themselves? Well, it's because these shares are more or less worthless. Though it might not seem so, considering the price they're asking for them. Sometimes, the share-issuer doesn't even exist. You're invited to send a fat cheque, but afterwards you won't hear another thing, not even the sound of shifty feet scuttling up dark alleys. Money out of sight and down the drain.

You are the recipient of attention from a boiler room – a well-known and widespread scam in the share world.

It's hard to believe it, but thousands of people, including a few lightly experienced traders, fall for this wicked con trick. The voice on the line is helpful, understanding and often cultured. It's said they use distressed public school boys and girls to add a bit of gentile credibility.

Don't worry about their finer feelings. They don't have any. You can't be a sensitive soul to work a fiddle as low as this. So just hang up on the bounders. Luckily, they are never foolish enough to ring you straight back. Though they'll often try again over the next week or so.

A trick I carefully worked out to play on them went like this:

"Hello, is that Malcolm?" asks the scammer.

"Um..." replies Malcolm.

"I'm David. How Are You Today?"

"Fine."

"Treacle Holdings shares are really cheap at the moment and we think they're about to take off..."

"Sorry, David, this isn't actually Malcolm."

"Could I speak to him, then?"

"I'm sad to tell you, David, that Malcolm is dead."

Silence.

"Between you and me, I killed him..."

The conversation ends abruptly as David hangs up. Sadly this is all in my imagination as I never dared claim a murder in case that's breaking the law. But you see it would leave the fraudster with a sticky moral dilemma – whether to report the conversation to the police or not. Doing the right thing would end up in a fraud charge. So, of course, we know what he would do.

Where do boiler rooms get your number from? Why didn't you hear from them until you bought your first shares? Easy. They check share registers for your name and address, then they use the phone book.

OTHER NUISANCES

There is another con trick being used on shareholders, or sometimes, in this case, people who are simply told they are shareholders. As someone known to be obsessed with shares, I receive loads of calls and emails from relatives, friends, casual acquaintances and sometimes strangers asking if I've heard of some obscure company or other.

It seems they have been phoned by a 'broker' who's told them they have thousands of shares in this company. But the targets of these calls knows nothing about their holding. The caller assures them they do indeed hold the shares and says they have a client who wants to buy them for much more than the market value.

My advice-seekers want to know what's going on. Do they own shares they've forgotten about or which have multiplied in value like wildfire? I have to disappoint them. Somewhere down the line they will probably be invited to send money to facilitate the deal. Or they may be invited to send their bank details so a huge deposit can be made to their bank account. They are not likely to receive a penny and their bank details will be blown.

Now perhaps there are genuine brokers out there who do want to buy shares you really do have. But I would advise extreme caution before you proceed.

Swindlers don't only contact you by phone. I've not had an approach to buy non-existent shares by email yet, but I'm sure others have. And crooks target share owners by other means of communication, too. I've been around the block a bit, but I was caught once.

Earlier in my career, a flyer dropped on to my doormat from an international company of currency traders. I sent for their expensive-looking brochure. They would use my money to trade daily on the currency market and take

a very small percentage of my profits. In those days, the only realistic way to trade currency was through a third party, so I sent some money to open an account. Within a few weeks the fraud squad pounced and closed them down. They had not traded on my account, just appropriated my money. I did eventually get some money back, but I wished the authorities had acted earlier – and I told them so!

Then there are canvassers for financial spread bet firms. Of course, they are not crooks. But some can be awfully persistent in trying to make you open an account. This time, they'll have your number because you have seen one of their many advertisements and have responded to them in some way. Perhaps you have applied for a free report on a popular share. You were only mildly interested because the report was free and you already hold the company's shares. But we all know that nothing is free.

Some pushy brokers choose firms with household names for their special reports because you're more likely to hold these shares, giving you an interest in reading more about them.

This time, I don't cut the speaker off dead. They're acting within the law. If I sign up, I won't be diddled. They're only doing their job.

But at the same time, these calls are an irritation. And I really don't like being called Malcolm by strangers. So thank the beggars for their interest and explain politely that you already have more brokers than you know what to do with. You've used them a long time and you trust them. So please take me off your list and don't trouble yourself to ring again. But thanks again for your time.

If you hear from them again – and I fear you probably will – you can get a little more brusque.

THE BIG LESSON

It's pretty clear isn't it? Never do any share business on the phone, unless you are the one who did the dialling. Some of these calls may not be dodgy at all – but it's not worth the risk of finding out the hard way.

If you hang up, it sends a clear message. But should you fail to down your phone, the pests are trained to keep you talking. They'll ask you questions which can't be answered 'yes' or 'no', such as "What's your normal trading strategy?" Try answering that in a few words!

The longer you chat, the more they'll think they've found a mug. You could leave the phone on the kitchen table and go out for a drink. That might discourage them trying again. But if the same lot don't call again, another gang surely will. Because they sell their beastly lists of shareholder numbers to other miscreants. Sorry, but it's just something we shareholders have to put up with.

You can't beat a beta

MOST SUCCESSFUL SHARE TWIDDLERS HAVE SOME high beta shares in their bag. Sounds a bit technical? Yes, but it's a simple enough concept. Betas are shares whose recent history indicates they will rise the furthest and fastest when the wider market bounds ahead. Sadly, the rule works in reverse when market rot sets in.

Obviously, there are some shares to be avoided more than most in grim times. In this respect, they are the opposite of defensive shares, which are considered to be safer during bear markets and recessions. Another way to put it is that high beta shares are more volatile than average.

Betas are measured on a simple scale. A beta of 1 means that a share is likely to move up or down at the same rate as the market. A beta of 2 shows it could move at twice the rate of the market. Which is nice if it's up, but slightly terrifying if it's falling back.

Defensive shares therefore tend to have a beta of less than 1 – a low beta. Technology shares, which often rely more than average on debt, usually have a high beta. A beta of 1.4 indicates that a share will rise 40% faster than average when the market is rosy.

My policy is rather obvious. It's to buy high beta shares when the market is on a roll and to sell a few low betas to pay for it. If the market has been falling for longer than is healthy, then out go some of my high betas. I may buy back some of them later, if the shares fall so heavily that they become bargains.

Betas are useful for assessing the probability of success. If your bag is waltzing along happily, you can afford to choose shares which carry a bigger risk. You will, after all, have a better chance of the share coming home to roost. A review of various betas, carried out as usual with the aid of our good friend Google, will help you find higher-risk shares.

It works better, by the way, for short-term trading; the kind that brings you more money faster if all goes right. Over extended periods, the story of a share is more likely to change, rendering the beta measurement quickly out of date. So don't rely on an old beta figure which you might find in a yellowing notebook. Hit the net.

The table below shows some examples of shares which usually have high and low betas.

High beta	Low beta
Ashtead	Centrica
Barclays	RSA Insurance
Kazakhmys	SSE
Persimmon	Unilever
RBS	United Utilities
Rio Tinto	

The chart shows the price performance of Persimmon (a high beta share), Centrica (a low beta share), and the FTSE 100 since 2000. This nicely illustrates how the shares of Persimmon are more volatile than both Centrica and the FTSE 100, while Centrica's price is more stable.

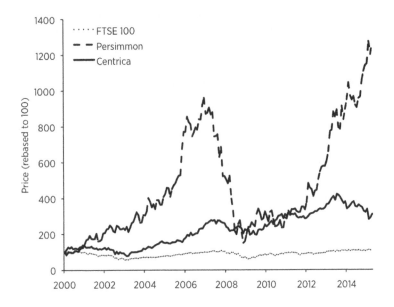

But, I hear you ask, how do analysts know with any accuracy what a share's beta should be? Well, the snag is that it's all based on past performance. It has to be. Yet we all know that a past triumph can turn into a future disaster.

So don't feel let down if a high beta doesn't live up to expectations all the time. Should it disappoint too often, its beta rating will soon come down, anyway. Remember that nobody can tell the future. Betas are a useful indicator, but not an infallible one.

The most tip top, top cats?

PICK FIRMS WITH GOOD MANAGERS. ALL RIGHT, IT'S not easy. But you can easily discover on the net if a chief executive officer or a chairperson (the only ones who really matter) has a stunning or a lousy reputation.

My hugely profitable buying of shares in Compass, the big catering and cleaning firm, is down to my admiration of a former clerk with Matchbox Toys. Sir Gerry Robinson became a big cheese at Compass and is now a TV presenter, specialising in turning around business situations. Elsewhere in his sparkling career, I was impressed with the money-making skill with which he chaired Granada Television, even though his background wasn't in broadcasting. Meantime, those Compass shares keep piling on value to this very day.

If the name of a company's top dog litters your search engine, then at least the luminary is doing a fine job in putting their name around. And that means his or her company will be in the public eye more often.

You will find accolades, too. And potted biographies. They are always worth reading. Look especially for top bananas who've turned around a struggling company after joining the team. This is management quality.

Of course, there's naff publicity, too. The net will soon show you which directors have been in hot water recently. Or have come under fire from the big institutions who invest in them. Repeated calls for resignation or allegations of fraud should sound the loudest alarms. You'll be surprised how many captains of industry are more likely to steer on to the rocks than return the share price safely back into its old waters.

Don't underestimate the affect of a corking boss on share prices. If someone renowned for delivering the goods steps down from a board, then the share price will plummet. If a replacement is found of equal standing, the price will take off again.

Why should this be? Certainly the share price depends on everyone in the company, plus all sorts of outside influences, like a healthy demand, growth in the economy and rising interest from big buyers. Well, the man or woman at the top brings so much to a company that the talents of all the other staff are chucked into the shade. This helps to explain the gargantuan salaries and bonuses which many of them enjoy.

So what are we looking for, then? Clarity of leadership, achieving targets and street cred in the City, that's what. Oh, and most important of all, is personal ambition. Think Sir Richard Branson.

Now, we all accept that a great captain could push forward a dinghy, but what about a heavy tanker, where surely his influence is going to be heavily diluted? Not so. Some of the biggest firms in the world owe it all to one person at the top.

So just to be clear. A top cat with experience and reputation increases share prices more than you'd expect. While derided leaders will cost you dearly if you buy into or stay with them.

Don't understand it? Then don't buy

HOLD MANY SHARES IN A CARDIFF-BASED FIRM called IQE. Too many, in fact, because they have lost me money. And that's my fault because I haven't much of an idea of what they do. Their website tells me they make wafers and they're not talking about ice cream.

The big product we are told is electronic wafers and apparently anyone who is anyone in the world of internet technology has to have them.

But have you a clue what they really are? Neither have I. And even if we find out, we probably won't comprehend how useful they are. So don't fall into my trap. Leave any investment in obscure electronic wonders to people who know all about them. You need to find something which you're more familiar with. Like ice cream, toffee apples or bicycles.

The greatest investor of all time, Warren Buffett, was, like Mrs Slocum, unanimous on this. We should not trust our money to an outfit who will use it to do something which is a mystery to us. We will never be able to tell if they are doing the right things or making horrendous mistakes.

If you find you're already invested with a firm which does, or starts to do, something you are ignorant about, don't sell the shares yet. Do some heavy research first, then you'll be in a better position to hold or sell fast. If you still don't get it, expunge.

Uncharted waters

YOU'LL HAVE HEARD OF CHARTING. IT'S THE artistry of tracing the path of a share on a graph and using that information to second-guess a share's near future. Fine, if you believe in it. I happen not to.

The predictions are based on history and you can't attach much weight to the past. Company stories change too often to be relied upon. And anyway, life's too short to learn all the different configurations that chartists rely on – candlesticks, double candlesticks, V-formations, double tops, and all that palaver.

We can still use graphs in a pretty basic way, though. If you draw a line through all the highest peaks of a share on the page, you get a straight line. Does it slant up towards the top right-hand corner of the page? Or does it lead down to the corner at the bottom? If it points up, we have a definite progressive trend. And as I stress elsewhere, a trend must be followed. An upward line on a graph tells me a share is worth buying.

Some shares in my bag whose graphs have followed a stairway to heaven are Compass Group, ITV, Arm Holdings, Ashtead and Inmarsat. The chart below shows the progress of Compass since 2000.

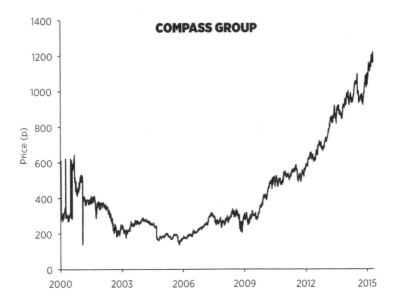

COMPASS GROUP

Another reason why we should peer regularly at the graph of a share's recent path is to comply with an old City saying: "You can spot company problems in a graph before they hit the headlines." What you're looking for, of course, is a line sharply and suddenly pointing south.

Leave value investing to the experts

PROFESSIONAL TRADERS, OFTEN WORKING FOR banks, insurance companies, hedge funds, investment trusts or other stuffy financial institutions, rely on value investing for their profits. So do a few private dealers. But only the talented ones who really know what they are doing.

Put crudely, value investing is the art of trying to buy shares on the cheap. Then you sell the shares dear, once the market has woken up to their real worth.

A value investor will pick over all the financial facts of a company to arrive at a true value for each share. If this price is higher than the current price in the market, he or she will hoot with joy at finding a bargain. The share will be snapped up and some serious sitting-back is done, until the market wakes up and the share is catapulted to its true price.

Sounds good. But sadly it is really hard to work out a share's true value. You need application, long experience and a keen analytical mind.

For example, you hope to find equities which have fallen too low because they were subject to news stories which caused them to decline unfairly. Then you have to study all the tiny facts available to see if those reports were justified.

To complicate matters, no single value investor will come up with the same true value as another. It's all subjective, you see. Some operators will put more stress on the recent past and current performance. Others will give more weight to the company's future, though of course this can only be guessed at.

I'll never pour scorn on value investing as I'm acutely aware that the richest man in the world, Warren Buffett, made his $50bn fortune by being a value investor. He's a real bargain hunter.

But personally I prefer to leave all of this hard work to the experts and concentrate on other ways to choose my shares.

The sector section

ALL COMPANIES OPERATING WITHIN THE SAME type of business are said to be part of a certain sector of the market. Thus producers of the black stuff are in the oil sector. Firms yanking stuff from the earth are part of the mining sector. Enterprises dealing with computers are in the technology sector. And so on.

If you hold all your shares in just one group of activity, you are taking your wealth in your hands. Supposing you only hold oil shares. Then the price of crude crashes. Or wind farm technology takes a leap forward. Or a really cheap petrol substitute is found. Or we all become fatally allergic to steering wheels. Every one of your shares will lose money. If you have no other shares but oilers, you could be wiped out. But if only 10% of your mazuma is in oil companies, you will be fine. One or more of your other sectors will take up the slack and keep you in profit.

While I was writing this book, the price of crude surprised everyone by crashing by half. This was serious for me because I hold far too much money in oil shares: BP, BG, Royal Dutch Shell, Tullow Oil, JDX, Gulf and Dragon. This glut was mostly caused by the oil giants having done very good business in the last 20 years. I lost a lot of my gains on the oil slump and – as the actress said to the bishop – it wouldn't have been so disastrous if I'd limited my exposure.

So, you spread your trades around companies in different sectors to limit your losses.

Sectors can also be useful in making money. What you can do is research a hot sector which is really in vogue. There will always be one ballpark where shares are pointing skyward across the board.

Let's use as an example the black stuff sector, again. If the price of crude is breaking all records, all but a few oil producers will be attaining records of their own. At the same time, another sector, supermarkets, say, could be suffering from the latest round of food price wars. It could be the worst performing sector.

In this case, I would recommend selling your supermarket shares and putting the money into oil producers, so that you can ride on the coattails of the trending sector. You still have a bit of research to do to see exactly which oil firms offer the best prospects. But it is not vital to sort out the very best, because you have the assurance that all oil companies are rising in tandem with the soaring cost of crude. Just be careful that you invest in oil producers who hold big reserves.

PICKING SHARES WITHIN A SECTOR

Even though you have identified a sector which is on a roll, you still have to take care to choose the shares within the sector that are worth your attention. Always select those that have performed the best in recent times. I'm talking about improving sales, reducing liabilities and growing dividends.

However strong a sector is at the present time, there will always be also-rans within it; shares that are still failing. Don't favour the laggards in the fruitless hope that they will be carried along by other firms in the sector with a better record. You'll almost certainly be let down.

Make it nicer with an ISA

YOU'LL KNOW THAT INDIVIDUAL SAVINGS Accounts (ISAs, or NISAs as some people now know them) are a useful way of saving free of tax. You can hold shares in a self-select ISA and you won't have to pay capital gains tax on your profits or income tax on dividends. Your brokers will list your shares in an ISA account just as they do in your ordinary trading account. There's no difference in the trading procedure.

Chancellors of the Exchequer set up these tasty accounts to encourage us to save. They have thoughtfully boosted the allowed annual amount year after year – and the rate of improvement seems to be accelerating.

There are estimated to be only a dozen ISA millionaires at the moment. They could not have done it in cash-only ISAs. And probably not in ISAs where only safe Footsie shares were chosen. No, those with more than a million pounds in an ISA must favour small, riskier companies. I'll bet my grandma to a penny that most of their ISA investments were start-ups, innovators, niche firms and techno pioneers.

ISAs can grow like rolling snowballs. Yet many private investors don't bother with an ISA account. They argue that they already get a generous tax break on the first £10,000 or so of gains. That tax break also goes up every year. As they don't expect to make much more profit than that, they allow their annual tax-free account to lapse.

But you, dear reader, are aiming to make much more than your capital gains allowance. So I think you should operate an ISA and feed it without fail by the maximum amount at the start of each financial year. Your dividends will also be paid into your ISA. I would also allow this extra money to build up to buy new shares within the account.

For self-select ISA owners, it's a huge relief to have so many shares immune to taxation. You don't have to keep records of your purchases and sales. You don't have to sell losing shares at the end of the financial year just to offset your gains to fit your annual capital gains allowance. HMRC just doesn't want to know. It's an ideal account for sluggards like me.

ISAs are well worth keeping up every year. Sell shares in your ordinary trading account if you need ready cash. ISAs should not be raided until you want a really large amount of tax-free cash for a second home in the Caribbean or a new luxury yacht.

This is not to say you shouldn't sell shares you hold in your ISA. It's just that you should reinvest the proceeds as soon as you can in more promising firms. Very few of my shares are now outside my ISA, so my tax administration is now almost non-existent, as is my tax bill.

A trade for all seasons

SOME COMPANIES HAVE A RUSH OF SALES AT certain times of the year. This means, of course, that they have abnormally quiet periods the rest of the time. The trading fraternity don't always realise that the surges and declines cancel each other out over 12 months. Consequently, share prices rise and fall depending on which month it is. We can take advantage of shares which jump around like jiving crickets on a red-hot stove.

Take it from me that seasonal fluctuations in sales do have a noticeable affect on share prices at certain times of year. It may seem utterly predictable that most stores will sell more stuff near Christmas, but it seems – like snow in January – to take the City by surprise every year.

EXPLOITING THE YULETIDE RUSH

A firm which traditionally does most of its business in the run-up to Christmas will find its share price in a perky mood in December. This is particularly true of high street shops. What happens is that everyone sees the shops are full and the cash tills are tinkling like runaway horse sleighs.

Even if traders never enter these shops themselves, they assume that sales this year will be strong. So the share price starts rising in early December and continues until Christmas Eve.

When January comes, a party hangover sets in and the price shudders back again. In fact, the share price of most stores tends to wobble in January. That's when they report on the results of Christmas sales and most of the time the report disappoints. So disgruntled shareholders divest in disgust.

The plan of action for astute traders is to buy shares in retail stores that sell stuff which makes good Christmas presents – which, I suppose, is most of them – in November. Some firms I often play this way at Christmas are Marks & Sparks, Debenhams, WHSmith, Signet (inc H.Samuel) and Poundland.

Then we sell in that very quiet period for the stock exchange – after Boxing Day and before New Year's Eve. Thus, we collect our cash before the announcement of those Yule sales which are usually so unsatisfying. Yes, there will be odd occasions when a store actually exceeds expectations, but we can't be right all the time.

The festive season can also affect the share prices of businesses which are not sellers of gifts. Drinks firms, restaurant chains, pastry shops, supermarkets and pubs can also see a cool Yule of share price surges. Sell those shares before New Year's Eve, too.

SUMMER SHARE ACTION

If the summer has included a few heatwaves, there are some opportunistic deals to be made. Get busy with the fizzy as soft drinks companies are likely to show increased profits in their next reporting wave. So are pubs. The list also includes DIY stores, ice cream makers, garden furniture manufacturers, purveyors of swimwear, sunscreen makers, bedding plant growers and so on. I won't insult your imagination by producing the whole boring list here.

On the other hand, there are some shares you might think of shedding if the sun has been out to play. Package holiday outfits will do worse than usual when people are already enjoying tropical sunshine at home. (I explained earlier why holiday firms may not be an investment for the future, anyway.)

The great chase

AVERAGING DOWN

THIS IS ONE OF THOSE PLOYS THAT DOESN'T WORK out every time, but on many occasions it's worth a try. It certainly merits addition to your profit-making armoury – as long as you don't put in too much gelt. You must also make sure that conditions are set fair before you go ahead.

Averaging down, which I prefer to call doubling up, is when one of your shares drops and you chase after the irksome thing on its backwards trek to buy more. Why should you do this? You do it when you think the selling has been overdone by other traders and you expect the price to bounce back up.

If the drop was fast and furious, there is every chance that the price will indeed stage a comeback. A big wave of fast selling is often caused by panic. Afterwards, bargain hunters may hone in like vultures, to send the price up again. Or the original sellers might decide to reclaim the shares at the lower level.

If you buy more shares at the bottom and the price rises to par, you are better off than you were before. At this stage, you might want to jettison the shares you bought in the basement, leaving you with your holding as it originally was, plus some cash profit.

During the 2008 banking crisis, I held a modest number of shares in Royal Bank of Scotland, now known as RBS. Before the crisis, the price was around £9 a share. As the extent of the bank's pickle slowly began to unroll, the price began to fall. Unable to believe that such a monolith was in serious trouble, I bought more shares at what I thought was a 'bargain' price. The chart below shows the RBS price in the last ten years.

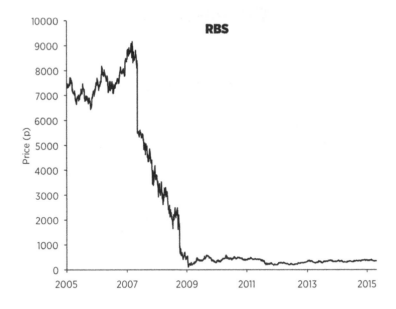

Every time the price fell a little more, I bought more shares. This has continued year after year. Now I have a shedload of RBS shares, but the share price is still trundling along, amazingly at only 5% of the pre-crisis share value. However, the price only needs to improve by 20% or so to see me recover all of my money. This is the beauty of chasing down a share price – the rally need not be spectacular to break even and perhaps even realise a tasty profit.

You see how it works? By buying more shares at the new, cheaper price you are bringing down the average price you paid for all of your shares – hence the tactic's name. The table below showing four purchases of Company A shares at a gradually falling price should help to illustrate the method.

Company A share price (£)	Shares purchased	Cost (£)	Total cost (£)	Total shares held	Average price per share (£)
1	1000	1000	1000	1000	1
0.95	1000	950	1950	2000	0.98
0.90	1000	900	2850	3000	0.95
0.80	1000	800	3650	4000	0.91

If Company A's share price now returns to £1, the initial price paid, the trader holds £4000-worth of shares that cost £3650 – a profit of £350. If the price rises to 91p (from its current level of 80p) the trader has broken even and could sell to get back their £3650 stake.

You can see that the risk is greater with every additional purchase – but the potential rewards are greater too. You would only want to undertake averaging down if you believe the price drops are just a blip and the company's business is still sound.

DOUBLE OR DROP

The more lucre you throw at the decaying share, the better your chances of turning failure into success. But is it worth all the stress? And what if the company goes bust?

This is why I refer to averaging down by the gambler's term doubling up. On a roulette wheel you might put £1 on red. When black shows, you risk £2 on red at the next turn of the wheel. As the scarlet slot fails to come up each time, you double your stake each time. Eventually, red will triumph and so you've lost nothing. Nerve-racking, ain't it? Averaging down is just like that. It's certainly more heart-pounding than most of the wheezes in this book.

There are some precautions to be taken before you average-down. If the price hasn't fallen badly, there's nothing much to worry about. It will probably right itself soon. But if the backward jump made you groan aloud, then you need to discover what the reason was. Consult the internet oracle.

Should it be something serious, like a profit-warning, a huge explosion in the factory or the chief executive being dragged away in chains, I would rush to sell the share, not buy more.

If the reason for the tumble is less drastic, such as a mildly disparaging note on the company by a broker, then you should loosen your purse strings. But first wait until you think the panic is over and the price has found its lowest level.

After a nasty topple, shares tend to take one of two courses. They bounce back the next day or they drift lower over the next few days. Therefore waiting three days before buying more shares would seem the most sensible approach. If there is a next day bounce I would not acquire any more shares, but still hope for the old price to be reinstated.

Should you buy even more shares if the value continues to retreat?

Probably not – unless you were absolutely convinced, backed-up by other trusted sources, that the share is truly underestimated and oversold.

Weddings made in heaven – and hell

PERHAPS THE BEST THING THAT CAN HAPPEN TO A share shuffler like you is for one of your minnows to be swallowed by a bigger fish. Takeovers can motivate the share price in an instant. A 20% or 30% rise in a flash. And this can be on the low side. Some companies that are snapped up often see a jump by 50% or even more.

I remember calling my broker to dispose of all my shares in Yorkshire Television. He phoned in a mortified condition the next day to say he'd made the deal the wrong way round. He accidentally bought the same number of shares, instead of selling them. Sensing the intervention of fate, I assured him I couldn't care less. Was he relieved!

A week later, at my weekly poker game in Islington, a fellow player asked "Have you heard: Yorkshire's been taken over by Granada?" This news added a little zest to my game as I realised I was £40,000 better off because of someone else's cock up. I've let mistakes by brokers stand ever since.

You can take advantage of a vaunted takeover even if the merger never takes place. This is possible because the rumour always comes first. The merest whisper that a marriage may take place will put some welly into the targeted company's shares. I'd say that the average rise on a wide rumour is around 15%. If the story persists it can swell by another 10%. And if the predator later makes a firm encouraging statement, the price will tick up again.

Should you begin to fear that this coupling will not take place after all, perhaps because of something one of the parties said, or the process seems to be taking too long, you should consider selling right then. But if the signs still look positive, I should hold on to your shares, because a confirmed takeover will make you tango into the night.

HOSTILE TAKEOVER JOY

Things can be even better if you hold shares in a firm which isn't happy to be courted by a rival. The predator will increase their initial offer per share to persuade the owners into accepting the deal after all. So up goes the price and you're sitting on even more happiness. If the offer is rejected again, a juicier bid can follow. This can go on for some time.

Though sometimes in the end you won't receive cash at all. This happens when the takeover is paid for in shares by the buying company. However, you can of course sell your new shares and make your profit anyway. It's also quite common to receive both cash and shares from the company's new owners.

There is another rewarding takeover scenario. This is when a company fancies a merger with your firm and puts in a bid, which is then bettered by a third party. This can lead to an auction between the two rivals for your firm. This is all very satisfactory, as things can spiral out of control until you get a really overblown price for your shares. Hurrah!

It's not so good if you have shares in both of the battling aggressors. The City can take a dim view of expensive duals over a target company. If you see such a battle looming with one of your babies as a predator, you should quickly hop out of the way.

FINDING TAKEOVER CANDIDATES

Over the years I've scooped big windfalls out of takeover battles. So you might want to follow one of my best ploys for obtaining easy bonanzas. It's to buy into companies which have attracted merger rumours in the past and now seem ripe for a blissful union.

My long love affair with BG is a top example. The share price had rattled along ever since it was suggested we should "Tell Sid" to buy British Gas shares in the famous 1986 ad campaign. In recent years, that nicely-inflated price has been kicked upwards from time to time by takeover rumours. Yes, BG, as it's now known, has always been an ideal target.

For though the company is a Footsie giant it is not as big as similar firms, like Royal Dutch Shell or Exxon Mobil (the world's biggest oil company, based in Texas). And when a moon circles a bigger planet there's always a possibility that it will be drawn in. Whenever the rumours grew stronger, I bought BG shares. And eventually, after three or four false alarms, it happened.

In spring 2015 Shell made an offer for BG at 50% more than the current share price. Golly gosh! You can see how the share price reacted in the chart below.

I'm playing the same game now with Dragon Oil. I've piled in each time rumours hit the fan, and each time the price has risen after I bought, and my investment has stayed in the black. But that bonus will pale into nothing, once Dragon Oil is finally subsumed, which I rather think it will be.

The most attractive takeover propositions tend to operate in the more competitive sectors, like drugs companies and supermarkets. Small oil companies are also enticing targets, especially if they've actually found the black and sticky. A bigger oil firm will find it cheaper to take over active wells run by a smaller rival, than to start expensive new explorations of its own.

Firms which have seen recent drops in their share price or appear to have weak management teams are also susceptible to takeovers. Companies with a nasty debt pile or other major problems will often put it around that they're open to takeover offers. It's an easy way to extract them from a hole. However, don't touch any firm with horrid debts. If the outfit's not taken over, your investment could be on the road to nowhere. And even if it is swallowed up by another firm, the share bid will be pretty poor.

There are times when takeovers and mergers became as rare as budgie teeth. These are within protracted bear markets. The first thing all companies do in hard times is to batten down their expenses. Taking over a rival is about the costliest thing you could do, so they'll wait till boom replaces bust.

I've also found mergers are thin on the ground at holiday times, like Christmas and the height of summer. It's not hard to see why. A welter of overtime has to be done by managers, lawyers, accountants and press relations types to get such a complex operation airborne. They won't relish doing it during their hols. So don't buy in the hopes of a merger in these lax periods.

Train your mind to behave itself

YOU'RE BIASED – SO DEAL WITH IT

THERE'S A MUCKY MINEFIELD IN SHARELAND called *confirmation bias*. It's the mind's trick of making us seek out views which bear out our own opinions. At the same time we ignore facts which show us we are wrong. Recognise it? You should do – it's common in all areas of life and it messes things up all the time. Scientists, journalists and politicians have a particular problem trying to overcome it.

When I was a writer at the BBC we would find out the worst things about a company we thought was exploiting the public. We would collect these facts and present them as a TV or radio programme. We would mostly ignore the positive bits about the firm.

Ok, there probably weren't many of those anyway. But you can see what happened here. We formed a view of the outfit we wanted to pillory – and then we gathered the facts to fit it. We rejected the bits which didn't substantiate our initial thought that the firm was iffy. Luckily, there were always wiser editors who would look at the facts from a distance and pull the programme back on track.

CONFIRMATION BIAS AND YOUR SHARES

Confirmation bias can strike as we consider buying shares in a company. We research likely firms on the internet but only take into account facts that confirm our personal point of view. We considered the shares to be worth a look in the first place, so we're already slightly biased. We list in our mind the things we like, we dismiss the snags, and we end up buying a lemon.

I was once very attracted to a children's TV company called Sleepy Kids. My reasons were laughable. Firstly I was tickled by the name in a world where most companies seemed to have stodgy monikers, like Amalgamated Cables or Consolidated Foods. I had three small children, so ended up rather liking one of their programmes, *Budgie the Helicopter*, even though it did not seem particularly original. And thirdly, I rather liked the idea of sponsoring art, even if it was only a noisy cartoon.

But I failed to appreciate that TV programme-makers have a hard time of it – the competition is immense and programme commissioners are a hard-hearted bunch who believe that, when bringing entertainment to the small screen, every expense should be spared. I should have known all this, as I was in the broadcasting game myself. But I went ahead and bought the shares, never made any money and was still in possession of some Sleepy Kids shares when the firm closed its eyes for good. I was just another sad victim of confirmation bias.

The dangerous condition can affect professionals, too. There are loads of analytical reports about companies on the net. Not all of them take a balanced view. Most present a glowing picture. They list all the reasons we should buy this share – a low price-to-earnings ratio, growing worldwide demand or spanking sales figures last time round. They might not stress, or even mention, the downside – sky-high debt, for example, or the number of distressed directors desperately disposing of their shares.

At the same time, the articles you read denigrating companies can leave out the hopeful signs. They might make you avoid an enterprise which is in reality very promising. The article might make you sell your shares when in fact holding on to them, at least for a while longer, might be extremely profitable. If armies of people read the article it might cause a selling spree, which would depress the price, before you could enter your trading account. If the article bumped you into selling your shares at this awkward stage, you would almost certainly be worse than if you had stayed put.

It follows, therefore, that you need to read both rosy and critical reports on company prospects with cynical eyes. Try to see what's missing – and then do your own reading to make up your mind.

Start with the company's official website. There may be lots about the firm that you like. Though be careful again. Because no firm is going to fill its website with destructive prose. Then try a more general search to see if anyone has written up the firm from the opposite point of view.

Like everyone else, financial scribes take a view then look for facts to fit it. The bits that don't accord with their initial theory are glossed over or missed out. And it's not just writers who have this weakness. So before you grab a share, search for any piece of information about a firm you've failed to take into account.

It's worth saying that confirmation bias can be so powerful that it's been put forward as the main reason why the markets rise or fall. Especially when there's no easy, in-your-face explanation why prices should be going either way.

BEWARE OF SURVIVORSHIP BIAS

Another mindset which gives a false picture of the true situation is survivorship bias. It works this way. If you sell a loss-maker in your portfolio, the total of your profits suddenly leaps. This is because the loss of the dumped shares no longer shows in the sums.

For example, your trading account displays a profit of £5,000. But it would be £5,500 if it weren't for one company which has lost £500. When you sell that losing share, your total profit will leap to £5,500 in the account. So you think, soon forgetting that you ever sold the loss-maker, that you have a profit of £5,500. Yet the total gain showing is 10% more than you've really made.

To deal with this problem, make a note of the losses you make on ditched shares and subtract them from the profit shown in your account each time you need to know how much you have really made. When working out your capital gains tax, for example.

Also, if you don't remember the losses, the danger of survivorship bias is that you might invest more than is safe for your particular circumstances. You may, in other words, become overconfident.

Another manifestation of survivorship bias is that the fund you invest in might be using it. As only surviving companies can be counted by the management, the fact that some firms have failed and been ejected from the trust is not always accounted for. Therefore, the trust may attract more clients than it deserves by appearing to perform better than it actually is.

THE DREADED FOMO FACTOR

FOMO is the fear of missing out. It makes us follow the herd in Shareopolis. We see everyone is buying shares because the Footsie has shot up. Or focus might fall on a particular share that everyone on the bulletin boards is excited by. So, frightened of missing a bonanza, we start buying too. Even though our hearts tell us that we should be staying away. This goes against the wisdom that you should sell when everyone else is buying. FOMO must be resisted.

Don't fear your broker

YOUR COMPUTER IS PLAYING UP. OR YOU'RE ON THE road and without it. Or you have an inconvenient message on your account saying the shares you're trying to buy can't be traded online at present, so please ring your broker.

Some employers of broking firms can be intimidating. In your mind's eye, you see big fat Scrooges with red faces in braces of the same hue, wearing green eye shades. You think they know all about the big bad City, and they know that you don't. Some of them yammer like machine guns in unintelligible jargon. They also like to show off their knowledge, falsely thinking you'll have more confidence in them.

But believe me, they don't want to dominate you, they need you to put through the trade. So don't feel intimidated. You're the boss. You're the one with the money. The hero who's taking the big risk.

State the share you want to buy or sell and ask the price. Don't be frightened to invite them to repeat it. Even if you're happy with the quote, it's quite normal to change your mind at this late stage. Don't hesitate to decline when your heart suddenly tells you not to bother. Nobody will be upset. No one will think you are daft. You can, after all, ring back a few minutes later and say you'd like the deal to go through, after all.

But remember, once you have said 'yes' to the deal, it will go ahead. Which makes it vital that you speak clearly, understand what is said and pull out if you're not entirely happy.

Don't give share tips to your friends

WHEN YOU COME ACROSS A COMPANY WHICH YOU think is going to the stars, it's very hard to resist sharing with friends and relatives. You naturally want to do them a favour. You might also reason that the more people that buy your tip, the more your shares, acquired a week earlier, are likely to soar.

But wait! If you promote a share to mates and it backfires, you won't be forgiven. They may say it doesn't matter, but they'll secretly hold it against you. Furthermore, you'll check the share every two minutes to see how it's doing. This is not for your sake, but in fear that your tip has gone pear-shaped, triggering your friend's dismay.

You can also bet that your chum invested far too much; more than you did, probably. For some reason, there's a Chinese whisper effect in these ill-fated engagements. Each time the share tip is passed on, the new trader goes a bit more over the top with money laid out. And even if you hammer home to your friend that this is a super speculative punt worth only a few quid, they will pile in with thousands.

Ah yes, but what if the share rises and your friend(s) make a killing? Well, they'll conveniently forget your part in the success story. It will be purely down to their own wonderful skills. This is human nature.

Take it from me, because I've been there so many times. Do not pass on hot share tips to friends. Both you and your pal will wish you had never met.

Inconvenient company announcements

COMPANY DIRECTORS, LIKE POLITICIANS, HAVE discovered that the best time to release bad news is when everyone is looking the other way. So you'll find that dire company reports are sometimes issued on Christmas Eve, New Year's Eve, bank holiday Mondays, election days, royal weddings and so forth.

News releases on profit warnings, or the departure of a top manager with a high reputation, can also be pushed out when attention is likely to be low. It's a shabby trick, but it often works.

It pays to keep up with business news, even on those special days when stock exchanges aren't open or closing early, like 24 December. This, of course, makes it impossible to sell shares immediately on bad news. But at the same time, if a lot of shareholders have missed the announcements due to their inconvenient timing, it won't matter if you sell as soon as the markets open again.

It's no real hardship to open up your computer on holidays and just check that one of your firms isn't making a difficult declaration. Even if it's done furtively, such reports will still appear somewhere on the internet.

The falling pound

WHEN WE SEE STERLING FALL AGAINST THE EURO or the dollar, we naturally feel deflated. It's something to do with all those foreign holidays when our money was too quickly swallowed by the beach bar. But a rising pound is not normally a joyous thing for bedroom traders as it bears down on corporate earnings and thus on share prices. So don't rejoice in a buoyant pound. The stronger it gets, the more you should think about selling some shares.

A bushy-tailed pound makes it hard to sell British stuff abroad. And when all the UK companies which do most of their business overseas – including the bulk of Footsie firms – are paid the conversion rate, their profits will be lower than they should be. So don't cheer a rising pound – it can be a signal to sell if your company does a heap of business in foreign climes.

Ten reasons to sleep well as shares fall

I CAN UNDERSTAND WHY TRADERS ARE UPSET WHEN their shares tumble for days on end. I used to twist my hands in despair quite a lot. Bad moods were no stranger to me on failed Footsie days. The family wasn't safe. But it no longer bothers me. Here then is a raft of ravishing reasons why tumbling share prices should not grind you down:

1. Share prices must decline some of the time or the market would not work at all. Nobody could make a profit as nobody would ever sell. Regular plunges in share prices are not only normal, they are essential.

2. Big traders have a herd mentality which deliberately arranges falls from time to time. The stratagem allows them to sell at the peaks and buy back more shares for the same money on the dips.

3. History shows that the market rallies after falls and always, over time, rises to a higher point than before.

4. Shares never travel north in a straight line. Even the strongest bull market has a recurring pattern of three steps up and two steps back.

5. Even in Shareland, what goes up must come down. The very best

shares run out of puff sometimes. After the fall, a good company will continue to post growing profits and dividends, and the rising process begins again.

6. World disasters, like typhoons, terrorist attacks and wars, crush shares. But the effect never lasts long. Sometimes, shares are back to normal after only a few days.

7. If your share falls it may well be nothing to do with your company's performance and prospects. Both could be very encouraging. It's just that the world's financial environment – not your shares – is giving concern. Your shares will revitalise when the world economy picks up, as it always does. Or even earlier, if the firm's next set of figures are better than expected.

8. The markets operate on boom and bust cycles. So when shares are all down, it's not a worry, it's an opportunity. A chance to buy cheaply.

9. Big traders sell the moment bad news is released. This causes thoughtless computers to kick in, ditching more shares. A domino effect begins. This instant selling nearly always sends the share price lower than it should be. The price usually improves within a short time.

10. The market has fallen fast. So what? Shares are cheaper now. That's great if you have spare money. If not, there's still nothing to fret about. Time will sort things out in your favour.

So the overall lesson is: do not sell all your shares when the market hits a selling spree. Tough it out. But if one share falls, while your others do not, find out why.

Make your mates interested

THE PHALANX OF ARMCHAIR TRADERS IN BRITAIN is thinner than it used to be. The bursting of the techno-bubble at the start of this century and the crippling credit crunch of 2007-8 take the blame. Those who are burned find their skin is slow to heal.

So the vast majority of shares are held now by City mandarins – hedge funds, banks, insurers and institutions.

But confidence always returns. If you encourage chums, relations, neighbours and colleagues to become interested in the captivating world of shares, I believe you will be doing them a favour.

Point out that trading shares has proved over and over again to be the best investment. The dividends alone eclipse interest from banks and building societies, even when the bank rate is high.

There's also a modicum of self-interest in suggesting your friends and acquaintances do shares. The more people who buy shares, the higher the prices will climb. There's nothing wrong in having this as your motive for involving your chums and colleagues, your cousins, nieces, sisters and aunts. As I've just said, you're still helping them out.

The folks I know who've followed my path into shares have mostly done well. They've become hooked, done their own research and learned fast. Some of them now work much harder at the great game than I do.

How do you suck them in? Give them a good talking to. Explaining how well your shares have done this week is a good start. Of course, you'll need to pick your week.

But don't try to interest every friend in shares. They should be resilient by nature. They must have enough resources to withstand any losses. As discussed earlier, don't hand out any individual tips. Just promote the general idea. You also need to stress the importance of starting small. Then they can build on any successes later. Give them all the help and advice you can.

It's not just about profit

SOME BLIGHTERS HAVE DERIDED ME IN THE PAPERS and on radio and television for trading shares. Some have been quite nasty about it. One chap on a Radio Wales phone-in was so disgusted with me, he could hardly speak. He and lots of people regard me as some sort of low-life scrounger. It appears they think shareholders are somehow picking the pockets of the working man and woman. That we are exploiting widows, children and pensioners by extracting money from them while doing no real work ourselves.

Well, I agree with the last bit. Trading shares from your living room doesn't require much more physical effort than turning on a computer and scanning a few pages on the internet. But as for exploiting working families, well, the opposite is the case.

By buying shares in a company, you are funding that firm and securing jobs. You may even be creating employment. You are also supporting suppliers of that company. There have been cases where I know I've saved small firms from going bust.

Share-pickers push forward the frontiers of science and technology, by supporting the companies who do work in those areas. We find new cures and treatments for disease. We help to keep people safe and we increase happiness by funding entertainment and travel, for instance. In fact, without shareholders the world economy would probably collapse altogether. We don't deprive others of money and jobs. Without us there would be an adverse impact on jobs and the strength of the economy.

If you believe in, use or approve of what your company makes or does, you are helping to make useful goods or services for a better world. And if you have any doubts whatsoever about the morality of a firm, then you should jolly well not buy their shares in the first place.

The probable truth is that your critics, especially the vitriolic kind, do not have the confidence to put their money on the line and are envious of your entrepreneurial spirit.

A final list of rules and hints never to forget

Throughout this book, I've tried to avoid clichés – like the plague. But there are some popular sayings in Shareland that are very true and very easy to remember, simply because they're clichés. I've made a list and added a few more hints which are less hackneyed. All of these ideas have been discussed earlier in full detail, but I present them here as a final tally. They should be remembered zealously if you want to make shares work for you.

1. Ride your winners and dump your losers.
2. The trend is your friend.
3. Buy on the rumour, sell on the fact.
4. Never catch a falling knife.
5. A rising tide lifts all boats.
6. Buy on the dips, sell on the peaks.
7. That big recovery could merely be a dead cat bounce.
8. You have all the time in the world to make a trade.
9. If a deal's too good to be true, it will be.
10. It's never wrong to take a profit.

The oldest lessons of them all

BY WAY OF LIGHT RELIEF, I LEAVE YOU WITH PROOF of my theory that the best tool we have in making real money out of share trading is old-fashioned common sense. You won't find anything more sensible than the ancient wisdom of great British proverbs. You'll be amazed how many of them appertain to the best ways to deal shares.

- A rolling stone gathers no moss. *If we keep chopping and changing our shares, we will not make much profit.*

- Too many cooks spoil the broth. *If you spread your money over too many companies, you will not make a killing when just a few of them rise like rockets.*

- A stitch in time saves nine. *It's better to sell a share as soon as its price starts to drop, rather than wait a few weeks when it may crash like a stone.*

- People in glasshouses should not throw stones. *Don't criticise other people's choice of shares until you have put your own under the microscope and thrown out your own pigs' ears.*

- You can't have your cake and eat it. *Once you've sold a share, don't look back. You've taken the money, so don't behave as though you still hold the shares.*

- Don't put all your eggs in one basket. *Buy shares in enough companies to make sure you can never lose more than 10% of your pile in one go.*

- A bird in the hand is worth two in the bush. *Made a cracking profit on a share? Take it and leave some over for the next punter. Holding out for more dosh may lose you the lot.*

- A fool and his money are soon parted. *Once a share comes up on your radar, it's wise to research it thoroughly before you leap.*

- A little knowledge is a dangerous thing. *So do your research thoroughly.*

- A new broom sweeps clean. *Look for a company whose new manager has a much better reputation than the old one.*

- A picture paints a thousand words. *Check the graph over the last two years. If the line generally points south-east, look for another firm.*

- Actions speak louder than words. *Rate concrete results in annual reports above the cheery annual speeches of the chairman and chief executive.*

- All good things must end. *No company has a perpetual licence to make money. Reject loyalty to your old firm and sell when the time comes. That's when profits dip, dividends fade, sales dry up and debt balloons.*

Now all's said and done

THAT'S THE END OF MY CHEERY CATALOGUE OF strategies, ploys, policies, hints, tips, dodges, wheezes and avoidable mistakes. You now hold what I humbly believe is the best kit of tools there could possibly be to guide you on the road to making a fortune from shares.

Oh, and when you arrive, don't forget to buy me a drink in the Punter's Return. It's where all the share millionaires go…

Fin

9 780857 194190

GOD'S END

THE FALL

MICHAEL McBRIDE

snowbooks

Proudly Published by Snowbooks in 2007

Snowbooks Ltd.
120 Pentonville Road
London
N1 9JN
Tel: 0207 837 6482
Fax: 0207 837 6348
email: info@snowbooks.com
www.snowbooks.com

British Library Cataloguing in Publication Data
A catalogue record for this book is available from the British Library.

ISBN 1-905005-61-X
ISBN 13 978-1-905005-61-1

Printed and bound by J. H. Haynes & Co. Ltd., Sparkford

For Kyler, Madison, Trent, and Blake…
My hope for the future.

BOOK ONE:
THE FALL

"Cursed is the one who trusts in man,
      who depends on flesh for his strength
      and whose heart turns away from the Lord.
He will be like a bush in the wastelands;
      he will not see prosperity when it comes.
He will dwell in the parched places of the desert,
      in a salt land where no one lives."

"But blessed is the man who trusts in the Lord,
      whose confidence is in him.
He will be like a tree planted by the water
      that sends out its roots by the stream.
It does not fear when heat comes;
      its leaves are always green.
It has no worries in a year of drought
      and never fails to bear fruit."

— Jeremiah 17: 5–8

CHAPTER 1

I

56 MILES NORTH OF
HAMADAN, IRAN

"Bring her to me," the man rasped into his ear. His febrile breath reeked of the septic infection festering in his abdomen. "I can ease her pain."

The little girl wailed in her mother's arms on the cot at the back of the tent. Writhing against the torment of even her mother's gentle caress, the charred, blistering skin on her arms sloughed off in chunks. Their morphine supplies were already exhausted, and it was all he could do to try to manage her exposed nerve endings with the remainder of the Lidocaine and topical Novocain. They served to deaden the pain for a few precious moments at a time, affording her the transitory respite of sleep. She couldn't have been more than seven years-old, reminding Adam Newman of his niece back home. Long, flaccid ebony hair, reflecting the lamplight like a stream of tar. Wide brown eyes that occasionally peered out from those pinched lids, issuing tears down her reddened cheeks. Light brown skin like a perfectly toasted marshmallow.

The entire tent was stuffed full of cots, brimming with men and women uncomfortably slumbering in the wan light. It was only a matter of hours before they awoke, needing food and painkillers.

The wind rose with a howl, battering the tent with sand like buckshot. The western wall bowed in, one of the stakes tearing loose from its mooring, the tether slapping the canvas.

The little girl's mother had carried her, flailing and screaming, for seventy-two straight hours, on foot through the rugged Zagross Mountains to the west, following the winding course of the Gave Rud River, out of Baghdad and to the northeast into the Kabudrahang Province of Iran. Twelve other refugees had arrived with them two days ago. Four had since moved on, two labored on the windbreak to the west of camp to try to keep the ferocious gale from tearing the group of khaki tents from the hard, sandy ground, and the other six were in the makeshift cemetery half a mile downwind, where they were buried beneath mounded stacks of rocks. Over the last three weeks they had treated more than two hundred refugees fleeing what had become of Iraq after the Syrian occupation, most of whom had only needed a meal and a place to sleep for the night, before rejoining the mass exodus to the east. Lately, the injuries were becoming increasingly severe, like the little girl whose arms had been sprayed by a policeman's flamethrower while trying to flee the melee surrounding a car, and the man on the cot before him now, who looked like he had taken a heavy dose of shrapnel to the midsection.

The girl reared back and screamed, her right forearm splitting like a hot dog to weep a pasty sludge of exudates.

"We can't risk passing your infection to her. She should really be in reverse-isolation in a burn unit, not some dirty tent in the middle of the desert," Adam said, drawing his weary gaze from the girl long enough to look the man in the eyes. He hadn't slept more than two hours in succession in the last week. There were only five of them manning the encampment that had been designed to service no more than a couple dozen refugees each week, not the constant deluge that flooded across the border. Nearly all of their medical supplies were gone, and even the ibuprofen was being rationed a single tablet at a time, so Adam was letting his headache bore though his skull before finally succumbing to the temptation. They were down to potatoes and carrots, stewed with whatever feral mongrel bayed at the moon long enough for its location to be triangulated in the sights of an automatic rifle, ending its melancholy song.

The man's face was heavily tattooed. Black designs fanned from his nose to his temples in such a way that when he closed his eyes they looked like large bird footprints with the heels touching at the bridge. Arabic words covered his forehead like dancing black flames, his long hair drawn tightly into a frayed braid on the pillow. Wavering lines like thin tiger stripes covered his cheeks from his ears. His lips were tattooed black. Various designs crept up his neck like ivy from beneath the formerly white sheet, stained with expanding amoebas of blood. There was barely enough space between markings to see the pallor creeping into his sun-leathered skin.

"Her wounds can be healed," the man whispered.

The girl's mother looked up from the corner of the tent, drawn by the sound of their conversation, but unable to comprehend their words.

"We're doing everything we can!" Adam snapped, pressing his fingers to his temples at the surge of pain.

"I can heal her wounds," the man said, producing a trembling hand from beneath the sheet. He held up a clawed fist, leaving only his index finger free to summon Adam closer. "Lean forward."

Never taking his eyes from the other man's wide brown irises, Adam scooted the chair forward until his knees were against the side of the cot, and eased his face closer and closer—

The man's hand moved with a speed and grace Adam never expected, grabbing him across the forehead, thumb on one temple, middle finger pressing into the other. His hand reeked as though he had been digging into his own wounds beneath the sheet.

"Let go!" Adam railed, swiping at the man's arm, but those fingers held tight. "Let me go right the f—!"

The words died on his tongue.

The man released his grip on Adam's forehead, then brought his hand back beneath the sheet.

"How did you—?" Adam started, brow furrowing. "The headache… it's…"

9

"Gone," the man whispered. His black lips drew wide, shimmering with the lantern light like an adder's scales.

Adam stared at him, shaking his head.

"Bring me the girl," the man rasped, his face pinching into a fist of pain.

Adam watched him a moment longer before finally rising to his feet and walking to the back of the tent.

"Please," he said, holding both arms out to the girl's mother.

She shook her head violently, pulling the girl tighter to her chest, eliciting a scream.

"I'm not going to hurt her," Adam said. His tan camouflaged shirt was black with blood. The matching pants streaked with it all the way down to his military-issued boots. "I'm just going to…"

Going to what? Give her to this psychotic-looking, tattooed man in hopes that his touch alone might alleviate her pain? Never in his life would he have pictured this scenario when he enlisted in the Army Reserves to let the government pay for medical school.

"Please," he whispered again.

The girl's mother looked across the room to the tattooed man, her stare searching his soft brown eyes.

She closed her eyes and nodded, reluctantly loosening her hold on the child. Adam slipped his hands beneath her armpits and carefully brought her to his chest, watching as more blackened chunks dropped from her arms. Amber pus seethed from the wound like tree sap.

The child screamed and stretched her arms out for her mother, frantically wailing the same Arabic phrase over and over.

"It's all right," Adam said, carrying her across the room to the man's bedside.

"Bring her lower so I can reach her."

Adam knelt beside the cot, propping the squirming girl on his knee.

"Relax, child," the man said. "You must endure only a moment longer."

His right hand emerged from beneath the sheet and wrapped all the way around the girl's arm. Thin tendrils of smoke wafted from beneath his touch, the smell like roasting an overdone slab of meat.

The girl's screaming ceased and she stared intently at the man's hand.

The charred flesh began to flake like ash. He drew in a deep, wet inhalation then blew his acrid breath across her forearm, chasing all of the charcoaled remains away as though they had merely been dust piled on her now smooth skin.

The child's mother moaned and hurried to the cot, throwing herself to her knees and kissing the back of the man's hand, but he jerked it away. She turned to him as though she had been struck, but he placated her with a weak attempt at a smile.

"I must still heal the other arm," he said.

A rivulet of blood trickled from the corner of his mouth, the beading droplet swelling and shivering on his painted jaw line. He offered his palm to the child, who didn't even hesitate to lay her arm on it. His fingers closed slowly around her burnt flesh like a Venus flytrap.

Again, smoke arose from their union, summoning an intoxicating scent that caused Adam's mouth to begin salivating.

Releasing her arm, the man drew another deep breath and blew across her skin, scattering the ashes of what moments prior had been a wound Adam was sure would soon take the child's life. Droplets of blood pocked her pristine skin, their origin trailing down the man's chin.

Adam stared at the man's hand until it was safely stowed again beneath the sheet.

"Thank you," he whispered, matching stares with the man. Though the tattoos made him look menacing, he had the warm eyes of a child, like gently-stirred vats of rich chocolate.

Adam reached out tentatively, prepared to touch the sheet covering the man's dwindling body, and then paused. He didn't want his tactile senses to spoil the illusion if the man weren't actually real.

"Newman!" a voice shouted from outside.

Adam looked up in time to see Peter Keller burst through the tent flaps. He had a jaw that appeared to be chiseled from granite and black that framed a nose broken a few too many times. His face was sheet-white in contrast to his black crew cut. Though he looked like the stereotypical grunt, he was their information specialist, running the gamut of duties from communications to recon with the hopes of entering the FBI Academy after his tour.

The large veins to either side of his neck bulged and pulsed.

"You've got to see this."

◉   ◉   ◉

The command tent was smaller than the others to make it appear less significant to any insurgent factions or aerial reconnaissance. There were only three chairs set in the middle, so Adam and Keller sat on the floor in front of the others, focusing their attention on the open laptop set on their reserve drum of water. Topographical maps detailed from satellite images lined the walls.

Behind, the radio communications crackled with static, having come alive with activity shortly after midnight. It was a secure channel, and even then, orders were coded. A sudden surge in relays always indicated that something big was about to happen.

"Oh my God," Thanh Vu gasped. She was sitting behind Adam with both hands clasped over her mouth, repeating those three words like a mantra. Stateside she had been a surgical intern and a reservist. At five foot three and a hundred pounds after a big meal, she wasn't a typical military gal, but she could wield a scalpel like no one Adam had ever seen.

Lieutenant Roy Kimball sat next to her, his fatigues thick with dust from heading the construction of the windbreak. His entire face was thick with dirt, save for an oblong stretch around his eyes like a raccoon's where the goggles dangling around his neck had shielded them. He still wore his camouflaged helmet, sand sifting from the edges to fall onto his shoulders with each slight movement. Customarily boisterous and commanding, lest someone forget who was in charge, he hadn't said a word since Adam had entered the tent.

David "Kotter" Cosgrove sat in the chair behind Keller. He was an excellent nurse, somehow managing to tend to all of the refugees at once, while Adam and Thanh could barely keep up with their half loads. He had a thick mustache and short curly black hair that could easily have been grown out into an afro, making him look just like the 70's sitcom star.

"Oh my God," Thanh sputtered again.

"…Syrian atrocities perpetrated on the former democratic regime. Again, these images were attained through undisclosed information networks and no further details are available at this point in time," the reporter said over the rolling footage. The CNN logo was clearly visible in the lower left hand corner, but the rest of the black and white picture was riddled with static. Fires burned as blinding white shapes to either side of a road littered with rubble. The camera zoomed to the right, drifting in and out of focus at the will of the flames then finally rectified the hazy image. It was the top of a man's head, a flap of scalp flopping on the breeze, exposing the red maw beneath from which a flower of his gray matter bloomed. His chin rested against his chest, his eyelids held partially open by a thick layer of crusted blood. Broken jaw set askew, his swollen tongue parted fractured teeth. The lens drew away, again fighting for focus before capturing the entire image. The man was nailed to a cross formed from cut telephone poles.

Crucified.

The camera panned down the street, revealing the shadowed silhouettes of a dozen more similarly posed corpses.

Adam couldn't concentrate his thoughts enough to formulate speech.

Static clipped the screen, which froze momentarily until they regained their connection.

"…lining the main roads leading into the capital city of Baghdad as deterrent to further insurgence, and as a warning to the United States that intervention will not be tolerated."

The image cut from the sketchy handheld video taped on the street to a much clearer image labeled with the Al-Jezeera television logo and Arabic subtitles.

"This was the scene this afternoon outside of what remains of the American Embassy," the reporter said. A towering blaze burned in the middle of the street in front of the charcoaled skeleton of the building, twice the size of the men racing around it, waving burning American flags. Firing rifles into the air. Throwing the bodies of US soldiers into a pyre fueled by their ranks. "Casualties are still estimated in the hundreds, but there has been no official confirmation.

"In an impromptu press conference at the White House, President

Wallace defended the decision to withdraw close to a quarter million troops from within Iraqi borders."

"This was not a result of abandoning the fledgling Iraqi government too soon," the President said. His thick gray hair stood up as though he had been tearing at fistfuls, the bags rimming his eyes so dark they looked like bruises. "It was this administration's—and this country's—decision to bring our boys back home after the election. We're saddled with the results of the former administration's inept foreign policies, and, unfortunately, it falls on my shoulders, and the shoulders of the greatest military force on the planet, to clean up this mess.

"We have been assured support from the countries neighboring both Syria and Iraq. Iran, Saudi Arabia, Egypt and a solid list of others have all pledged military support, while offering staging grounds within their borders for our infantry. The Syrian occupancy of Iraq violates international law and should be seen as an aggression against a developing nation under the protection of the United Nations and the American umbrella. Our country will not stand idly by while the oppressive fist of tyranny closes on these people who only recently tasted heir first breaths of freedom, nor will we allow these people to be tortured and killed in defiance of the Geneva Convention. We liberated Iraq once. We can do so again if necessary. Let this serve as warning to Ali Ak-Abbat and his Syrian forces that the United States will not stand for this unprovoked aggression. Pull your forces out now. Leave the sovereign state of Iraq.

"Or face the consequences.

"While the president declined to comment on the deployment of US forces, reports indicate that a fleet of battleships are already well on their way to the Persian Gulf to join the more than ten thousand soldiers currently afloat on warships both in the Gulf and the Caspian Sea. Fully loaded military transport planes have been taking off from Army bases lining the eastern seaboard all afternoon," the reporter said, the camera cutting to a shot of him sitting at a desk on a news set. "Is this the beginning of World War III? At this point, one can only speculate, but with this administration's platform of 'Hands Off' Diplomacy and the large cuts made in the military budget, the US appears at its most vulnerable since the dawn of the First World War.

With the UN convening in an emergency session later tonight, only time will tell—"

He paused, pressing his right hand to his ear. His eyelids closed and his lips moved over soundless words. After an interminable moment, he looked up to the camera, the color drained from his face, his plastic hair reflecting the stage lighting. At that moment, he looked like a lost little boy in an adult's suit.

"We've just received word that Al-Jazeera television has just broadcast a tape purportedly from Al-Qaeda operatives within the United States."

He sat there a moment, staring at the camera.

"What's going on?" Kotter asked, his voice a strained whisper.

The radio cackled with life behind them. Sharp, fevered voices snapping back and forth.

"We're at war, kids," Kimball said. Unblinking, he stared at the screen.

The reporter was replaced by an image shot on a camcorder, jiggling up and down in someone's unsteady grip. Four men stood against a plain white wall behind a table, upon which rested what looked like an enormous garbage disposal unit lying on its side. Each man wore a black sack covering his face and a novelty white T-shirt. Disneyland was stenciled across one man's chest with a picture of the Magic Castle, while another's bore the Statue of Liberty. The third wore a Denver Broncos logo. The American flag graced the final man's chest beneath the words "We Remember: 9/11". He had scrawled a hurried slash across the flag with a marker.

The man second from the left started to speak, his words garbled by both an electronic voice-altering device and his Arabic tongue. He gestured to the apparatus on the table.

"This is a Uranium-235 explosive device," a narrator translated with a thick accent, "the same bomb the infidels themselves used to annihilate Hiroshima. This is a two pound device capable of releasing 75 million joules of energy, or, in other words, able to create an explosion large enough to demolish half of New York City; more than enough to remove Salt Lake City, Las Vegas or Denver from the face of the earth."

He paused.

"And we have four."

The other men reached beneath the table and hefted matching units up across their chests.

"Oh my God," Thanh whispered, tears streaming down her cheeks.

"Control order four two six alpha," a voice commanded from the radio behind them. All eyes turned from the computer monitor to the radio setup behind. "Repeat: four two six alpha."

"What's four two six alpha?" Adam asked.

Kimball turned to him, blue eyes set like stone in that pale strip against his bronzed skin.

"Immediate evacuation of all units within two hundred and fifty miles of Iraq."

Adam looked to Thanh, who buried her face in her hands, then back to the lieutenant.

"We have forty-eight hours to fall back to the Caspian Sea for retrieval."

"What happens then?" Kotter asked.

Keller turned around, jaw muscles clenching and unclenching.

"Boom," he said.

II

12 MILES WEST OF
BARSTOW,
CALIFORNIA

Evelyn Hartman sat on the roof of the dilapidated barn, her eyes fixed on the western horizon, where the desert terminated against the ridged foothills, speckled with small pines and Joshua trees. The last hint of the sun stained the sky a pale pink, which bled into the encroaching deep blue like a receding tide. She could remember sitting in this precise spot when she had been a little girl, imagining that on the clearest of nights, she could see the Hollywood sign stenciled into the mountains and the brilliant turquoise of the Pacific beyond. Like every other girl, she had dreamed of testing her fortunes in the magical city, fancying herself the next Carrie Fisher or Margot Kidder, but after making her first sojourn to the coast, those fancies had been relegated to a small locket she clutched to her heart. She wasn't drop-dead gorgeous and blonde like Kim Basinger, nor did she have the curves of Christina Applegate. She'd been a gangly fourteen year-old with chestnut hair lightened by the sun to dirty blonde, skin that was apparently allergic to every form of makeup, and clothes that had been clearly in style in Barstow, but were eons behind what they were wearing in Hollywood.

Her dream had officially died the afternoon her father had driven them down the Sunset Strip in their dusty old Ford pickup and she had seen all of the phenomenally beautiful women walking down the streets in clothes straight out of a rock video. Not one of them appeared flawed in any fashion. This was where the perfect people migrated. Her clearest memory from that trip had been sitting at a traffic light. There had been a pretty blonde waiting to cross the street in a herd of tourists. Evelyn could remember staring at the girl, her face familiar. The girl looked down as she crossed the street, her eyes on her comfortable black shoes, greasy hair pulled back into a bun, smoke trailing from the Marlboro Light between her dainty fingers. She wore a tan waitress uniform, stained with blotches of grease and oil.

The girl had looked up, her eyes locking on Evelyn's through the front windshield where she was pinned in the seat between her parents, before quickly looking back down to her feet and tugging her heavy brown purse back up on her shoulder.

Evelyn finally recognized her. The girl had been one of the boarders during the first couple seasons of The Facts of Life and even had a good part in Adventures in Babysitting. She had watched the girl blend back into the crowd as they drove on toward Mann's Chinese Theatre, tears blossoming from her own hazel eyes, all illusions shattered in that one bleak moment.

The trip hadn't been for naught though, as a couple days later they went to the Scripp's Aquarium in San Diego and Evelyn found her true calling. It had been her first time ever seeing the ocean in person, and what she had found was a world beyond anything she could have ever imagined. Fish of every color and hue, every shape and size. A million varieties of crustaceans from electric blue lobsters to clams with lips that glowed fluorescent pink. Clown fish that actually lived in the stinging tentacles of anemones, immune to the toxins that killed most other fish. It was a society far more complex than even that of the world above the sea. There was definitely a food chain, but there were also amazing symbiotic relationships between separate species that defied logic. Crabs growing anemones from their shells; corals made of different species of colonial polyps; even jellyfish were composed of two different types of organisms functioning as a collective whole. It made the dry world of dust she grew up in seem like something from an old black and white reel.

She knew her parents would never be able to afford to pay for her to go to college, not on what they made with their hatchery. Granted, a half-dozen Lady Amherst pheasant eggs could bring in a hundred bucks, but the market sure seemed to be dwindling even as the cost of scratch was rising. They had taken to growing their own corn, wheat, and sunflowers, but factored against the cost of their time, it was even more expensive. So she had to make sure that when she graduated there would be scholarship money, and after four years of killing herself in high school, there had been a full ride to the University of California at San Diego waiting for her.

The money had covered the tuition and books, but had barely touched her cost of living, so she had worked during the week at Sea World and weekends at an organic grocery store, running a register for a year before landing a better gig in produce. She graduated fourth in her class with a Bachelor of Science degree in Biological Sciences, majoring in Ecology, Behavior, and Evolution, and went on to graduate school at the Scripps Institution of Oceanography.

During her first year of grad school, her mother, Karen, had been diagnosed with esophageal cancer, which had metastasized so quickly that by the time they diagnosed it, the end was a foregone conclusion. She died within two months, leaving Evelyn's father to handle the whole poultry operation single-handedly. A year and a half later, Gerald Hartman fell while patching a hole in the roof of the ringneck pen. It took close to two days to drag himself into the house a half mile away with a matching pair of hip fractures and three compressed vertebrae. Evelyn had been home within ten hours of receiving the phone call from the hospital.

That had been three months ago now.

Evelyn sighed and slid down the rusting corrugated aluminum roof, dropping into the mounded haystacks they used for litter in the pens. It wasn't nearly the thrill it had been in her youth.

The school had granted her a semester's leave, but the way it looked now, her father wasn't going to be in any condition for her to go by then. He was finally able to get out of bed, though every step he took came with a wince of pain. He wore an enormous plastic clamshell that held his torso firmly in place to take the weight off of the recent spinal fusion and prevent any sort of oblique torsion. The hip replacements had both been successful, but he was only now trying to teach himself to walk again.

So now she was up before dawn, raking the desecrated hay from the pen floors and replacing it with a fresh layer, toting buckets full of scratch and water back and forth, tending to the incubation cabinets, packing and shipping eggs, taking care of the downy chicks in their red lamp-heated enclosures, and even releasing birds for hunters on the back acreage. Somewhere in between, she found time to fix the meals and look after her father, manage the business books and make sure both the doctor and the veterinarian stopped by when they were supposed to.

But at the end of the day, she still managed to spare just a few minutes for herself. The following semester she was to begin work on her Master's Thesis, which was pretty much the culmination of all of her life experience. Oceanic Agriculture: Industry and Conservation. Her working theory was that through the use of farms and hatcheries, more actual ocean could be set aside as preserves free from commercial fishing and transoceanic shipping lanes could be consolidated, creating hundreds of thousands of square miles free from the taint of man. The way she saw it, the ocean was the last remaining natural resource left that mankind had yet to pillage and plunder to the point of eradication and it was only a matter of time before there were people packed shoulder to shoulder on every continent, and all that was left was to look to the sea.

After all, the entire beef industry was based on the premise of using large ranches to raise and butcher cows exclusively to meet the food demands. It wasn't as though they hunted free-range cows. The chicken industry—all livestock industries, for that matter—were built upon the premise of captive propagation and wholesale slaughter. Why then were there still fishing boats trolling the coastlines, snaring dolphins with their tuna nets and raping the natural populations of crabs and lobsters? Surely fish and crustaceans alike would be able to be harvested in farms in the very same manner as chickens and cattle. Aquatic kelp was one of the very best foods on the planet as far as nutritional value. She'd sold a ton of it through the market. For every square acre of corn produced, a hundred times as much kelp could be grown, and harvested twice as often.

And then man could leave the ocean as he found it.

It was a pipe dream, she knew, but one she had dedicated her professional life to living... a life that was now hundreds of miles inland.

Brushing the hay from her dirty jeans and flannel shirt, Evelyn crossed the windblown, packed-sand drive and scaled the rickety wooden steps to the back door of the house. The white paint was nearly peeled back to the bare wood, browned with age and smoothed by the torrential dust storms; the torn screen door stood ajar as the latching mechanism had broken, preparing to bang against the side of the house with the first heavy gust.

She threw in the door and closed it behind her, noticing the dust she'd allowed to accumulate on the avocado-colored linoleum floor and matching counters. Half of the mail scattered across the kitchen table was unopened. There was a stack of poorly-rinsed dishes in the sink and the entire place still reeked of the meatloaf she had burnt the night before.

There just weren't enough hours in the day.

Crossing the worn carpet through the living room, she ducked down the hallway and slowly cracked the door of the first bedroom on the right, just far enough to be able to see through with one eye. Her father was still asleep beneath the heap of patchwork quilts her mother had sewn, his microwaved lasagna untouched on the TV tray beside the bed. He had apparently knocked the TV guide from the nightstand in his hurry to get at the bottle of Vicadin that lay open on the polished wood amidst a scattering of its contents.

Some baseball game played on the tube to her left behind the door. She debated turning it off, but didn't want to wake him. Not if he was comfortable and sleeping. These moments were precious to her. It caused her physical pain to see her father lying on his back with tears in his eyes as he couldn't find a comfortable position to lie in for more than a few seconds. So, with a sad smile, Evelyn closed the door and crept down the hallway to her bedroom.

Porcelain unicorns and stuffed animals still lined the shelves on the wall, interspersed with theatrical posters she had bought from the guy at the video store in town, running the gamut from The Goonies to Prizzi's Honor. Her old single bed sat beneath a pair of shelves supporting an old stereo and her small collection of CDs, complete with the same quilt that had adorned the bed since she was eight years-old. Lately, though, she had taken to passing out atop it in the same clothes she had worked in all day, barely messing it as she slept, still with exhaustion. She didn't even need the overhead light anymore; it had burned out months prior regardless. The entire room was lit day and night by the high-intensity sodium halide lights in little silver domes, strung from the ceiling to hang above the seventy-five gallon fish tank in the middle of the floor. Pumps whirred and filters churned, connected by plastic hoses over the lip of the tank. A mud-filled refugium sat beside the tank, growing tall stalks of red mangrove, which leeched the nitrates and phosphates from the constantly circulating system.

"How are we doing tonight?" She dropped to her knees then lay on her stomach, propping her chin on her hands.

Inside the tank, long greenish-brown leaves of kelp wavered side to side at the whim of the current produced by the constant influx of filtered saltwater. They took up nearly every inch of space on the floor of the aquarium, planted into a sandy medium she had procured from a hydroponics store on her last trip to the coast. Miniature blue- and red-legged hermit crabs sifted through the sand, aerating the roots.

"Someday," she whispered, tapping on the glass.

Closing her eyes, she drifted weightlessly into unconsciousness, knowing full well that her "someday" might never come.

III

EAST OF
BETHLEHEM,
PENNSYLVANIA

Phoenix closed his eyes in preparation of the inevitable. The woman had told him they would be coming. This was octavusdecimus dies, she had called it, his eighteenth birthday. He could hear them beyond the heavy wooden door, shuffling expectantly back and forth, crammed shoulder to shoulder in the tight hallway amidst the crumbling plaster and betrayed framework. Their breathing was always heavy, always creeping beneath the doorway across the concrete floor, reeking of despair, heated by their fervor. This was what he both desired and dreaded the most. To be among other people, to have physical contact of any kind, to for just a fleeting moment feel as though he was loved and special, but that feeling would be erased as they crammed in around him, all of them reaching for him, tugging at his bare skin, moaning and pleading for him to touch them, to spare their bodies from the evils that ravaged them. And when they finally left, he felt as though every ounce of blood had been drained, every inch of flesh torn away, leaving him little more than the festering bones housing what little of his life force remained.

The Swarm, as he had come to think of them, scratched at the other side of the door. He could imagine it carved into a million grooves, ribbons of wood peeled back and littering the floor atop the tatters of nails ripped from bloodied fingertips, tracing parallel lines on the walls.

He would never know for sure though, as the only times they ever took him from this damp cellar he was bound, blindfolded, and

23

carried so as not to even place his feet on unblessed ground. Being blindfolded was really no different than being in this room all the time. Seeing nothing but blackness was a nice change to the rattling pipes, rusted and staining the concrete walls with orange patterns that crept toward the condensation on the floor. The room was lit by a solitary light bulb, which cast an antique brass glare over everything. He fancied that in that light, the straw they used for his bed looked like spun gold.

His only real friends were the enormous black flies that buzzed around the rusted bucket in the corner where he relieved himself, by now no longer even smelling his refuse as he was so accustomed to being near it. All he knew was that the woman came every day to take the bucket, though he knew not exactly what she did with it, but when she returned it was always empty and reeked of stagnant water. He imagined she washed it in a lake with a thin skein of green growth rimming the edges, feeding the multitude of ducks and geese that nested in the cattails. The sun always glimmered from gentle ripples where fish leapt out of the depths, shimmering with scales like mirrors, before splashing back down as though they had never even existed, leaving the mystery of their genesis spreading out in ever-expanding concentric circles.

That thought always made him smile.

Sometimes there would be turtles sunning themselves on driftwood and doves mourning in the trees. Other times there would be a doe and her spotted fawn drinking from their own shimmering reflections while red-tailed hawks and golden eagles circled high above, screaming down to taunt the fish to rise for their meals. And still there were times when he pictured the woman crouching on the bank, sloshing the vile, larvae-riddled water in that rotting bucket. The lake would be the color of mud, carcasses of decomposing fish rimming the shore, the turtles snapping the flesh from the furry, maggot-softened remains of the glass-eyed fawn, while cottonmouths skated across the water toward her through the cattails.

In those times, he felt afraid. Not for the woman, but for himself. It was wrong to wish her ill, for she was the one who brought his bread and oats, who gave him warm milk to drink from the wooden chalice. Yet still, he prayed that when the stomping would begin above, when The Swarm started flailing around on the hardwood floor, convulsing with The Spirit, that the ceiling above would give way and bury him beneath the cracked concrete shrapnel, but then he could see the lake reflecting the startling blue skies and the purple mountains that held them aloft, the blaze of autumn aspen spreading through the forest around him, and could almost taste fresh sap on the breeze and feel the warmth of the sun on his outspread arms.

That was enough.

It had to be. There was nothing else.

Sometimes he could find his friends during the night while he was sleeping so he could see the world through their dreams… the trees, the mountains… all of it. He knew there was more outside of this cellar, or the one before, or the string that preceded that cell. He knew all about mothers and fathers and brothers and sisters and grandparents and friends and lovers, though the realization that such things existed beyond his little room was often more than he could bear. He wished for a mother to stroke his cheek and dry his tears; a father to clap him on the shoulder and beam with pride; a girl his own age to hold his hand between hers and steal him into her soft eyes. Instead, there was the shrouded woman, who covered every inch of her flesh but her hands and feet, her face hidden behind her flaccid black hair, and the man with the white square on his collar who never spoke directly to him, but always brought The Swarm.

Phoenix didn't even know what he looked like, for he had only seen himself through the eyes of The Swarm. To them he looked like a filthy rag soaked with mud and refuse, long hair in clumped strands, cowering in the dirty straw like one of the mice that scurried from the darkness to greedily take the pinches of bread he spared for them and run back into the crawling darkness.

Nothing in this world was his. Not even his name.

The Swarm called him Messiah and Lord, though he much preferred the name Phoenix, which he had heard numerous times in his former home, the sweltering basement into which all manner of hairy spiders and whip-tailed scorpions materialized to torment him.

There was a brief sparkle of light from the doorknob as it twisted, causing Phoenix to gasp. The thud of the bolt being withdrawn. The jangle of the length of silver chain. The clatter of snapping latches.

He closed his eyes and stretched out on the straw as he knew he was supposed to: arms stretched out to either side, palms to the ceiling; legs straightened, one foot balanced atop the other; naked but for the crusted dirt and filth.

Bare footsteps slapped across the cement, heading straight toward him. Voices cried out as several fell and were trampled beneath the others in their hurry to touch him. He was surrounded by their rasping breaths and the stench of disease. Hands grasped at him, poking him, scratching him, caressing him, leeching his essence through his pores. They wailed and moaned and floundered in ecstasy, waves of human flesh writhing all around him.

Tears streamed down his cheeks, but he refused to allow a whimper to part his quivering lips. He felt like they were peeling away his flesh one strap, one severed muscle, one snapped tendon at a time.

"Lay your hands!" the man with the white on his collar shrieked over the din. His square teeth were decayed to the texture of wood, his tangled silver hair framing a face like melting wax with deeply-set, hollowed eyes. "Lay your hands on the Caulbearer, the Prophesied One!"

Eager fingers crawled over his skin like so many spiders and Phoenix thought of the lake with the deer and the turtles and the sun and the fish...

"Lay your hands on the Son of God!" the man raged, his voice cracking to a shrill wail. "The Second Coming of the Christ!"

...and the purple mountains and the cattails and the ducks, but as it always seemed to, the darkness obliterated the image and drew him into its black heart where there were only the tearing fingers and the oily film of disease that formed on his flesh.

"Come and be healed!" the man screamed with the last of his voice, chasing Phoenix's mind from the terror of his flesh.

Even in his dreams, he could never see the woman's face. Maybe it was his fear that to do so would somehow lessen her magic, or maybe it was because that so long as he didn't have to see her, she wouldn't be able to see him. She had told him several times, always from a distance, from the shadows as though if he could not see her, he would be unable to pass judgment, but rather hear her confessions from afar. Her eyes were always there, irises as brown as a diseased liver, streaked with green like bile from a ruptured gallbladder.

"You were born beneath God's Veil," she would say, her voice a whisper, glancing toward the floor above at every creak of the settling house. He knew the sounds of the house dying around him. It spoke to him, but the woman didn't know the language. She was listening for the man's footsteps, he knew. To Phoenix, the man's tread sounded like hatchets being driven into his skull, the metered beat of his own demise. "His thumbprint was upon your face. The Chosen. I saw it with my own eyes as I was there when you were delivered. I was the one who tore the holes through the caul with my own teeth to keep you from suffocating, who ripped the seal over your mouth so you could draw the breath to cry, and who eventually pried the congealed mask of flesh from your face, the loops from around your ears."

He hardly ever spoke while she was talking, hoping she would betray just a little more of the story; a hint, a single word that might one day lead him out of this cellar and into his mother's arms again, wherever she was…

"We knew you would be coming. The signs were easy to follow. They led us to several before you, though all were still-births, delivered both from and to the grave. But we knew when we found your mother that she had been the one we were looking for all along. It resonated from her like a struck tuning fork, making it so that the world itself shivered against her presence. As The Father had promised, as he had prophesized, we found her in the City of Angels, though cast far from His grace into the very heart of purgatory. Pocked and scarred, she delivered you into my hands in an alley behind Sodom, amidst the screams of the dead and dying. She delivered you to us, our light, our savior, while the rest of God's Children knelt around us in prayer."

"Is the man upstairs God?" Phoenix had asked once.

"No," she had said, the only time he had ever seen a smile in her eyes. "He is God's servant, a shepherd, a prophet. God speaks through him, gathering His sheep into the fold so that we may commune with Him through His only son."

She loved him. He was sure.

Then why did she steal him from his mother and lock him in these dreary confines? If he was God's son, then where was his father? Certainly not down there in that rank cellar to hold his hand when he was scared or warm his prickled skin when he was cold.

Only The Swarm came to see him in the dark.

Only The Swarm touched him.

Only The Swarm.

That night he dreamed of the hum of a million insects, vibrating the very floor of what he assumed would one day be his tomb while myriad voices screamed a cacophony of horror above.

That dream eventually bled into another, where he sat at the edge of a crystalline stream, his bare feet pruned beneath. Another pair of slender, pearl-white legs splashed beside him. He felt a warm hand slip into his own, his heart accelerating like a hummingbird's wings. He looked to the right, blinded by the sun behind her, her face bathed in shadow.

"More man tears," she whispered.

Even though he couldn't see it, her smile radiated more warmth than the fiery orb behind her.

He awoke on the heap of defiled straw with a blissful smile on his face, though, for the life of him, he wasn't sure which dream had caused it.

IV

NORTHERN IRAN

"Get on the truck!" Keller shouted, leaping from the driver's seat of the tan transport vehicle and sprinting around to the back to open the gates, leaving the door wide and the engine running. The enlarged bed was framed with an aluminum infrastructure, canvas roped around it so it looked like a moving van. He had backed it right up to the line of tents.

The sand blew sideways on the rising wind, muting the darkness.

"Go! Go!"

The more ambulatory patients were the first to their feet, crowding around the rear of the truck while Keller tied back the canvas flaps. They clambered over the gate and scurried toward the front, standing up and packing themselves forward like sardines cramming themselves into a can. None of them spoke, as all knew what was transpiring around them and how fortunate they were that they weren't being left behind in the camp. Holding bloody gauze to foreheads and shoulders, arms and legs in slings and makeshift casts, they pressed back as far as they could to make room for as many more as possible.

"You go first!" Adam yelled, shoving the woman toward the truck's gate, then giving her a solid boost from behind. As soon as the woman clambered to her feet, he passed her daughter to her. "Get up against the side so you can still get air!"

With a final shove, he propelled her toward one of the sides where the canvas was seamed together then sprinted back toward the tent. A lungful of the black smoke churned and coughed from the tailpipe.

"Newman!" Kimball yelled, the radio and laptop stacked across his arms, cords trailing around his legs. "Get on that truck!"

"There are still patients."

"We save the ones we can," Kimball shouted over the patter of sand hammering the tent. "The rest can fend for themselves."

"Not in their condition. We'd be leaving them to die."

"They'd have died already if it weren't for us."

"We can't leave them."

"We can and we will, soldier. Now, get on the truck. That's an order!"

Adam's stare locked contemptuously on his commanding officer. "Yes sir."

Kimball held his gaze a moment, before finally turning and heading out of the tent. As soon as Kimball turned, Adam sprinted back into the tent.

Lieutenant Kimball clambered up into the driver's seat of the truck, setting the communication devices carefully on the seat next to him while still leaving enough room for a passenger. Sighing, he rubbed the grains of sand from his eyes and pounded his fist into the horn.

He looked to the side mirror, but could only see various bodies pressing into each other to try to force their way onto the truck through the thick black exhaust and the blowing sand. The entire cab bounced gently with the transferal of weight from the tailgate to the bed.

He triggered the windshield wipers, dragging twin intersecting arcs through the dust.

Something moved through the sideways blowing sand like a specter through the mist. He leaned forward, squinting to try to make out the details. Whatever it was appeared to be the same color as the desert sand, flirting in and out through the dust storm, a mere shade of gray apart from the black night. Slowly, he was able to decipher a vague impression of the outline.

"All right, boys!" he whooped out the door. "We've got ourselves an escort!"

Kimball immediately recognized the model as he had served on one during the Gulf War. It was a Challenger 1 tank: seating for three with a 120 mm L11A5 gun, two 7.62 mm MG's and two five-barrel smoke dischargers. Challengers had destroyed more than three hundred Iraqi tanks without suffering a single casualty of their own. They were the biggest and baddest land animals to ever slither across these deserts.

He clambered out of the seat, shielding his eyes from the dust with his left hand while flagging them with his helmet in his right.

"Yee-haw!"

"We're out of time!" Adam shouted as he sprinted into the tent.

"We need five more minutes," Thanh snapped nervously.

"Kimball's orders. Grab everyone you can and move it!"

"We can't leave any of these people behind."

"I don't intend to," Adam said.

She looked up to him from her patient while hooking him to a fresh tank of oxygen that she knew would only last for the next six hours if they were careful, forcing her to turn down the flow from four liters to one and a half and hope he didn't become hypoxic.

Adam smiled and gave her a squeeze on the shoulder as he passed to the adjacent cot.

"What do you want us to do then?" Keller asked.

"Just start grabbing people and getting them onto that truck. We can treat them in the back while we're driving if we have to. So long as they're on the truck."

"That truck isn't going anywhere until we're all on board. I'll see to that."

"Kotter!" Adam shouted.

"Over here!"

Adam spun around to see the nurse kneeling next to one of the cots trying to pack the patient's IV's into a backpack.

"Get him on the truck. We can worry about the details later."

"I'm not pulling his tubes!"

"I don't care if you have to load him up holding those bags in his mouth! Just get him on the truck!"

Kotter struggled, winced at the exertion then heaved the man into the air, holding him across his chest with the man's head lolling over his left shoulder, legs draped over his right arm. Grunting, he pushed his way out of the tent and toward the truck, letting in a gust of sandy wind.

"I can't carry this guy by myself!" Thanh yelled.

"Keller?"

"I'm on it," Keller said, draping the woman he had across his chest over his right shoulder like a roll of carpet. He leaned precariously down to heft the slender man from the cot in front of Thanh.

"Come on!" Adam yelled, sliding his arms beneath the tattooed man's shoulders and knees. "We've got to go now!"

Kotter breezed back into the tent.

"We have a few more minutes. Looks like we're going to get a chaperone after al—"

A bang like boulders slamming together cut him off, followed by a high-pitched scream.

"It's about time you guys got here!" Kimball shouted over the howling wind, battered from the side by the rising gale, still waving his helmet over his head. "I was beginning to think that we were going to have to—"

He slowly lowered the helmet to his side, his face falling slack.

There was no combat dozer blade on the front of the tank. The external fuel tanks were mounted to the sides rather than in the rear. It was the same design as the Challenger 1, but a previous model. A Shir2. Made by the British.

An Iranian tank.

"What's wrong with this picture?" Kimball asked himself as he donned his helmet and slowly walked out to meet the tank.

They were barely thirty miles from the Iraqi border and smack-dab in the middle of nowhere. Any armored convoy would have to have been sent out of Hamadan, which was close to a two hour drive in one of those tanks. They would have had to have been dispatched before Kimball had even been given the order to fall back.

He looked back at the truck. There was a nine millimeter in the glove box.

Fifteen feet away.

It would have made more sense to send an aerial escort. A chopper. Able to cover them from the air should things get nasty. Not a tank.

A tank was too slow. They could have moved nearly twice that speed in the truck alone.

The only reason they wouldn't have sent a chopper was if—

He stared down the turret as it leveled at the same height as his head.

—they didn't want to show up on radar.

If they didn't want anyone to know they were coming.

Kimball shook his head and looked to the sky. There was a clap of thunder and a furious scream.

"Double crossing sons of—"

He saw the flare of muzzle fire, but didn't even have the time to close his eyes. The mortar impacted his skull with such force that it drove his facial bones back through his occipital bone, demolishing the entire works, cleaving his body from the ground. His left boot still sat erect on the sand while his body was launched like a twin missile beneath the spiraling shell.

The missile slammed into the front of the transport vehicle, lifting it from the ground and tossing it back over the line of tents in a swelling fireball of molten metal and smoke.

"Down!" Keller shouted, throwing the bodies from his shoulders to the ground and then covering them with his own like a human shield.

Flaming shrapnel tore through the tent as though it were made of tissue paper, instantly setting fire to the canvas shreds and everything else that got in its way.

Adam pinched his eyes shut, grinding his teeth, and dropped atop his patient.

A fiery wash of gasoline spattered the roof of the tent from the disemboweled truck as it careened over their heads with a grumble like an avalanche. The flames consumed the canvas with such speed and ferocity that they had no way of even getting back to their feet before the fiery tatters dropped down upon them.

Adam smelled burning hair before he even felt the heat on his shoulders. A metal sliver stood from his shoulder like an angel's broken wing, issuing a river of blood that sapped into his clothing.

All he could think was to run. He had no conscious control of his body as he hefted the man's weight from the ground and raced away from the source of the explosion, leaping through what remained of the burning wall into the all-consuming smoke. Retching convulsively, he stumbled, falling to his knees before summoning the strength to again stand and continue sprinting away from the intense heat behind. Hair burned black up past his singed ears, smoldering in an attempt to rekindle itself against the tumultuous wind, he sprinted across the blowing sand until his legs finally gave out and sent him sprawling to the dirt. The tattooed man let out a bleat of pain when Adam crashed down onto him, driving his right knee through the man's left fibula as though it was made of glass.

The man bucked back and released a scream that was drowned out by the wail of the second missile that pounded a crater into the earth where the tents had once been, throwing up enough sand to fill the sky around them.

Adam grabbed him by the back of the shirt and started crawling away, dragging the man behind him, choking on the sand and smoke.

Severed appendages and unidentifiable body parts littered the ground all around him between melting monitors and the mangled frames of cots, charred and blackened to the point that the flesh was split clear down to the charcoaled bone.

Adam collapsed, dragging the man atop his chest to try to scrabble backward on his elbows.

He thought of the little girl he had forced into her mother's arms in the truck, trying not to gauge the size of the fiery arms attached to the clenched hands, the tattered straps of burning scalp and disembodied torsos, trying to determine if they had belonged to her. There was no point now, as whatever remained of her diminutive form could surely be scooped into a shoebox.

What kind of monsters would attack a refugee camp?

"She's with God now," the man whispered into his ear through pain-clenched teeth. Another missile screamed, obliterating the remainder of the truck's metal frame. "They all are."

Adam groaned as he tried to roll back over to all fours, feeling the sharpened tip of the metal lance grind against his scapular spine. Cocking his head back to scream, a hand slapped over his mouth, pinching it tightly shut again. His eyes raced skyward. Keller crouched over him, half of his face charred to a ghastly black. A wide white eye leered out from the blackness, scanning the horizon through the sand and dirt, waiting for the enemy to betray its location. In his left hand, he gripped another hand, smaller, dainty, like the hand of a child in his meaty ham-fist. Thanh lay face down in the sand behind him as though he had dragged her the entire way. Her formerly silken black hair was tangled and knotted, singed in sections to curled black wisps.

"We need to find survivors," Adam spat through the thick dust coating his tongue.

"No time," Keller rasped, seizing Adam by the shirt collar.

Adam barely had time to wrap his arms and legs around the tattooed man before he felt the sudden jerk, the sand packing against his fried neck like the stingers of so many hornets. He laced his fingers together, crossed his ankles and prayed the knots would hold as unconsciousness swelled like a wretched black tide.

V

Dover, Tennessee

This time of year, the Cumberland River didn't meander as it did in the spring, winding slowly like any righteous southern thing down out of the Kentucky Bluegrass country and toward the country music capital of the world, but rather raced the migrating birds south for the winter. The dogwoods were no longer in bloom along the banks, having shed their flowers and leaves onto the speeding river to race away like their own funeral procession. All of the 'possums were already tucked away in the hollows of the trees and the last of the late summer's over-ripened fruit had leeched through the luxurious Tennessee grass and into the hardening turf.

Today was a late fall anomaly and Melissa Stringer intended to take full advantage of it.

Slipping off her Doc Martens and socks, she tiptoed across the dewy grass, a shade this side of frozen, and plopped down on the matted weeds beside her little section of the river.

"I know I'm going to regret this," she said, biting her lower lip in preparation of thrusting her feet down into the river.

She shrieked with the cold, but forced her goose-bumped legs to stay their ground. Her toes turned brighter than the last of the red maple leaves clinging to the branches for dear life.

The water raced past so quickly that the molecules felt sharp, as though somewhere further into the industrial north this same section of river had been frozen over. Maybe it had. For all she knew, there could have been igloos and penguins north of the Mason–Dixon Line. The farthest she'd traveled from Dover had been to bury her grandparents in Boca Raton, though she hadn't really known them at all. They never approved of her mother Anne marrying her father Donnie. She'd been southern aristocracy, raised in an antebellum mansion that bordered the Savannah River just outside the town of the same name. To say they were stereotypical southerners would be to do them a great injustice. They were the forebears of the standard, the last remaining bastion of an era gone by, but sworn never to be forgotten in the General Lee-striped heart of Dixie. Her grandparents never forgave her mother, not even after she died of a cancer they knew to be breast, but surely would argue grew from shame. Maybe it was that Missy and her younger brother Mare represented some diseased limb of the family tree in need of pruning, some tainting of the pure Trafford blood, or maybe it was just that her grandparents were so self-involved that they wouldn't have acknowledged their own grandkids unless they saw them looking back out at them through a mirror.

Missy preferred to think of it as the latter, though there were definitely more times than not lately where she wished she could wade into a pond filled with enough leeches to suck that Stringer blood right out of her.

Her father hadn't been an Appalachian hillbilly: a five-toothed, gun-toting McCoy peddling the moonshine out of the back of a rusted wood-framed cart, but he probably lived close enough that they'd have heard him hollering. "You can take a boy out of the mountains," he was apt to say, "but you can't take the mountains out of the boy." He'd used that motto to explain how he was often inclined to walk around barefoot or the thrill he got from knocking the gray squirrels out of the trees with his old slingshot. Later, he used it to explain his Jack Daniels breath or the loud crashing that awoke them in the middle of the night during one of his tantrums. A couple years prior, he'd driven them down a long dirt road, winding into woods so thick that she wondered how any bird could be small enough to fly through there. They'd passed a house that looked to have been made with wooden slats stolen from a collection of old fences, hammered together with nails long since rusted. The roof had collapsed and the moss had already moved in and invited the vines to slither up the face of the shack. There were no windows, and no one had bothered to board up the holes either. The drive was long since overrun by weeds.

"Must be dead," her father had said with a shrug, turning back to the muddy road without slowing. That was the only time she had heard him utter a word about her paternal grandparents.

It wasn't long after that sojourn that Staci, who dotted her "i" with a cute little heart, moved into her mother's room and filled her bureau with gaudy clothes and baubles. They'd moved Mare into Missy's room to make way for Staci's girls, Amber and Ashley.

That had been three years ago now. Three of the longest years of her life. Three years of listening to Staci squeaking like a chipmunk while her father banged the headboard against the wall until the noise ceased, as it always did, with a groan not so different from the noise he would make while hunched over the toilet a few moments later. Three years of having to make breakfast for herself and her brother while her dad and Staci ate at the kitchen table in their sweat-stained underwear. Amber and Ashley barely swallowed dry toast long enough to vomit it back up in time to squeeze into whatever cleavage-revealing, belly-ring-flaunting outfit that would undoubtedly be crumpled on the floor of a Mustang by third period. Three years of listening to her father's drunk footsteps shuffling down the hallway in the middle of the night and pausing outside of her brother's old room, standing there breathing heavily for a few minutes before lumbering back to his own room to bang on the adjacent wall some more.

She saw how he looked at them. Just a quick glance over the top of his glass, a sideways look from the couch…

The sooner she and Mare were out of there the better. They just didn't know that when she went off to school down the Cumberland at Vanderbilt, that her sixteen year-old brother would be moving along with her.

She knew her father loved them, and, eventually, when they ran out of cold beer in the fridge or clean plates in the cupboard, he'd miss them as well.

It was too bad her mother's parents hadn't been alive to see that the man they disowned their daughter for marrying had become just like them, cutting his children out of his life like a canker for the blood that he could no longer stand the thought of.

Feet finally numbing to the wiles of the river, Missy leaned her head back and let the unseasonably warm sun caress her face. In that moment it was summer. The scent of the sumac was thick as tar and the water tickling her toes slowed to a crawl. She stretched both arms out and let the warmth trace every inch of exposed flesh, shimmering on hair blacker than a raven's feathers, trailing over her shoulder to the middle of her back. Finally, like a cat stretching on a window sill, she arched her back and opened eyes bluer than the heart of the thickest glacier and clearer than a stream in spring. She felt the comfort of another hand settle over hers and smiled, finally turning to her left, expecting to find Mare sitting there beside her.

She looked at her hand, held by nothing.

"More man tears?" a voice asked from behind her.

She repeated it in a whisper.

Missy suddenly realized that the initial voice had come from someone else and jumped, jerking both hands back into her lap as though he had caught her doing something she shouldn't have been. Her face paled quickly beyond its normal porcelain, highlighting the handful of freckles on her cheekbones. Her heart pounded so hard that her vision throbbed.

Even in her lap she could still feel the warmth of another hand within her own.

"I said 'warm in there?'" Mare said, chuckling.

"Absolutely freezing," she whispered.

"I can imagine, it being nearly winter and all. It was sarcasm, Missy."

She smiled, the rose slowly blooming back into her cheeks.

Mare plopped down beside her on the bank, tossing off his Vans and socks and thrusting his feet beneath the water beside her with a splash. He stood just over six feet with hair a shade lighter than hers, spiked into a ruffled mess atop his head. From the side, he looked remarkably like she imagined her father must have looked at that age, though Mare was thinner, his limbs taut and wiry.

"You sure you're ready to do this?" Mare asked, his eyes fixed on the river. He didn't want to see any indecision in her eyes.

"Of course," Missy said without hesitation. "You're my brother for crying out loud."

He smiled and nodded, but still stared straight ahead.

"What's wrong?" Missy asked. "You starting to get nervous?"

He shook his head.

"I don't want you screwing up your education trying to take care of me," he said, finally turning to face her.

"Jesus!" she gasped, jerking her feet from the water and propping herself on her knees, cupping either side of his face with her hands. "What the hell happened to you?"

He smiled, but couldn't bring himself to look up to her face. His left eye was swollen into a purplish mass, the eye a slit of black amidst the knotting bruise. Two streaks of blood drew diagonals from the outer corner of his eye, dribbling thin rivulets of blood.

"It's not as bad as it must look," he said, his forced smile never wavering.

"Did he do this to you?" she nearly screamed, forcing his chin up so he had no choice but to meet her stare.

"I had it coming." His smile appeared to bear a twitch of mirth.

"What did you do this time?"

"You know we don't have enough money to get us to Nashville—"

"You didn't."

"She keeps all that cash in their closet."

"Put it back."

"No way! They owe us at least the gas down there!"

"We don't need their money."

"I consider it a 'bon voyage' gift."

"We don't need anything from them at all!" she huffed, lurching to her feet.

"The hell we don't!"

"Lord only knows what she does to get that money."

"I don't care if she's thieving jewelry off of corpses—"

"Was it worth the black eye? Hmm? You've got nothing but that shiner to show for it!"

"Who says I don't?" he said slyly, the left corner of his mouth curling upward.

"You didn't give the money back?"

"What money?"

"You're really starting to piss me off!"

"There's no money missing from their closet."

She sighed and felt her teeth grinding. Planting her fists on her hips, she cocked her head, raised an eyebrow, and waited.

"Like I said. All of the money's still in their closet… just not exactly where they put it."

"What if they went looking for it and found our hidden money?"

"They won't."

"What if they did? Then what?"

He shook his head.

"They won't, okay?" Mare said with a shrug. "Besides, I only pulled a twenty from Staci's stash. She usually doesn't even notice."

"You've done this before, I take it?"

"Don't tell me you haven't gotten into one of those rolls."

"Never," she said. "So what did you do with the money?"

"I put it with the rest."

"Mare…"

"Okay, okay. You know that hole in the ceiling of their closet leading up to the attic?"

"Of course."

"Well, if you push the panel up and reach toward the back, you'll find a manila envelope filled with cash. For us, Missy. For us."

"Look at you," she sighed, gingerly touching his mashed eye. "It's not worth this."

He smiled.

"Like I said, I can't have you throwing away your future for your screw-up of a brother."

She couldn't stay mad at him. He was her baby brother after all.

"You're not a screw-up," she whispered, ruffling his gelled hair.

He nodded, pulling a smooth stone from the bank and pressing the cold surface to his eye.

"I want to go now," he said softly.

"We just have to wait a couple more months. I can't start classes until after Christmas, and we can't afford to get a place of our own yet. We'd run out of money way too soon."

"There's easily a couple grand up there."

"What?"

"I've been pulling a twenty from her wad once or twice a week for the last few years."

"Years?"

"I didn't want you to get upset."

A couple grand? That was first and last month's rent on a decent apartment with money left over to stock the cupboards. Throw in the four grand she'd set aside from waiting tables, all of her tip money since she was sixteen, and the grant money she'd receive with her first student loan check, and they just might be all right after all.

She looked up into the clear blue sky, shaking her head.

She was scared.

Missy leveled her eyes on her brother's face, studying the deep black ring swelling around his eye like a decomposing donut. She hated her father for hurting him. How would he feel? she wondered. How would he feel if he walked down the stairs in the morning and I was waiting there with a baseball bat—?

That wasn't her. That wasn't the Melissa Stringer who graduated first in her class and served as student body treasurer all four years. That wasn't the Melissa Stringer who fancied herself growing into the woman that her mother would have wanted her to become.

The frightening thing was that it easily could be. She could almost feel the grain of the wood against her palms as she clenched her fists around the bat, twisting and tightening, jaw muscles clenched, Louisville Slugger raised over her right shoulder...

"Two weeks," she whispered.

"What?" Mare asked, his face dripping with bewilderment. He dropped the rock back into the river and climbed to his feet, walking to where Missy stood with her back to him.

"I get my next paycheck in two weeks," she said without turning. "We'll go then."

Mare turned his sister slowly, both enraged and terrified by the sheen of tears glimmering over her eyes. He pulled her to his chest and wrapped both arms around her. She shuddered against him, a soundless sob releasing the flood of tears onto his shoulder.

He wanted to say something to make everything all right, wanted to whisper something reassuring so that she would know that no matter what happened, everything was going to work out for the best, but he knew if he even tried to open his mouth to vocalize his feelings, he'd be standing there by the river crying with her. So he lowered his chin and kissed the top of her head.

Two weeks.

He stole a hand back and winced before his fingertips came into contact with his eye.

Two weeks.

VI

Eugene, Oregon

"Oh, yeah! Stick that ugly head of yours around that corner again and give me a clean shot at it!"

A skeletal manifestation slunk onto the screen only to be barraged with bright blue laser bursts to the thorax and face. Electric blue lightning snapped from one side of the screen to the other before the monster exploded with a pixilated spray of gore.

"Who's your daddy?" Rick gloated, nodding and shifting the joystick from the right side of the keyboard to the left. His thumbs ached and his elbows were bruising his thighs.

"Dude," Darren snapped from where he knelt on the couch, the curtains pinched in his fingers and parted just enough for him to see out into the sunlight while still wallowing in the anonymity of the shadows within. "You've got to check this out!"

Rick Megget paused the game and arose from the computer for the first time in three hours. His knees popped loudly as he walked, his pale legs trying to readjust to his weight. His hazel eyes were bloodshot from staring at the monitor all afternoon, his face scruffy with a couple of days' worth of growth. Were it not for the backwards Seahawks cap and the jean shorts that hung below his knees, he would have been a dead ringer for Shaggy from Scooby-Doo.

"Why don't you just go across the street and see if any of them require the services of a future doctor?" he asked, nudging Darren aside so he could see through the slit.

It appeared as though every Kappa Delta

in the house was out on the lawn sunbathing. Bikini season had long since come and gone, but the majority were out there on towels in their shorts and belly shirts. One had to take advantage of the sunny days in the Pacific Northwest, as it could cloud up at any moment, and Lord only knew how long it would be before the sun burnt off the rainstorms again. That was why they paid a thousand bucks a month for a three bedroom dump when they could have had a much nicer house a little farther from the university.

"Oh, to be a bottle of Coppertone," Darren mused, wiping his damp lips with the back of his hand. His wavy, streaked hair was pulled back as flat as he could manage, though it was only a matter of time before it frizzed again. He had a slender face with sharp features and a long thin neck. His shamrock eyes betrayed his O'Neal roots every bit as much as his love for Guinness.

"Seriously, Dare. Are you going to waste this whole year staring at them across the street or are you going to get up the nerve to cross it?"

"What chance does someone like me have with someone like...?"

"Gina Andrews," they said in unison as a blonde with long tanned legs strode out of the open front door in heeled sandals. A loose sundress made of material as thin as air hovered about her form, the low cut of the front split in two by a swell of cleavage they could clearly see from all the way across the street. She had lips the color of maraschino cherries and eyes a blinding color of blue that nature had reserved just for her. There was just an aura about her, as though she was something so special that even the air around her had to take a step back admiringly.

Three other girls flocked to her side from the lawn, their tanned bodies already glistening with a mixture of sweat and tanning oil. While a moment prior, each would have been considered gorgeous, by merely coming within her vicinity they were made plain by contrast.

"What I wouldn't give for just five minutes—"

"What are you guys doing?" Ray Gorman shouted from behind them.

Darren and Rick nearly left the ground, loosing the curtains to flutter back into place. Neither had heard him descend the gray carpeted stairs from the second floor.

"You trying to give me a heart attack?" Darren gasped, while Rick merely took a step away from the couch and socked his roommate in the shoulder.

Ray laughed. "Man you guys don't even have a pair between you."

"Easy for you to say," Darren said. "You've already got a girlfriend."

"I certainly didn't get her by stalking her from across the street."

"Funny."

"Come on, guys. We're pre-med. Don't you know what that means?"

"It doesn't mean jack until we have that M.D. after our names," Rick said. "You know... many dollars, mucho dinero."

"Microscopic di—"

"Shut up, Gorman!" Rick said, pounding Ray in the shoulder again.

"Do it again," Ray said, raising a fist.

Rick socked him in the exact same spot again before Ray even saw Rick move.

"Damn," he groaned, turning and rubbing at his shoulder.

"Who's your daddy?"

Ray's face was bright red, and beneath his T-shirt, he was sure the forming knot was a miasma of blue, purple, and black.

"Who's your daddy?" Rick demanded again.

"For God's sake, Rick," Ray huffed, his bangs hanging in front of his eyes. Usually, he would have dragged them back over his ear, but one arm was nearly paralyzed with alternating tingling sensations and outright bolts of pain, while the other kneaded at the swelling bruise.

"Incoming," Darren said, having resumed his position by the front window after tiring of the macho posturing. "Three bogeys, moving fast."

"That's why you're still single," Ray said.

Darren leaned farther back to ensure that he wouldn't be seen, watching as the girls stepped out onto the street from the walk in front of the sloped lawn of the sorority house. Browned fern leaves littered the gutter, but they simply hopped over and looked to either side before slipping out from between the cars parallel parked along the road.

"It's only Tina," Rick said over Darren's shoulder. He sniffed. "Are you wearing Axe?"

Darren ignored him, watching the three sets of long, tanned legs striding confidently across the weathered asphalt.

"Who's with her?" Ray asked, heading through the doorway into the kitchen in anticipation of her arrival. Two Pepsi cans popped open, one after the other, and fizzled in either hand as Ray came back into the living room.

"Looks like Jill and April," Darren said.

Rick rolled his head back on his shoulders and sighed up into the ceiling.

"Jill's a great girl," Ray said. "And besides, no beggar ought to turn down a burger."

"It'll take a six pack for me to want fast food when there's filet mignon right over there."

Both Ray and Darren knew exactly who he was referring to. What had begun as something of a crush for Gina had turned into a full-blown obsession. She was way out of Rick's league, and everyone seemed to know it except him. Of course, the best he could manage to muster was a nervous "Hi" in passing, though once he had driven her home from class during a rainstorm. They still heard about that on a daily basis.

Ray transferred both cans to his left hand, stacked one atop the other, and opened the door before the doorbell rang, looping his arm around Tina's waist and drawing her inside.

"S'bout time," he said with a crooked smile.

"We've got a test in microbiology tomorrow, and you know as well as I that we weren't going to get any studying done here."

"Micro was cake," Ray said.

"Someday you're going to actually have to work for something," Tina said, smirking.

"Not today, I hope," he said, mashing his lips against hers.

"Get a room," Rick said, shaking his head as he walked back across the room and plopped down in front of the computer. He unpaused the game and took hold of the joystick.

"What crawled up his butt?" April asked, but Jill silenced her with an elbow to the side.

Electronic laser-fire echoed from the corner of the room where the computer was set up on a rectangular desk beneath a set of shelves displaying an array of empty beer bottles.

Ray Gorman smoothed back his bangs with one practiced motion and lowered his eyes to find Tina's azure stare. Their hair was nearly the same shade of brownish-blonde, though hers was streaked with a blonde so white it almost looked as though the locks had been ripped from someone else's head entirely and sewn into her scalp. Her legs were well-toned, but her exposed stomach showed a bit of paunch over the tight waist of her shorts, her cropped shirt held away from the stomach by the massive swell of her chest.

Ray broke the lip-lock and handed her a Pepsi before taking her by the hand and bounding up the staircase.

"So," Darren said, clapping his hands in front of him and nodding self-consciously. "A microbiology test, huh?"

"Yeah," April said. They were still freshmen, having rushed and been accepted into Kappa Delta, but still living in the dorms across campus. It was somehow much more adult to be away from the campus, whether actually doing something or not. Still these guys were sophomores and had their own place, which made them a whole lot more attractive than the guys back in the dorms. "It's a lot harder than I thought it would be after the first test."

"I did pretty well when I took it last year," Darren said, trying his hardest to keep his southward drifting eyes focused on her brown eyes made blue by her contact lenses. She had chestnut hair pulled back into a ponytail and an otherwise nondescript face. Her shorts were a little snug over her hips and she tugged unconsciously at the bottom of her shirt to keep it from displaying her little gut. "I could, you know… help you…"

"Do you mind?" she asked with a tilt of her head, looking up at him to showcase her long lashes.

"Not at all," Darren said, unable to hide the beaming grin. In his own way he had been trying to flirt with April since the first time Tina brought her over months ago. Really, Rick thought it was a pathetic thing to watch, especially considering he could tell that April liked him anyway. He could always tell these things. "Let me just grab my book and I'll be right back."

Darren grabbed the railing and sprinted up to the second story, his feet hardly touching the ground.

"Go on," April whispered to Jill, raising her eyebrows and giving her friend a nudge. Jill gave April a subtle nod and walked tentatively into the middle of the room. She was shorter than her friends and on the thin side. Her legs and hips were tight from her cross country days in high school, her stomach rippled with muscle, though she never allowed it to show. To her, it seemed almost masculine, especially with her small breasts. They weren't nonexistent, just… cute. Everything about her was cute: her button nose, her timid smile, the ridges of freckles beneath her pale blue eyes, even her cropped blonde hair that fell just to her shoulders.

"Hi, Rick," she said, easing up behind the desk chair.

"Hi, Jill." He jerked his shoulders to the right, using his whole body to make the joystick fire a battery of flashes at some mutant creature crawling toward him through a dark hallway.

Jill looked quickly back to April, who just waved her on.

"I like that hat," she said, biting her lower lip. Had she really just said I like that hat?

"You a Seahawks fan?" he asked dubiously.

"Yeah," she said, wincing in preparation of a barrage of questions designed to discredit her. She hadn't watched a game since she had gotten her driver's license two years ago. They weren't still playing at U Dub; what was the name of their new stadium?

"Cool," was all he said.

"Yeah."

She looked back over her shoulder to April for guidance, but Darren pounded down the stairs with a beaming grin on his face.

"We can sit at the kitchen table if you want," he said.

"Sure," April said, following him through the doorway into the adjacent room.

Shoot, Jill thought. She was on her own.

"So what's Gina really like?" Rick asked without slowing his finger on the trigger.

Jill sighed dejectedly, unable to maintain the façade of a smile.

"She's nice enough, I guess," Jill said, letting her arms fall to her sides with a slap.

Rick was absolutely clueless.

Shaking her head, she walked over to the couch and leaned across, parting the blinds. All of her sisters were out on the lawn, each of them the epitome of beauty in a different regard. She wished she was more like them. She wished she had more provocative curves. She wished she could pull off the outfits the others wore without a second thought. She wasn't really one of them. Sure, she got along just fine with all of them, but when she stripped the matter down to the bare bones, she got in because both her mother and grandmother had been Kappa Delts.

She looked back at Rick, his whole body absorbed by the game, wishing she had half of the confidence of the other girls. Why did he have to be so oblivious?

April giggled in the kitchen, and Jill could almost picture her friend place her hand atop Darren's, the laugh ending in a silence through which their eyes met, locking a moment too long.

She turned her gaze back to the window.

The bodies of her sisters lie scattered across the lawn in bloodied heaps like fallen leaves, ashen limbs tangled, large bruises like eyes staring back from withering flesh. The grass was bled black. Clouds of insects swarmed over the carnage, the bodies crawling with them.

Jill screamed.

"What?" Rick blurted, spinning around in the chair.

"Oh, my gosh. Jill!" April gasped, dashing into the living room.

Jill looked from Rick's face to April's, all of the blood drained from her own. Her right fist curled into the drapes to help her manage her balance as the room had begun to spin.

"What the hell's wrong with her?" Rick asked from beneath raised brows.

"Jill?" April called, rushing to her side. She took the smaller girl by the left arm, steadying her.

Jill opened her mouth to speak, but nothing came out.

Her face a twist of conflicting thoughts and emotions, Jill turned back to the window, jerking the curtains away with a trembling hand.

Her sisters were still sprawled out all over the lawn, only they were as she knew they had to be: reading books beneath the shade of the trees, browning with their headphones on, turning the pages of schoolbooks with oily fingers, sipping tea from glasses sweating with condensation. The grass was bright green, and the air around them was rife with nothing but the precious rays of the pristine sun.

Her knees gave out, dropping her onto her rear end on the couch.

"Are you okay?" April whispered into her ear. "Jill?"

Jill opened her hands on her lap, turning her palms to the ceiling. Her jaw fell slack.

What's wrong with her?

Is she all right?

He was holding my hand.

Is she drunk?

I think she'd let me kiss her.

I hope we don't have to take her to the hospital.

Voices called chaotically to her from all around the room, though when she was able to steal her stare from her trembling hands, she saw that they had all crowded around her, claustrophobically leeching the air from her. She started to wheeze, laboring to draw breath.

She's hyperventilating.

I could cop a feel and no one would know.

What's going on down there? Can't this wait another five minutes?

She's wigging out.

The voices assaulted her from all sides, attacking in a riot of sound from the spinning room like so many flying fists.

None of their mouths were moving.

"Jill?" April said, her voice resonant with fear.

"I'm okay," Jill managed to say, pushing herself from the couch to her unsure legs. She wobbled from side to side before righting herself and heading for the front door.

Something was wrong. Really wrong.

By the time she hit the street, she had to bury her face in her hands to hide the tears.

VII

Northern Iran

It was only when he smelled his own burnt flesh that Adam knew he was alive, and the sudden rush of pain made sure to drive the point home. His neck buckled back with the throes of a scream that was never able to rip through his parched throat. The warmth of the sun permeated his closed eyelids with an orange glow. With all of the sand packed into his tear-crusted eyes, opening them was like raking sandpaper across his orbits.

"Don't try to move too quickly."

It was Keller's voice.

A wash of cold water passed over his lips and he had to sputter to force it to go down. It tasted like it had been pulled from a river downstream from a herd of yaks, and his first thought was of giardia ravaging his intestines, but it was still the most divine thing he had ever consumed.

"There isn't much," Kotter said, a black shape blotting out the rising red sun and the wavering aura of the desert heat. "We need to make it last."

"One more," Adam croaked, propping himself up on his elbows despite the raging protests from his field-bandaged shoulder. He could barely peel his tongue from the roof of his mouth to allow his lips to open wide enough.

Kotter leaned over him and tipped the helmet just enough to splash across Adam's mouth. He no longer looked like Gabe Kaplan. Only the right side of his head still had hair, while the left was singed back to the blistering scalp. His left eye was encircled by angry-red skin, and there was no hair left on his eyebrow or eyelid. What little remained of his formerly thick mustache was fried to scorched curls burnt nearly to the flesh. Fresh blood seeped through the cracks in his lips when he spoke.

"Think you can walk?" he asked. "There's no way we can drag you guys any farther."

Adam nodded and somehow managed to roll over onto all fours and tentatively push himself up on legs that felt like noodles. He reached gingerly over his shoulder toward his back. It felt as though the metal was lodged all the way clean though.

"We removed the shrapnel and were able to bandage it, but it's jimmy-rigged at best," Keller said.

Adam's legs gave out and deposited him again to the sand on all fours. He panted, trying to force his pinched eyes open against the ferocious agony. The pain in his shoulder abated just enough to allow him to open his eyes and look around. Red rocks towered over them, reaching like skyscrapers into the blood red sky. It reminded him of the Garden of the Gods back home in Colorado, though there were no purple, snow-capped Rocky Mountains behind. No pale blue sky. Just these sheer cliffs already beginning to come to life with brilliantly-colored lizards with spiked tails and thickly-scaled serpents staking their claim to the prime basking surfaces, and the dust-riddled sky above leeching the sun's rays. Squinting against the glare, he rolled over onto his rear end, bracing himself on his arms.

Uninterrupted desert stretched to the eastern horizon, shimmering like a field of diamonds before the dawn.

"Are you sure you'll be able to walk?" Keller asked.

"Yeah," Adam whispered, finally mastering his equilibrium and rising to his feet. "Where are we anyway?"

"I'm not precisely sure, but I'd guess roughly 10 miles southwest of Ali Sadr Village. If I'm correct, from there we can find transportation to Tehran, which ought to get us to the Caspian Sea in time for retrieval, so long as we keep moving."

"What happened back there?"

"Tank."

"The Syrians crossed into Iran?"

"Best I can figure. I wasn't about to stand around waiting for an introduction."

"I never even saw it."

"I guess it snuck in under the dust storm, but that's also what allowed us to get away."

"Don't you think the Army will send choppers out for us once they notice we're missing?"

"If they ever notice," Keller said, shielding his eyes against the sun. The right half of his face was still black. Tears poured unimpeded from the right eye, thickening with dirt, but it didn't move with the left eye scouring the horizon. It just stared blankly ahead. "For all they know, we loaded up in our trucks and are on our way to the removal site. I keep watching the sky, but so far nothing."

"So we're on our own, then," Adam sighed.

Keller nodded, turning back to the desert to the east where he could see nearly to the end of the world, and wondered why a Syrian tank would have attacked a refugee camp on Iranian soil. It made absolutely no sense. Surely they couldn't be preparing an offensive against Iran, who had already entered the nuclear age. The only reason they would have even considered being so brazen was if—

"Saddle up," Keller said, turning his attention to the north. If he was right, the journey was going to be a lot more perilous than he could even imagine.

Adam could tell something was eating at Keller, but, under the circumstances, that was only to be expected, though he couldn't shake the feeling that there was more than the soldier was letting on. They had been traveling north along the foothills of the Zagross Mountains for close to two hours, or so he surmised by the position of the rising sun, which was turning the day into a sweltering oven. If they were headed toward Ali Sadr, then surely they would have already begun heading away from the mountains. Unless they weren't going to Ali Sadr after all. But where else could they be going?

Keller trudged a good half dozen paces ahead of the rest of them, his eyes fixed to the north, only turning around long enough to ensure that the others were following in his footsteps to mask their tracks. Sweat glistened on his skull, an aura of heat emanating from him. His service pistol never left his right hand, while the sun glinted from the serrated blade in his left.

Adam lagged behind, doing his best to just place one foot in front of the other while he supported the weight of the tattooed man, whose left arm was wrapped around his neck. The man's abdominal wounds had nearly completely healed overnight, leaving little more than ugly crescent scars that almost looked as though the scar tissue had grown across the gaping lacerations and closed them like so many small mouths. And Adam was certain that he had heard the man's left fibula snap beneath his knee when they had been fleeing the assault at the camp, but the man walked on it as though nothing had ever happened. Even the color was starting to come back to his face between the ominous markings, but there was something about his eyes that had changed. They were no longer fathomless pits of warmth and softness as he had seen them when the man had healed the girl's arms, but now looked to be carrying a weight of sadness that hurt Adam to look at. So he kept his eyes on the sand, making sure that one foot proceeded the next, occasionally looking back to make sure that they hadn't lost the others.

Kotter trailed in the rear, and by now it looked as though Thanh was supporting him every bit as much as he supported her. His face was dripping with sweat, his eyelids blinking frantically to keep the stinging droplets from creeping into his eyes. Every so often, his irises lolled upward, but with obviously great exertion, he forced them back down and concentrated all of his strength on staying on his feet.

Thanh struggled to balance the much taller man, though she didn't really appear to be in any kind of shape to be doing so. A long gash bisected her face from her hairline, over her right eye, and all the way down to her chin. Whatever had sliced her had torn her tan jacket as well. She held it tightly closed with her free hand as though to allow it to open would expose her chest.

There had been another patient with them as well, but he had died during the night while Adam was still unconscious. There hadn't been much time to bury him, so they had done what they could and hurriedly mounded sand atop his corpse.

Adam tried not to think of the little girl and her mother, whom he had personally shoved into the back of the transport vehicle that had proven to be their deaths.

"Shouldn't we be heading to the east?" he called ahead to Keller, forcing the thoughts from his mind.

"We're on course," Keller called back, but even Adam knew that wasn't the case.

"We have to avoid Ali Sadr," the tattooed man whispered into Adam's ear.

The man hadn't spoken since they had begun their trek that morning.

"Why?"

The man just looked to him with those pained eyes.

Adam looked away.

"Wait!" he called.

Keller froze, his stare fused to the horizon where the foothills advanced into the desert from the west, forming jagged castles of stone directly ahead. Spotted clusters of withered palms were barely discernible like toppling columns from the rocky ruins of that natural structure.

"Everyone take a break," Adam huffed, removing the man's arm from his shoulders and helping him drop to the increasingly hard terra.

"We don't have time for this!" Keller growled, storming back toward them. The lid had dripped halfway down over his dead eye, while his good one blazed.

"What aren't you telling us?" Adam demanded, squinting to blot out the sun so he could see Keller's reaction. Thanh eased up on his right side while Kotter plopped down onto the ground amidst the random tufts of yellowed wild-grasses.

"Everything's under control." The harsh edge in his voice betrayed his words.

"If we stay on this course, we'll overshoot the town," Thanh said.

"We should have been headed far more to the east by now," Adam added.

"I want to stay close to the mountains. If anyone were to come upon us in the middle of the desert, we'd have nowhere to hide," Keller said, sighing and removing his helmet long enough to run his fingers through his sopping hair.

"If we stay this far to the west, no one will be able to find us. They'll be looking over the desert while we're climbing through the foothills," Thanh said, exasperated. "We're not catching a bus from Ali Sadr to Tehran, are we?"

Keller turned back to the north. The back of his neck was bright red already.

"Those trees ahead signify that there must be some supply of water. We just need to push a little farther—"

"What's going on?" Thanh nearly screamed.

Keller turned to face her, smoothing his hair back and donning his helmet.

"Something about the tank doesn't sit right with me," he finally said, rubbing the crusted dust from his eyelashes.

"Like the fact that it destroyed our entire camp?" Kotter said.

"Tanks aren't long range assault vehicles. They're meant for combat, not reconnaissance. And this tank was alone. The only reason a single tank would be deployed was if someone didn't want to draw attention to the objective and if the expected resistance was to be minimal. There's no way that a tank crossed from Baghdad through the mountains along the Gave Rud. The slopes are nearly vertical. This has all of the signs of an ambush."

"You think it was one of our own?" Thanh asked.

"Maybe not American, but I'd wager a vital organ that it was dispatched from somewhere within Iranian borders."

"While we do not look at the things which are seen, but at the things which are not seen. For the things which are seen are temporary, but the things which are not seen are eternal," the tattooed man whispered.

"Corinthians," Kotter mused.

"What?" Adam asked, turning to the man who now drew Arabic symbols in the sand with a dirty finger.

"Treachery," the man said, looking up to Adam with those wide, hurt eyes. "Can't you taste it in the air?"

Adam looked back to Keller.

"So where are we headed then?" he asked.

Keller sighed. "We stay as close to the mountains for as long as we can. After I'm sure we've passed Ali Sadr, we head due east until we run into the Caspian Sea… unless anyone has a better idea?"

"You think they'd be watching for us in Ali Sadr?" Kotter asked.

"Are you willing to take that chance?"

"If we don't, then we'll never make it to the retrieval site before our time runs out."

"And if we do and they're waiting for us there, we'll never make it at all!"

"Mûwth," the man said. He retraced the markings he had carved into the ground: תרפמ

"What does that mean?" Thanh asked, lowering herself to her haunches to look into the man's eyes.

"It is my name," he said, matching her stare with fathomless brown irises.

"It's Hebrew…" Kotter said.

When the man turned to face him, the markings on his face glistened like the black scales of a viper.

"It means death."

CHAPTER 2

I

NORTHERN IRAN

"There's a way through Ali Sadr," Mûwth said when they were nearly upon what looked like a fortress crafted from stone. The foothills themselves appeared to have grown toward the desert, leaving a massive pile of debris as though the mountains lording over them had broken free and tumbled eastward in the form of enormous rocks. Its walls were steep columns of sandstone, between which a multitude of wide fissures formed thin passageways leading into the heart of the monolith. Where the desert sands met with the abrupt uprising, they formed sloping dunes.

There was no way of scaling the nearly vertical walls that stood more than one hundred and fifty feet above their heads, not without the proper climbing gear, and even then, the sandstone was likely to crumble before allowing a post to be driven into it.

From where they stood in the shadow of the mountainous crag, there were only two options. Either they could head to the west into the mountains and risk the treacherous terrain, slowing their progress to the point that they were unlikely to reach the retrieval spot in time, or they could follow the face of the stone outcropping to the east, which would surely bring them right into Ali Sadr.

"We're not going through Ali Sadr," Keller growled, his jaw thrust forward from his reddened face in obvious frustration. He pressed himself to the cliff and reached for the first handhold he could find, which immediately crumbled away, dropping a scorpion the size of a man's hand onto the sand. Even as the black creature arched its stinger to prepare to strike Keller's boot, Mûwth raised his chapped and bleeding bare foot, and smashed the scorpion, grinding it beneath his callused sole.

"I did not mean that we must go through the town," he said, raising his foot to pluck the carcass from where it was lodged into his sole by the stinger. He ripped the entire tail portion from the squashed exoskeleton, innards squirting out in gray gobs, tossed it aside and offered the remainder to each of them in turn before taking several quick bites. "I only meant that we could bypass it entirely without detouring from our present course."

Adam stared at the man. His voice dripped with an Arabic accent, but his English was nearly flawless. He was the furthest thing from the typical refugee who had passed through camp. Of course, none of them had shown the ability to heal with their touch, either.

"How?" Keller asked. He pinched his one functional eye against the desert sun.

"Forty years ago," Mûwth began, his molten irises glazing over, "a young boy discovered a series of caves while looking for a lost goat. He was a shepherd, a simple peasant boy of no means. His mother died during his birth and he never even met his father. He was taken in by his maternal grandparents, who were the only surviving blood relatives as his mother had no siblings, and there was no way to even begin tracking his father's lineage. He began shepherding the goats by the time he was seven, and it was said that the animals held an incredible affinity for him, that he could speak to them in their own tongue."

"We're wasting valuable time," Keller said, eyeing the sun that was now descending from the apex of its journey. "Do you know a way around this or not?"

"All will be revealed if you will allow me to continue my story," Mûwth said, looking patiently to Keller, who finally threw up his hands. "I was saying that the boy was able to communicate with the goats. When one wandered off from the herd, he could simply listen to the others to find out where it had gone.

"There was one day in particular when the boy was ten… a mischievous male slipped away from the herd. This was the biggest goat in the herd: long sharpened horns that could easily gore a man, a shaggy gruff like a lion's mane, and a head so scarred from battling the other males that it looked as though his lumpy skull was exposed. When the boy noticed that the goat was gone, the others in the herd pointed to this very ridge before us, only several miles to the east. Many times the boy got close enough to the goat that he was able to see it, but each time he got close, the animal's hind-quarters caught fire with a brilliant orange and red flame like the setting sun. His twin horns glowed like two golden spires pointing to the heavens. So the boy continued following this animal, over hills and around stone pillars for many hours, each time the beast allowed him to come just a little closer until finally he cornered the creature before this very cliff.

"The goat stood before him for an eternal moment, fur ablaze, a fiery beard beneath his chin, horns forming a divine golden 'V'. His eyes glowed a deep blue to shame an amethyst, to pale the sky, but before the boy could run to him, the goat turned and disappeared into the very mountain itself.

"It was this crevasse directly in front of us right now."

"The same crevasse," Keller repeated, no longer able to contain his frustration. "What the hell does this have to do with anything? By the time you're done telling this story and my head stops spinning, we might as well just cut right through the center of town. Maybe a bullet might even be able to cure this headache you're giving me!"

"Please," Mûwth said, his soft eyes falling on Adam. "Come stand precisely where I am now."

Adam walked over to Mûwth, who stepped aside just enough for Adam to sidle up next to him.

"What do you want me to—?"

"Look," Mûwth said, his voice dripping with reverence.

As if by magic, the shape came into focus before him. The fissure in the rock formed the long bridge of a nose. Halfway up, a recessed ledge to either side created ovular shadows that looked to be eyes chiseled from the stone face. Long ledges stretched to either side, furling with small plants to look like the curled hair on the tip of triangular ears, which sloped back toward the face to form the rounded swelling of the cheeks. Two more cracks, each symmetrical to the central crevasse arose from above the ears to the very top of the rock, tapering as they climbed until they reached twin points through which the early afternoon sun shown like the golden horns of the mythical goat.

He took a step to the left and the face vanished as though it had never been. One step to the right and it appeared again. That particular point was the only such vantage to bring the features into alignment.

"What is it?" Thanh asked.

"Stand right here," Adam said, pulling her directly in front of him so that he could still see over her ebony hair. His hands cradled her shoulders.

"You've got to see this," she said, looking first to Keller, then to Kotter.

"So this boy stood on the same ground that is beneath your feet right now, and watched the burning goat slip into that crack and disappear," Mûwth continued as Keller slid into place behind Thanh. "The boy followed, led by the flicker of flames staining the walls from the goat that stayed just ahead of him, just out of sight, leading him deeper and deeper into the mountain itself until the boy reached the end of the path.

"The goat was no longer there. Instead, four hoof-prints burned around a crumbled section of sandstone, as though the creature had balanced himself against the wall and then disappeared. The boy fell to his hands and knees between the rear prints, still burning a bright red, and began unstacking the crumbled boulders and moving them to the side. Finally, with the setting sun staining the sky as red as a goat's blood, the boy uncovered a dark hole. He continued shoving the rocks aside until it was wide enough to accommodate his shoulders and slithered into the hole like a snake.

"Within this mountain of sand and stone were wonders that took his breath away. He found himself in a cave filled with water that stretched clear off into a darkness as thick as tar. Droplets fell from the stalactites above like the patter of feet on the still, hidden lake.

The boy realized that this had been a gift revealed to him by the spirit of the goat, a gift presented to him and him alone. Wading into the warm water, he swam deeper into the darkness, until the first cave opened into a second, and from there a labyrinth unfolded before him. He swam through the night, winding through cave after cave until finally he reached a point where the rising sun shone like a light from God's eye through a hole in the earthen roof above. The water shimmered with a pristine clarity as though the fluid itself was made from liquefied diamonds. Deeper down, where the sunlight pierced the water's depths and spotlighted a halo on the cavern floor, something blazed with brilliance even more breathtaking than the light itself.

"The boy dove beneath the crystalline surface, swimming deeper and deeper until the glow hurt his eyes and he had to shield them from the glare. Deeper still he swam until his breath had nearly staled in his chest and he began to doubt that he would be able to reach the surface even if he turned around right then. Yet something spurred him on. His eyes closed, he slid his hand along the smooth bottom until his fingertips touched the arced edge of the creation, wrapping it tightly in his palm and swimming swiftly toward the surface, this time propelled from beneath on an unseen current.

"When he breached the surface, he held the circular medallion high over his head in triumph. The boy took too much credit for his discovery though, and was thus pricked by the prize, allowing but a single drop of blood to roll from his hand and over his wrist. When that lone drop of blood slipped free and dropped into the clear water, the entire lake around him changed to blood.

"Eventually, he emerged from the caves, on the other side of this mountain before you now, dripping with crimson fluid. No one believed the boy's story. The boy was accused of slaughtering the goat and received a lashing that nearly killed him. You see his mother's parents were simple shepherds themselves, working the land for a powerful man who provided the scraps from his table in exchange for the sweat of their toil. The boy knew that the golden medallion would more than cover the cost of the goat, yet he kept it hidden from his master, preferring instead a hundred lashings that opened his flesh as though the cords had been knives, disfiguring him to the point that people feared his hideous visage."

"So, you're saying there's a way around Ali Sadr through a system of caves ahead of us?" Thanh asked.

"If the folklore is true," Keller amended.

"Oh, I assure you that it is true," Mûwth said.

"I'm sure," Keller sighed. "We're burning daylight. I'm the ranking officer now, so—"

"I was that boy."

The revelation transported him to that time in his mind. He clearly remembered holding that golden disc in his small hands, turning it over and over with the kind of innocent curiosity granted only to a child. One side had seven points encircling it, while the other had seven smooth circles backing them; a metaphor in gold for the creator of the very earth, in whose likeness it had been cast. Two sides of the same coin; one representing His loving and nurturing nature, the other His promise of fire and brimstone. The same duality He had fathered into His children. For every good there was an evil, for every right a wrong. For every savior there had to be a destroyer.

"You said that was forty years ago. There's no way you're fifty! You don't look a day over thirty," Kotter said, chuckling. "We're just losing time now."

"Is it proof that you require?" Mûwth said, a sly smile creeping into the corners of his upturned lips. He grabbed either side of the tattered, blood-stained fabric across his chest and ripped it wide with a sound like tearing denim.

His chest was covered with deep black markings that reminded Adam of the tribal designs of the Pacific Islanders: parallel lines turning to squares, widening into sweeping arcs, then turning back on themselves before moving in another direction entirely. It almost looked as though if he placed the tip of a pen at the man's jugular notch, he could weave through the design like some sort of maze.

"It's a map," Adam whispered.

"As I said, the scars were unsightly, so I hid them beneath this design so I could find my way back again."

"So where's the medallion?" Keller asked.

The man pointed to a small whorl above his navel.

"It is waiting for us right here. It is the heart of the mountain. You will feel its pulse the moment you set foot in the water as though you've tapped the very lifeblood of the earth."

"This is absurd!" Keller blurted.

"I assure you, sir," Mûwth said, "I make no attempt to mislead you. I believe God showed me this place to prepare me for this very day, to lead you through the heart of the mountain. I believe this to be my destiny."

"If my theory's right, we can't trust him," Keller said, turning to the others, making sure to match their gaze one at a time. "For all we know, there could be a dozen Syrian troops in there waiting to slaughter us! We're at war now, remember? We can't afford to trust anyone!"

"Keller—" Thanh started.

"No, no. Why don't we just go ahead and follow this Arab we don't know into a dead end and hope that whatever mystical fate he believes to be—"

"Shhh," Mûwth whispered.

The man moved with fluid grace, eliminating the distance between himself and Keller before the much larger man even suspected that he was coming. Keller tried to throw himself backward to the sand, tried to raise his firearm, but the darker man was so fast. He clapped his hand over Keller's face, thin tendrils of smoke issuing from beneath the man's palm.

Keller opened his mouth to scream, but nothing came out. His legs gave out beneath him and dropped him to his knees before Mûwth.

"Arise," Mûwth said, peeling his hand from Keller's forehead. A red palm-print crossed the bridge of his nose, the blunt edge of the palm circling his right eye, four fingers drawn across his left. "I trust that now you can see more clearly."

Keller's eyelids fluttered as though adjusting to a bright light after walking out of a dark room. No more than a moment prior, his right eye had been a useless, deteriorating sphere of dehydrated flesh. Now, that iris looked all around as though seeing everything for the first time.

"Christ," Keller said, waving his hand in front of his face. "What did you do to me?"

"Are you ready to follow the path ahead?" Mûwth asked.

All of the others watched in silence.

"Yeah," Keller said, rising from his knees. He rubbed his eye with a balled fist, then opened it quickly as though he expected it all to have been an illusion. "Lead the way."

Keller whirled to face the crack leading into the side of the mountain.

Thanh recoiled, slapping her hands over her mouth to stifle a gasp.

Keller's left eye was still as blue as a Caribbean coast, while the right had turned grapefruit red, the pupil a fathomless pinprick of darkness.

●   ●   ●

The hole had been there as promised, though it had taken a few minutes to drag away more of the fallen sandstone to widen the opening enough to accommodate Keller's broad shoulders. Mûwth was the first through that ragged maw into the impregnable darkness. A skittering of small stones trailed his skidding descent down a short slope, followed by the muted sounds of splashing.

Keller crawled through next, sliding down into the water with a splash.

"Can you see anything?" Thanh bellowed through the opening.

"Not much," Keller called back, his voice echoing, betraying the enormity of the cavern.

Thanh slowly dropped her right leg through the opening, transferring her weight gingerly downward while she ducked her head. The darkness swallowed her whole, issuing but the sound of a pair of soft footfalls before a splash.

Adam looked to Kotter, who simply nodded and lowered himself to all fours and climbed through the opening into the pitch black. Adam was already on his hands and knees, scurrying through the opening and down the smooth rock surface inches behind. Loose gravel gave way to some sort of slime or mold, slicking the already polished surface. Adam heard Kotter suck in a deep breath a split second before he dropped into the waiting water.

"I can't see a thing," Adam whispered, the sheer size of the cave inspiring a sense of awe as though he had just walked into a European cathedral. "How in the world are we supposed—?"

He was swallowing water before his body even felt the fall.

Jerking his head above the surface, he spat out a mouthful of the vile fluid, and then retched until he finally caught his breath.

"For Chrissakes," he coughed, dredging up more filthy saliva. "It tastes like sulfur!"

"Smells like we've just crawled into a giant's ass," Kotter said.

"This is a natural hot spring," Mûwth said. The faint hint of his silhouette drew contrast against the darkness. He was a good ten feet out from them, though his voice sounded like it was coming from everywhere at once.

"Feels like it's got to be close to ninety degrees," Thanh mused. "And I don't know if it's the sulfuric content, but I almost feel like a buoy, like I'm floating."

"You sure you know your way through here?" Keller called after Mûwth, who was already swimming away from them, judging by the clamor of his stroking arms and kicking legs.

"Follow me to your destiny."

II

Evelyn awoke to the sound of screaming. Her eyes snapped wide and she shot upright, blinking as she tried to rationalize her surroundings. For a fleeting moment, she thought her entire adulthood had been a dream and here she was again, thirteen and asleep in her old bedroom. It took the kelp beneath hanging lights as intense as the sun to draw her back to the present.

Had it been a nightmare?

The faint residue of an all-consuming dream lingered in her head like a slowly dissipating fog. Her last vanishing thought was of a lake stretching away as far as she could see. Or was it an ocean? All she could remember were sands as white as snow rimming the bank. And smoke. Smoke washing over from behind on an unseen wind, bringing with it the scent of burning meat. Thick black smoke as though whatever was burning had long since been consumed.

Her eyes steadily dripped closed, sleep summoning her back into its warm embrace.

Shrill screaming.

She was wide awake now, eyes darting from side to side around her room. The glare of the sodium halide bulbs turned the middle of the room to daylight, chasing the darkness into all four corners. Behind a shelf lined with dolls their shadows stood twice their height, stretching clear up to the ceiling where a wash of darkness pooled like crude oil.

The sound echoed through her head, slowly dissipating as her mind tried to comprehend the noise. It hadn't been screaming; not like a wailing baby or a terrified woman. It had been more shrill, hundreds of voices mounting one another in a discordant cry of terror.

"The pheasants!" she gasped, lunging to her feet.

The tingling of sleep still infested her legs, yet she dragged them out of the bedroom, bracing herself on the hallway wall before propelling herself toward the main room. Through her father's closed door she could hear the buzz of static from the television, a stain of gray creeping across the floor from beneath the door.

She slapped at the kitchen light, which blossomed like a quasar before popping with a snap, leaving a lingering blue glow. The rear door rattled when she slammed into it, barely able to grab the knob before twisting and tugging it inward far enough to slip through.

The sound of screaming assaulted her like a slap to the face.

Launching herself from the stairs, she barely maintained her balance on the hard, windblown dirt, skinning her palms as she caught herself.

All she could see ahead were the vague outlines of the rows of bird pens against the night horizon to the east. A mass of flapping wings pounded together, the air filled with short downy feathers and long multicolored quills. Her first thought was that the coyotes who stalked this area of the Mojave Desert had found a way into the pens, but the shrieking of the pheasants was beyond anything she had ever heard. Usually a single mongrel managed to dig beneath the netting or squeeze through a weak spot, but it would steal the first bird it could snap it jaws around and dash off into the night before even startling the other birds. And that was just one pen. Every enclosure she could see was alive with activity, shadowed forms battling in the air in their attempts to tear through the nylon netting surrounding the twenty-foot rectangular cage.

Sand kicking from her heels, heavy feet scraping the hard earth, she reached the ringneck pen first. There were only about sixty birds in there, but it appeared as though every single one of them was hurling itself against the netting in a frenzy.

She tried to say something soothing to calm them, but her voice was drowned out by the frenetic shrieking and the thunder of pounding wings.

The holes in the netting were smaller than those of a chain link fence, yet many of the birds had managed to shove their green, red-splotched heads through to the point that they lodged themselves there, wings beating furiously to try to either propel themselves through or tear themselves away. Spurred feet ripped like claws at the webbing.

Evelyn tried to shove as many heads back through the netting as she could, clumps of feathers tearing from their breasts, sharp beaks slicing into her palms. It seemed as though each pheasant she forced back was immediately replaced by another. Minuscule droplets of blood patterned her face and arms like a mist from the tiny holes where the feathers had been plucked.

"Stop it!" she screamed, shoving at one last ringneck before dashing to the adjacent pen, filled with black pheasants mimicking their brethren.

She had no idea what to do.

"Daddy!" she whirled and screamed back over her shoulder, madly pressing at struggling, floundering bodies.

After an eternal moment of battling the birds with blood-soaked palms, wan light spilled across the ground from the porch light behind her, followed by the bang of the withered screen door against the side of the house.

"What's wrong?" her father called in a weak voice still resonant with the overwhelming effects of the Vicadin and a dreamless sleep.

"They're going crazy! What am I supposed to do?"

Darryl Hartman eased down the crumbling cement stairs, gripping the wobbling railing. He could barely keep his legs beneath him, let alone force them to bear his weight. Pain raced from his feet all the way up into his hips where it exploded like a powder keg. Tears streaming from his eyes, reflecting what little moonlight permeated the roiling black cloud cover, he nearly cried out with each step, stifling it by biting down and refusing to let his teeth part. By the time he reached the bottom of the staircase and took his first step toward the pens, it was over.

The screaming of the pheasants ceased abruptly like air through a slashed trachea. With a resounding thump, all of the panicked airborne pheasants hit the ground at once, staggering and swaying in a momentary daze before finding the strength to scurry back through the hole in the wooden coop at the back of the pen.

Feathers descended like snowflakes inside the cages, alighting on the mangled lumps littering the ground.

"My God," Evelyn whispered, curling her fingers through the mesh and leaning forward.

The hay substrate was bled black in sweeping arcs, blotched with corpses with stiff, outstretched legs forked to the sky, bare breasts poking through in diseased-looking swatches where the feathers had been torn away. Even from where she stood, she could see the dead birds in the adjacent pen: mounds of twitching and already stilled flesh.

A howl erupted from the distance, across the sea of dirt and dying Joshua trees.

Evelyn walked between the two pens toward the source of the sound. The sun was only now beginning to bleed light blue onto the otherwise blackened eastern horizon, yet she could still see them… lined up at the edge of her range of sight, shoulder to shoulder, sitting and watching as though no longer caring if they were seen. They were usually timid and ducked back out of sight when they even suspected that human eyes had fallen upon them. But not tonight.

Light flashed from their minion eyes like so many halogen headlights.

She'd never seen so many coyotes together in her life. There had to be hundreds of them, all sitting patiently like obedient dogs waiting for their master to fill their food bowls, a line of sharp triangular ears cutting the darkness like a saw blade.

"What's going on here?" Evelyn whispered.

With a moan, her father made his way to her side, grabbing her shoulder and transferring an inordinate amount of weight to her small frame. She widened her stance to accommodate him, slipping her arm around his midsection so she could help provide just enough balance to take some of the pressure off of his hip. The pain must have been excruciating, yet he stood beside her, trembling lips clamped over gritted teeth.

"My father used to say that all things eventually come home to roost," he said, barely able to speak through the pain. "I don't suppose he meant it quite this literally."

She smiled meekly and kissed him on his scruffy cheek.

"Let's get you back to bed," she whispered. "I'll take care of the pens."

"Best do so in a hurry 'fore those coyotes figure out they aren't scared of us and decide to rush the pens. Lord knows they've already caught the scent. You know I'd help you, but…"

"I know, daddy," she said, laboring under his weight. She couldn't bring herself to look him in the face as she could clearly hear the tears in his voice. He felt helpless, useless, and in a very tangible way, for her father, that was a fate worse than death. "I know."

She walked him slowly toward the back door of the house, his feet hardly rising from the ground. Evelyn hated herself for allowing this to happen to him. He was the strongest man she had ever known, the kind of man who could eat nails for breakfast and pass an anvil without breaking a sweat. His skin was coarse and callused from working his entire life with only the tools the good Lord gave him, though even now it felt comfortable against her skin, as though that by itself was enough to let her know that it was still her daddy inside that failing form.

Evelyn eased him up the first step, grabbing hold of the back of his trousers in case he needed a boost.

Another howl pierced the silence, followed by another and another until there was a chorus of coyotes baying hauntingly.

Then silence.

Evelyn stood there with her father a moment, enrapt by the sudden stillness around her.

"You need to use the bathroom first?" she asked, her soft voice like a shot in the quiet.

He just shook his head, hating what he'd been reduced to.

"I can make it from here," he said at the top of the stairs, leaning onto the open door as he had on her. He shuffled his slippered feet across the threshold and onto the linoleum, grabbing onto the counter to use it as a guide and a crutch to the living room.

"Are you sure?" she managed to ask before the tears bloomed from the corners of her eyes.

Her father just grunted and edged further into the kitchen, the chapped soles of his slippers scraping like sandpaper on rough timber.

She turned back to the night, wiping the tears across her cheek but refusing to sniff and betray her emotions. It would absolutely kill her old man if he was forced to see his current state through her eyes, if only a glimpse.

Evelyn trod across the drive, wary of the feral silhouettes against the coming dawn, now showing their true browns and grays, silver eyes flashing. Jerking the latch on the barn door, she threw it wide and eased into the pitch black, feeling along the edge of the dusty workbench until she found a pair of old cowhide gloves, crusted with mud and blood, and shoved her hands inside. There was only one acceptable way of dealing with this many dead and dying birds. They couldn't afford to take any chances. If some disease were to develop and get back to the live birds in the pens, it could easily wipe out their entire stock and cripple them financially.

Beneath the bench she found the gas can and sloshed it around, content with the amount of fluid and the resultant thick fumes. Hanging from one of the multitude of hooks on the pegboard above was a lighter with a long silver snout designed for outdoor grills and pilot lights.

They couldn't risk drawing the coyotes in any farther either. Once they lost their fear...

Her face ashen, features expressionless, Evelyn walked out and set the can of gas and the lighter on the far side of the barn by a circular depression surrounded by a ring of scorched earth.

With a final tug on her gloves, Evelyn opened the hatch to the closest pen, and with the first red stain of the rising sun permeating the cloudy sky, she began the arduous task of gathering the bodies.

III

EAST OF
BETHLEHEM,
PENNSYLVANIA

Phoenix sat in the corner of the room on the cement floor. Cold though it was, he reveled in the feeling of the walls behind him, the warm water sliding across its surface. It was as close as he could get to an embrace without feeling like the life was being sucked out of him. And so long as there was concrete behind him, he only had to worry about what was coming directly at him.

The morning after being descended upon by The Swarm, he always felt as though he had been turned inside out. His throat was beyond parched, even licking the fluid from the slimy walls wasn't enough to dampen the discomfort. His eyes burned like he hadn't slept in weeks. His limp arms cradled his trembling legs to his chest, his numbed bare feet flat on the floor.

He knew she was out there even before she disengaged the series of locks.

"Breakfast," she said, hurrying into the room and setting a bowl on the floor before him. Tepid oatmeal slopped over the side onto the ground.

Phoenix reached for it with a flaccid hand.

Watching nervously, she took a step forward and nudged the bowl closer with her toe.

"Thank you," he croaked. His trachea felt as though it had been shredded by the words.

The woman just looked at him then down to the shin-length black apron she wore over an aged brown sweater, unraveling from the shoulders and collar. Dirty jeans covered what little leg reached the floor beneath the blacksmith-style smock. Thick yellow toenails capped dirty, plump toes, the soles of her feet callused and flaking. Long, oily black hair hung in front of her face, hiding eyes like jagged chunks of ore.

She looked at him again, only parts of her eyes peeking between the greasy locks, then reached into one of the front pockets of the apron and produced a tarnished spoon. Bending at the knees, eyes still watching him carefully, she leaned forward to the extent of her reach and barely slid the business end of the spoon over the lip of the bowl. Before she could jerk her hand back, Phoenix's arm shot from his side, his hand clasping her firmly around the wrist. She tugged against him, but was unable to wrest free.

"Why do you hate me?" he whispered.

Darkness flooded over him, pouring from her flesh like a crashing tide.

The man with the white collar towered over him, fingers tightened to the point that they turned white around a belt folded in half. He raised it over his head, but the arms that reached out to ward off the coming blow didn't belong to Phoenix. The fingers were stunted and pudgy, the nails gnawed nearly back to the quick, flabby skin hanging from the arms, wriggling with fear.

"Accept him!" the man raged, eyes maniacally wide, pupils like dots in his fiery irises. Lightning bolts of ruptured blood vessels struck through the whites. His lips stretched back from square, wooden-looking teeth bared so wickedly hard they appeared to be close to cracking. Wild hair framed his head like briars.

The belt snapped forward before the arms could even flinch. A spatter of blood fired out from the right side of his vision, which swam in and out of focus as though beneath water.

"Accept him!" the man screamed, raising the belt again.

"Please," the woman moaned.

Another snap of the belt and he was looking across the floor at the man's black leather shoes, scuffed in spots to a dirty brown. The hardwood floor was riddled with deep grooves, the frayed wood peeling away like truffles.

The man crouched down before him, tilting his head from side to side like a vulture. Calmness washed over him, the anger vanishing as though it had never ravaged his face at all.

"Your mother was a saint," he said, smiling. For a moment there was a twinkle in his eyes. "She was quite possibly the most divine woman to ever set foot on God's earth, shy of the Holy Virgin Mother herself. She would have laid down her life for the Lord. She would have gladly borne the sins of man in her own frail body had she been able."

The man reached into the front pocket of his black jacket, producing a baby food jar, which he quickly closed in his fist.

"Purity of mind and body. Do you know what purity is? Purity is the form beneath the flesh, the soul as God initially breathed it into your heart, the hidden body that only He can see."

She whimpered.

He leaned forward until the rancid stench of breath like festering raw meat filled her nostrils.

"I can see it too," he whispered, thrusting out one large hand to clamp over her nose and mouth. "Do you know what I see in your soul?"

Panicked grunts of fear pushed through his fierce grip on her face.

"You've a taint on your soul. When the day of reckoning comes, when God reaches through The Rapture and summons His flock to His side, you would be left behind. I cannot allow that... my own daughter abandoned on the earth to cavort with the sinners and heathens."

He opened his clenched fist to display the small glass jar. The label had been peeled away, leaving small rings of tacky paper.

Phoenix heard her scream.

"We must purify your soul, dear heart."

Inside the jar was a tiny coiled snake, blacker even than the darkness behind Phoenix's closed eyelids in his basement cell.

"You must give the evil back unto the serpent, allow it to consume your sins," the man said in a patient, loving tone. "Let it purify your body. Your soul."

He maneuvered awkwardly until his right knee pressed her sternum toward the floor, freeing his other hand to open the jar. A tiny serpentine head arose from within like a cobra from a basket. Its forked tongue flicked several times, tasting her scent, eyes appearing to come to life.

The woman screamed, thrashing and bucking, trying to knock him from atop her. Her clawed fingers tore at his clothing, carving seams wherever her nails could bite into his skin.

With the jar in his right hand, he grabbed her to either side of her face with his left, squeezing her cheeks hard enough to force her lips to part, her teeth threatening to snap at the roots and fly onto her tongue. Slowly, he lowered the jar, the eager snake arching into striking position. Phoenix watched as the serpent struck at the air, hissing and spitting, then slithered over the rim of the jar directly before his terror-widened eyes, dangling down toward her open mouth.

Phoenix gagged ferociously, finally tearing his hand away from the woman's wrist. Blinking dazedly, he scrabbled back into the corner, slapping even more of the cooled oatmeal onto the concrete. He heaved several times, back arching like a startled cat, loosing naught but a long strand of thick saliva to connect him to the floor. When he returned his attention to the woman, she was already to her feet and staggering toward the door.

"Wait!" he called, uneasily pushing himself to his feet and stumbling after her. She stopped, outstretched hand grasping the doorknob. Phoenix tempered his voice. "Please."

She neither turned around nor opened the door. She just stood there, rooted in place.

"Why do you let him hurt you like that?" Phoenix whispered, unable to shake the horror of what he had seen, what the woman's own father had done to her.

He had seen it through the eyes of her memory.

Her greasy hair whipped side to side as she answered him with a shake of her head. She still didn't turn around.

"He's a very angry man," Phoenix said.

"He's a humble servant of God," she whispered in a voice so tiny he could barely hear it.

"No man of God would subject anyone, especially his own daughter, to that kind of cruelty."

"You don't know him. He's saving my soul."

"What have you done that would require your soul to need saving?"

She stood there silently, shifting her weight nervously from one foot to the other as she appeared to be contemplating his question.

Rusted water dripped from the pipes running along the ceiling.

"The Rapture is coming," she whispered. "You of all people should know that."

"I know nothing of the world outside by what I see in my dreams... through the eyes of others."

"You will bring the end of days. My father has foreseen it."

This time Phoenix was quiet.

"Is that why you keep me here?" he finally whispered.

"I've said too much already."

"Please," Phoenix whispered.

She could feel his stare on her back, her skin positively crawling.

"He knows he can accelerate the Second Coming through you. You'll be the one to help carry us all to Heaven."

The room was silently still between them, as though all time and reality had frozen, interrupted by the click of the doorknob, urged by a flick of her wrist. She drew it inward.

"Please," he whispered. "Help me."

She stopped, still holding the doorknob, but didn't turn around.

"Don't let him hurt me anymore. Not like he hurts you. Not again," he begged.

"He's saving my soul."

"You can save it yourself."

She hesitated, her back still to him, her free hand clenching and unclenching with a grinding of knuckles.

"How?" she whispered.

"Help me."

"I would only end up damning my soul," she said, stepping through the doorway and slamming the wooden slab shut behind. The locks thunked into the woodwork as he imagined that must be the sound one hears from inside his coffin while the final nails are driven in.

Phoenix slunk back into the corner, pressing his back to the wall and slumping to the floor. He thought about the girl at the edge of the stream, the girl from his dream, her porcelain legs dangling in the cold water prickling her flesh.

More man tears, she had said.

Phoenix needed to get out of that basement. The urge had become imperative, stirring his guts and aching from the marrow of his bones. He knew that if he didn't get out of that cellar soon, it would prove to be his tomb. He was as sure of that fact as he was of anything he had ever known in his life. And the only way he was ever going to be able to get out of there was to convince the woman to help him.

His fate was in her hands.

He just wished he knew how to get through to her. Today she had spoken to him, but more importantly, she had listened. A seed of doubt must have taken root somewhere within her. He needed to feed it, nurture it, coax it into blossoming.

Time was running low. He could feel it as though with each grain of sand that passed through the hourglass his life force drained from him. Phoenix may not have known what it felt like to truly be alive outside of this godforsaken room, but he sure knew what dying felt like.

Closing his eyes, he focused on the sounds of his breathing, which often made it at least feel as though he wasn't alone in the room.

Small clicking sounds filled the muted darkness.

Phoenix held his breath, willing his heart to slow, and listened.

The clicking grew louder, coming from all around him now. He opened his eyes, but could still glean no detail from the darkness.

Something small crawled across his foot. He reached for it, but it easily evaded his grasp and raced away. A dozen more tiny creatures scurried over his feet, several veering and scuttling up his legs. He grabbed one, pinching a crisp shell between his thumb and forefinger, and brought it to within an inch of his face. Small legs waved at the air.

"Hello, friend," he said, setting the insect into the middle of his open palm. "I haven't seen you around here before."

The roach raced down his wrist and dropped into his lap.

Once he knew what they were, it was easy to decipher the sounds around him. Scuttling feet tapping on the pipes above, scurrying down the walls like geckos, carpeting the floor. Phoenix carefully rolled onto all fours, sliding his hands and knees through their crawling ranks. They circled the mess of oatmeal on the floor, venturing no further. The lip of the bowl was resplendent with them, though none dared to take another step.

"Where did you all come from?"

The roaches crawled all over his arms and legs in response.

"Go ahead," he said, smiling. "Eat up."

The insects attacked the mess of soggy oats, swarming all over it with the frenzied sounds of clicking and legs scratching on exoskeletons. The bedlam lasted for several minutes, until finally Phoenix heard the sounds of miniature legs climbing up the walls all around him, clamoring over the pipes and woodwork overhead, slipping through the cobwebs on the ceiling.

Silence settled over the room like a tarp.

He slid his hands over the cold concrete where the oatmeal had been. It was barely damp. The bowl was completely empty as well; every last oat had been consumed.

His stomach growled, but he could live with some minor discomfort. He'd finally made some friends after all. Where had they come from? Where had they gone? He slid his hand across the floor beyond the bowl, his fingertips knocking the spoon with a metallic clatter. Tracing the edge, he followed the shaft of the spoon toward the end, but it didn't terminate in a widened scoop as it had moments before. He picked it up, turning it over and over in his hands. The spoon had been whittled away and the handle now terminated in a sharpened tip. The roaches had consumed more than the oatmeal. He closed his fist around it, sharpened blade pointing at the floor, and swung it through the air several times. It screamed like a diving eagle.

Scrambling back to the bed of straw, he plucked out the longest and thickest stem he could find, parting it cleanly down the center with the knife. It provided only the slightest resistance.

Phoenix opened his left hand and ran the tip of the blade across his palm. He felt the warm blood spilling from the wound long before the bite of the cut.

Flopping onto his rear end, he stared at the weapon in the darkness. The razor-honed edge glinted even in the absence of light. Left hand clenched to staunch the bleeding, he slid the utensil beneath the straw and lowered his body atop it.

Though his heart was pounding and his palms sweating, he smiled excitedly.

The time had finally come.

IV

NORTHERN IRAN

Adam's shoulder was killing him. He didn't know how long they'd been swimming, but it felt like forever. Occasionally the bottom would rise enough to stand on, giving them a few precious steps to take the strain from their aching limbs before dropping back off into the deeper water. Now, they were in the middle of who knows where, and he was lagging behind the others, whose splashing sounds grew farther away. How long would it take them to notice he was gone?

The wound in his shoulder stung as though someone was sifting through the gash with a branding iron.

"Hey," he gasped, taking in a mouthful of warm water that tasted like the business end of a match. He tried to call out again, but he was barely able to keep his chin far enough above the water level to breathe, let alone form words. His fingers tingled, simply beginning to fall asleep.

"Guys," he sputtered, blowing bubbles across the surface.

Their splashing had grown faint, now echoing like a distant plane on a summer's day.

"I will help," a voice whispered, so close he could feel the warm breath tickling the fine hairs in his ear.

A hand settled over the wound on his shoulder. A radiating feeling of warmth blossomed from the wound, pulsating through first his rapidly numbing arm, then flooding his entire body.

"I saw the way you looked at the little girl," the voice whispered.

"Mûwth?"

"It has been a long time since I have seen what I saw in your eyes."

With renewed vigor, Adam treaded water, spinning himself in circles to get a glimpse of the man he knew to be within inches of him, yet neither his kicking legs nor swooshing arms brushed against anything.

"What are you talking about?" Adam asked in the same hushed tone.

"Hope."

Two hands suddenly clasped his head over each ear with a loud clapping sound.

Damp breath on his forehead.

Pursed lips.

A kiss.

The hands withdrew and Adam jerked away, nearly submerging himself as he thrashed.

"The seed is in you, Adam," the voice whispered in a thousand tongues. "Cultivate it. Allow it to take root and blossom. Nothing can stop what must come to pass, for it has already been set in motion. You have been spared this day. Go forth Adam, and spread your seed."

With a whoosh like air being sucked through a crack in a pressurized seal, the voices merged into the wind, and then were gone.

Adam floated there, amidst the slight sloshing of water from his exertion, the gentle lapping of the resultant waves against the rock walls around him, the dripping of condensed fluids from the ceiling above.

Smothering darkness.

Plip.

Ploop.

There was no sound of paddling ahead.

No sound at all.

"HEY!" he screamed, buckling his head back and shouting into the darkness above him. His voice echoed away into oblivion.

Plip.

Plip.

There was no resultant sound of leathery wings pounding against one another, having been startled from their slumber to swarm like gnats. No flapping sounds. He tried to pry apart the darkness to ascertain any detail at all.

Ploop.

In fact, he couldn't remember having heard any sort of life down there beneath the mountain other than them at all.

No fish or aquatic life more complex than single-celled protozoans could survive in the alkaline water.

The world was dead down there in the darkness.

He rocked back and screamed to the heavens, splashing violently.

Plip.

Rolling onto his stomach, he started swimming as fast as he could in the direction he thought he had been facing when last he had heard the others.

Keller's knuckles grazed solid ground first. He palmed the smooth rock surface beneath and propelled himself the last yard with his dwindling strength. He crawled forward, peeling away crusted reams of sulfuric salts and moss dried to the consistency of lichen before heaving and launching a putrid spray of aspirated water onto the cavern floor. He retched until there was nothing but dry heaves and a strand of repulsive saliva dangling from his lower lip.

"Everyone…" he gasped, sucking for breath while trying not to inhale any of what he had already cleared from his system. He huffed and wheezed before finally pushing himself to his knees and slapping the dangling spindle of sludge from his lip. "Everyone all right?"

"I think so," Thanh whispered from somewhere to his left. She gagged and rolled from her stomach to her back, finally regaining enough energy to drag her legs out of the hot water.

"I didn't think I was going to have to be a damn Navy Seal for this tour." Kotter's effort at levity sent him into a throng of convulsive heaves punctuated with a splatter of fluids. "I think I must have swallowed half of the water down here in this sewer."

He let out a wet belch that stirred Keller's gut to roil, but he shunted it quickly by pinching a hand over his mouth and nose and swallowing whatever rose in revolt.

"Are you all right, Adam?" Thanh asked, leveraging herself against one of the stone walls so she could sit up. She pulled her hair into her fist and wrung the water out in a stream that reminded Keller of his biological priorities. The silence was disturbed only by the scuffing of Keller's boots and the metallic zip of his zipper.

"Adam?" she asked, louder this time.

The water lapped against the ledge they had crawled out upon with a slurping sound.

"Come on, doc," Keller called through a shake of his body and the quick zip that followed. "We don't have time to screw around."

Plip.

Silence.

Ploop.

"Adam?" Thanh called, rising to her feet.

"Adam!" Kotter added his voice to the chorus.

"Newman!" Keller bellowed, his echo thundering through the caverns both ahead of them and behind. A chunk of rock broke free from a wall somewhere in the darkness and splashed into the water.

"We are near the place I was telling you about." Mûwth's Arabic accent was unmistakable. "Surely he will have caught up with us by the time we have found my medallion."

Neither Thanh nor Kotter cared a whit about the man's stupid medallion. Right now their only thoughts were of finding Adam and getting moving again. Time seemed to stand still there in the pitch black beneath the mountain, but undoubtedly it was still flying by in the world above. Neither intended to find out what would happen if they were late for the extraction.

Keller, on the other hand, had a keen interest in the man's medallion. If, indeed, the stories the man told were true and not simply fabricated to convince them to bring him along and provide safe transport for him through a desert about to become a war zone, then a solid gold disc may prove invaluable if they missed their transport liaison. He wasn't about to be stranded on Iranian soil when their deadline passed. Granted, he didn't know precisely what sort of offensive the US would launch, but he was sure that based on the threat of an atomic holocaust on American soil, their response would be both swift and proportional, which meant more than strafing Baghdad with some tomahawks and cruise missiles from the 'Gulf. They already knew precisely what swift meant; the fuse had been lit. But what was proportional to an atomic threat against four of the most heavily populated cities in the western world?

He had never agreed with the new administration's reactionary politics and knee-jerk responses to everything from the astronomical cost of oil to the rising interest rates at home. The American infrastructure had degenerated to the point that everyone from congressmen to the President himself acted like dogs at the pound barking at each other through the chain-link cages.

Some moderate sized town, probably somewhere between Iraq and Syria, would be mercilessly annihilated. The sand would be turned to glass and whatever remained of its former inhabitants would be carried on the nuclear wind.

If that meant Keller was going to have to take that man's medallion and trade it to some freighter captain to get himself anywhere beyond the Caspian Sea, then so be it. If he had to kill this man Mûwth to take it from him, then he would do just that. He was not going to be stranded here in the Middle East, watching for death to rain from the sky. He'd sooner peel the Arab's skin from his bones and wear it as a disguise than face the fate these sand jockeys had coming.

"And said to the mountains and rocks," a voice whispered into his ear. "Fall on us, and hide us from the face of him that sitteth on the throne, and from the wrath of the Lamb: For the great day of his wrath is come; and who shall be able to stand?"

"Jesus!" Keller spat, stumbling backward. It was obviously Mûwth's voice, though only a moment prior he had heard the man a good ten yards deeper into the adjacent cavern.

"Mûwth," he called hesitantly.

"Follow the sound of my voice," he called back with that thick accent. He sounded even farther away than he had before. There was no way he could have been standing beside Keller to whisper in his ear and managed to get so far away in that span of time. But he had felt the warmth of the breath on his cheek, and the voice… the voice had been identical.

I've got to get out of here! he screamed inside his head. *I'm losing my mind!*

It was the darkness. That had to be it. It had been so long since he had seen the outside world that he was beginning to feel like the darkness itself was settling over him like a wet blanket, smothering him, sucking the very air from his lungs and forcing him to the verge of hyperventilation. He just needed to get out of the darkness, get out of his head—

"Keller?"

He flinched from her touch, causing her to immediately recoil.

Fall on us, and hide us from the face of him that sitteth on the throne, and from the wrath of the Lamb.

"Are you all right?" Thanh asked.

No! I'm losing my damn mind!

"Yeah," he said through rapid, jerky breaths. "Just… just starting to feel a little claustrophobic, you know?"

She nodded, though in the darkness she knew he couldn't have seen. Where was Adam?

"I can see the light!" Mûwth exclaimed from somewhere beyond the cavern, his voice echoing as though through a long tunnel.

"Wait!" Keller called, grabbing Thanh by the arm and dragging her quickly toward the source of the voice. They couldn't afford to be lost in here without the Arab. He was sure they wouldn't be able to find their way back, let alone to the other side, without the man's help.

"Kotter?" Thanh called back over her shoulder.

"Right behind you."

Their footsteps clapped back at them from the narrowing corridor.

"One of us should stay behind and wait for Adam," she said.

"You heard Mûwth. By the time we grab this thing, we'll be able to come right back and rendezvous with Adam. I'd bet anything that shoulder slowed him down and he had to take a rest. He'll catch up in no time," Kotter said.

The air stirred around them as though some ambitious breeze had managed to penetrate the mountain's husk. With it came a stench like nothing they'd ever smelled before. Worse than the sulfuric water. Worse than the makeshift graveyard they used for the refugees. The smell reminded Keller of one of his earliest childhood memories, of standing in a dark forest with his father and uncle. There had been a stag strung by its rear hooves from a thick lower limb of an ancient pine. His uncle had pried a six-inch, serrated hunting blade from its sheath and offered it to Keller, who had taken it in his small hand, surprised at just how light the weapon was. Keller could remember rising on his toes and pressing the sharp point into the soft skin of the taut belly, tightening both fists around the sculpted bone hilt, feeling the design of the wolf against his palms even through his gloves.

His father clamped his large hands atop his, shoving forward fast enough to drag Keller from his feet. A gust of air had exploded from the hole they created. A stench he would smell again in a small shack they liked to call "The Confessional" in Kirkuk where they had disemboweled an Iraqi insurgent to learn the location of the enemy's staging grounds; in a hidden cave beneath the desert sands where Mahmud Al Sharah, a known terrorist, had killed himself a week prior to finding him and exhuming his bloated, scarab-infested corpse.

He felt it, smelled it, tasted it against his face as clearly as he had as a small child when the blast of warm air had blossomed from the deer's underside, tousling his hair and melting the snow from his cap, before pouring forth in a flood of heat that drenched his legs and boots.

For the great day of his wrath is come; and who shall be able to stand?

The smell of death.

"Oh," Thanh gasped, pinching her hand over her mouth and nose.

"Hurry!" Mûwth called, his voice cracking, unable to contain the excitement.

Following his voice along a bend to the right, tracing the rugged earthen surface of the wall beside them, the darkness began to fade from a palpable black to a muted gray, until finally, the narrowing tunnel opened into a large chamber. A beam of light lanced from the ceiling to the center of the stagnant water, filled with swirling motes like glitter.

The smell intensified the moment they stepped into the wide cavern, as though the entire room around them were filled with rotting corpses.

Keller opened his mouth to speak, but instead, he simply stood in awe of the ray of light that came through the stalactite-riddled ceiling as little more than a fiery dot, but widened to the size of a spotlight's beam. While he had reluctantly resolved to believe the man's story, he assumed much of it to have been either fabricated or stretched from a child's imagination. But this... This was like nothing he had ever seen in his entire life, as though the light itself didn't just penetrate the rocky roof, but grew from it, becoming increasingly blinding the farther it traveled from the source. Where it touched the water, the circle of light took on an orange tint, not like the banal coloration of a tangerine, but like the intense rustic tinge of the inner layer of flesh surrounding an over-ripened peach pit. The water around it appeared black, though the beam attenuated beneath the surface, fading from an impossible sunset stain to a deeper red like molten lava. And there upon the floor of the cave, shimmering like a coin at the bottom of a well was the medallion, so bright he could only look at it for a moment.

"Does it not call to you?" Mûwth said; a shadow against the black lake wading down its rapidly descending slope.

Keller was certain that it did, as though there were invisible strands of cord sewn through the prickled skin on his chest, urging him forward.

"Yes," Thanh whispered, freeing her arm to descend the stony embankment.

"I took it with me once," Mûwth said, propelling himself forward into the water that didn't splash around his paddling arms, but rather absorbed him, as viscous as tomato soup. "But I had to return it. Nothing can live without a heart. And this medallion is the heart of this mountain. Of this entire desert. Without it, the sandstone would crumble to dust, plants would cease to grow, and the precious water would be sucked back into the earth to fill the void."

He had always known that he was God's child, but he had never been clear which half of his Father's dichotomous nature he had inherited. Until now. His destiny was to be the savior of the Lord's children, but as he now understood, there was more than one was to save them. His lot was to save them from themselves.

Thanh crouched at the edge of the lake, cupping her palm and immersing it momentarily before drawing up a handful of the warm liquid.

She brought it to her nose and recoiled. It was definitely the source of the stench. It was thicker than water, a viscosity she knew intimately through her experience as a surgeon. She rubbed her fingers together, the fluid redolent with corpuscles that popped like citrus vesicles.

It was blood. There was no doubt about it. Not smooth and clean as though from a tapped artery, but thickened and mealy as though wrung from a cirrhotic liver.

"Is it…?" Kotter asked.

Thanh nodded, affixing her eyes to the back of Mûwth's head, his long braid trailing along the surface like a crocodile's tail. He paused in the wash of light, looking up into its depths momentarily, his features bled white. His shoulders rose with the great inhalation, and then he dove beneath the surface, his form wavering like a mirage beneath the tranquilly-rippling fluid.

"He should have reached it by now," Keller whispered. He watched the man's arms reaching deeper into the abyss, seeking leverage to draw himself toward the glowing medallion.

Mûwth's shape became smaller and smaller, the bottom fathomless.

"He's going to run out of air," Thanh said, realizing that until that precise moment she'd been holding her breath as well.

Kotter waded in to his knees, the fluid seeping through his clothing and clinging to his bare skin, trying to clot against it. He was a heartbeat away from throwing himself forward into the putrid fluid when Mûwth's hand closed like a black clamshell over the medallion.

"Come on," Kotter whispered, edging deeper into the water.

"We shouldn't be here," Keller said, finally granting voice to the panic.

"We can't leave him down there," Thanh gasped, watching the now miniaturized form try to plant its feet on the floor of the cavern and propel itself upward, but though the medallion had appeared to be resting on the stone floor, it had been illusory.

"It's a lake of blood!" Keller snapped.

"You don't think I'd be able to tell it was blood even without smelling or seeing it?"

"I'm not questioning your assessment, doctor. I'm a little more concerned about the fact that this entire cave is filled with a lake of blood. Where the hell do you think it all came from?"

She looked at him. Had she even stopped to wonder?

"How many animals or people or God knows what had to be killed to provide this much blood?" Keller asked. Something was dreadfully wrong here. He could feel it in the knots in his spine, in the frigid fingers prickling his flesh, in the tremors that set in upon his hands. They needed to get out of there right now or they weren't going to be able to at all. He was sure of it. If he didn't grab Thanh and Kotter by the scruff of their necks and run as fast as he could, they were going to die here beneath the mountain. Or worse. It was the same overwhelming urge that triggered him to flee the market in Basul before it was swallowed by a fireball; the same compulsion that drove him not to walk around the corner of the demolished building that had allowed insurgents to snipe three of his friends.

Kotter sloshed out until he was in to his waist. He appeared to be debating whether or not to dive away from the shore into what smelled like a cutting room floor.

"We're going to die here," Keller whispered, turning to try to decipher the black tunnel's mouth from the swarming darkness.

Behind him, Mûwth broke the filmy surface with a gasp that sounded like a scream. In his hand he held the large coin, the seven sharp tips prodding his palm. His fingertips pressed on the smooth circles on the opposite side, which dimpled ever-so-slightly. The time had come. For His gentle nature to succumb to His wrath, the smooth would have to give way to the sharp, the seven seals between them broken.

It was too late now.

For the great day of his wrath is come...

V

DOVER, TENNESSEE

Mare checked the garage before hurrying up the stairs into his father's bedroom. Neither his dad's black Charger nor Staci's yellow '85 Mustang were in there, but it was only a matter of time before they came home. Undoubtedly, his father had knocked off early at the mill and was already slouched over a stool down at The Still finding the courage to drag himself back home. He knew his old man felt terrible about belting him and dreaded that first confrontation between the two of them. He'd probably spent his day at the lathe checking over his shoulder every thirty seconds waiting for the cops to show up to haul him away. Served him right, Mare thought.

He entered their bedroom, leaving the door standing wide open. He wanted as much notice as he could get when those first footsteps hit the stairs. This had to be done before Missy got back from the river. He couldn't stand the thought of risking her getting caught too. It was one thing to incur a beating for himself, but there was absolutely no way he would ever allow anyone to raise a hand to his sister, which is what frightened him the most. With their father becoming increasingly violent, it was only a matter of time before he lost his cool with Missy, and at that point, Mare knew he'd do whatever he had to do.

With a quick glance across the room, Mare went straight toward the closet.

The bed was unmade as usual, the covers crumpled in a heap at the foot. Empty bottles crowded the nightstand, hiding the clock, its red digital readout staining the glass. Clothes were strewn all over the floor, socks bunched inside overturned shoes. Cobwebs made themselves at home above, connecting the corners and encircling the light fixture. The dresser was buried beneath folded clothes Staci had been too lazy to shove into the drawers. There were a couple of glasses that looked like they'd been sitting there forever and bowls crusted with Lord only knew what. The bathroom door stood ajar, through which he could see the toilet seat standing guard over the bowl, the dark blue, mildew-lined shower curtain drawn closed in front of the tub.

Mare jumped and popped up the square of drywall, seated in a frame of painted trim, over the top shelf of the closet. Dragging a roughly-kept, black leather chest with brass corners from beneath the hanging clothes, he hopped up and rose to his tiptoes, reaching over the lip. He slid his hand side to side, fingers probing through the dusty fiberglass insulation.

"Looking for this?" a deep voice asked from behind him.

Mare closed his eyes and turned his face to the heavens. His heart stalled and his lungs refused to fill. Legs trembling, his first impulse was to propel himself upward into the attic, but then what?

"Why don't you come on down, son?" his father said. His voice was cool and even, but Mare heard the manila envelope crumpling in his tightening fist.

If he knew what was good for him, he'd come right down before his father's anger boiled over, but for the life of him, he couldn't make his quivering legs move.

"Come on down," his father repeated, this time through bared teeth.

Mare was caught and there wasn't a thing he could think to do but to just clamber down and face the music. Where had his father been? His car wasn't in the garage and the bedroom had been empty.

The shower curtain had been drawn closed.

After noticing the missing money, they must have gone looking for it. They hadn't found it in all the years it had been up there. Couldn't they have just made it another couple of weeks?

"I said 'come down!'" his father bellowed.

Twin fists slammed into Mare's back, twisting into his shirt. Before he could even begin to comprehend what was happening, he was in the air, feet cleaved from the top of the chest. He saw his arms flailing above him, then flashes of light exploded across his vision, the entirety of his breath firing past his lips. The back of his head pounded the floor with a resounding crack, releasing a metallic taste to slither from his sinuses. He tried to roll over onto his side, tried to curl into fetal position to suck in the deficit of air, but his old man was already on top of him. Sawdust-crusted jeans were tight over the knees that pinned his biceps to the floor, his father's weight sitting squarely on Mare's already compressed chest.

"Think you're smarter than me, huh?" his father demanded, eyes wide, face blazing red. Vapors of whiskey heated his breath. "You left your damned footprints on the chest!"

Mare tried to gasp, but he simply couldn't force his lungs to expand to fill with the oxygen he so desperately needed, blotching his field of view with metamorphosing pink shapes like amorphous blooms. Tears pinched from the corners of eyes he didn't dare blink.

"You know how much money's in here?" his father screamed, rearing back and smacking Mare across the face with the cash-stuffed envelope. Mare could instantly feel his hot lip begin to swell. "Twenty-three hundred dollars! You stole twenty-three hundred dollars from us!"

Mare scrambled to come up with any sort of plausible explanation, anything at all, but when he opened his mouth, all that came out was a dry cough.

"What were you going to do with this? Huh? Do you have any idea how we've been scrimping and scrounging just to pay the bills? Do you even care?"

Another furious swat with the envelope opened a wide seam in his lip, the stack of bills exploding from the torn package. His father followed with his left fist, clattering Mare's teeth and starting a flood from his right nostril. Mare turned his head away and finally stole a breath that sounded more like a scream, sucking a stream of blood into his lungs, launching him into a coughing fit.

"Christ!" his father spat, pawing at the crimson speckling his face, only succeeding in smearing his son's blood in swatches over his cheeks.

"Get off!" Mare gasped through the throng of coughing.

"You steal from me and then have the nerve to make demands?!"

"Please, dad." A line of blood drained from the corner of his mouth.

His father answered with his right fist, dimming Mare's vision.

"Leave him alone!" Missy screamed, throwing herself at her father's back. She'd barely entered the house when she'd heard what sounded like thunder from the bedroom above.

Mare groaned with the addition of her weight slamming onto his chest, flinching when both of his father's hands flew at his face, slamming to the floor by his ears to catch himself.

Missy wrapped her arms around her old man's neck and started jerking at him, finally prying him off of her brother. The two toppled awkwardly backward. Missy hit first, dragging her father along to slam down atop her. The crown of his head battered her right cheekbone, immediately causing swelling around her eye.

Her father moved more quickly than she even thought possible. She was used to seeing him slouching in his armchair, half-conscious, barely moving a muscle for hours at a time. He pounced like a cat, flipping from his back onto his stomach, and just like that, he was on his knees above her, both fists raised. His eyes glowed with blinding rage.

"Daddy," she whimpered, throwing both quivering hands in front of her face.

Her right hand bent backward with the impact from his fist, hardly slowing what felt like a brick pulping her left cheek. She wailed and clasped both hands over her face, tears spurting from beneath.

Maybe the blow had taken the edge off his liquor-fueled fury, or maybe an ounce of humanity had slipped through. He froze above her, both fists still raised like rattlers preparing to strike, staring down at her trembling, sobbing form. His face ran the gamut of emotions, finally settling on a shocked stupor. All he could manage to do was blink, his mouth working soundlessly around incomprehensible words.

He lowered his arms and inspected his fists, the split knuckles dripping with blood. As he watched, entranced, the fluid formed crimson rivers running between his fingers.

"Get out of here," he whispered, mesmerized by the shimmering blood.

Missy easily knocked him from atop her, depositing him onto his rear. He dropped the bloody hands into his lap, head falling slack, chin resting on his chest.

"I'll kill you!" Mare shouted, lunging from the closet. His eyelids were so swollen and purple that he could barely see. Blood flew from his lips when he spoke, his entire mangled face awash with it.

Before he could slam his mass into his father, Missy stepped in front of him, forcing him to relinquish his momentum for fear of clobbering her.

"Let him be," Missy whispered to her little brother, frightened by the look in his eyes. In that moment, they looked precisely like her father's had before he struck her. It physically pained her to see such emotion that she should have been able to shield him against.

"I promised that if he ever hurt you—"

"Mare."

He shuddered, his pause giving the tears a chance to overcome his puffy eyes.

"It's all right," she whispered, drawing him closer and cradling his head to her shoulder.

Her father still sat in the middle of the floor, staring at the slowly drying blood on his shaking hands, dripping onto the carpet.

Mare sobbed against her, his whole body convulsing.

"Time to go," she whispered, pushing him gently against the chest and trying to force a reassuring smile.

He fought to steady his quivering chin, sniffing back the tears and doing his best to look brave.

"Pack only what you can carry," she said.

"What about the money?"

It was scattered around the room, crumpled and folded from the scuffle, spattered with droplets of blood.

"Forget the money! We'll get by with what we have."

"Missy…"

"Mare," she said, taking him carefully by either side of his misshapen face. "Everything is going to be fine. Pack your things and meet me downstairs. We don't want to be here when he comes back to his senses and realizes what's going on."

Mare lumbered down the hallway, using the wall to steady himself, drawing bloody fingerprints along the faded white paint. Missy followed him into their room. Rushing to her desk, she grabbed her backpack from the back of the chair and dumped her old notebooks and supplies out onto the floor, kicking through the resultant pile on her way to the closet. She tugged a handful of shirts from their hangers and shoved them to the bottom of the bag, hurrying to the dresser and cramming in all of the pants and sundries she could fit. Unable to bring herself to look at it, still neatly made as she could only imagine it would stay until either Ashley or Amber claimed it as their own, she confronted her bookshelf, brimming with hardcover texts and paperback, wishing there was at least time to grab her Chronicles of Narnia. But there wasn't, she knew. It was only a matter of moments before her father broke out of his funk. She didn't want to be anywhere within shouting distance when he regained his faculties.

Missy reached for the top of the bookcase and grabbed her old stuffed Winnie the Pooh, hurriedly stripping its red shirt. She flipped it over and ripped open the Velcro she had sewn into its back, thrusting her hand inside. Fistfuls of cash came out, the majority hundred dollar bills in stacks of five rolled as tight as cigarettes. There was a crumpled mess of fives and tens she had yet to take to the bank to have converted into larger bills. She zipped open the front pocket of her backpack, pulled out all of the pens, tossing them to the floor and shoving the cash in their stead.

Every lingering relic of her childhood tugged at her heart: the swimming trophies lining the windowsill; the dried corsage from her junior prom; the pictures rimming her mirror, mainly of her as a toddler with her mother; her Barbie Dolls and Beanie Babies; and her jewelry box filled with everything physically left of her mother. She forced the images and the memories they conjured from her mind as she imagined this would be the last time she would ever see them.

Tears streamed down her cheeks, stinging the angry swelling rising from her cheekbones. Closing her eyes to the still waters of reflection and the wonderful times that had once upon a time been hers, she threw the backpack onto her shoulder and bolted into the hallway. Her legs quivered as she pounded down the stairs, alighting in the living room and ducking to the right into the kitchen. Mare was already there, his duffel resting on the table. Fruit Roll-Ups bulged from his overstuffed pockets.

"Ready?" she asked, her voice tremulous.

Mare nodded.

"We can't come back, you realize," she said, unable to bring her eyes to meet his.

"I know," he whispered, slinging his bag onto his back.

They stood there a moment in the silence, neither daring to take the first step toward the door that would lead them to Missy's Escort, parked against the curb beneath the nearly skeletal dogwood. There were so many ghosts there with them in the kitchen, so many meals shared over laughter and tears.

Whatever love had once lived in this house was now as dead as her mother.

"I can still grab the money," Mare said, though Missy could tell from his voice that the last thing in the world he wanted to do was to go back upstairs.

"Would you forget about the money, Mare!" she snapped.

"After what he did to us, he owes us that mo—"

BANG!

It sounded as though a lightning bolt had hammered through the ceiling and nearly blown the entire roof off.

Missy looked to Mare in the quiet that followed, unable to mask her wide-eyed fear.

"Oh, God," she whispered, casting her bag to the floor. She sprinted through the living room and up the stairs, bursting through the closed door to her father's bedroom.

His legs hung over the side of the bed, his body sprawled across it. Blood rained from the ceiling, shimmering amidst fragmented bone and chunks of gray matter, falling back down to his body. Crimson poured from his jaggedly rimmed crown, across the tattered flaps of singed scalp. Curls of smoke wafted from the .44 Magnum, still clenched tightly in his twitching right fist.

VI

Eugene, Oregon

Jill didn't know what to make of what she'd seen. She tried to convince herself that it had all been some sort of waking nightmare, but the harder she tried, the more unlikely it seemed. Obviously, she hadn't actually seen her sorority sisters lying dead and bleeding on the lawn or they would still have been there. Wouldn't they? It hadn't been a trick of the sunlight or some heat-cast mirage. She had clearly seen it, though. There was no persuading herself otherwise. She could still recall the awkwardly folded limbs, the seething open wounds, the still eyes, unblinking while swarms of insects buzzed around them, crawling across them like a living skin.

What had she seen, then? She had to approach it from a logical and rational perspective. It couldn't have been a dream, as she was positive that she had been awake. She wasn't sick and she'd been inside of the air-conditioned house at the time, ruling out any sort of fever-fueled delusion. She wasn't taking any medications and there wasn't a chance in hell that she might be pregnant. What did that leave? A vision? A premonition? That sounded absurd. Of course, there had been the time when she was twelve and was convinced that she had seen her grandmother at her bedside in the middle of the night. When she went downstairs for breakfast the following morning, she'd been prepared to tell her parents all about what happened, but instead found her father stroking her mother's back while she sobbed into her hands. Logic dictated that it couldn't have been her grandmother since she had died during the night.

She'd experienced several cases of déjà vu, especially in recent years. Several times during the homecoming dance, she'd had the feeling that she'd already lived that night before, making her just uneasy enough to head back to her house early, avoiding the car wreck that put her friend Allison in the hospital. When Jill had moved into the dorm, she'd known her way through the labyrinth of hallways to her room by instinct, but had chalked it up to a series of lucky guesses. Even Rick. The first time she saw him, she felt as though she had known him for years, but that was easily explained away as attraction. Still, though, there were times when she saw him where she could almost touch the dream of him, imagining him through a swirling mist of steam, his face framed from above and below while rain and hail drove him sideways.

This was something different entirely.

Jill didn't have the slightest clue what she was supposed to do about it, but she felt as though she needed to do something. It was eating at her like a parasite, refusing to allow her a moment of peace, even inside her own head.

"Earth to Jill," April said, waving a hand in front of her face.

"Sorry," Jill said, clearing her throat.

"What's going on in that head of yours?"

"Nothing," Jill said, forcing a smile.

They were sitting on the porch in front of Rick's house, staring past the parked cars to the front of their sorority house. The lawn was still covered with sunbathers, but the thunderheads building over the distant horizon had brought out thicker T-shirts and shorts. Jill just couldn't look at the house the same anymore. Rather than seeing the aged stone façade riddled with flowering ivy, huge rectangular windows covered from within by multicolored curtains, all she could see was a cold, stoic house like a European castle. No life within: simply stone walls standing against the elements where once there had been nothing but laughter and life.

"Don't let him get to you," April said.

"Who?"

"Rick! I can see right through you, Jill. Sometimes you have to practically hit a guy over the head with a brick before he realizes you like him." April smiled. "And no offense, but Rick is definitely denser than most in that regard."

Jill laughed.

April had caught up with her across the street before Jill made it up the lawn to the Kappa Delta house and had managed to get her turned around and walking back in the direction of the guys' house. She hadn't felt like going back in. Not yet. Not after her complete meltdown and the looks she had seen on their faces as they leered down on her.

"You ready to try going in again?" April asked, draping an arm over Jill's shoulder and giving her a squeeze.

"Not just yet."

"No one's going to hold it against you, Jill. I think everyone's just more concerned with making sure that you're all right."

"And not a head case?"

"You did freak out pretty well."

Jill smiled and stared across the street. All of the girls were still there: every bit as alive as they had been the moment prior. She'd heard that people suffering from strokes or aneurysms had similar episodes. Maybe she'd just had some sort of transient ischemic attack, momentarily blocking the flow of blood to her brain, and now everything had gone back to normal. That had to have been what happened. She'd just make an appointment with the doctor and he'd be able to work everything out for her. Yeah, that sounded like a prudent course of action, but still...

"Have you ever... dreamed of something and then had it happen?" she asked nervously.

"All the time," April said. "Just last week I dreamed that I got an A on the psych test, and that's exactly what happened."

"I mean more..." Jill paused to carefully formulate her words. "Have you ever dreamed something so real that you could remember every detail clearly: the sights, the sounds... the smells—?"

"Lucid dreaming?"

"In a sense, and everything is so lifelike that you can't tell the difference between reality and the dream?"

"Sure, sometimes anyway. I had this nightmare once where I was running through a cornfield. I couldn't see who was behind me, but I was sure that someone was. I could hear my own heartbeat, feel the cold sweat on my skin, the stalks tearing at my clothes. I couldn't scream or I knew he'd find me. Finally, when I reached the point where my legs were burning and I couldn't catch my breath for the life of me, I turned to look over my shoulder, but he wasn't there. When I turned around again, he was right in front of me. This dark shape that I can still remember precisely to this day. He raised his arms and that's when I woke up.

"I jumped out of bed, expecting to find my feet covered with dirt from the field, scratches up and down my arms, but there was nothing. My heart was pounding like crazy and I was on the verge of popping my bladder, but after I went to the bathroom and got back in bed, I could tell it had been a dream. But I sure as heck haven't done any sort of running in any cornfields since. It was a dream after all. Just a dream."

Jill nodded.

"Come on," April said, hopping up and dusting off the rear of her shorts. She extended a hand to Jill to help her up. "Have one of more man tears. That'll make you feel better."

"What?"

"I said let's go in and have one of Gorman's beers. That'll make you feel better."

Jill grabbed April's hand and rose to her feet. "I'd swear you said 'more man tears.'"

"What in the world is that supposed to mean?"

"I don't know; that's why I did a double-take."

"Maybe you've got some sort of inner ear thing," April said, *or maybe you're crazy.*

"What?"

"Geez, Jill. I said maybe you've got some sort of inner ear thing."

"No, after that."

"That's all I said."

"I'm sure you said…" Jill started and then stopped. "I must have heard someone across the street." She smiled. "Now, you said something about having one of Ray's beers?"

"That's the Jill I know."

They walked through the front door. Rick and Darren were already sitting on the couch, having dragged the corner table into the middle of the room. Each had an opened bottle of Killian's Irish Red, preferring that to the canned Olympia in the fridge while they could still taste it. On the table was a leaf from a wooden table that had been flipped over and converted into a board game of sorts. The guys called it "Doomed," and Ray had specifically designed it with the end result of leaving everyone hammered.

"Sit down," Darren said, scooting to his right against the arm of the chair to make room for the girls. April plopped down beside him, while Jill stepped over her friend's legs and eased onto the couch between April and Rick.

"Come on, Gorman!" Rick hollered. "It's time to be Doomed!"

"Did someone say Doomed?" Ray called, peering around the staircase from the second floor. "Go ahead and start it up. We'll be down in a second."

His footsteps pounded quickly over their heads.

"Okay," Rick said. "You're first, Dare. Roll them bones."

Darren cupped the dice and sent it clattering across the wooden board.

"Four," he said, grabbing the blue piece and tapping it four spaces down the hastily drawn board. He leaned over to read what was written beneath his piece. "Take two drinks and sing your favorite commercial jingle."

"Drinks first," Rick said, the self-designated enforcer of the rules.

Darren took two long swigs, downing half of the bottle.

"Mr. Clean gets rid of dirt and grime and grease in just a minute," he started, before giggling. "Mr. Clean is stronger longer 'cause there's—"

"Ultra Power in it," April finished for him.

They all laughed.

"Your turn," Darren said shyly, biting his lip in anticipation.

"I'm going to need a beer if you want me to play."

"Way ahead of you," Rick said, dragging a Styrofoam cooler from beneath the table. He reached into the melting ice. You could see in his eyes that he was debating whether or not she was truly worthy of one of the Killian's. Darren shot him a glance. Rick just rolled his eyes, pulling two of the Reds out by their necks.

"Okay then," April said, shaking the dice and casting it onto the board. "Two!" She grabbed one of the red pieces. "One. Two."

"Two chugs and a peck," Rick read. "And that means chugs, not sips."

April twisted off the cap and brought it back, easily swilling a third of the bottle while everyone watched her throat rise once, then again. She transferred the bottle to her left hand and leaned toward Darren, tagging his lips with hers. Their eyes lingered long after the kiss.

"Go, Jill," Rick said.

"What did we miss?" Ray asked, leading Tina down the stairs by her hand. Though she had tried to wipe it from his chin, the residue of her lipstick still lingered. They sat on the floor on the other side of the table.

"Not much," Rick said.

"Judging by how red Darren's face is," Tina jibed, "I think we missed something good."

Laughter.

Jill shook the dice and threw it down, grabbing a yellow piece and tapping it down the line.

Ray rolled over and flipped on a lamp, then pressed the power button on the stereo. Mudvayne throbbed from the speakers as the sun vanished for the day behind the swelling bank of clouds. An eerie blue light emanated through the curtains behind the couch from the bug zapper affixed to the overhanging roof beyond. Beneath the thrum of low-strung chords, several invisible bugs sizzled, leaving flaring blue sparks as fiery testament to their former existence.

Across the street, the sunbathers had vacated the lawn, those with afternoon classes preparing to start their day while the others arrived home from their morning classes.

Somewhere through the descending cloud cover, the sun settled behind with a sigh. Thunder grumbled ominously as the first drops of rain pattered the rooftop.

More man tears, a voice whispered to Jill.

She looked back over her shoulder, but there was no one there, only the popping of bugs on the zapper. One after the other after the other. Flashes of light like fireworks.

A lot of bugs out today, she thought, chasing away her imagination before it could rise and assault her with the images of the girls across the street.

She took a sip of the beer.

The coming storm swelled outside as God turned away.

VII

"These have power to shut heaven, that it rain not in the days of their prophecy," Mûwth's voice whispered in her ear, though from where she stood, Thanh could clearly see the man's silhouette against the even darker water a dozen paces away, "and have power over waters to turn them to blood, and to smite the earth with all plagues."

Her auditory senses must have been playing tricks on her, for even beneath the whisper, she had distinctly heard Mûwth, in the exact same intonation, summon Keller closer to his hip.

"And when they shall have finished their testimony, the beast that ascendeth out of the bottomless pit shall make war against them, and shall overcome them, and kill them."

She felt the tip of a tongue against the outer conch of her ear, enunciating the final words.

"Who's there?" she whispered.

She spun a slow circle as she walked.

It felt as though a curtain of darkness had descended around her, gently constricting until she had to swat it away like a cloud of gnats. Even then, she could feel it regenerating its oppressive mass like a pressure front and quickened her pace to catch up with the others.

"It doesn't look like he's come through here," Keller said, wiping his palm across the dry stone floor.

"He still will," Mûwth assured him. "We, however, must press on."

"What if he's back there, floating on his back because he's too tired to tread water, waiting helplessly for us to come back for him?" Thanh asked.

"Would you sacrifice your chance to flee this country for him?" Mûwth asked. There was something about his tone that intimated a second question hidden beneath the first, though for the life of her, Thanh couldn't imagine why.

"No," Keller answered quickly. The others looked to him in the dark, waiting. "We can't risk missing the extraction," Keller said, his voice a firm monotone. "It would be suicide."

"What about Adam?" Thanh asked softly, though she already knew the answer.

"I'd want you all to go on without me," Kotter said in the same hushed tone, as though to speak up would tug on God's ear. "I wouldn't expect you all to risk your lives for me."

"Nor would I," Thanh said.

Silence settled in their midst like a fog.

"We will give him a means of following us," Mûwth said. "Should he make it this far."

"You were certain he would a moment ago," Thanh whispered.

And when they shall have finished their testimony, the beast that ascendeth out of the bottomless pit shall make war against them, and shall overcome them, and kill them.

She immediately clutched both Keller and Kotter by the arm, drawing them closer, though she was certain that she had been the only one to hear the corporeal words.

"I pray I have not misjudged him," Mûwth answered, though this time in a voice sprung from his own mouth.

"What do you propose, then? Leaving a trail of bread crumbs?" Kotter asked, though his voice lacked any semblance of humor.

Mûwth laughed, raising goosebumps on each of them.

"Keller," he said, the one word thrust between them. "Your knife please."

"What are you going to do with—?" Thanh started, but her words trailed off.

She knew.

There was a clap as Keller slapped the hilt of the blade into the man's expectant palm.

"No... please," she whispered, but his head had already buckled back with the force of the first scream.

Flesh parted for steel.

The edges yawned wide.

Slashing sounds she recognized even in the dark.

These have power to shut heaven, that it rain not in the days of their prophecy.

Droplets of blood pattered the smooth stone beneath their feet.

And have power over waters to turn them to blood, and to smite the earth with all plagues.

Tearing sounds as Mûwth curled his fingertips beneath the self-inflicted seam and yanked like tugging worn carpet from floorboards.

Thanh covered her ears to muffle the man's cries, closing her eyes even against the darkness.

Adam floundered from the water onto the slab of rock, grateful for even one blessed moment with something firm underneath him. He retched up a phlegmy wash of that foul water, coughing until he expelled the last of the fluids from his chest, though he was certain he would never be able to scrape the taste from his tongue.

"Seek and ye shall find," a voice whispered.

"Who's there?" Adam asked, but he was beginning to feel as though he knew that other voice every bit as well as he knew his own.

He crawled forward, pulling his legs out of the warm water, listening to the drainage pour from his pruned body and trickle back into the source.

"Hello!" he screamed, listening for a response as his own voice repeated the same word over and over through the hollow caverns until the darkness swallowed it. "Can anybody hear me?"

Sighing, he pushed himself forward, though his arms felt as though they had been wrenched out of their sockets and his legs were noodles, he knew he couldn't afford to fall any farther behind. He feared that he wouldn't be able to catch up with them, but he dreaded the prospect of them waiting for him even more. Bad enough to miss the pickup himself, but to know he was the cause of the others missing their extraction, consigning them most assuredly to death... He didn't think his conscience would be able to bear the weight of their lost lives. Just that one little girl's life weighed upon his shoulders like a boulder.

"Anybody!" he bellowed, listening to the echo to try to determine the size of the cavern.

Reaching forward to prepare to push himself to his feet, he felt something other than the wet stone beneath him against his palm. His first thought was that it was some sort of sludge one of the others must have dragged from the water, but something deep down inside of him knew otherwise. Running his palms over the surface, he encountered twin knobs on the otherwise flat surface. About ten inches apart, the center of each a small prickled pillar of what felt like flesh. He traced the ragged contours of the rectangular shape, pinching it between his fingers and peeling it from the rock. It was roughly the consistency of leather, though much thinner. Nearly congealed fluids coated the back side like sap, though he was still easily able to peel his fingers apart. Bringing them to his nose, he recoiled, immediately recognizing the smell.

"Oh, God," he moaned, dropping it back to the rock with a slap like a rotting fish.

His eyes rolled upward before he pinched the lids shut.

Those little knobs…

Jesus.

They were nipples.

His first impulse was to scream and throw himself headlong in whichever direction his momentum led. Surely they would eventually hear him. They couldn't be that far ahead. They would have to hear his cries at some point. Surely they would want him to catch up if he could…

His heart stopped; his blood flowing like slush.

They did want him to catch up.

He reached tentatively down for the flayed skin, pinching it gingerly by the upper corners, holding it up before him. Sloppy wads of clotting fluids dripped to the ground.

As I said, the scars were unsightly, so I hid them beneath this design so I could find my way back again.

They'd left him the only means they could think of, somehow knowing he would crawl out of the spring-water onto this very outcropping of rock.

Staggering to his feet, holding the curling strap of flesh at arm's length, he eased forward into the darkness, shuffling his feet to make sure that he didn't trip over any imperfections in the rock or run himself straight into a wall.

He was only a dozen paces down the stone corridor when the screaming started.

●   ●   ●

They must have been steadily rising toward the surface world as the water was now only knee deep in the cavern. Their sloshing was deafening, like a herd of horses fording a stream.

A faint amber glow illuminated the room. Swatches of phosphorescent algae glimmered from the stalactites overhead, reflecting back up from the water beneath. It was as though the air was filled with fireflies; not enough to clearly visualize the cavern around them, but it drew contrast against the formerly impermeable blackness. Their silhouettes stood out against the rocky walls, splashing water glimmering around their legs.

Keller didn't notice they were slowly beginning to stoop until Kotter's head hit the lowering ceiling, summoning a flurry of cursing.

The walls to either side were closing in as well. Though he couldn't see it, he could feel it. It was resonant in their panting breaths, which echoed back much more quickly than before, nearly as loud as the original sounds.

Keller couldn't shake the image that they were walking deeper into something's mouth, with the sharpened teeth looming overhead, the throat constricting before them.

I don't want to die! a voice screamed from somewhere inside his mind, but he just shoved it back down as he was so accustomed to doing. He was a soldier. Fear was a luxury of the weak.

"Are you sure we're going the right way?" Thanh whispered from behind him, unable to hide the tremor in her voice.

"We are nearly there," Mûwth said. Thanh thought he sounded more resigned than elated.

She could only imagine the kind of pain he must be enduring, but it was neither reflected in his steady stride nor his rhythmic breathing.

"I don't like this," Thanh whispered, catching up with Keller. She gave his arm a tug. "Something's not right. Can't you feel it?"

"No," he said, though every hair on his body had risen electrically and his heart was pumping so hard he could feel it throbbing in his temples.

"Here," Mûwth said.

He stopped before what appeared to be a solid wall, the tunnel terminating in a dead end.

"Now what?" Kotter asked.

Without their thrashing footsteps, the silence was a presence surrounding them.

"We must break the seal," Mûwth said, raising the medallion in his right hand. The metal glowed a dull copper color between his fingers. He placed it against the wall, sliding it side to side until it latched into place with a loud click.

He pulled his hand back and they all watched as the disc spun like the wheel on a safe, first one way, then the other, whizzing with the sound of startled bees. Four copper posts rose straight out from the medallion, slowly curling forward like the tails of so many scorpions, then stabbed directly into the rock. With a crack, veins of light opened in the rock wall, spreading to either side like lightning bolts. A gust of heat bellowed from those fissures, blowing their hair back and sapping the moisture from their skin.

"What in the hell's going on?" Keller gasped. He lurched forward and grabbed the spinning medallion. Blood flew in arcs from his fingers where the sharp edges cut through his flesh clear to the bone. He let out a scream and tried to rip his hand away, but with a sickly snap, a golden shaft capped with a pyramidal tip like an agar bit lanced through his palm and tore through the back of his hand.

Thanh flinched and closed her eyes when she felt his warm blood spatter her face.

Kotter watched in awe as the wall itself seemed to deteriorate into a spider web of crevices through which a light more blinding than the sun ate away at the rock. He couldn't tear his eyes away, though his retinas constricted furiously against the glare and his vision was taking on a reddish hue.

"Help me!" Keller screamed, grasping his right wrist with his left and planting his foot against the wall to try to tear his hand free.

Thanh smeared the blood from her eyes and raced to his side, grabbing hold of his arm and adding her weight to his efforts. The veins in Keller's arms glowed with the same light that ate through the wall.

There was a loud snap.

The prong ducked back through Keller's palm and he and Thanh stumbled backward and splashed down into the water.

Mûwth stepped back up to the wall and closed his fist around the medallion, which turned to glitter in his palm and was swept away like shimmering dust. With a grumble, the wall collapsed before them, exposing a gaping maw of darkness barely wider than a doorway. Dust swirled on the warm breath that sighed through that mouth, swallowing Mûwth, who stepped right through the veil of shadow and disappeared within.

"Are you all right?" Thanh wailed.

"Mm-hmm," Keller groaned, clenching his right hand into a fist to try to slow the bleeding. He wrapped it in the front of his shirt and applied as much pressure with his left as he could, unnerved as he could feel the tip of the middle finger of his right hand through the hole in his palm. The third metacarpal was shattered, fragments poking from the wound like a bony ring. He growled with the strain of forcing himself to his feet. "Don't let him out of your sight."

Kotter charged through the opening, the dust beginning to settle like snowflakes.

"Don't go through there!" Thanh shouted, but Kotter was already gone. "Keller—"

He shoved past her and lumbered through the earthen doorway.

"Keller!" she screamed, her voice like a shotgun report in the close confines.

She looked back over her shoulder into the darkness from where they had come.

"Don't leave me alone," she wailed, tears streaming from her eyes.

Forcing her trembling hands into fists, she sprinted after the others.

CHAPTER 3

I

NORTHERN IRAN

Kotter dashed through the darkened corridor, running with his arms stretched out before him to provide that split-second of warning should the tunnel terminate suddenly or bend away.

"You can't leave us here!" he shouted, grinding his teeth in frustration.

As far as he could tell, there had been no branches in the tunnel, so he could only assume that Mûwth was still somewhere directly ahead of him, though he couldn't hear a thing over the pounding of his own footsteps and the resultant echoes. Though he couldn't see it, he could feel the walls constricting, the smooth, almost-polished stone seamless, without any rock outcroppings, as though a funnel of water had glazed this tube for billions of years.

He didn't like this at all. They were deep within a mountain in a country half a world away with their lives in the hands of one whose appearance made him the enemy. He cursed his liberal leanings and the political correctness that had been beaten into him during his public education, when the army had trained him to be able to recognize the enemy on sight. As soon as he saw that man's dark skin and even darker hair, as soon as he heard that Arabic accent, he should have known not to trust the man. Now, because he was too blinded from the truth, he was going to die down here in the darkness. His family would never be able to claim his body. He imagined his mother kneeling in front of a list of names engraved into a wall like the Vietnam Memorial. Tears streamed down her wilting face, channeling through the wrinkles.

Kotter realized he was crying too, the tears stinging the abrasions surrounding his eyes.

"Where are you?" he shouted, enraged at the thought of his mother's sorrow, at the bitter pain lancing his face like so many scalpels, at the man who had abandoned them to their fate.

He stopped, doubling over to try to replace his spent breath, the air in the tunnel was hot and oppressive. Sweat bloomed in droplets from his pores. He sucked in a deep breath and screamed with fury.

The echo bled away into the darkness, stretching before him into infinity.

He didn't want to die. Not down here. Not like this.

His breaths started coming faster and faster. He was hyperventilating and he couldn't even begin to calm himself enough to compensate. Staggering forward, dragging his feet beneath him with his arms searching through the darkness for anything at all, he prayed for air, a hint of light from the surface, anything but the darkness that wrapped around him like a layer of cellophane. He couldn't... couldn't breathe... his vision... spotted with red blobs... choking...

Kotter fell to his knees, slapping his hands to the smooth floor. His throat felt as though it had closed up. He doubled over, a long strand of saliva slipping from his mouth.

"Come!" a voice boomed in front of him, the force blowing his wet hair from his forehead. A gust of warm air filled his lungs.

He rose slowly to his feet, carefully taking that first hesitant step forward.

"Who's ther—?"

Crack.

Something had broken beneath his right foot. He could still feel its remains beneath his tread.

Never allowing his eyes to stray from the darkness directly ahead, he lifted his foot from atop whatever he had stepped on and took a small step backward. Kneeling, he brushed his hand along the floor, refusing to so much as blink as he stared down the tunnel. His fingers traced the outline of a circular shape set directly into the middle of the floor. A thin channel ran away from the circle to either side, perpendicular to the progress of the tunnel. Set perfectly within those precisely straight grooves was a thick length of chain; he could feel the rectangular links, the rust crumbling away like dust. Tracing the chain toward the center from either side, Kotter's fingers reached the edge of the circular seam. Set in the middle was what felt like a flat plate made of clay. Ornate symbols had been carved into its surface. Delicately, he traced them with his finger. A long crack ran diagonally through the circle, so sharp that it sliced open his fingertips.

"What the hell?" he whispered, finally looking down at the ground before him.

He again found the top of the circular seam and curled all four fingers from each hand to pry the plate upwar—

The chains.

God, please don't—

The plate had been part of a mechanism that held the chains in place. A seal. The moment the crack began to widen, a pair of hooks arose from the center of the hole where the plate had once been, lancing through the dust of the broken seal.

Kotter opened his mouth to scream, but it all happened too quickly.

One sharpened hook drove through his left palm, while the other pierced his right. With the thundering sound of a drawbridge falling, the chains started to move, yanking his arms out to either side. Two gigantic stones fell from the ceiling in front of him, a flash of the iron chain trailing their descent. He was jerked up from the ground, his hands racing straight up to the earthen roof. It felt as though the hooks had ripped his hands right off, but he hadn't been that fortunate. Dangling there, suspended from a horizontal beam of petrified wood where the stones had been precariously balanced for eons, his legs flailed helplessly beneath him.

He could hear the flesh and muscle in his hands tearing as gravity urged him back down to earth. It was a pain beyond anything he could have ever imagined.

Steaming blood rolled down his forearms, around his elbows and into his sopping shirt. It slithered beneath his clothing, all the way down his legs before draining over his shoes with a steady splatter. Each kick of his legs splashed arcs of blood across the smooth floor two feet below, marring the stones holding the opposite ends of the chains, tearing the skin and muscle in his palms more and more with each attempt to loose himself until finally he had no choice but to hold his legs still and try to control his shaking arms. He began to beg for the hook to shred the remainder of his hands and erupt between his middle- and ring-fingers. Dear God, regardless of the damage, just having those hooks out of his hands would be reward enough; just to feel the ground beneath him again...

"Help," he gasped, trying to raise his voice without creating any additional movement.

"Where are you?" a voice echoed from somewhere far behind him in the darkness, a world away. "Kotter! Answer me!"

"Help!" he screamed at the top of his lungs, bucking back to force his diaphragm to propel every ounce of air from his lungs. The word trailed into an agonized wail, which he nipped off with his bared teeth, pinching his eyes tight and trying not to breathe.

Something tickled his hands, starting from the tips of his fingers and moving down his arms. At first he thought it was his lifeblood fleeing him in a massive deluge, but he was able to discern the difference. Whatever crawled over his arms had something small and pointed on it, which poked his flesh like bramble. They were legs, insect legs, crawling all over him, pouring down the chain from the rafter above. In seconds they had covered his neck and chest and were making their way toward his toes, swarming over his face. Tiny, fur-tipped appendages scurried in and out of his nostrils, tunneling into his ears with a sound like crunching potato chips.

Footsteps approached from ahead, though he couldn't force his eyes to open with the sheer mass of bodies crawling across his eyelids. He didn't dare open his mouth to scream.

"Desert Locusts," Mûwth said, his voice emotionless. The man had broken the seal, hidden within the mountain following the death of the first Messiah, who had foretold of the end of days to his apostles alone. They had installed seven safeguards against the apocalypse, seven seals concealed from humanity until such time that all hope was lost and a child of God was sent again among them, not to die himself for their sins, but the exact opposite. "Each day they must consume their weight in vegetation to survive. Each subsequent generation increases their numbers tenfold. Such beautiful and simplistic creatures."

Kotter wasn't listening. His breath had staled in his chest, and soon he was going to have to open his mouth to breathe. Those that filled his nostrils were already flattening themselves and squeezing into his sinuses, where they expanded like popping corn within the skeletal infrastructure of his face. They felt like the grasshoppers they'd had back home stateside, but they were much bigger, their tiny feet sharper.

His chest was ablaze and his head was beginning to feel like it was filled with helium.

"Do not fight it," Mûwth said. "Yours is a grand destiny."

Kotter ripped his lips apart and sucked at the air, giving the locusts the opportunity that they needed. A channel of the insects poured across his tongue. His teeth snapped shut over and over, crunching as many as he could, but unable to stop the flood that poured down his throat. He bucked and thrashed until what remained of his hands parted with the sound of a phone book torn asunder.

His body crumpled into a still heap on the stone floor, lumps rising and crawling beneath his skin. It looked as though he was boiling, with those bubbles scurrying beneath every inch.

"Arise," Mûwth said, raising his arms.

Kotter's body floated from the floor, limbs hanging weakly. He opened his mouth, but the sound that erupted was of a million buzzing wings and the chirping of rear legs rubbed together. His skin was pasty white like children's glue and the hair on his body had been bleached white from sheer terror. Eyes without irises snapped wide, as though the former orbs had been removed and replaced with cue balls.

"Take to the saddle, first of the God's Horsemen."

Kotter's body twirled back to the floor, where legs unaccustomed to bipedal locomotion staggered, then finally rooted themselves to the ground.

"You are the first, the chosen purveyor of God's wrath. You will sow His anger from the coasts to the mountains and drown them with His tears. You are the white horseman. Turn the soil unto salt, the forests to ash.

"Ride, Famine, scourge of the fields. Let no man stand in your way."

◉   ◉   ◉

"Where are you?" Keller shouted. "Kotter! Answer me!"

He clenched his knife in his left hand, blood crusted to the serrated edges from Mûwth's recent use, the rest wiped in two dried smears on his fatigue pants. He swung his service revolver side to side in front of him, though with the constant immersion of swimming through the caves, he wasn't sure whether it had any hope of firing or not. Part of him almost hoped he'd get to find out, though with the gushing hole in his palm, he couldn't even hold it steady.

His heavy footsteps pounded back at him from the smooth walls, louder even than the drumming of his pulse in his temples and the screaming of the voice in his mind, crying for him to just turn tail and flee. There was another equally insistent voice, however, one that yearned for blood to be spilled, begged for the chance to sink that knife to the hilt into forgiving flesh, to coat the walls with a spray of fluid and chunks of gray matter from the passage of a bullet.

There was no way he was running blindly through the darkness and making himself an easy target. He walked quickly but carefully, the butt of the gun in his right hand balanced on the base of the knife in his left, blade pointed to the floor, barrel directly ahead. He could hear Thanh calling for him from behind, but he forced the sound of her voice from his ears, peeling apart the layers of silence that cocooned him in the passageway.

He slipped, his arms wind-milling wildly. The blade of the knife clacked off of something hard while his right forearm slammed into solid rock with a crack. Bracing himself, though his entire upper body screamed in protest from what was assuredly an ulnar fracture, he transferred his weight back to his legs, kneeling on the smooth stone floor. Warm fluid leeched through his pants to heat his knee. Whatever mess he now crouched in was the reason he slipped, he was certain. Still holding the pistol directed into the emptiness ahead, he placed the knife flat on the ground and dabbed his fingers into the liquid, bringing them to his lips. Unblinking, he scoured the pitch black down the tunnel. A dab of his tongue confirmed what he already suspected.

The metallic tinge, the biological taint... it was blood. And it was still warm.

Wiping his palm on his shirt, he took the hilt of the knife in his fist and rose carefully to his feet, swinging the sharpened tip before him like a blind man's cane. It grazed a large stone to the left, from the top of which a thick, rusted chain stretched to the rocky roof. He reached across his body and examined a matching boulder to the right, an identical chain connected to an enormous eye-ring drilled into the surface. Both were slick with blood.

"Kotter," he whispered, taking a tentative step forward. Something crunched beneath his feet like cereal. He didn't even have to look down to know that he was walking on a carpet of insects, their exoskeletons snapping and crackling almost rhythmically.

They arose and buzzed in a cloud around him, wings beating at his face. He could feel them crawling all over him, thrumming in his ears, tapping his exposed skin. Where had they all come from? It was as though they had materialized from thin air. He swung his left arm through their midst, slicing through the cloud of swirling locusts just to have them refill in his passage.

If there were this many flying bugs, then logic would dictate that somewhere nearby there had to be some sort of exit to the surface. After all, locusts needed vegetation to survive and they certainly weren't going to find anything growing down there. He felt hope float up in his chest. He just needed to make it to that opening. Damn them all, he was getting out of that tomb.

Keller was barely able to keep his eyes open a slit against the barrage of bodies and wings. He slashed to no avail, swinging the blade against the creatures was like trying to cut a cloud, but what else could he do? If he tried to outrun them, maybe he would be able to leave them behind, but he'd be hurdling blindly toward who knows what, and turning back wasn't an option he was prepared to consider. Whoever's blood he had slipped in... their fate would not befall him.

The swinging blade met with resistance, cutting through whatever it was as though it were no more substantial than a cobweb. With a zipping sound, rope was drawn through a pulley somewhere in the blackness, causing a small avalanche of stones to cascade down the wall to his left. A pinhole of light blasted into the darkness just higher than his line of sight like a mote-infested laser. Frenzied wings flashed in the light like fireflies, the locusts swarming toward the hole, crawling frantically through one atop the other until the buzzing faded to a whisper.

Keller held up his hand, reflecting the nearly blinding light from the blade. If there was sunlight, then there was a way out. There had to be. Even if he had to tear through the stone wall with his bare hands, he was getting out of that hole in the ground. He'd sooner face a dozen armed Iranians than something he couldn't even see down there in that passage to hell.

Sheathing his knife, he eased toward the wall, carefully watching the hallway to ensure that if there was something coming, he'd see it immediately. He rose to his tiptoes, but still couldn't see through to the world without. A final glance down the tunnel produced nothing discernible from the darkness. He tucked the pistol into the front of his pants and reached up for the small hole, slipping his index finger through. The rock surrounding it pushed away in a larger circle, lighter than he had expected, the force cracking what appeared to be a stone disc before it fell. The opening was now large enough to shove his fist through.

Running his palms along the smooth wall, he probed for any sort of leverage. He found a small outcropping with his right hand, gripping it fiercely until he secured a similar handhold with his left. Forearms bulging, he pulled himself up, scrabbling with his feet until his toes caught hold. Veins popping out like cords in his neck, he leveled his eyes with the hole.

The sunlight felt blissfully warm on his face, though the sudden change in luminescence struck him temporarily blind. His eyelids batted against the flood of brightness, fighting to adjust from the near-absolute pitch black to the sudden influx of light which cast red blobs across his vision. He was staring out at the same level as the ground. A wall of sandstone stood before him, three feet away and stretching upward well past the extent of his limited view. Several symbols were carved into the rock's face, directly across from him, no more then six inches from the sand as though chiseled to be viewed specifically from this vantage. תורת. He squinted to try to decipher the writing, and though he recognized it as old Hebrew script, he couldn't translate it.

An orange and blue Uromastyx lizard scurried across the sand in front of him; stunted, round body dragging a thick gray tail like a pinecone. It climbed onto the disc of stone he had knocked from the pinhole to widen it, spreading its legs as wide as it could to lower its belly to the rapidly warming surface. It didn't look like stone now that he could actually see it, but rather a circular clay plate with a tiny hole like a vinyl record. More symbols lined the edges, but with the fat lizard sprawled across it he couldn't make any out.

What was this ornamental relic doing here of all places? He had heard the wall crumble away from the hole after slicing the vertical rope, so it couldn't have been lodged there from the inside. Had someone placed the plate over the hole in the cavern wall from the outside? Was it because someone out there didn't want something escaping from within, or to prevent it from gaining entry? The characters on the sandstone face were designed to be seen through this hole in the wall, which he never would even have been able to see through had he not knocked that clay saucer to the ground... a saucer etched with similar Hebrew characters.

The whole scenario seemed too... elaborate. Too much effort had gone into the design of what should simply have been a crack between the inside of the mountain and the outside world. It could easily have been covered by a single rock, though how anyone would have been willing or able to scale the mountain for the sole reason of carving a word in the sandstone and widening a fissure to a circle large enough to press a clay seal into was beyond him. It was absurd.

And why the hell was he getting so hot?

His entire body was damp with sweat, though at first the difference had been indistinguishable as he'd only recently crawled out of a warm slough of filth-water. His clothes were sapped tightly to his body. It felt as though there was a fire burning behind him; a dry heat baking the backs of his hands and neck. The first curls of black smoke drifted into his line of sight, ripped out into the otherwise clear air outside. Something was definitely burning.

The lizard readjusted, sliding forward on the cracked plate to escape the swirling smoke, settling just across the middle of the fissure. With a snapping sound, the clay seal broke in half, startling the Uromastyx to scurry across the sand.

A grumbling sound came from behind Keller, shaking the wall he clung to. A crack formed in the stone floor behind him where he had stood only moments prior. Fissures raced away from it like a spider-webbing windshield, each of the crevices glowing a brilliant orange. The floor finally just gave up and fell away, dropping into a molten pool of boiling metal like lava, consuming the stony remnants of the cavern floor.

The ledges began to crumble beneath his hands, threatening to deteriorate and drop him into the source of the heat that was already beginning to melt the rubber soles of his boots. He glanced back over his shoulder. Beneath where the floor had once been was what looked like an open lead sarcophagus, brimming with bubbling liquid metal heated to a flame orange.

His right foothold crumbled away, but he managed to compensate with his straining arms. He was going to have to try to leap across it to the stone floor beyond before his disintegrating handholds dropped him to his death.

"Come!" a voice bellowed from behind him, storming up and down the tunnel like a steam engine.

On three, he thought, bracing his right foot against the wall to launch him backward.

One.

The ledges crumbled to dust, leaving him flailing at the otherwise smooth wall and then the empty air. A scream burst past his lips, intensifying to a crescendo of unadulterated agony the moment his feet splashed down into the magma. His flesh burned with a sickening smell like scorched pork rinds. His legs buckled, and the last thing he saw before his head sloshed beneath the surface was his arms catching fire, his skin blackening in response.

The plane of the boiling mess slowly resumed its former calm, betraying the fact that Keller ever splashed into its melted embrace.

"Arise," Mûwth said, stepping from the darkness. An orange glow stained him from head to toe, shimmering on the fluids that covered the muscles on his chest where there had once been skin. "Arise, fist of God's fury, second of His Horsemen, first to join the battle and lead the legions of His righteous rage."

A hand rose from beneath the surface of the metal, deep crimson as though the blood now flowed on the outside. The air cooled it with a hiss; what had at first looked like liquid fire on the flesh cooling to the consistency of leather. The joints fit together like sections of a wasp's exoskeleton… like a living skin of armor.

Another hand erupted from the left side and both grasped the sides of the smelting pot, pulling upward until the head emerged, followed by the thorax. A single smoothed plate covered the entire face like a shield, minus raggedly slashed seams through which a pair of eyes blazed like embers, and a mouth without lips showed sharp, layered teeth like those of a shark. His faceplate met with what looked like large leather scales where the hairline had once been, spikes rising in a series of long, four-inch spines like those tracing an iguana's back. Wide plates covered the neck, making it as thick as the head, seamed together with leathery shielding like a knight's suit, stretched taut to precisely mimic the musculature beneath.

His knees flexed beneath him and he finally rose to his full height, now only a couple inches shy of seven feet, flaming metal draining down heavily scaled legs. He raised his clawed hands in front of him, opening and closing them, watching the way the plates covering each hand fit together like the talons of a bird of prey.

Whatever had once been Peter Keller had been burned away like his pathetic layer of human skin, dead beneath intricately sculpted biological armor.

"Go forth and champion His Word. Let all who have cast Him asunder know the glory of His Wrath. You are the hammer of His Vengeance and the harbinger of His Eternal Love: the red horseman, he who will leave lakes of crimson on the battlefields in his wake."

The creature Keller had become stepped out of the molten sludge and raised his fists, inspecting the spines that ran along the backs of his forearms, the wickedly sharp scales that projected from his knuckles.

"War, most feared and beloved of His children: angel of mercy, angel of death."

A solitary tear crept from Mûwth's eye.

"Ride, War, and let the earth tremble beneath your advance. May no quarter be sanctioned and no warning given."

"Where is everybody?" Thanh screamed. "Somebody answer me!"

Her pants were saturated with Kotter's blood, having slipped in it between the boulders and been unable to get back up. She'd flailed around in the warm mess, trying desperately to get her legs beneath her, before dragging herself atop one of the boulders. Her hair was sapped with cooling blood, drying on her cheeks and hands, making it feel as though her skin was shrinking, tightening to the point she was certain her epidermis would crack.

She spun in a circle, suddenly unsure of which direction she had come from and which way she was going. The walls were closing in on her, sucking the air from the room. Panic seized her in a stranglehold. Rocking back, she screamed into the cavernous ceiling above, her legs breaking into a sprint of their own accord. She ran as fast as her legs could churn, her alternating sobbing and screaming trailing through the darkness, their echo haunting her.

"Oh God, oh please!" she wailed the moment she saw the aura of light filtering through the darkness. Thanh barely saw the burbling cauldron of liquefied metal in time to throw herself to her rear end, skidding to a halt with her toes hanging over the fiery pit. Kicking at the smooth earthen floor, she scrambled backward, her palms smoldering. The heat was ferocious, baking the mask of blood to her face. "Just let me out of here! Please!"

The light crossing the tunnel from her left was sheer torture. She could see the circular hole in the wall and the sunshine beyond, but so far as she could tell, there was no way of reaching it. It tormented her: promising freedom, yet offering only death in the flaming magma.

"Keller!" she screamed, burying her face in her hands. She didn't care about the twin streams of mucus running from her nose or the ragged hitching of her breath. All she wanted to do was find someone, anyone, and get the hell out of the darkness. Conflicting urges paralyzed her; she wanted to run as fast and as far as she could, and yet, at the same time, she wanted nothing more than to curl into a little ball and just simply disappear.

"Give me your hand," Mûwth said.

"What happened to the others?" Thanh whispered.

"They are waiting for you at the end of the corridor."

"Why didn't they come back for me?"

"They have both already passed through into the light. Take my hand, child, and I will lead you there as well."

"I don't want to be here anymore," she sobbed.

He walked closer, to the far edge of the smelting pot and stretched out his open palm. The glow from the molten metal stained his visage, revealing striated muscles seething with blood.

"I know," he whispered. "Take my hand and this will all be over for you very soon."

She rocked back and forth, cradling her legs to her chest.

"Do you want me to make all of this go away?"

"Yes," she whimpered.

"Then take my hand." His words were firm, his outstretched arm strained.

"I just want to go home."

"Come!" a deep voice boomed from somewhere in the tunnel like a clap of thunder.

Thanh screamed, shielding her face with her shaking hands. The world was spinning around her. She couldn't breathe, couldn't speak. Her body simply shut down.

"Rise to your feet, child. Take my hand and you will know peace."

Her wide eyes were blank, tears rolling unimpeded. She didn't realize she was climbing to her feet until she was standing opposite Mûwth, her quivering hand reaching tentatively across the steaming lava. If there had been a point when she could have stopped this, it had long since passed. As a doctor, had she been in control of her faculties, she'd have known that she was in shock. Her blood pressure had dropped significantly, her heart rate accelerating. Her skin shimmered with a cold sweat. All of her follicles prickled; every hair standing erect.

"One more step," he coaxed.

The rubber soles of her boots peeled off in a gooey mess like black gum, but Thanh no longer thought of anything at all. Mûwth clasped her hand, drawing her across the burbling volcanic emission like a princess from a carriage. His flesh was febrile, so hot it hurt her hand, but she no longer cared, allowing him to usher her deeper into the darkness. The light from the hole in the wall and the orange glow of the molten metal faded behind her.

"Just a little farther," he said.

The smooth walls absorbed their footsteps, as though the only sound in the world was their harsh breathing. She didn't know how far they had walked, only that the heat from his hand flooded up her arm, warming her entire body. She was as light as air, yet somehow her feet still touched the ground.

"You must go the remainder of the way by yourself," he said, slowing her. Nothing was distinguishable from the blackness. "I can only lead you to the light. I cannot make you see."

His hand fell from hers, the warmth sucked away with it. She was cold again, shivering. The shock of the transition allowed a surge of fear to rush back in. She didn't know exactly what she was looking for, but she could feel it drawing her closer. She stopped after three paces and looked at the wall to her right. It appeared just like the rest of the channel: smooth, barren of any sort of crags or imperfections. Her right hand rose from her side of its own accord, pressing her flattened palm to the surface and gliding it back and forth until she felt a thin vertical seam.

Thanh took a small step forward.

"Beyond that doorway lies freedom," Mûwth's voice drifted from behind. "Will you go willingly?"

She nodded, still staring at the wall as though beyond was her heart's desire.

"Then kneel before your salvation."

Thanh dropped to one knee, blood-crusted hair slapping her face like dreadlocks.

"Before you is the key," he said, watching carefully as she reached down to the stone floor and produced a circular disc. Her fingers grazed the indentations of several etched symbols.

She looked back at him over her shoulder.

"Break it," he said, his voice resonant with a deep sorrow. "Break the seal."

There was a moment of hesitation as she turned the clay piece over and over in her hands.

"On the other side of the door you will find redemption."

Gripping either side of the seal, she snapped it cleanly with the slightest effort, the halves disintegrating to dust in her palms. With a grumble, the stone door began to open away from her. Chains clanked and gears groaned, so loud that the mountain itself quivered. The screech of stone being dragged across stone finally ceased, followed in short measure by the grinding of chains coming to rest on sprockets. A humming sound crept from within on the first breath of stale air to seek refuge in the tunnel, like millions of tiny voices made high-pitched by helium.

"I don't see the way out," she whispered, her own voice a thousand miles away.

"You must have faith, child."

Her leg tensed, but she couldn't bring herself to take a step. She looked nervously back to him, though all she could see was darkness.

What was that humming sound? She could see nothing in the darkness that seemed to intensify within that room. All she wanted to do was get out of there, and if there was an exit beyond the humming shadows, then by God she'd turn cartwheels through there if she had to.

Thanh's jaw jutted forward, her lips a determined tight line. Her fingers curled into fists and she willed the tears to cease. Her right foot moved, followed by her left. Each step made the next that much easier. Before she knew it she was through the doorway, a sense of excitement rising within her. She was going to get out of that godforsaken darkness and the hellish catacomb of passageways. A smile warmed her lips. She wanted to run toward her salvation.

"How much farther?" she asked, daring to turn to look in the direction she had come.

Even though she couldn't see him, Mûwth just lowered his chin to his chest in response, tears dripping straight to the floor.

The chains began to grind.

"No!" she screamed, sprinting toward him.

With a screech, the slab of stone began inching across the floor.

"Please! Don't close me in here!"

"I am truly sorry," he whispered.

"Help me!" she trilled, her voice cracking. She reached the closing door and grabbed the corner of the enormous rock. Her fingertips bit for leverage, but the force of the closing door ripped it right away from her.

Mûwth dropped to his knees in the hallway.

"Thy will be done," he whispered.

"Nooo—!" Thanh screamed, her voice silenced sharply by the closed door.

Thanh pounded at the rock wall with insane vigor. She screamed and raged, sobbing convulsively, hurling her diminutive form against the sealed stone.

The humming grew louder.

Thanh slapped at the back of her neck the moment she felt the first stinger pierce her epidermis. More mosquitoes landed on her cheeks and arms. Staggering backward, she swatted at the air around her, feeling countless bodies swarming her like a tangible fog. They covered her skin in a living sheath, planting their small legs and then driving their stingers in. It felt as though she was on fire; the fleshy layers of her skin ablaze with intense pain. She threw herself against the cavern wall, desperately trying to kill as many as she possibly could, but as soon as one fell, two more filled the gap left by the squashed carcass.

The sensation of lightheadedness came on suddenly, sending her crashing to the floor, flailing uselessly. They were draining her blood; she completely understood that now. She was growing increasingly dizzy and gasping for air, yet still they inhaled her lifeblood, squishing when she rolled on them, covering the stone floor with a sheen of her blood. It coated her body, the scent driving the rest of the mosquitoes into a feeding frenzy.

Thanh screamed, the last fearful note passing her lips on breath never to be replenished. Her skin turned to parchment, crumpling over what little substance clung to her bones. Emaciated, her corpse lie on the floor, beneath a seething layer of feasting insects intent on securing every last drop of her blood.

The swarm rose at the first clank of the chain, buzzing back to the walls where they merged with the darkness, out of sight, a gentle, contented humming filling the room. The stone slab scraped back into the room, the stench of death belching out into the tunnel.

"Arise," Mûwth said sternly.

The task was almost complete.

Thanh's paper-light, nearly mummified body floated from the floor, levitating before alighting on its feet once more. Her eyes were cracked and yellowed like ancient paper, merely resting in sunken sockets suddenly far too large. The graying skin was pulled tight over her cheekbones, clinging to her jaw. All that remained of her nose was a skeletal nub flanked by a pair of triangular black holes. What little hair still protruded from her skull was scraggly and clumped. The wiry strands no longer even came close to covering her crusty scalp, the rest congealed on the floor in what little remained of her rapidly drying blood. Her arms and legs were merely dehydrated skin on bones that looked like the slightest touch would shatter them.

"Rise, third of God's horsemen, let your plague follow the fall. Go forth and spread disease enough to decimate all that is left."

The thing now inhabiting Thanh's body opened her mouth wide, exposed teeth like withered corn kernels, and drew a deep breath. With a furious hum, the mosquitoes flew from the walls, swirling around her head like a cyclone. They funneled into her open mouth, crawling on her lips, creeping through her nostrils until the entire swarm had vanished down her throat.

She closed her mouth, silencing the incessant hum.

"Ride, God's chosen daughter, let your minions scour the earth and lay waste to all. Take to saddle, Pestilence," Mûwth said, voice splitting, tears flowing unhindered. "Prepare the path for him that is to follow: ender of suffering and bringer of life eternal.

"The end of times is nigh."

Mûwth knelt in the darkness at the end of the tunnel. His tears were all but dried. He had known all of his life that this moment was coming, yet he had prayed to never see the day. It was only a matter of time before they destroyed themselves anyway. They had already destroyed God. This was simply the culmination of a series of events that had been building since the first man evolved from ape and raised a fist against his brother. Violence was in their nature. It had always been, but he had never imagined that man would be willing to destroy himself to claim such a hollow victory. Especially in the name of God.

Jihad.

Man had fallen from His grace. And like the rabid dog he was, man would be put down. There was not enough compassion in the world to spare it a moment longer. No love, no light, no hope. The doctor he had spared, the one who had helped the child of the enemy, would have been better served by a mercifully quick death, not what he now had in store. The man had shown him compassion and he had sentenced him to a grueling, painful death. Rather than trying to cultivate that little blossom of hope, praying for it to bloom, he would eliminate it with the rest of the rage and hatred. It was like stomping a bed of flowers to kill the weeds.

Mûwth was God's fourth horseman, rider of the black steed.

The fourth seal rested on his legs. He grasped it with his sweaty fingers, barely able to hold the clay disc, tracing the engraved symbols with his thumbs. The children have lost their way, it translated roughly from a tongue never meant to be spoken by human mouth. It was his lot to call them home. Sorrow permeated every pore, leeching into every bone and muscle. He'd never felt such overwhelming remorse and regret. A solitary tear, the last he would ever shed for his flock, swelled from beneath his eyelid, rising up over the lashes. It shivered there at the tip of those fine hairs, growing until finally victimized by gravity and snapping free. The tear fell onto the seal in his grasp, which shattered at the moment of impact.

He buckled backward, his knees still beneath him, shoulder-blades touching the ground. Thrashing about, the base of his skull pounding the stone floor, his eyes slid up beneath flagging lids. His mouth opened to scream in agony, but instead fired a flume of white smoke up to the ceiling. He swelled from within, plumping like a cooked sausage, his neck growing thick and riddled with bulging veins, chest sealing over the formerly open wound. When it looked as though his skin could stretch no more, it began to rip open in bloody seams, peeling back and curling. Dead skin sloughed off, littering the floor around him in long strips like a snake slithering out of a shed. The skin beneath was blacker than the darkness, so smooth it felt like satin. Serpentine scales melded together seamlessly, covering the entirety of his form, what remained of his humanity on the cavern floor disintegrating into piles of dead cells like dust.

Rising to his feet, his movements fluid, Mûwth arched backward, arms stretched to his sides, and screamed up into the ceiling in the voice of a thousand tortured souls. His body was still human in shape, but that was the totality of it. No hairs originated from anywhere on his body, only scales that appeared to absorb light rather than reflecting it. His scalp was coarse where the tips of the scales pointed up like the short spines as the base of an adder's head, a crest running down his spine like a short, rocky dorsal fin.

The others crept from behind him. He could feel them beside him there in the darkness as though each were an extension of his flesh. Their breathing was out of synch, haggard.

Mûwth's eyes snapped down from under twin black eyelids, yellow as the rising sun, slit with a slash of darkness.

There was no longer any need to speak, for their thoughts were one. They knew him as Death, and before the sun set that night, countless souls would speak his name as well.

Death placed his hands on the stone wall before him, which crumbled away, sending a small avalanche of rocks thundering down the face of the mountain.

The late afternoon sun beat heavily on them as they emerged from the mouth of the mountain, the earth trembling beneath their feet.

The day of reckoning had arrived.

II

NORTHERN IRAN

Adam stood knee-deep in the lake of blood, studying the map beneath the celestial light from cavern roof. He tried to remember Mûwth's story, recalling a point where the man had said there had been a lake of blood where his medallion had been. He had illustrated that spot by pointing to his tattooed map above his navel. Adam could clearly see the small hole in the drying skin where it had been torn from the umbilicus. Black lines spread from that location like the sun's rays, branching into a maze of passageways. As he watched, the long dried ink became damp, moving rhythmically, wavering as though trying to peel from the very skin it was stitched into.

He had heard the others screaming, sounds that had assaulted him for what felt like an eternity. Trying to follow the anguished cries, he'd sprinted blindly through the passageways, splashing through shin-deep water and stumbling on the uneven rock. By the time he reached this room, the screams had ceased. All that he could do was pray that they were still alright, but deep down, he knew otherwise. The abrupt end to each voice's cry and the subsequent silence that followed was enough to convince him that his speculations were correct.

Long, formerly straight lines of ink peeled from the skin, draining off into the blood where they wriggled away like snakes. The majority of the swatch of flesh was now bereft of the tribal-looking design, save for a lone series of lines that stretched toward where the skin would have covered the right ribs from the precise spot where he stood right now.

Adam ran his hand across the crinkly surface, but none of the remaining ink rubbed off.

He didn't know what to think or what to do. The whole situation had crossed from real to surreal the moment they crawled through that hole into the mountain. The refugee camp seemed a million miles away, fading like a memory lived in another lifetime entirely. The imperative to make it to the extraction point was overwhelming. He needed to get out of these caves before…

Before what?

Adam didn't know, but there was a dreadful sinking feeling deep inside that insisted he didn't want to hang around long enough to find out. As a doctor, he'd become familiar with the scent of death. It may have come in a variety of fragrances, but when boiled down, all of them were composed of the same biological foundation. There was that rich ammonia component from when the bladder ceased to work and the urine crystallized; the mealy stench of cellular decay, as though the whole body breathed a foul last breath; and the smell of the bacteria now breeding unchecked in the abdomen and bowels. He'd smelled it at the camp long before the refugees emerged from the concealed trail following the river.

That smell was all around him now: filling his nostrils, settling on his skin like a skein of oil, dripping down his pores.

He'd never smelled it this intense. It overrode whatever qualms he may have had about following a tattooed map peeled from a presumably dead man's chest, the physical impossibility of the ink bleeding back out of the epidermis and leaving but a single route to follow. Besides, he had no clue how to get out of this labyrinth. He couldn't have even followed his own path back out the way he'd come. The map at least pointed him in some direction, which was far better than he was able to come up with on his own.

If his interpretation was correct, it appeared as though if he swam across the lake, on the other side would be an entrance to a series of passageways. He needed to make sure that he memorized his path now while there was still light to read by. Once he was back in the absolute darkness, there'd be no way he could follow the map. Rehearsing it in his mind, he rolled the flap of skin like a scroll and tucked it beneath his waistband, wading forward until the ground fell away from his feet. He paddled on, careful to keep his chin above the water level so as not to accidentally drink any of the blood.

Passing beneath the light, he looked down into the fathomless depths, unable to see the cavern floor. The light was blinding, making everything else seem pitch black after passing back through. By the time he reached the far shore, it felt as though he'd been doing the butterfly for hours. Every muscle ached, but the urge to hurry out of there superseded his fatigue.

He didn't immediately see it, but after crawling around on the smooth boulders, he eventually found a crevice wide enough to accommodate his shoulders, but not quite tall enough to allow him to walk fully erect. Stooping, he clomped onward, arms held out before him. Cobwebs parted for his probing fingers, which felt as though they were now glazed with filth. The passage wound steadily to the right, often opening to either side over another silent cavern, where every drip from the stalactite-riddled ceiling sounded like the thump of a bass drum. He didn't even realize he was ascending until his ears popped.

Exhaustion set in long before he saw the first hint of muted light. It took all of his strength to drag his tired legs forward, but the moment those first rays of light permeated the darkness, it was all he could do to keep from breaking into a sprint.

A rocky slope led upward toward the source of the light: a crescent-shaped opening through which he could see the sky. It was the most beautiful thing he'd ever seen. The dry desert air poured down on him, the leading breath sheer ecstasy. The air down there had been so humid and dense that it had felt more like swallowing than breathing, but this was exquisite. Tears streaming down his cheeks, he crawled upward, fingertips tearing open, pants shredding from his bloody knees. The dust clung to his face, forming a layer of mud. He could barely catch his breath with the excitement, spurring him on over boulder after boulder until finally he crawled out into the sunlight. After so long in the darkness, the glare felt like needles driven through his retinas, but it was so blessedly comforting against his skin that he moaned in relief.

He forced himself to his feet, laughing excitedly while still crying.

The world came slowly into focus. The desert stretched away from him as far as he could see to the north. He was standing on a rocky crag about a dozen feet above a steep, boulder-lined hill leading toward a town set like an oasis amidst a clump of trees. There was even a small lake beyond. It had to be Ali Sadr.

Adam raced toward what looked like the least treacherous path down the mountainside.

◉ ◉ ◉

The steppe leveled off, the ground, once steep and hard enough to hold vegetation, turned into sand that sunk beneath his weight. His throat was parched, the sun baking him red. Ahead, a dirt road appeared from the wavering heat. He stumbled onward, coughing up the last of his body's moisture as he pulled up before it. The tracks were well-worn, the sand not given much time to drift across it before being scattered again. Shielding his eyes from the sun, he looked down the road to the east where it led into Ali Sadr. To the west, a cloud of dust rose from the road at the end of his range of sight. The signature of a car headed toward him at a high rate of speed.

His heart jumped.

Whatever bore down upon him could either be carrying his salvation or his doom, but there was no way of knowing for sure until it was too late. He was fifty yards out into the open from the nearest suitable boulder to hide behind, and besides, he was completely drained. By the time he made the sprint, were he even able, the car would already be on top of him.

His legs buckled, dropping him to his knees on the shoulder of the road.

He wasn't going anywhere. All of his strength had deserted him, leaving him barely able to watch the cloud of dust growing larger beneath the late afternoon swelter, the dust merging with the clouds. A car materialized through the angry cloud stirred by its passage. It looked like a transport vehicle of some kind, painted tan to blend with the never-ending sand.

Adam plopped back onto his rear, barely able to steady himself. He swooned as a result of the heat and exhaustion. His eyes were beginning to cross of their own accord, the ground beneath him tilting back and forth.

The front grille of the cab looked almost like that of a Jeep; framed from behind by a canvas-covered cargo hold. Sunlight reflected from the front windshield as the first sounds of the engine and the pebbles clanging from the undercarriage reached his ears. He could taste the dry dust on the mild wind.

Adam toppled to his side. His arms were unresponsive, his legs crumpled beneath him. All he could see through his left eye was the sand pressed against his forehead, the blazing sun through his right. Darkness converged from the corners of his vision, forcing his eyelids closed.

It felt as though they'd only been closed a second, but when he opened them, the cloud of dust was all around him. The transport vehicle was idling on the road beside him, gushing black exhaust into the brown cloud. The frame of the truck shuddered as the engine roared; the passenger door standing ajar.

"He's one of ours!" a man yelled, dropping to his haunches.

He filled Adam's vision: camouflaged helmet; sunburned, heavily-stubbled face; white stripe across his eyes like the negative image of a raccoon; tan and brown camo fatigues. McMAHON was stenciled into the black strip over his breast pocket.

"Get him on board!" a voice bellowed from within. "Clock's tickin'!"

Adam's eyes closed again. The lids felt as though they each weighed a ton, but he finally forced them open again, his lazy eyes taking their sweet time finding the opening and focusing.

Dust exploded from the rear tires through the square of the open back flap of the cargo bed. Someone had already started an IV in his right arm, the cold saline creeping up his biceps and spilling into his chest. Another red-faced man leaned over him from the right, stethoscope hanging from his neck. He flashed a penlight into Adam's eyes, triggering him to look away.

The corrugated metal bounced and vibrated beneath him; gravel pinging in the wheel-wells, grinding under the truck's weight.

The swirling cloud of dust trailing them shifted long enough for Adam to glimpse the landscape falling away behind them. He could see the mountain he had barely survived, a cluster of strangely-formed rocks atop it like a crown. Boulders and bushes lined the hillside, and higher up, his eyes were drawn to movement. Atop a rocky ledge, four silhouettes stood out against the pale sky.

Dear God, was his last thought before unconsciousness claimed him. They're still alive.

A bend in the road returned the swell of dust, closing behind him like a mouth.

III

DENVER,
COLORADO

When Dr. Charles Eagan awoke that morning, it had felt like a day like any other. The coffee from the drive-thru stand tasted every bit as bitter as usual, the donut as dry as every day before. He'd decided on his navy blue suit and the red power tie, like he had so many times before, slicking his rich black hair perfectly into place. Thin gold-rimmed glasses framed his Pacific blue eyes, his Italian loafers buffed to a reflective shine. He'd driven the same route to work he had taken every day, parking his sleek black Lexus in the exact same spot he'd used for the last five years. Charles always believed that the measure of a man was in the details. It was a philosophy that had served him well, from graduating fourth in his class at the University of Colorado Medical School to landing a cardiology fellowship at the University Hospital in downtown Denver. Some might have called him obsessive-compulsive, but for Charles it was a gift of unerring focus. Routine eliminated surprise and promoted accomplishment.

Instinctively, there was a part of him deep down that suspected that something was amiss. He'd checked to make sure that the car doors were locked twice, and patted down his pocket to ensure he had his wallet. His watch was on his left wrist; both cufflinks were in place; his keys were in his right trouser pocket; his hospital identification badge was clipped to his shirt pocket; and the creases in his slacks were straight and firm. Yet something seemed out of the ordinary, somehow... wrong... but he'd gone through the checklist and everything was in place.

He looked up to the withering gray sky.

"Might snow," he said aloud, tugging his sleeves sharply into place.

Grabbing his soft leather briefcase, Charles strode across the reserved parking lot, walking briskly through rows of Mercedes, Beamers, Porsches, and Jaguars toward the front of the hospital. The asphalt scuffed the fine leather soles, but he'd feel better once he was in his office where he could change into the pristine loafers he kept beneath his desk.

On the north side of the hospital was a wide, stone-paved courtyard surrounding a heaping pile of snow-spotted soil where during the summer flowers of all colors bloomed to spite his allergies. Further ahead, there was a raised walkway, shielded by tinted glass, connecting the older wing to the newer construction across Ninth Avenue. Charles turned crisply to the right, taking a precise forty-five degree angle across the courtyard toward the wide set of stairs leading to the revolving doors as he did every day.

The state flag with its large C flew to the left of the American flag. A patient stood beside an ashtray to the far side of the front steps, holding onto the silver IV pole with his right hand, a thin tube connecting the drained bag to his elbow, a smoldering cigarette in his left. His powder blue gown hung past his knees, from which two pasty lower limbs stretched to bare feet as red as arterial blood. There was a woman sitting with a screaming child on one of the benches flanking the circular patio across the dead flowerbed. He could tell she'd been trying to quiet the child for quite some time as she was now squeezing the child's arm so tightly her fingers were red in contrast to his white flesh. She'd spent the night in the emergency room, he assumed, based on her ratty hair and wrinkled clothes. The only bags she'd managed to pack were the bruised-looking ones beneath her eyes. A pair of nurses sat on the opposite bench, now directly to his right as he swiftly stepped past. Both wore scrubs that had obviously belonged to surgery before they were permanently borrowed.

He snapped his wrist before him so he could read the time.

In precisely eight minutes he would be sitting in his office chair with his suit jacket draped carefully over the back, a fresh pair of indoor shoes on his feet. He would check his messages for the next seven minutes before donning his scrub top over his shirt and tie and heading for the Cath Lab, where for the following three hours he would place Swan-Ganz lines until he rotated into the OR where he'd complete one coronary artery bypass graft after another until he took a dinner break exactly at the six hour mark.

By the time he had crossed the courtyard, Charles was halfway through his work day.

Stick to the routine.

No surprises.

His right shoe clacked on the first cement stair, his hand closing around the cold iron railing that bisected them.

"Help me!" a woman screamed.

Charles stopped. There was a moment of hesitation where he was forced to close his eyes to concentrate. Don't turn around, he told himself. Just walk straight through those doors into the lobby. If you quicken your pace toward the elevator, you can make up the time you're losing right now. Let the ER staff handle this. It's their job after all.

Besides, if he turned around, he'd surely end up ruining another shirt and tie, and maybe the jacket as well. He would begin his afternoon off-schedule, and he would never be able to catch back up. And the amount of paperwork he'd have to file if he interceded…

"Please!" the woman shrieked.

The briefcase fell from Dr. Charles Eagan's hand, landing squarely on the stair. He turned around slowly to face the courtyard.

A woman ran toward him, wheeling a long tandem stroller at a full sprint. She wore a thin dress that covered her from her neck all the way to her ankles, made of an almost satiny material that reminded him of the scarves his mother had worn when he was a child. A shawl of the same material was pulled over her head, completely swaddling her hair and wrapped around her face to cover everything from the bridge of her nose to her dress. All he could see were tiny black irises set into extraordinarily wide eyes against creamy caramel skin. The sockets were sunken, the rims of her lids red, as though she hadn't slept in ages.

He looked back over his shoulder to the revolving doors.

When he turned back to her, he'd closed his eyes.

"I'm a physician," he said, shaking his head as he reopened his eyes, his attention falling to the contents of the stroller as she came to a stop at the foot of the stairs.

The seat back had been folded flat, and where he had expected to see twins sitting one behind the other, he saw instead mounds of tangled blue and pink blankets.

"What's wrong?" he asked, reaching into the stroller and tugging back the blankets.

He looked hurriedly up and into her wild eyes.

She screamed into his face in a foreign tongue.

"I can't understand you. Please... slow down. Try to..."

His stare darted back into the carriage.

There weren't two children covered under those blankets. There wasn't even one.

She continued screaming at him, the sash falling away from her mouth and allowing her words to speckle his glasses with spittle. He recognized the single word 'Allah'.

A long silver canister rested in the stroller. At first he thought it was some sort of new oxygen tank, but he realized what it was when the red LED lights started flashing sequentially.

He caught the word 'Jihad' as her fingernails tore at his cheeks.

This was really going to throw off his schedule.

A light even brighter than the sun exploded from the canister.

IV

BARSTOW,
CALIFORNIA

Evelyn plopped down on the back porch, finally removing the filthy blood- and soot-stained gloves and tossing them aside. A tower of black smoke rose from the other side of the barn, funneling up into the early dawn sky. She felt guilty for the sudden rise of hunger at the scent of so many birds cooking on the open pyre. She'd lost count at one-hundred thirteen, or maybe she'd just stopped keeping track. There had to be over two-hundred pheasants of all breeds burning to charcoal in the fire ring. That was literally thousands of dollars of their sole means of income turning to ash and blowing away into the desert. With her father unable to work and accruing medical bills, this was likely to be the straw to break the camel's back.

She didn't know what to do.

She'd failed her father. She'd failed herself.

It was only a matter of time before the creditors came calling. Then what? The medical bills were the obvious priority as her father would still need to be cared for, but she couldn't lose the house in the process. She'd considered the notion of taking out a second mortgage on the house and land, but she'd only end up using the money to pay the combined mortgage payment for the two loans. It was a stall-tactic at best. All it would do was buy them more time to sink.

The time had come to consider every alternative. If they put the house and accompanying acreage on the market now, then, even if it took a while to sell, the equity should end up being enough to balance out the deficit, but little more. What were they supposed to do then? There would be no money to pay the bills unless she got a job, and while she was at work, who would take care of her father? Without her Master's Degree, she wouldn't be qualified to work in oceanography. Even with the higher degree, it wasn't an industry that made many people rich.

"What am I supposed to do?" she whispered to the sky, holding her breath awaiting an answer she knew would never come.

Sighing, she finally dropped her chin, tears clearing lines through the caked soot.

For a fleeting moment, she wondered what might happen if the wind were to shift, blowing the flames onto the barn to eventually spread to the house. If they were well-insured, that could solve a lot of problems... Even if they were, she could only imagine her father's torment having to walk through the charred remains of his dream. The dream he had shared with her mother.

Evelyn couldn't see the coyotes anymore, but that certainly didn't mean they weren't still out there, undoubtedly circling wide around their land, preparing to converge on what must have smelled like an open invitation to a barbecue to them. An occasional howl interrupted the constant crackling of boiling blood cracking through bones in the blaze.

The smoke rose into the sky like a mighty fist preparing to smite their house.

Maybe that would just be for the be—

The ground shook beneath her with a sound like thunder.

"Daddy!" she shouted, leaping to her feet. Her first thought was to stop beneath the doorframe leading into the kitchen and ride out the quake, but she couldn't just leave her father lying in the middle of his bed to be crushed if the roof came down.

The ground steadied beneath her as she raced through the living room and into the hallway, only to begin shaking again when she grabbed the knob and threw open his bedroom door. She could hear all of the framed pictures falling from the walls and shattering behind her.

Her father was already on the floor, having pulled himself off the bed out of instinct, but he'd been unable to balance on his weak legs with the ground rising and falling beneath.

Evelyn dove beside him, wrapping her arms around his chest from behind and dragging him toward the doorway. He cried out with the pain in his hips, but right now, she knew her only priority was to get him to safety. Then she could worry about medicating him and getting him—

The ground stilled.

Evelyn's eyes met her father's.

That hadn't felt like an earthquake, not like any she'd ever experienced anyway. Usually, the shaking would go on much longer, varying in intensity. Nearing the end of a normal quake, you could almost feel the pressure abating, like an echo dissipating to nothingness. That one had gone from rumbling to stillness far too abruptly.

"Turn on the TV," her father said through gritted teeth.

"We should wait out the aftershocks before—"

"That wasn't an earthquake."

"What are you talking about? What else could it possibly—?"

"Turn on the TV, honey."

She propped him against the dresser and crawled from behind him. His face was drained of all color, making his eyes appear sunken, his cheekbones bruised. His hands shook with the pain, forcing him to finally close his eyes as she rose to her feet and crossed the room for the remote control on the nightstand.

She pressed the power switch, but there was nothing but static.

She switched channels.

Static.

She switched it again and again, unable to produce anything but black and white snow.

"My God," he gasped. "Try the radio."

Evelyn tossed the remote onto the bed, leaving the TV blaring white noise. Flipping the power on the flashing clock, she sat on the edge of the bed, her finger poised on the dial. Static hissed in stereo now.

Slowly, she combed through the stations. Nothing but fuzz.

Cranking up the volume, she went back to the beginning, this time going even slower and listening for the slightest sound. Peeling apart the multiple layers of static, intently focused on gleaning even the faintest whisper from beneath.

"There," she whispered, holding her breath as she wiggled the dial ever so slightly, then blasted the sound.

"...electrostatic discharge affecting signals... several hundred miles... of the detonation."

"Jesus," her father moaned.

"...satellite images confirm... atomic bomb, destroying... city blocks... no way to even begin estimating... casualties. Again, no contact... established with anyone... Los Angeles..."

Evelyn gasped, clapping her hands to her mouth.

A loud hiss of static.

"... Christ!" the announcer screamed. "Did you feel...? What in the name of God... earthquake in New Yor—?"

Static.

Evelyn cranked up the volume until it was deafening, standing there, holding her breath.

Nothing.

She released her breath in nervous jerks through her fingers.

The hiss of static.

Evelyn turned and sprinted out of the bedroom, tears streaming down her cheeks. She hurdled her father's legs and blew through the living room and kitchen. A fine layer of dust covered the linoleum. Swirling sand tapped at the window over the sink. Bursting through the back door, sending it pounding against the side of the house with a sound like a gunshot, Evelyn leapt from the top stair and dashed to the middle of the drive. A monstrous cloud of smoke rose over the distant mountains. It expanded to the sides, the bottom portion curling back under.

The air was thick with dirt like a sandstorm on the torturous easterly gale, the grimy texture covering her skin. Dust devils arose from the desert all around her, swirling angrily.

"What's happening?" she screamed, dropping to her knees.

The already dark sky clogged with dirt and dust, slowly cresting the mountains like a wave and thundering toward her. All around her she could smell it: the reek of burnt timber, the bitter tang of melted glass and plastic, cooked flesh.

Death.

V

BETHLEHEM,
PENNSYLVANIA

◉

Phoenix sat up in the darkness when the cement floor shivered. Concrete dust powdered from the walls and rust flaked from the rattling old pipes. The air grew heavy, pressing in on him, squeezing his body until it felt as though his flesh might burst, his bones grind to grains. Millions of screams erupted in his head as one, rising to a pitch that cut through his skull like a circular saw. Blood drained in rivulets from his ears, welling before dripping from his lobes, running down his neck. He slapped both hands over his ears, spattering fresh blood onto his cheeks.

As quickly as they had erupted, the voices ceased.

Phoenix opened his eyes, having not even realized he had pinched them tightly against the pain. A sonic thunder echoed in his mind like a concussive blow.

What had just happened?

He tried to stand up, but there was no strength in his legs. It was as though every ounce of energy had been drained from his useless form, leaving him flopped across the straw like a rag doll. Pins and needles assaulted every inch of him, a tingling beneath his skin as though his entire body was going to sleep. But it wasn't. He could feel it.

His body was becoming aware.

He didn't feel pain, but a passage, as though an ethereal wind were blowing straight through him. He could feel every cell in his body like he was composed of sentient glitter, each atom resonating with an intense sorrow that overwhelmed him, bringing a rush of tears and an expulsion of sobs. His shoulders shuddered convulsively, forcing out a long moan that took hold of his guts and threatened to turn him inside out on its way.

He'd never experienced a feeling even remotely like it before: such intense pain and sadness. Millions of lives reaching out to him before being quickly ripped away. Their scents were all around him, lingering in the room like he imagined it must be like in a subway station. So many people trying to touch him, filled with fear, confusion, and rage, buffeting him in the confines of his cell. None of their touches felt familiar, none of their smells recognizable.

With a great inhalation, he breathed them in like the swelling of a great bellows. The tingling sensation, the electric prodding… all of it disappeared as though it had never been. Normal sensation resumed, and he was again alone in the cellar. Alone in the darkness.

Alone.

He rose effortlessly to his feet, aware of the sensation of straw between his toes, the dust shaken loose from the foundation and the metallic tinge of rust forming an invisible mist. Slowly, he walked toward the lone door. A fresh crack had opened in the cement against the soles of his feet like a wound inflicted upon the earth itself. Pressing his hands on the door, he brought himself against it, the cool wood prickling the flesh on his chest. He leaned his cheek on the door, mashing his ear into the unforgiving slab of wood and held his breath to listen.

All was quiet beyond. There were no footsteps on the stairs, no hushed voices. He had never heard The Swarm leave: herded clomping through the door above. They always moved together, in unison, like an enormous centipede. He was completely unaccustomed to this kind of absolute silence. Usually, floorboards creaked above or someone crept down to his door, either just listening to him breathe or trying to plot a way to have him all for themselves.

It was too quiet. The world around him had taken in a deep anticipatory breath, waiting… waiting for something… though what he couldn't imagine.

"Is anyone out there?" he whispered, though from the chill of the door he was certain that no one was.

He tested the lock, but the door didn't budge, hardly groaning in its wooden frame. There was a small creak of transferred weight on the floor above, followed by daintily placed footsteps.

Phoenix took a small step back from the door. Even in the darkness, he could sense the exact location of his pike buried beneath the straw. Perhaps this was his chance.

The footsteps descended the stairs, slowly, gracefully, though from their sound he could tell that such large weight was unaccustomed to being borne in such a manner. Whoever was coming wanted no one else to know.

He leaned his ear against the door again. The footsteps stopped just beyond.

Phoenix looked back to his bed, debating how quickly he could make the sprint. Just because he couldn't hear The Swarm didn't mean they weren't up there. He had to plan this perfectly, for he may never get the chance again. They'd take the shiv and that would be the end.

"Who's there?" he whispered.

"Why didn't you stop it?" a weak voice whispered from the other side, a million miles away.

"Stop what?"

A hand settled gently on the knob outside.

"Don't pretend you don't know."

It was the woman. He could feel her body heat through the door, hear her rasping breaths. There was something else in her voice, something he'd never heard there before.

Fear.

"Why did they all have to die?"

Silence, broken only by a slight squeak of the doorknob.

"Are you still there?" she whispered.

Phoenix didn't know what to say. He hadn't known at the time, but that feeling he'd had… that feeling of passage through him. He'd felt them die.

"Who were they?" he whispered.

"Everyone."

She opened the door a crack, the salt from her tears creeping through on her foul breath.

"You could have stopped it," she said. "You could have saved them."

"I don't understand," he said, taking a small step away.

"They all died because of you."

He shook his head, unable to comprehend.

"New York, Los Angeles. Atlanta, Denver. All gone," she said. Her voice fell below a whisper to the point he could barely hear it. "All dead because of you."

It couldn't have been his fault. How in the world could it have been?

He dabbed at his face. His cheeks were soaked with tears.

"It's not my fault," he whispered.

"Your very birth triggered this string of events. We thought if we found you in time and hid you, we'd be able to change things. I think all we ended up doing was making it worse."

"The only thing I am faultless in is my own birth, though beyond that, I have known little but suffering. Were I able, I would gladly take it back and wish myself into the grave."

"My father read the prophecies that foretold of your birth, and he was able to find you before any of the others. Only his followers know of your existence. It's both for your protection... and our own." She sighed. "I always thought you'd be able to change things. I thought that here away from the evils of mankind, away from the all-consuming hatred, you wouldn't be able to feel its pull, and wouldn't feel the need to bring forth its end."

She opened the door wider and slipped her girth through. He could feel her in the darkness with him, her form positively trembling.

"I'm sorry we failed you," she sobbed, no longer able to contain it.

"If I am to blame, how could you have failed me?"

"We should have killed you," she whispered, staring at the floor, bangs sapped to her tear-dampened cheeks. "Then none of this would have happened. My father... my father and the others got greedy. They wanted what you have. It's your light. It's blinding to all who behold it."

"I am just a boy."

"You are more than that and you know it."

"I know nothing but what you've told me."

"Then all of this is my fault."

Phoenix listened to her meek crying. He looked to the door, which still stood ajar, then to the bed of straw. He could hardly see her silhouette in the darkness; she would never see him make a move for the sharpened spoon.

He stood there, unable to decide what to do.

In the end, he reached out and took her by the hand. She squeezed it and pulled him to her chest. It was the first time he had ever been held. The feeling was magnificent: her heart beating against his, the heat of her body wrapped around his suddenly trembling form. Her wet tears against the side of his neck. Her pain and fear raced into him electrically, as though a current flowed from her shuddering body.

He could vaguely remember her from his childhood, her voice so much younger, so full of wonder. She used to sit outside his door, though it had been a different basement in a house far away, and tell him stories of life outside his cell. His favorite had been about the cocoon she had found in the bush out back and the vibrant red butterfly that had emerged. He often fancied the darkness his cocoon, from which one day he would arise into whatever lie in wait beyond. In her own way—though she now feared him, or rather, what she thought him capable of—she loved him. He could sense that as clearly as anything he had ever felt.

"Will you help me leave this place?" he whispered.

She pulled him tighter, in an embrace only a mother might know.

"My father will never allow it," she sniffed. "He's too powerful."

Phoenix wanted to end the hug, to free himself from her arms, but at the same time, he never wanted it to end.

"He'd kill me," she whispered.

"I don't want that," he said, surprised by the truth to the words.

She sniffed back the warm sludge from his neck.

"Can you make the killing stop?" she whispered, the strength returning to her voice.

"I don't know."

Silence.

"You have no idea of the power you possess. You can do anything."

He didn't know what to say.

"More man tears," she whispered. "You told me that in a dream. You said to remind you 'after the fall.' What does it mean?"

"I wish I knew."

"I'm sorry," she said suddenly, pushing herself away from him.

"Please forgive me."

"For what?" He felt cold now away from her heat. It struck him how similar the sensations of cold and alone actually were.

"For touching you," she said, scurrying to the door. "May God have mercy on my soul."

Phoenix shook his head, unable to rationalize anything.

"I've wanted to do that since the day we found you," she said, hurriedly closing the door.

With a click, the lock engaged.

He dropped to his knees in the cold darkness. The room felt so much smaller.

Tears spilled down his cheeks.

VI

DOVER, TENNESSEE

Missy was crumpled in a heap on the couch, sobbing, when the floor began to shake. At first, she thought that it was just her trembling body... until a thunderous report grumbled through the valley. Framed pictures fell from the walls, shattering on impact. The overhead fixtures rattled. Books toppled from their shelves.

When it was all over, the silence in the house was deafening.

"Mare!" she screamed, sitting up and pawing the pooled tears from her wet eyes. She could barely see through the swelling.

He descended the stairs, arms thick with a crusting of blood to match his face.

"What was that?" he gasped, still holding the crimson sponge he'd been using to try to scrub off the mixture of his father's blood and his own. He'd tried chest compressions, but all that did was pump blood from his father's mangled jaw. Rescue breathing hadn't even been an option as there'd been no way to form a seal over what remained of his father's mouth. Yet still, he'd tried everything he could think of, breaking ribs and cracking the sternum, until finally he had no choice but to relent with an anguished scream.

The police and paramedics were on their way, though neither appeared to be in much of a hurry. It had only been a few minutes since Missy made the blubbering call, but it felt like eons had passed in the interim. They weren't supposed to touch the body. They weren't even allowed to start cleaning the mess. The police still had to investigate the scene, though Missy couldn't imagine what they thought they might find other than a single bullet somewhere in the attic.

Mare had closed the door to his father's bedroom, leaving what remained of their lineage to congeal into the carpet and bedspread.

"I don't know," Missy whispered, unable to bring herself to look at her brother.

"I've never felt anything like it."

"Plane crash?"

"Maybe."

The phone rang. Missy and Mare looked at each other. Neither wanted to answer it. They'd put in a call for Staci at work, but the lady who answered the phone said she hadn't seen her all day. Neither of them wanted to be the one to have to tell her what happened.

"I got it," Mare finally said, swallowing hard and swiping his hands on his shorts. He lifted the phone from the cradle, silencing it mid-ring. "Hello?"

He closed his eyes in anticipation of what he was sure was to follow.

"Jason?" he said, recognizing the voice. "Listen, man, now isn't the best ti—"

His face crinkled and he looked at his sister.

"What?" she asked.

"You've got to be kidding me."

"What is it?" Missy nearly screamed.

"No way! What channel?" Mare asked, then covered the phone. "Turn on the tube, sis."

"What channel?"

"Any," he said, then brought the phone back to his lips. "Look, dude, we've got problems of our own here."

"…nothing left of downtown Atlanta," the panicked voice called from the television, the background redolent with sirens. "The bomb detonated nearly simultaneously with the other three in New York, Los Angeles, and Denver. Casualties are estimated in the millions."

"Yeah, I've got it on," Mare said into the phone. "Gotta be a hoax… No, my dad, he… Sorry, Jason, I've just… just gotta go."

He dropped the phone onto the cradle with a clatter.

"What's happening?" he whispered.

On the TV was a static-lined black and white image, flickering like an old news reel. All they could see at first were treetops framed like skyscrapers against a pale gray sky. The camera bounced up and down as an enormous cloud of smoke arose from the horizon, spreading to either side as it swelled, blocking out the clouds and sun and everything else. It hovered there, roiling, swirling furiously, then exploded outward. The treetops shook violently before all of the leaves and needles were blown from their bowed branches, assaulting the camera like buckshot before the cloud rumbled through, absorbing everything in its way with a rush of smoke and dust.

"That was footage obtained from our sister station in Savannah," the reporter said. "Transmitted shortly before we lost all contact. Citizens are asked to stay in their houses and off of the roads. If you have a basement, please take your family down there and wait until authorities are able to confirm that it is safe to come back up."

"The cops aren't coming," Mare said, scratching at his blood-knotted arm hairs.

"A state of national emergency has been declared. Please stay off of your phone lines unless it's an absolute emergency so as not to overload the circuits and help emergency units to be available for those in dire need of help."

"Aunt Mary lives in Atlanta," Missy said.

A raging wind kicked up outside, the walls and floorboards of the old house groaning in protest. Debris hammered the windows, the wind screaming in through the weakened seals.

"Army and National Guard units are scrambling to get to the sites of the tragedies, while the Red Cross has already begun setting up relief stations in neighboring communities to help the survivors. All medical personnel are asked to join their efforts to treat the thousands of victims expected to show up with mild to severe radiation poisoning and injuries of all kinds."

"What are we supposed to do, Mare?"

"I… I don't know. We don't have a basement…"

"We now go live to the Capitol Building in Washington D.C. where the President is expected to arrive shortly to brief a stunned nation."

The image switched to a podium beside an American flag. Various uniformed military bigwigs milled behind, in front of the seal of the President of the United States, while countless reporters fought in front of the camera for seating.

"Get in the closet!" Mare snapped, grabbing Missy by the hand and jerking her toward the front door. He opened the door to the left and shoved her inside.

"What about you?" she screamed.

"I'm right behind you!" Mare shouted as he grabbed the coats and hangers and threw them out onto the floor. He dashed through the living room and kitchen into the garage, slamming into the workbench in his hurry. He grabbed the staple gun from the shelf by the paint thinner and knelt. Under the worktop was a shelf littered with half-empty gallons of paint, atop which were crumpled several large plastic drop-cloths. He snatched them and ran back into the house, throwing them toward the closet, on his way past and up the stairs.

Without even looking at the closed door to their father's bedroom, he grabbed the doorknob of the closet beside it and yanked. On the second shelf was a stack of folded blankets, which he pulled to his chest before bounding back down the stairs.

"Where are you going?" Missy sobbed.

"I'll be right there!"

Leaping the plastic sheets, he sprinted into the kitchen and turned on the sink, shoving the blankets under the stream of water, soaking them thoroughly before hurrying back to the closet.

"Get under the blankets!" he yelled, throwing them to the floor by Missy with a wet slap.

The front door blew inward, slamming into the open closet door. A flood of leaves and dirt raced in on the wind, scattering across the living room floor. Mare grabbed the drop-cloths before the gale could steal them away and rushed to the closet, fighting to open it against the pressure applied by the front door. He slipped inside and the front door slammed the closet door with a bang. Spreading out the plastic sheet, he started stapling it to the doorframe, trying to stretch it tight as he went to seal off the doorway behind the shut door. Stapling and stapling, cracking through the shoddy trim, he squeezed the handle over and over until it simply clicked.

Outside the closet he heard the crash of the television falling from its stand.

Tossing the spent stapler into the corner, he dropped to the floor beside Missy, jerking the wet blankets over his hunched shoulders. The water soaked through his clothes, matting his hair to his head. The humidity was unbearable, almost like trying to breathe beneath a lake.

"How did you know to do this?" Missy whispered.

"What makes you think I have any idea what I'm doing?"

He'd meant it to sound like a joke.

"What about dad?" Missy asked. "Are we just supposed to leave him up there?"

"Do you have a better idea?"

She lowered her head, closing her eyes. It was already starting to get hot.

"How long do we have to stay in here?"

"I don't know if we have to at all. It's not like the plastic—or even the walls for that matter—will protect us from the radiation, but if there's some sort of germ warfare going on out there, we just might get lucky."

Silence descended between them, scarred only by their heavy, wet breathing. Missy's mind conjured an image of Hansel and Gretel in the witch's oven. It was getting harder and harder to tell whether the wetness covering her was from the blanket or her own perspiration.

The front door banged into the closet door at the wind's urging.

"What do you think's going to happen?" Missy whispered.

"I don't know."

"Do you think we're going to war now?"

"I'm not sure. For all I know, they could be nuking the entire Middle East right now."

Missy was quiet for a long moment.

"Is it wrong to hope they do?" she asked, so quietly that her voice merged with the wind.

"I don't know," Mare said. "I hope not, 'cause I hope they nuke 'em all."

"Me, too," she said softly. "I wish it didn't have to come to that."

"Sometimes to save lives, you've got to be willing to take them." He fell silent. "How many people would have been saved today if we'd already blasted them all to hell?"

"That's genocide."

Mare nodded beneath the blanket, loosing streams of sweat from his brows.

Missy placed a hand on his, squeezing tightly.

"We'll get through this," he said, trying to keep his voice firm as the tears finally came. "You and me, Miss. We'll be fine."

"It isn't just us that I'm worried about," she whispered. "What's going to happen to all of us? What's going to happen to our souls?"

VII

EUGENE, OREGON

The lamp on the stand behind Ray flickered. The disc in the CD player skipped almost imperceptibly. Outside, the bug zapper flared with a bright blue light from a surge of power.

"What was that?" Tina asked. Her cheeks were already blushed from the alcohol.

"I think I felt the ground shake," April said.

"Couldn't have," Rick said. "We're too far north of the fault lines. Must have been a truck passing or something."

"I didn't hear a truck," Tina said.

"You're halfway gone. A truck could park on your forehead and you'd miss it."

"Don't be a jerk, Rick," Ray said.

"I think she's right," Darren said. "I felt something too."

"You're just saying that because you've got a thing for her," Rick said.

"No, really." Darren rose from the couch. He swayed momentarily, fighting to regain his equilibrium. "I'm positive I felt something."

"Have you forgotten this is Oregon?" Rick snapped. "When was the last time—?"

"Wait," Jill said. She closed her eyes to focus her auditory senses. "Listen…"

Ray turned down the music.

There was the snapping and popping of bugs frying outside, crackling like kernels of corn in hot oil. The wind had risen as well, swinging the blue light like a lantern on a trolley. Dry leaves tumbled along the shingles, racing down the gutters. Another sound lurked beneath, a resonant thunder vibrating beneath the patter of rain blowing against the siding like pebbles.

There was something else, nearly indistinguishable from the wailing wind.

Someone was crying.

Jill rose and turned around, jerking open the curtains behind the couch.

Mandy Lewis, jet black hair beneath her almost white locks, was crumpled on the lawn in front of the sorority house, face buried in her hands. Liz and Sarah stood over her, looking helplessly at each other before kneeling and wrapping their arms around her.

"Something happened to Mandy," Jill said, unable to tear her gaze away. Anything at all going wrong over there brought the sobering effects of her waking nightmare.

They all jumped when the phone rang.

"Get the phone!" Rick barked.

"I've got to go see if Mandy's okay," Tina said, staggering toward the door.

The phone rang again.

"For the love of God, man! Get the phone!"

"Settle down," Ray snapped, crawling toward the computer table. "You could always get up and get it yourself, you know!"

Jill watched Tina shuffling between parked cars, hair already wet, the wind buffeting her sideways as she crossed the street without looking. The wind shifted too quickly, hammering the window with raindrops that sounded like hail, then ripping them away on the same breath.

"Hello?" Ray answered, sliding beside Jill to watch his girlfriend out the window. Tina was across the street and on the lawn now. She held her right hand over her eyes to shield them from the rain. "Oh… Hi, mom."

"Something's wrong," Jill said, her hand trembling as she drew the curtains further back.

"No, I haven't. We've been—"

The wind picked up with a roar, nearly knocking the group of girls from their feet. Tina started to fall, but caught herself on Sarah's shoulder. Jill could only think of her vision… of corpses piled atop each other where her sorority sisters stood at that very moment. She reached out and touched the glass over Tina.

It was warm.

"No way!" Ray said, turning from the window and clapping his free hand over his left ear. "You've got to be—"

Static buzzed in his ear.

"Mom…?" he whispered, then louder: "Mom!"

"What is it?" April asked.

"Come on, Gorman. It's your turn," Rick said.

"Mom?" He hung up the receiver. "We got cut off."

"Is everything okay?" April asked, tension forcing its way through her voice.

Ray had noticeably paled.

"My mom… she said terrorists hit LA."

"Seriously?" Rick shouted. "Turn on the TV!"

Ray looked past Jill out the window. Tina was hurrying back across the street, arms wrapped around her chest, face down to shield it from the pounding rain.

Darren grabbed the remote control from the coffee table and turned on the television.

"…in an unprecedented attack on the most powerful nation in the world…"

Darren switched the channel.

"…Al-Qaeda operatives have already claimed responsibility for…"

Click.

"…the devastation. All we can clearly see through the massive wall of smoke is that there are no buildings left standing in downtown Manhattan."

"Mom?" Ray gasped.

Click.

"Turn it back!" Ray shouted.

Click.

"…five boroughs, roughly thirty times the population of Hiroshima in 1945, when nearly one hundred forty thousand people were killed. The crater is estimated to be roughly six miles in diameter, with the shockwaves from the blast being felt hundreds of miles to the north past the Canadian border."

"Oh, God," Ray sobbed, dropping to his knees.

Tina burst through the front door, the wind rushing past her.

"Mandy just found out that terrorists nuked Atlanta," she said, spitting through the sheen of water soaking her face. "Her family lives down there."

She looked to Ray, who was curled in fetal position on the floor.

"They got New York, too," Darren said softly.

"Ray…" she cried, dropping atop him and wrapping her arms around him.

"…details are still unclear, but massive amounts of radiation exposure should be expected within five miles from the edges of the blast zone. Late effects may be felt as far west as Philadelphia, and there's no way of knowing how long it will take the biological damage to manifest itself."

"They're probably fine," Tina whispered, stroking Ray's hair. She looked to the others with tears mingling into the streams of rainwater draining down her face.

"Guys…" Jill whispered.

"…officials have vowed that reprisals will be swift and proportionate…"

The bug zapper flared with blinding light and a sound like stomped bubble wrap.

"…reports indicate that nuclear-armed warships are already in place in the Middle East and awaiting the order…"

"Guys!" Jill screamed.

"What is it, Jill?" April shouted, whirling to see what had her friend so panicked.

What looked like a baseball bounced in the middle of the street, followed quickly by two more. The front yard was already dotted with them.

There was a bang on the roof. Then another. The crash of a shattered window and the wail of a car alarm. The banging grew so loud that it was all they could hear. Even shouting over it proved to be to no avail. Hailstones bounced from the hoods and roofs of the parked cars outside, leaving dents that could hold grapefruit halves.

A loud boom from upstairs.

Ray whirled in time to see a ball of ice bounce down the staircase onto the landing.

One of the upstairs windows shattered.

"Everyone get away from the window!" Darren screamed.

He grabbed April by the arm and yanked her from the couch, sending her sprawling to the floor. His next move was to reach for Jill, but before he could, the window shattered, dropping piles of wicked shards onto the couch, throwing smaller fragments into the room.

Jill screamed and whirled away, covering her head with her arms. Streams of warm blood already coursed down her forearms from slanted gashes. Hail the size of fists fired through the open window, striking their soft flesh hard enough to draw unheard wails of agony.

The drumming from the roof was deafening.

Slowly, the barrage of hail tapered off until it sounded like a dripping faucet from the heavens slapping what remained of the tattered roof, cracking on the sidewalk outside.

Jill rose, glancing across the demolished living room. Tina lay atop Ray, moaning. There was a tangle of hair knotted with blood where one of the stones had bludgeoned her above the right ear. Darren had managed to scurry across the shattered glass to cover April, his bleeding hands trembling atop his head.

Jill didn't see Rick at first, not until she took her first step toward the remnants of the shattered window and noticed his wide eyes peering up at her from beneath the coffee table. She crawled across the couch, knocking dozens of cue-balls to the floor, glass fragments grinding beneath her knees, slicing open the thick skin covering her kneecaps.

A few straggling hailstones struck outside like the last lingering effects of a meteor shower. It looked as though there was a good three inches of snow covering the lawn and cars.

Car alarms were drowned out only by sirens rising from the night.

Jill screamed.

Across the street, Mandy, Liz, and Sarah lie still on the lawn, piled atop each other. Crimson flowed freely from a hole in Mandy's head like a toppled bucket. The bruises were already blossoming on her skin like spots on a Dalmatian. Neither of the other two moved, though from the way Liz's lower leg bent to the side, revealing the sharpened ends of the splintered tibia and fibula, Jill didn't suspect that they might any time soon.

"Is everyone okay?" Rick asked sheepishly as he crawled out from under the table.

"Tina!" Ray yelled, rolling out from beneath her and slapping her cheek. Twin rivulets of blood rolled from the wound down to her chin. "Wake up! Tina!"

The bug zapper still glowed a sickly blue. One of the thin vertical bulbs flickered and died. With a loud snap, a spark popped between the lights. Then another. And another, until it started to more closely resemble a fountain firecracker.

Jill looked through the shattered window frame, jagged shards protruding from the rubber seam like a wolf's teeth. The bodies across the street. Still. Unmoving.

Her vision assaulted her.

"We have to get out of here," she whispered, chest starting to heave.

She whirled and faced the others, oblivious to the blood running down her forehead from the seam along her hairline.

"We have to get out of here!" she screamed at the top of her lungs.

CHAPTER 4

I

NORTHERN IRAN

In another life, Death had known this ranch well. His grandparents had toiled in the sand, trying to grow vegetation where it had never been meant to grow, herding goats through the barren desert, leading them between small pockets of wild grasses. He had never been this far down the dirt road, especially this close to the main house. The memories of that life were now only spectral reminders of a dying world, and what he had become did not come back to reminisce.

He led them past the side of the house, which now appeared far smaller than it had through the wide eyes of his youth. The masters were within behind boarded windows, cowering beneath the floor in shelters that would never withstand what was to come. He didn't feel pity for them, nor did he feel anger. Though they had whipped his body to within inches of the afterlife, he didn't wish what was to come upon them. They were simply flickering flames atop candles down there in the dusty darkness, and with a single breath they would be extinguished.

Even the bleating child, whose cries he could feel beneath the sand under foot as his mother tried to comfort him, held no emotional sway. Their souls would soon be released to join with God, where there would no longer be any pain.

Death led the others past the house toward the structure behind, listening to the scuffle of their tread across the windblown sand. A long barn stood at the rear of the homestead, a rickety wooden structure more than a hundred feet long, surrounded by a split-rail fence that enclosed more than an acre of sand and weeds gnawed all the way to the ground. He had never been allowed here as a child, yet he knew this was where he was supposed to come. Frantic neighing and whinnying erupted from inside as the occupants sensed their approach.

They moved like shadows, dust blowing sideways from their heels, leaving scorched earth in their wake.

Pounding hooves echoed from within amidst equine screams.

Death stopped before the front doors of the stable, where he lowered his black head and knelt before the structure. The others stayed behind him, their long shadows stretching past him.

He raised his right fist to the sky, which responded with a crash of thunder. The clouds grew darker, racing in circles around them in the stratosphere, grumbling angrily. Slamming it down into the ground, it parted easily, allowing his arm into the crusted sand well past his elbow.

He jerked it back like a rattler from a gopher's den, a circular clay disc in his palm.

Reverently, he held it from his body, symbol-etched side to the sky, and laid it before him on the well-tread sand. The sky roiled and coughed, causing the ground to tremble. A bolt of lightning stabbed from the clouds, striking the center of the seal. Connected to the sky, the stream of electricity snapped back and forth, warring between the earth and the heavens. The ground shuddered and the sky boomed, the lightning trying madly to tear free.

With an explosion of thunder, the seal split down the middle. The electrical lance drilled into the ground, splitting the hard tundra, a crack racing away from the point of the impact toward the barn door, and then beneath. The earth opened behind it in a soundless scream, molten lava spilling forth like blood.

The lightning bolt vanished back into the clouds, which slowly dissipated like ripples from a cannonball.

Flames caught on the weathered wood, racing up the doors toward the roof.

Death rose from his knees, planting one foot to either side of the seething fissure. Reflected flames flashed across his serpentine eyes, shimmering on his scaled flesh.

The animals within bucked and thrashed, kicking hooves through the decrepit walls. Their screams sounded almost human. The desert trembled beneath the contained stampede. Smoke poured out the small windows from each stall, flames creeping up the outer walls toward the roof, where the raging tongues already chased the thick black ashes fifteen feet into the sky. Sections of the charcoaled thatch crumbled inward, releasing a swell of curling blackness into the sky, showering the hay-lined stables with fiery embers. The smell of burnt hair crept out from beneath the closed doors, followed by the mouthwatering aroma of cooking meat.

"Rebirth," Death said. "Baptism by fire."

The doors exploded outward, blasting flames and smoldering chunks of burning wood across them where they stood. An enormous stallion charged through the billowing smoke, flames rising from his long mane.

Death moved fluidly: taking a step to the side and then reaching for the burning strip of hair. He was jerked from his feet, but before the burning beast could rise to buck him, Death was astride him, fists curled into his burning mane, legs gripping his smoldering sides. The steed bolted another ten yards before his front legs crumpled, driving his snout into the sand.

Dust swirled around them, blending with the ashen smoke.

Though it lie still, the stallion still burned, issuing flames up Death's arms, small fires burning from the beast's long tail and eyelashes. Its heaving breaths and pounding heart shuddered and then stilled between Death's thighs. As the flesh cooked, it blackened and sloughed off, breaking apart and disintegrating on contact with the sand. Yet Death still sat atop its back, engulfed in flames as muscle gave way to bone, burning until there was nothing of substance left to consume. A smoldering, scorched skeleton, held together by knotted joints of cartilage, knelt beneath its master as though praying before an altar.

"Arise, Harbinger," Death said in a voice that boomed like an avalanche.

Flames burst from the blackened eye sockets, flaring with sentience. Snorting twin plumes of smoke from what remained of its nostrils, the stallion rose to its feet with Death perched on its exposed vertebral column, knees pressed to its scapulae. Wisps of fire crackled from the spinous processes of its long neck where once the lush mane had grown, a matching tail flaring from the stub of the terminal end of the spine.

Death grabbed hold of the flames with his reptilian claws and gave them a stern tug.

Harbinger made a screaming sound like wind through a tunnel and rose to its full height on bony hind legs, exposing its vacant abdomen, the charred ribcage enclosing nothing but emptiness. It flailed at the air with its front legs, capped with the smoking remains of its hooves, before slamming them to the ground with force enough to cause waves in the sand.

It lowered its head and blasted steam from above its bared teeth, melting the sand to glass. Tendrils of flame crawled over its brow from the white hot orbs within the sockets.

Death trotted the beast in a circle until he again faced the blackened barn, drifting in and out of the smoke that consumed it. War rode from the flames atop an enormous mare, his crimson armor scored with scorch marks. Spikes jutted from the beast's neck where the mane had once been: twin sharpened rows forming a ridge of V's like so many gazelle's horns. He held a pair of the spines underhand in his fists as though curling them, razor-sharp ridges protruding from his knuckles. Flames lapped the mare's frontal bone from eyes that burned redder than a branding iron. It exuded power with its wide stance, burning eyes seeing everything at once. The sand caught fire where its hooves stabbed the earth.

With War upon it, the mare towered over Death and his steed. Its name was Thunder, for with each fearful stride, the heavens shook.

Famine followed through the belching midnight cloud atop a skeletal mare. No fire burned in its hollow sockets, only a rich blackness that sucked in the light with ebon rays like tendrils. Smoke as black as the breath of a charnel fire poured in a steady stream from its nostrils. Bramble filled its mane, riddled with thorns and barbs that snaked around its master's wrists like reins. Thistle trailed as a long tail from its haunches, dragging the ground, grinding even the smallest grains of sand to dust. Scourge was its name, for in its passage the earth itself grew infertile for all but the most feral of vegetation; greenery metamorphosing into inedible briars.

Locusts crawled beneath Famine's taut flesh like wriggling tumors. The smaller mare clopped forward, sending a wall of dust along the wind in its wake, sidling up to the others with a snort and a shake of its head.

Pestilence was the last to emerge from the burning stables before the roof collapsed with an explosion of fiery embers. The walls toppled behind the transformed steed, blasting a gust of smoke and flames across the stallion and its diminutive rider. Its master's mummified body perched atop its strong back, from which an inordinate amount of ribs emerged. Serpentine tails grew from its skeletal neck like so many hairs, slithering all the way over the crown of the skull between eyes like the reflective surface of a placid mountain lake, held in spherical drops despite gravity. Ripples crossed through the water as though something swam beneath. Its long tail was crocodilian, swishing from side to side as it dragged through the sand. Twin ridges tapered from the pelvis to where they joined at the tip of the tail, which lightened in color steadily until it became indistinguishable from the desert sand.

The writhing tails forming the creature's mane lightened as well, constricting around Pestilence's tiny wrists until her arms disappeared beneath the slithering bodies.

The stallion's name was Harvester, for its station was to separate the souls of the deceased from their flesh, leaving their carcasses to feed the ranks of the damned.

As one, the four riders turned to face the north. Smoke from the burning barn blew sideways across them, alternating between hiding and revealing their inhuman visages.

With a yank on the flowing, fiery mane, Death spurred Harbinger to its hind legs, kicking and screaming like a chorus of strangling children.

The smoke enveloped them.

When the wind arose to chase the lingering cloud of ash to the east, the horsemen were gone. A trail of fire burned in a straight line atop the sand to the south, while a wide path of blackened, smooth sand crossed the desert to the west.

A small circle of clay lie smashed in a dozen pieces amidst myriad hoof prints.

The sixth seal had been broken, rattling the gates of heaven and hell alike.

The end was at hand.

II

When consciousness returned to Adam, he thought he was dead. He couldn't find the strength to open his eyes, and there was nothing lurking behind his closed lids but darkness. At first he thought the roaring sound that surrounded him was surely the fires of hell, but he rationalized them to be jet engines by the high-pitched scream piercing the constant thunder. It was then that the pain descended upon him, convincing him once and for all that he was still alive.

His throat burned as though someone had shoved a flaming sword down his trachea. There was no specific pain, but a generalized ache that went from the blistered tips of his toes to his throbbing head. It felt like he had the world's worst hangover, a sign of severe dehydration.

Adam coughed.

"Hey!" a voice called over the roaring turbines. "Welcome back to the land of the living!"

His eyelids were thrust open, a penlight stabbed first into his right retina, then his left.

"Equal and reactive," the man said. He was a blot of shadow against a smear of orange glare. "You're lucky those boys came across you back there or some vulture would be flossing its teeth of you by now."

Adam peeled his tongue from the roof of his mouth.

"Where…?" he retched, pinching his face and grabbing his throat.

"You're thirty-five thousand feet above the Atlantic Ocean, my friend. Again, you're

169

about the luckiest man alive. A chopper went down outside of Tehran on a training mission. Otherwise you'd still be on the shores of the Caspian Sea waiting for an airlift to Frankfurt."

"Every—," he coughed, "all right?"

"Oh yeah," the medic said. Though Adam's eyes had yet to adjust to the light, he could tell from the man's voice that he was smiling. "Between you, me, and the wall, one of the kids we picked up from the 'crash' site was a Private named Rutherford. You know, General Rutherford's son? I'd be surprised if the chopper ever even left the ground, let alone wrecked. That right there tells me everything I need to know about what's about to go down. A Three-star General gets his boy airlifted directly back to the 'States, bypassing the standard medical once-over in Germany? I wouldn't want to be one of them towel-heads tonight! No, sir!"

Adam felt his eyes rolling back into his head, but he fought it.

From the man's candor and slang, Adam was sure he was an army grunt, which meant that they were more than likely in the cargo hold of one of those behemoth transport planes.

"Name's Kyle Norman," he said, shaking Adam's limp hand. "Fifth infantry. Four hundred and first. Like Stormin' Norman from Desert Storm. No relation. Too bad, though. If he was my old man, I'd sure as shootin' be treating sunburns on Virginia Beach instead of lugging GI's halfway across the world.

"I guess I should thank my good graces that I wasn't stateside today. Especially 'round Atlanta. All things considered, I suppose I'm probably safest in the air anyway."

"Atlanta?" Adam rasped, struggling against his sinking lids.

"Just came over the wire. Terrorists hit Atlanta. Denver, LA, and New York, too. A-bombs like we used on the Japs in dubya–dubya two." He paused, for the first time his voice bereft of levity. "Like I said, man. I wouldn't want to be no Arab right now."

Adam's lids closed. It had to be a dream. His grandparents lived near Denver. It couldn't possibly…

"That's right!" the medic said.

"Hmm?"

Adam's eyes rolled momentarily downward.

"You were talking in your sleep, buddy. You kept saying 'Norman's here.'" He beamed and clapped a hand on Adam's shoulder. "I didn't realize I'd had such a profound effect on you."

"No," Adam whispered, his voice garbled by gravel. His irises fluttered skyward. "More man tears. The boy said 'More man tears.'"

Darkness swelled again, stealing him away from the roar of the engines. The voices of the other grunts faded to nothingness, and again, Adam landed in the middle of a dream.

Before him stood a house like any other built in the '50's. It was a single-level, rectangular creation with wood showing through the weathered light blue paint. The roof was missing shingles, those having fallen rotting beneath the unkempt juniper hedges. Through the dead and brown lower branches, Adam could see the window wells had been filled with concrete. The lawn was yellow and infested with shin-high crabgrass. A single garage sat to the left of the house at the end of a cracked driveway, from which clumps of weeds grew unchecked. A flap of screen had peeled loose from the front door, which itself hung slightly askew. The blinds were drawn tight over the front windows, blackened so as to let light neither in nor out.

Adam took a step forward, his hand reaching of its own accord for the chain-link fence framing the front yard. He pulled it back with a rusted squeal and stepped into the yard. The ground leading to the porch was beaten flat into a dead stretch of worn earth, guiding him smoothly up the single step onto the concrete pad that passed for a porch. A brown, heavily-bristled welcome mat sat before the front door, leaves from the prior fall rotting in spider webs in the corners. Pulling back the screen door, he raised a fist and brought it down on the front door three times. The door shivered and slowly opened inward.

Darkness crept out on stale breath reeking of death, issuing a loud buzzing sound.

A handful of unnaturally large, bloated flies tapped at his face. He swatted them aside and stepped into the house, letting the screen door slam awkwardly into the frame behind him. He fumbled at the wall to his left, toggling the light switch several times, but no light ever came.

The smell of remains was all around him: a vile, pungent stench that dripped down the back of his throat from his sinuses like battery acid. A darkness as thick as mud embraced him, ushering him deeper into the house. The floor was tacky, each footstep peeling from the hardwood flooring as though coated with molasses. Adam was a dozen steps in, waving his arms in front of him to keep from wandering headlong into something, when the front door closed silently behind him, culminating in a solid thunk of the bolt burrowing into the wall.

Eyes snapped open all around him, twin slits of phosphorescent yellow focusing on him from the periphery of the room. None so much as blinked, mottled gray and black irises causing him to shiver.

A door burst open ahead of him at the back of the room, the doorknob pounding into the drywall beside it.

"You've got to hurry!" someone screamed. "The change is coming!"

The eyes turned to focus on the source of the voice.

"More man tears!" the voice railed. "We're running out of time! We have to find 'more man tears' before they—" The door slammed closed again, silencing the voice like a guillotine. The eyes turned back to Adam.

The buzzing resumed louder than ever, though this time more rhythmic. Buzz… buzz…

"Get up!" Norman screamed into his face, jerking him up by two handfuls of his shirt.

Adam stared into the man's wide eyes, blinking his way back to consciousness.

It sounded as though the plane was flying through a wind tunnel. The scream of the wind-shear was nearly deafening. A red light blinked over the side door of the plane, flashing in unison with the buzzing sound.

"We're going down!" Norman shouted, voice cracking.

He hauled Adam from the gurney and staggered backward. The floor rose and fell beneath them, forcing Adam's weak legs to drop him to his knees, but Norman still dragged him forward. Bags, helmets, and anything else not strapped down slid past them down the increasingly steep slope toward the nose of the plane.

"Help me!" Norman shouted over his shoulder.

Dozens of men were strapped into the jump-seats to either side of the cabin, dressed in desert camouflage, helmets pulled down so far that all that could be seen were their eyes. Some were wild with fear, others shut so tightly their faces were a mess of wrinkles. To a man, they clenched the shoulder harnesses in both fists, gritting their teeth against what was to come.

One of the men unfastened his harness and launched himself toward Adam, seizing him beneath his right arm while Norman took his left. They hauled him onto one of the black vinyl seats, slipping his arms through the straps and buckling them together across his chest.

"Keep your head down!" the man shouted at Adam, then buckled himself into the adjacent seat. Norman buckled in on the other side of Adam.

Blood dripped into Adam's lap, welling inside his elbow from where he'd been ripped free of his IV.

"What's going on?" Adam yelled, his heart leaping as the floor dropped beneath them.

"I don't know!" Norman shouted back. "All instrumentation failed and it felt like we were rammed from behind!"

Adam was wide awake now, unable to so much as blink. Beneath the screaming wind he heard a man reciting the Lord's Prayer at the top of his lungs. The turbine engines died with a sound like an agonized wail in reverse. The feeling of weightlessness was intense, as was the suddenly conspicuous lack of the roaring engines to keep them aloft. Adam looked at the soldiers directly across from him, lips moving over unheard prayers and desperate bargaining. The clouds were slanted through the porthole windows behind them, angry black storm-heads swelling like a tsunami. Blue bolts of lightning crackled from their bellies as they outraced the plane, bucking the tail end from behind and nearly inverting the plane before tossing it out of the way.

Adam closed his eyes and prayed.

III

The Persian
Gulf

The USS Talon, mightiest of the Virginia-class aircraft carriers, floated twenty miles off the Kuwaiti shore awaiting orders. No pilots scrambled atop the deck readying for takeoff. None of the fighter jets would even be required for what the President would soon call The Campaign to End All Campaigns on a nationally televised address. The Talon's orders were simple: maintain a visible presence until the submarines were in place, and then get the hell out of there.

They didn't want to be anywhere remotely close when those subs delivered their payload.

The USS Liberator was stationed a thousand yards to the left; the HMS Brittania a thousand yards to the right. For the last twenty-four hours, fishing and other commercial boats had been passing between them, loaded to the gills with refugees. They were like rats jumping overboard before the whole ship sank. While the operation was still technically considered top-secret, there was no mistaking what was about to happen. With the war shifting onto American soil, the mass casualties from the attacks on Atlanta, Denver, Los Angeles, and New York, the conflict needed to be resolved quickly and decisively. The world needed to see that any direct attack on America and her people would not be tolerated.

Each of the Seawolf-class nuclear-powered subs was armed with eight long-range ballistic missiles with 750 kiloton cobalt-59 doomsday devices capable of complete annihilation of anything within a forty kilometer radius. With a half-life of 5.26 years, any life form not killed by the strategically targeted missiles would be subjected to acute radiation poisoning, and the desert deemed inhabitable until the fission-activated cobalt-60 decayed. When the dust finally settled, there would be absolutely nothing left to war against.

Tensions were exceedingly high aboard the USS Talon as Gabe Wilcox would attest. He was a senior foreign correspondent with The Washington Post, a position he'd earned during the Gulf War in '91. This was his first tour on a destroyer since he ended his military career as a Seaman First Class following the invasion of the Falklands. His sea-legs had apparently abandoned him sometime in the interim, which was why he was now leaning over the railing, feeding the fish what remained of his lunch.

Until the prior evening, he'd been poised to move on Baghdad with the hundred and twentieth advance infantry. They were to begin Operation: Reclamation the following morning, moving via Bradley vehicle in the midst of a tank convoy into the heart of the beast to put an end to the Syrian atrocities. And he, Gabe Wilcox, senior correspondent, was not only going to get a front row seat, but he was also going to be giving his first live broadcast for CNN. The 'Post wasn't small potatoes, but this was the big time. This would be his audition into the elite world of journalism, halfway to Dan Rathers's desk.

When the order had come through to fall back, at first he'd thought that was the end of his dreams of glory, but when his air retrieval deposited him on the mother of all aircraft carriers, he knew that though he may have been a hundred and fifty miles southwest, he was still on the front line. History was about to be made and he had the perfect vantage. Not since Truman's decision ended the war for Japan in 1945 had there been a moment this monumental.

He was certain the planet would see its first true nuclear holocaust and he would be fortunate enough to be the first to share the news.

Gabe's crew, consisting of a single cameraman, Dave, and a tech named Peter, who could relay a signal through a network of satellites like most people could dial a phone, had been topside all morning broadcasting images of the Iraqis fleeing the Middle East by whatever means they could manage. They even had great footage of an inflatable raft carrying more than twenty refugees, packed like matches in a matchbook, sinking due to the absurd weight while women and children were sacrificed to the ocean for the sake of the others. It was human tragedy at its finest, though nothing compared to what was still to come.

The Gabe Wilcox who'd earned his stripes exposing the terrible conditions of the Iraqi people under Saddam Hussein's rule would have been sickened by the new Gabe Wilcox, who watched boatload after boatload of men, women, and children pull beside the carrier, screaming for help, pleading to be hauled aboard, falling into the ocean while pawing at the smooth steel hull, searching for a single handhold.

"The new Gabe Wilcox is going to win the Pulitzer," he said aloud, not caring whether anyone had heard him or not.

He swiped his silver bangs back into place and adjusted his thin, gold-rimmed glasses. His dark blue eyes matched the cresting waves surrounding him. Blotting the corners of his mouth with the underside of his tie, he tucked it back beneath the gray Washington Post jacket and smiled out upon the choppy waters.

The XO hadn't been above deck in hours and even then the captain had looked like he labored under the weight of the world, the tips of his bushy black mustache fading to gray.

"Gabe!"

He turned to see Dave the cameraman running toward him, camera tucked beneath his arm. Dave was fresh out of school with his L.L. Bean-bought cammo top, khaki shorts, and Teva sandals over wool socks. His face was burned bright red in contrast to his Norwegian-white hair. He pulled up in front of Gabe, looked cautiously back over his shoulder, then leaned in close.

"I've got news," he whispered into Gabe's ear, again glancing back.

"Not here!" Gabe snapped, grabbing Dave by the sleeve and tugging him over behind the nose of the nearest F-14. "Now spill it."

"I have it on good authority," Dave whispered, repeatedly checking to see if anyone at all was within earshot, "that these ships are just here for show."

"For what reason?"

"Keep your voice down!" Dave said. "If anyone finds out that this leaked, we'll both be swimming home."

Gabe mimed zipping his lips and tossing the key overboard.

"Okay, so here's the deal: we're decoys. Show 'em the left, bring the right, you know?" Dave looked nervously to either side. Gabe couldn't blame him. If this was leading where he thought it might, this was dangerous information indeed. "Right now, there's an entire fleet of nuclear-armed subs headed this way from the Philippines. When we get the go ahead, we turn and run, while the subs blow this whole area to smithereens."

"You're sure of this?"

"Dead."

"If they give the order to fall back, we'll miss the whole thing!"

"Are you out of your mind? That's good news!"

"I want this on camera."

"You'll be able to see this from a thousand miles away!"

"But we won't be the closest—"

"But we'll be the first," Dave said. A sly smile crept across his face. "The moment the order comes through, we go live under a bogus story. We'll be able to catch it when it happens."

"Did you sell it to the network?"

"That's what Peter's doing at this very moment."

"What's the hook?"

"We lead with the sinking raft images, then focus on the refugees. That ought to be a nice human-interest angle to lead into the... well, to what's going to happen next."

Gabe beamed. His heart rate accelerated, pumping pure adrenaline.

"I'll let you hold my Pulitzer," Gabe finally said, clapping Dave on the shoulder.

"Are you kidding? I won't have time for that with all of the offers that'll be pouring in for me!"

"Ha!" Gabe whooped triumphantly, fist held high in the air.

"Shh!" Dave hissed, though he couldn't hold back his toothy grin. "Not yet. We're going to need a good twenty minutes of lead so the other networks don't get wind from our broadcast."

"Well... What are you waiting for?"

"You're the boss."

"Let's make history," Gabe said, snatching the microphone and cord from Dave.

He walked to the edge of the deck, feeling his stomach rising, but he forced it down.

"How do I look?"

"Aces," Dave said.

"The hair?" Gabe patted the hair-sprayed crown.

"Perfect as always."

"On my mark then," Gabe said. He took a deep breath and blew it slowly out, shaking his hands to spread the blood flow. "Pulitzer time in five... four... three..."

"This is Gabe Wilcox on the deck of the USS Talon, the most fearsome aircraft carrier to ever sail the sea. Twenty miles to the northwest is the Kuwaiti shore, barely a line on the horizon from where we are stationed in the Persian Gulf. Even the Iraqis thousands of miles from U.S. soil realize the potential ramifications of today's terrorist attacks. Behind me you'll see boatloads of refugees fleeing the Middle East in whatever fashion they can. Many of these vessels are hardly what would be considered seaworthy, but these brave men, women, and children would rather take their chances with Mother Nature and the denizens of the deep than face the wrath of the United States Armed Forces."

Gabe could feel the juices flowing, the words coming smoothly and superfluously. From the corner of his eye, he caught sight of a fishing boat tossing on the sharp waves, trying to get close to the hull of the Talon.

He gave Dave a discrete wave and leaned over the railing to better see the smaller ship.

"Down here you'll see what appears to be a fishing boat trying to get our attention to haul the refugees aboard."

The camera panned across the twenty-foot tugboat through the black clouds of smoke churning from its sputtering engine. An enormous tarp covered the cargo hold, where Dave could only assume dozens of Iraqis lay packed like sardines beneath. The captain stood on the bow, waving frantically. His tan face contrasted his blindingly-white serape, freshly bleached as though he had gotten dressed up for the occasion. The white paint had faded to feather-brushed timber rotting to the point that it looked close to crumbling to pieces.

The vessel bore no name; just a weather-beaten ship probably found abandoned on some decrepit pier.

Dave zoomed past the man through the shattered glass, where another man commandeered the helm. He had a black cloth sack over his head, twin holes torn for his black eyes. His clothes were startlingly white as well.

"The order came through," Peter whispered into Dave's ear. He hadn't even heard the smaller man sneak up on him. "We're pulling out. The feed goes live in fifteen minutes."

Dave signaled he understood with an okay sign, never removing his eye from the lens.

"The Seawolves have already snuck in beneath us," Peter whispered even more quietly.

This time, Dave stole his eye from the camera, looking down to the deep blue water for what he knew was now somewhere far beneath. It was staggering to think that the very weapons that were about to extinguish millions of lives were directly beneath his feet. He thought there should have been some sort of radiating aura of power, some sort of announcement like a giant's pounding footfalls, but it was much worse. Death moved silently like a shark down there, preparing to attack without the slightest warning.

"Holy crap! What was that?" Gabe shouted.

Dave spun the camera toward the reporter, seating his eye against the viewfinder.

A streak of flames tore south across the ocean between the two battleships, throwing up walls of water to either side like a jet skimming the surface.

"Was that a missile?" Gabe gasped. "Zoom in on it!"

Dave fought to focus the camera on the wall of fire, leading it just enough to get a glimpse of the source of the flames.

"What in the name of...?" Dave whispered.

In that split second, he thought he'd seen a red man atop a skeletal horse.

The flames disappeared at the horizon, leaving Dave to follow the dwindling wake back toward the ship.

"Did you get that?" Gabe asked.

"I don't...?" Dave started to say, but lost his train of thought.

The man from the bow on the small ship below and the other from the cabin were both at the back of the boat. They'd pulled the tarp all the way off and cast it to the ocean, where it floated momentarily before starting to sink. There wasn't a pile of frightened civilians lying on the deck as he had expected. No one at all.

There was only a silver canister about four feet long and the width of a snare drum. A mess of wires trailed from the front end to a control panel atop a small pedestal. Dave's eyes locked on those of the masked man below, whose stare told him everything he needed to know.

Gabe's footsteps raced away from him along the deck.

There was a flash of blinding light.

The lens struggled to focus only briefly before incinerating.

IV

War sat atop Thunder on the Bandar-e Zahedan Atoll, six miles off the northern shore of Al Khuwayr, Qatar at the southern rim of the Persian Gulf. The wind blew the salt foam from the crashing waves into his face, patterning the shield covering the mangled mess of tissue beneath like shotgun pellets. Thunder blasted a gust of fire from its nostrils, bucking nervously, hooves clattering atop the jagged rock formation. The beast could feel it coming too.

War studied the horizon, his stoic gaze focused intently on where the sea met the horizon. His job was to give them a nudge of they needed it, but as he suspected, they'd been more than anxious to do it all by themselves. His battles were still to come. His armies would bleed the fields black, but this here was not his fight. Soon, he knew. Soon he would be waging war as he had been created to. Whatever managed to survive The Fall would be ground beneath his heels.

This was merely the prelude; his symphony to conduct.

The crash of nuclear thunder was music to his ears.

He watched the cloud of darkness rise straight up into the trembling sky, the column expanding at the base until it stretched from all the way to the west to where the horizon died to the east. Lightning stabbed through its roiling black belly, flaring angrily, flashing across the entire billowing mass.

The wind changed directions, forcing Thunder to lean back into it, bracing its hooves against the stone outcroppings as the fission explosion drew in a great breath. It screamed past him, the specters of the pain and bloodshed to come, stealing the crashing tide from the break beneath him. The ocean fell a hundred feet, exposing rock formations and corals that had never known the light of day. Crustaceans scurried for cover and fish floundered on their sides.

War raised both arms to his sides, and as if on cue, the ocean rose against the churning black clouds, towering hundreds of feet over its former level. It expanded outward in a giant ring of tsunamis larger than the world had ever seen.

Thunder fired another gust of flame and rose to its hind legs, kicking at the air, which had suddenly become still. The heavens were silent.

The wall of water raced outward at a speed that may even have surprised War. He gripped the spines from the beast's neck and braced for impact.

The ocean receded half a mile from the coast of the island, the swelling wave blocking out the sky hundreds of feet above his head. The smell of burnt flesh and melted metal hit him a heartbeat before the wave, which submerged the entire island. As the waves continued racing south, the water resumed a more normal level behind, still beating the face of the now bludgeoned atoll, dragging the crumbling boulders back out to sea.

Where War had once been, there was now just a disintegrated pile of rubble. The black cloud enveloped the crushed remains of the island, lightning stabbing every inch of the ground.

Nuclear winter descended with flakes of human ash, covering the ground like snow. Dead fish floated to the surface of the ocean, dragged against the rocks to be beaten to pulp in the crimson foam. No gulls cried overhead, though their bodies pocked the surf. The furious roar of the cloud of radiation was the only sound, drowning out even the thunder that blossomed from its belly. Palm trees withered, the bark peeling free and catching fire. Bushes shed their browned leaves. Sand melted and fused. Dried grass burned all over the scorched ground.

No life remained. That which wasn't incinerated on contact continued to burn against the finality of a charcoal backdrop.

Stillness fell over the land and ocean alike, forks of electricity connecting the earth to the infinitely black sky. Soon the rains would come, washing away the remains of man's stain, killing the soil.

Fissures would open in the sea floor, spewing enough molten magma to boil the Seven Seas, the earth bleeding red from the critically-deep wounds.

Those to die in the blast zone were the saved. The end would come far more slowly for those who remained; stretching painfully into the terminal future.

The earth shuddered with its death rattle, and then lie still.

Dead.

V

"My fellow Americans," the President began, looking to his right to where Brigadier General Alan Barnaby stood like a statue in front of the American flag, hands clasped behind his back. He gave a subtle nod and the President turned back to the teleprompter. "At precisely 6:16 pm Eastern Standard Time, thirteen minutes ago, a nuclear warhead was detonated in the Persian Gulf. Our entire forward fleet, including four aircraft carriers and a dozen Seawolf nuclear submarines were destroyed at the epicenter of the explosion. Preliminary indications suggest a terrorist attack as none of our captains had yet been given their launch codes. While we are unsure of the exact specifications and kilotonnage of the warhead, we can confirm that the resulting explosion was sufficient to extinguish all life within a radius of several hundred miles, while effects of the radiation may well be felt in Europe, Africa, Western Russia and China."

He looked again to the general. There was a rumble from the crowd of nervous reporters.

"Exactly seven minutes ago now, our early warning systems confirmed that the Chinese have launched a battery of surface-to-air nuclear-armed missiles, strategically targeting various cities between our western and eastern coasts. We can only assume that they fired their weapons in response to the detonation in the Middle East."

The audience of reporters fell silent.

"We are confident that our satellite defenses will be able to shoot down the missiles while still over the Pacific and Atlantic Oceans. We assure you that none of these nuclear devices will even come close to American soil.

"But that brings us to the greatest dilemma a nation has faced since the dawn of time. Negotiations concerning trade and US-sponsored sanctions against the Chinese have been permanently halted. While we cannot verify that the missiles were launched as anything other than a knee-jerk reaction, we cannot afford to take that chance. Our venerable defenses are capable of withstanding a single nuclear assault, leaving us vulnerable to a second wave of attacks. That is a gamble that I, as your President, am unwilling to take. It is the first priority of this government to ensure the safety of the American people. This was a decision not taken lightly, and the direness of the consequences carefully considered. It is my duty as the President of the United States of America to ensure the survival of the millions entrusted to my care and the future generations of God-loving children to follow."

He took in a deep breath and let it out in a long sigh. Deep circles ringed his eyes, his hair tousled from nervously running his hands through it. A tear blossomed from his right eye.

"Prior to commencing this address, I gave the order to launch a reciprocal strike against the People's Republic of China."

He looked out upon the sea of reporters, waiting for the wave of hands to rise.

None did.

"May God be merciful and just," he said, his voice cracking. "May He bless you and keep you."

He stormed off the stage and disappeared through the door where a dozen Secret Service operatives ushered him hurriedly toward the waiting helicopter that would speed him to a secure location where the First Lady was already safely stowed.

"Let the warmongers have their day," he said, then burst out into the raging wind and rumble of swirling blades, encircled by his entourage.

"Your questions will be answered in due course and in orderly fashion," Jack Remington, the Secretary of Defense said, taking the podium. He looked like he hadn't slept in a month.

The clamor that had ensued following the President's departure died promptly.

"With the conflict in the Middle East escalating due to the hostile Syrian occupancy of Iraq, the resultant deployment of nuclear-armed vessels into the Persian Gulf stalled already precarious negotiations with China. It was their justified fear that any sort of nuclear detonation in Iraq would inevitably affect the Chinese people with the fallout and subsequent radiation poisoning. Foreign ambassadors have already indicated the willingness of the Chinese people to go to war against the United States following the 2008 Olympics in Beijing if trade sanctions and United Nations-mandated disarmaments were not repealed.

"While it is not this government's stance that war with China was a foregone conclusion, we do feel that an opportunistic Chinese regime seized this opportunity to attempt to secure world dominance while we were trying to rationalize the tragedies both at home and abroad."

He smiled a wooden grin, loosing the beads of sweat from his brow.

"It is our official contention that the Chinese believed that we launched a nuclear attack against the Syrian-occupied Iraq without concern for the detrimental fallout that would cross into Western China. We can now state with one-hundred percent surety that the initial detonation was caused by a warhead other than our own, however it triggered a chain reaction that led to the detonation of our nuclear arms stationed in the Persian Gulf. Xiao Hung and the Chinese government made no attempt to contact the United States government to verify the facts before firing weapons of mass destruction at selected targets within American borders. Such an unprovoked act of aggression required swift and proportionate resolution to ensure the survival of future generations of our children... American children."

He hung his head momentarily, a tear slapping the podium.

"So it is with heavy heart that I stand before you today to confirm that a nuclear strike has been launched against the United States. We trust that our Star Wars defenses will effectively target and eliminate all incoming missiles, but we regret to inform you that the People's Republic of China has no such protection.

"As of 7:03 pm Eastern Standard Time, the threat against America and her children of freedom will be no more."

VI

OVER THE
ATLANTIC OCEAN

Terror forced Adam's eyes open. The floor rose and fell beneath him; the harness tattooing his shoulders the only thing holding him in his seat. Electric blue lightning pounded the opposite wing through the windows above the heads of the GI's across from him. The wind roared past and turbulence battered the lifeless bird from side to side.

The ocean rose into view at the bottom of the windows, the tumultuous, white-capped sea reaching for them to welcome the plane into its watery embrace with waves that had to be close to three stories tall. Bugs spattered the windows with streaks of guts as they passed through what appeared to be a living cloud of them.

Wind-shear vibrated the body of the plane, rattling bolts loose from the fuselage. One of the engines ripped from the wing behind him with a metallic scream, banging the wall against his back before flying off into the raging storm. Everything canted to the right with the sudden shift in weight. The Atlantic was clearly visible now, obscuring everything in the lower third of the porthole windows. They couldn't have been more than a thousand feet above it and falling fast.

Adam couldn't catch his breath. His lungs had deflated like balloons and were unable to expand. His teeth ground so tightly together he felt the pressure in his nose and chin.

A rocky shoreline appeared through the window a heartbeat before the right wing snapped free and flew past. He pinched his eyes shut again and tensed in preparation of impact, imagining the monstrous rock formations, evergreens, and scrub they were about to slam into. The scream of their descent became deafening, the ground echoing the sound back up at them.

Bang!

The remainder of the left wing folded back into the plane before launching into the wilderness. Pine needles clawed at the metal shell.

It sounded like a million hammers were pounding the plane under their feet. There was a crash of shattering glass from the cockpit. With a hideous wrenching sound, the seats tore from the wall across from Adam, slamming forward into the steel wall separating the cargo from the cabin. The sudden jolt threw Adam sideways, but the harness held despite the moaning of the bolts. Glass blasted the back of his head and then there were branches and needles slashing at his face.

The belly of the plane slammed into the rocky ground with an angry grumbling like an avalanche. Metal shrieked and was torn away; tree trunks banged against the side of the plane as the tail kicked out, sending them skidding sideways.

Adam clenched the harness and prayed.

With a bang, the plane tipped, dropping them onto their backs to stare through the shattered windows opposite them directly up into the roiling sky. That final impact nearly ripped Adam's shoulders through the belts.

The silence that washed over them was worse even than the battering of the plane.

He opened his eyes, the blood pooling in his head. The wall across from him bowed inward like it had been repeatedly rammed by a semi, the row of seats formerly attached to it crumpled to his left with black boots standing from it like so many headstones. Blood pooled around it, draining slowly toward the men beside him still latched in their seats.

Adam unfastened his harness and slid onto what remained of the window frames. He rested there a moment, watching the flaring azure lightning snapping back and forth from the jet-black clouds.

Someone groaned from the left.

"Sound off," Norman said, his voice shaking.

"Merton."

"Samuels."

"Peckham."

"Carter."

"Newman," Adam said.

"Anyone else?" Norman asked.

Buckles clicked and bodies rolled onto the warped metal. Footsteps pounded on the steel shell and Adam felt hands beneath his armpits. He coughed as he was pulled to his feet, his head swimming while the blood drained back toward his feet.

Samuels stood well over six feet tall with a cleanly shaven head, smeared with blood from a gash that ran from above his left eye clear past his ear. With a neck like a sycamore and the shoulders of an ox, he appeared to lumber more than walk to the front of the cargo bay. He grabbed the exposed underside of the row of seats smashed against the wall, braced himself, and pulled with all of his might. A dozen lower legs dropped to the floor pouring blood from the severed knees like so many overturned glasses.

"God," he gasped. He pinched his eyes shut as the warm rush of fluid covered his feet.

The seats thudded back down, their cargo flopping forward. All that was left of the men were so many purple sacks of skin in crimson uniforms, bones shattered to chalk, their payload gushing out onto the ground with a wet slap.

"All dead," Samuels said, vocalizing what was painfully apparent to all.

He gingerly skirted the crumpled jump seats and piles of humanity, placed his left foot on the end seat, and propelled himself upward. Grasping the door frame, he pulled himself up and balanced there, reaching up and tugging the latch on the door. It fell away from him into the cockpit, banging loudly against the wall behind.

"Pilots are dead," he called back over his shoulder before dropping out of sight.

"I can't be in here another second," Carter said, on the verge of hyperventilating. He was much thinner than his compatriots: all arms and legs with a neck like a turtle. Bounding up onto the seats, his boots squishing in his former battalion-mates' blood, he clambered over the side of the door and flopped with a thud into the cockpit.

"Wait a minute," Peckham said, holding the ragged lips of a laceration closed on his forehead. Blood ran from beneath his fingers down his face. "Without Jefferson, I'm in charge."

"You think now's the time for a power trip, Peck?" Merton asked. He had the thick brows and heavy stubble of an Italian, but spoke with a soft southern accent.

"I'm just saying we need to stop and think," Peckham said, stealing his hand from the weeping wound long enough to tear a long strap from the bottom of his shirt. He tied it tightly around his head, though it became quickly saturated. "We're at war. We don't abandon this bird without weapons and a com-link. Lord only knows what's waiting for us out there."

"We can't wait for the fuel tank to catch fire either," Norman said, tasting the black smoke slowly filtering through the shattered windows.

"Agreed," Peckham said. "Norman, help get the new guy out. Merton… you and I will grab as much as we can carry, and then we're out of here."

"That's a plan, boss," Merton said, hurrying toward the storage compartments at the rear while Norman guided Adam to the front of the plane, kicking one of the corpses to the side and helping Adam up onto the seat.

"I can make it own my own," Adam said, hoping he sounded more confident than he felt.

"You sure?"

"I'm fine."

Adam used the wall to steady himself, rising until he was able to prop both forearms on the doorframe. His arms trembled, but he pulled himself up, crawling over the door and falling onto a wall of computer components before once again pushing himself to his hands and knees.

The cockpit opened ahead past the end of a narrowed hallway. Even with their backs to him and still strapped into their seats, there was no doubt that the pilots were dead. Heads leaning awkwardly to the left with gravity, blood drained rapidly from the multitude of deep gouges torn through their faces from the implosion of balled glass from the smashed windshield.

He could barely see Samuels and Carter through the churning black smoke swirling around the plane, but he was able to make out rugged rocks jutting from the hard earth and dense pines flirting in and out of the fuel-rich cloud. There was only one place in the world where the loam was so rich and black, yet rife with stones... only one place where the deep green pine forests mingled with thick elms and maples.

It may have been an inauspicious arrival, but they were home.

CHAPTER 5

I

VIRGINIA BEACH,
VIRGINIA

Gus Rangle sat on the same park bench that he sat on every afternoon, staring dreamily out across the Atlantic, looking for the life he had once led. He'd been a seaman, from the fishing boats he'd worked on as a fourteen year-old boy to his first naval battleship as a seventeen year-old enlistee. He'd seen Pearl Harbor beneath a sky filled with kamikazes, and worked his life away as a customs inspector on this very stretch of coast. He'd met his Lorna on this beach and given his daughter away in nearly the exact same spot. He didn't know exactly what he waited out here for day after day, watching the children dashing in and out of the distant surf, the gulls his only companions, but he knew he'd recognize it when he saw it. Lorna had always said that he only had that sparkle in his eye when he was near the sea. Maybe that's all he was waiting for: his lost sparkle. He hadn't felt it since the day the cancer took her from him.

Five years ago today.

Perhaps that's why it felt like such an abnormal day, darker than usual with an oppressive weight in the air. Or maybe it was because there were no children playing in the waves, no lovers walking hand in hand. There was no one out at all. It was as though the world had ended and completely forgotten about him, which wouldn't have surprised Gus a bit. People strolled past him all day, but never even spared him a glance. He was a spectral vision, and almost began to think of himself as haunting the park, waiting for something magical to roll in with the tide.

He coughed. The fluid rattled in his lungs. Usually, that spooked the gulls, but today there wasn't a single bird circling in the dark sky or rummaging through the piles of refuse by the trash barrel. There wasn't a sign of life at all but the scrabbling of the dead leaves across the grass and their brethren rustling overhead.

His chest was heavy with pneumonia, but the way he saw it, it was simply one more nail in his coffin. He couldn't hear without the hearing aids, couldn't see without the glasses, and couldn't walk without the cane. What did that leave? Without Lorna's divine cooking, everything tasted bland and gray. He was simply marking time by the ticking of his pacemaker.

Earlobes flagging on the rising breeze, he inhaled the salty air, taking in as much as his sickly lungs could hold before coughing it back out. Something wasn't quite right. While his sense of smell certainly wasn't what it once was, he'd smelled this exact same air for so long that he quickly recognized that something had changed. At first he couldn't place it, closing his wrinkled eyelids and savoring it, feeling the long gray hair combed across his bald pate flopping against his forehead. He smacked his lips a couple of times, tasting it, jiggling his jowls.

It was a familiar scent, though the last time he'd encountered it had been lifetimes ago. He'd been a nineteen year-old boy at the time, green as an aspen sapling, loading drums of fuel from the dock onto pallets that would find their way onto the battleships filling the harbor. The smell had come, carried inland on the humid air. He could clearly remember standing tall, wiping the back of his work glove across his forehead, and staring out across the turquoise water. None of the others had noticed, it seemed, as they still labored around him, obliviously moving in and out of the warehouse. At first he'd thought it might have been a distant fire, but it didn't smell of wood, but more like… burnt motor oil. There'd been bitterness to it, almost like inhaling aspirin powder. While he stood there deciphering it, he'd heard the distant roar of engines, the first sounds of prattling gunfire, but it wasn't until the gates of hell flew wide and unleashed their wrath on that Hawaiian bay that he truly knew what the smell was.

Death.

Gus tugged up the collar of his plaid wool coat, buttoning it with arthritic claws. Tucking his chin under the warm lining, he looked up from beneath wild white caterpillar eyebrows to the horizon through glasses as thick as storm windows. The wind battered his face, assaulting him with clouds of sand. Lightning as blue as a Bunsen burner's flame flashed from one roiling black cloud to the next, grumbling inland like a landslide atop the increasingly-choppy sea. The clouds rose like a wall to the heavens, swirling and churning as they expanded. Leaves were torn from their branches and garbage bounded past him across the rippling grass.

After five long years, he finally knew what he'd been waiting for.

Another cloud, impossibly darker than even the storm-front, appeared like a massive flock of geese from the heart of it, stretching from one side of the horizon clear to the other. It moved faster than the other clouds, fueled by the now raging torrent.

Gus rose from the bench, leaning into the stiff gale, stabbing his cane into the earth. He raised a hand to shield his face, sand tagging him as though fired from a shotgun. He took one uneasy step forward, and then another, his knees knocking.

A faint hint of white bloomed from the midst of the low-lying cloud, rushing straight toward him. As he watched, the shape drew contour, emerging from within the cloud, a ship through the fog. It was still small in the distance, but growing steadily as it sped toward him. There was a constant banging, like a hammer on an anvil, beneath the relentless roll of thunder.

His eyes were old, but they'd never played tricks on him in the eighty years they'd shared a head. For an instant, though, he thought maybe they were trying to deceive him.

It sounded as though someone was humming in his ear.

The form came into focus: a long skeletal head with mirrors for eyes, flashing with the same intensity as the lightning. Enormous hoofed front legs pounded through the sky, supported by nothing at all, and with each footfall the hammer fell. The rider was a pale gray blur, the black cloud swirling to either side as though she was its origin.

The humming intensified, growing louder until it sounded like an electronic scream.

Gus staggered forward despite his body's protests, dragging himself into the ferocious wind by the cane.

The horse's hooves descended from the swirling cloud, alighting on the beach with force enough to shake the earth. An immense wave rose behind the rider, taller than any building along the beach, crashing down behind the beast's advancing stride. Piers shattered to toothpicks and the backs of warehouses and markets were knocked in by the giant swell of water, another immediately rising behind to fill the void.

He had to stop and brace himself against the shuddering of the ground for fear of falling. The rider thundered straight toward him, the cloud dissolving to black static. Finally realizing that the cloud was the source of the humming, Gus closed his eyes and tried to picture his Lorna, not the lifeless, blue-lipped woman in the hospice bed, but the vibrant teenager he'd fallen for the moment he first saw her.

The cloud of insects hit him with enough force to cleave him from his feet and slam him onto his back. His breath exploded past his lips, replaced by a mouthful of mosquitoes, which flooded down his trachea. Hundreds of needles lanced through his flesh and he felt his life leaving him in fluid ounces. The muscles in his back pulled so tight that he nearly folded in half, bones grinding through cartilage. His fingers curled so tightly that the nails peeled away from the cuticles and carved into his palms. Neck snapping violently back and forth, the last sound he heard was a popping in his head, and then everything went black.

A skin of mosquitoes seethed over every inch of his bruised flesh before rising as one and rejoining the cloud of their species as it pushed inland, passing through open windows and beneath doors, down chimneys and through swamp coolers and air conditioner ducts. The cloud rolled like a tide across the city, bathing everything in a wash of winged insects.

The demon horse paused beside where Gus's body rested, staring up into the sky through sunken eyelids. His skin had taken on a necrotic black and midnight blue appearance like a diabetic's dead toes.

Pestilence watched him, waiting for the muscles to twitch, the eyes to flutter, anything... but nothing happened. The corpse just lay there atop its evacuated bowels. This man was one of the chosen. There would be plenty of others who weren't, Pestilence knew. This one she would leave to rot into the grass to fertilize famine's wrath. He was of no use to her at all.

Curling her fists tighter into the serpentine mane, she jerked and brought Reaver to its hind legs. She opened her mouth in what looked like an agonized wail, but all that came out was another flume of mosquitoes to thicken the cloud. The creature's front legs slammed to the ground, rippling the sand, crocodilian tail thrashing from side to side.

Screams erupted from the city all around her, a mystical cacophony of pain and suffering, blended with the frenetic humming of the mosquitoes.

Reaver raced forward, throwing a plume of sand from its heels, black insects swirling in its slipstream.

II

EAST OF
BETHLEHEM,
PENNSYLVANIA

When the news of the nuclear holocaust in the Middle East broke on CNN, her father and the others had been lost in prayer, sitting in a large circle, holding hands and pleading for the spirit to take them. This was the day they'd both been fearing and dreaming of their entire lives, the day when the Father would reach down from heaven and summon them home. They'd spent the morning anointing one another, slathering balms and oils over their flesh to purge all but their initial sins. They would be pure of body and mind when the Lord set The Rapture into motion. The entire house reeked of feces and vomit from the massive amounts of castor oil, ipecac syrup, and laxatives ingested and then purged. Toxic sweat seeped from their glistening pores, but even that was far better than the rage to follow.

Sarah hadn't partaken of the ritual, as it was her lot to usher the others into God's graces before being allowed to do so herself. She'd always known this, and thus felt no bitterness. It simply was what it was. She would continue baking the unleavened bread, the body of Christ, for their continuous communion until she found herself alone in the house.

The others had knelt in a circle in the middle of the room, clasping hands and writhing as the spirit possessed them. That had gone on forever it seemed, as she watched discretely through the greasy bangs that hid her face. The twisting, contorting, and shouting in tongues had grown to a fever pitch, until as one, they ceased. All had looked to her father, waiting for him to give the good word, but he had been without answers. She had seen the fear in his eyes, but it had quickly been replaced by anger. That was the hour when God fulfilled the prophesy and called the souls of the chosen to his side. Why hadn't He called them? Why were they still on the mortal plane of sin's wages? Why had He forsaken them?

Sarah knew why, though. They'd brought the devil into the house when they abducted the boy and locked him away in the darkness. He'd been just a child, a tiny human being who screamed and cried for but the most transient moment of kindness, for the kind of touch an infant needed from his mother. She'd begun to doubt what they believed him to be. Could he really heal wounds and work all kinds of miracles, or were they simply deluding themselves? The longer he lived beneath them, the longer he went without summoning the angelic armies of the Lord to his aid, the more she started to wonder if perhaps her father had been wrong.

Her father was a man of God. He lived and breathed the Holy Word, embraced poverty and denied sin, but he was still human, after all. Was it possible that he'd misread prophesy? The child and his mother had been in the alley as he had predicted; the child was born beneath a caul, but what if he wasn't the son of God? What if he was simply a child delivered by normal means into a world where he'd known no love and been held prisoner down there in his own filth?

Perhaps they were all damned.

If she was indeed cursed to spend eternity in hell, then what could it possibly matter if she committed one final affront? Or perhaps this was the mission she needed to set her soul free.

Her father and the others were occupied with their indignance and fear. None of them so much as looked at her, let alone acknowledged her existence. They had learned to see right through her.

Sarah eased back into the kitchen and removed the last batch of unleavened bread, setting it atop the grungy stove to cool. Silently, she drew the drawer to the left open and removed the sharpest knife, lifting it from the clutter and sliding it carefully beneath her smock. Turning on dirty bare feet, she walked back to the doorway between the kitchen and the main room, her heart trilling like a hummingbird's wings. They were all still in the center of the room, the threadbare couches pushed back against the walls to allow for their large circle. Naked, glistening in the light that crept around the seals of the boarded windows, they held hands, chins hanging against their chests. Silent. It was as though they had all fallen asleep standing there.

Pressing her back to the wall, she inched sideways, her sweat pouring down her face, wet bangs slapping her skin, until she finally reached the thin hallway leading down into the darkness. Carefully easing her weight down upon the aged wooden planks, she descended, planting her feet all the way to either side by the walls to keep the bowed boards from moaning. She couldn't risk turning on the light and drawing attention to herself, so she felt her way toward the small landing and down the second, steeper flight of stairs to the closed door.

Hands trembling, she gingerly turned the locks one at a time, the bolts slamming back into their housings far too loudly. She held her breath as she opened the door, the stench of rotting gruel and human waste accosting her.

"Child," she whispered, her nerves sharpening her voice.

"I'm ready," he said softly, palming the roach-sharpened pick, the lance running up the underside of his forearm.

She pulled her black smock over her head and shoved it at him.

"Hurry and put this on!" she whispered.

"I don't…" he started, turning it over in his hands.

She took it back from him, found the neck, and slipped it over his head, letting the long fabric fall over his chest, hanging to the middle of his thighs. At first, he panicked at the sensation of the cloth draped all over his skin, constricting him. Fighting against it, he finally shoved his arms out through their designated holes, which helped to calm him.

Sarah took his hand and jerked him toward the doorway. He'd left many basements through the years, but never with his eyes wide open and without being tightly bound and carried. His heart leapt at the prospect of freedom, but he was simultaneously frightened nearly to the point of paralysis. He shook uncontrollably, barely able to keep his feet beneath him as she tugged. Finally, as they reached the threshold to the staircase, he stopped.

"What?" she gasped.

"Thank you," he whispered. "For everything."

That caught her off guard. They'd kept him locked away in the darkness all of his life, and yet here he was, thanking her. It finally dawned on Sarah that this was the only life the boy knew. He'd seen nothing of the world outside. All he knew of the universe outside of his walls was what she had told him… and she hated herself for it. The sin of keeping him as their prisoner was unforgivable, but turning him loose into the outside world was so much worse.

"Don't thank me," she whispered, tugging harder.

He resisted.

"What will happen to you?" he asked.

She smiled sadly. The truth was that she really didn't know. If it was indeed this child who brought the end of the world, then he'd already fulfilled his destiny. What more could he possibly do? Millions upon millions of people were dead, and the boy had never taken a step outside of his room. Was it possible that this entire time they'd been wrong and simply torturing an innocent boy out of religious fear and superstition?

"Quietly," she whispered, deliberately planting her feet to either side of the staircase to show him how, easing him slowly upward. Each slightly audible protest from the rickety old stairs was amplified a thousand-fold. She cringed with every movement, releasing the wobbly railing. With each step, she felt her burden growing lighter. This was the right thing to do. She was sure of it now. Her father would understand. He was a man of God after all. He could see through her flesh and to her soul. There he would find the truth, and he would undoubtedly forgive her, and together they could ask the Lord for His forgiv—

"Put on all the armor that God gives you, so that you will be able to stand up against the Devil's evil tricks. For we are not fighting against human beings but against the wicked spiritual forces in the heavenly world, the rulers, authorities and cosmic powers of this dark age," her father said.

She closed her eyes, her right hand instinctively clasping the handle of the knife tucked beneath the top of her overalls. With her left, she pulled the boy behind her onto the landing. There was no exit behind her; the only one through her father.

"Try to understand—" she started, but he cut her off with the booming voice of a giant.

"Hold thy tongue!"

He barred exit from the top of the stairs, legs planted against the wall to one side, the banister to the other. His naked flesh glimmered as though coated with glitter, all but a wash of blood that flowed from holes on the tops of his feet, running down the stairs toward them. Blood poured from the matching wounds in his hands, draining in ribbons down the white wall and the banister rails. His forehead was covered with scratches and puncture wounds no larger than had the damage been inflicted by needles, but a skein of crimson covered his face like a mask.

The others crowded in behind him, smears of blood crossing their chests from where they'd wiped their palms after laying their hands on him. Their eyes were hollow, soulless.

"He's just a boy, father," she whined, tears flowing freely. Her fist tightened on the hilt of the blade, but she kept it against her belly.

"Even Satan can disguise himself to look like an angel of light," he spat.

"I know the scriptures," she sobbed. "You just want to keep him for yourself!"

She'd said it, the words hanging in the air between them like a wraith.

What little skin showed through the rivers of blood on his face turned red, his eyes growing impossibly wide. His entire body trembled with the rage building beneath his taut skin, teeth grinding like gravel.

"We no longer need the child," he growled through gnashed teeth. "The End of Days is at hand. Bring him before me, girl. Let the child meet the righteous welcome of the Lord."

"No, daddy," she whispered in a voice from her childhood to the father he'd once been.

Her eyes fixed on his, she slowly drew the blade from beneath the bib of the overalls.

The rictus of anger spread to a toothy smile that threatened to tear his cheeks, his eyes narrowing to slits.

"You have become estranged from Christ, you who are seeking to be justified by law; you have fallen from grace!"

He slapped a bloody foot down a step.

Sarah slashed at him, the tip of the blade opening a bloody seam beneath his kneecap.

"Blessed are those who hunger and thirst for righteousness, for they shall be filled," he said, taking another step.

"Don't come any closer!" she screamed, slicing across his stomach, which opened like a mouth preparing to yawn. Freshets of rich crimson spilled over his groin.

He flopped backward, grabbing the lips to close them for fear of what might fall out.

Two of the others bounded down the staircase to his side, grabbing him under his flexed arms and hauling him to the top of the stairs. The swarm of bodies closed around him, the floor now positively drenched with his cooling fluids.

"Come on!" she shouted, yanking on the boy's arm.

She led him up the stairs at a lumbering sprint, careful not to slip in her father's blood. The front door was ten feet to her right, but it might as well have been a mile. The moment she took her first stride in its direction, the group of faceless zealots erupted from the cluster around her father. She slashed at the hands reaching for her, but there were far too many of them. Arms wrapped around her legs, bodies flew at her from the side. She heard the knife clatter to the floor before she even knew it had left her hand. Her wrist broke. Fists pummeled her from all sides, driving her back toward the stairs. Teeth tore into her flesh, yanking it away in meaty bites.

Sarah screamed as they knocked her down and hauled her by the hair into the kitchen.

Everything was happening so quickly that Phoenix couldn't even think. He held the sharp spike out in front of him, but the action before him was a blur of motion. His hands shook and he couldn't breathe. He could only stand by and watch as wounds opened up on her like blooming flowers. The only sound he could hear was her screaming. He searched for the man on the floor, the one she called "daddy," but the others were already carrying him to the kitchen behind the tangle of glistening bodies splotched with his blood, which covered the floor like a slug's trail.

Phoenix staggered around the corner, hardly able to see through the mass of humanity packed into that room. Barely able to steal his eyes from where they were hauling the woman up onto the countertop, he glanced back at the front door. There was only one man standing guard in front of it, a hairy man with a grizzled beard that hung nearly to the middle of his chest, the coarse gray and black strands tangled into a ratted mess. His long hair framed his head like rays from the sun, his body an ugly, patterned mess of wiry hairs slicked smoothly over his flabby, sagging skin. The man looked at Phoenix like a starving dog eying a steak.

Phoenix was sure he could get through the man. If he ran at him and drove the dagger through any part of his body, he'd be able to pass, and once he hit the door, he'd just run and…

And what? He didn't know where he was any more than he knew where he'd go. His memories of the world outside were fuzzy at best, glimpses stolen from dreams. Images swirled together. Everything he had ever seen came in the form of intangible nighttime visions. And if the muted light in this room hurt to look at, what did he expect from the radiant sun outside?

But this was his chance and he knew it.

The hairy man locked stares with him, but Phoenix turned away and forced himself through the maze of bodies into the kitchen. Feet pounded the floor and there was the raucous roar of indistinguishable voices. He shoved through the slick bodies, all of whom shrunk from his touch. Able to see neither over nor through them, he followed the woman's pained wails. Finally pressing close enough to see her, he lunged forward near where one of The Swarm held her head in the sink, neck hyper-extended over the rim. Behind her head was a long spike, dripping with blood. A similarly soaked hammer had been cast aside on the stovetop. Crimson poured from the counters, draining down into the basin, and puddling on the floor. Dear Lord, the man's wounds were no sign from above, no stigmata. He'd driven that enormous nail through his own hands and feet to keep his followers from doubting him.

"Please!" the woman screamed, before her jaw was forcibly closed. She tried to flail her legs on the countertop, tried to buck her body free, but she was held firm.

They brought The Man to her side, his human crutches stepping away and allowing him to sway there on his own. Someone pressed the woman's knife into his bloody right hand. He could barely close his fist around it. His entire body was now either blood red or stark white. Phoenix had to wonder if there was now more blood outside the man than within.

"A soft answer turneth away wrath," he said, his voice faltering. The room around him fell silent, save for the muffled screams of the woman through the hands clasped over her mouth. The man cast the knife aside, not caring where it landed. "This is not the way of the Lord."

"Please don't, fath—!" she screamed, freeing herself from the hands pinning her head, but they struck like vipers, squashing her head into the sink and forcing her mouth closed.

"We must purge you of this evil, child," he whispered, raising a dripping hand over her features. Her eyelids reflexively closed against the blood spattering all over her face.

The hands loosened and she screamed, which was precisely what they wanted. The man slapped his hand over her mouth. More hands fell atop his to hold it there. With a muffled cough, she patterned their hands with a mist of blood from her nose. Another hand pinched it closed.

"This is the new covenant in my blood—" the man started.

"Stop it!" Phoenix yelled.

He raised the pick and slammed it into the shoulder of one of the men holding the woman, jerking it back with a slurp and an arc of warm fluids. The man didn't even notice.

The woman tried to thrash, her eyes inhumanly wide. As Phoenix watched, her irises rolled back beneath her bruised lids, her face an eggplant. Her legs twitched, her fingers curling into claws, but they soon relaxed and she stilled, blood pouring from the sides of her mouth.

"I am sending an angel ahead of you to guard you along the way..." the man whispered.

"No!" Phoenix screamed, raising his pick.

The Man turned to face him as Phoenix swung the weapon.

A humming sound arose beneath the frantic voices and the clamor of movement.

The man didn't have enough time to react. The tip of the blade split his forehead in two, then opened his eyebrow and eyelid like a butterflied shrimp, before clipping his cheekbone and gouging through his cheek. The implement stood from the side of his head, his mouth opened in shock to reveal the silver spike driven clear through his upper gums and into his tongue.

He dropped to his knees, the metal lance poking out from his cheek like a snaggled tooth.

The others fell silent, all movement ceasing.

Humming. From all around.

"Get him back to the basement!" one of The Swarm shrieked, followed by another.

Before the man even toppled forward into the black pond of his own blood, Phoenix was wrenched from his feet. Hands pinned his arms behind his back and ground his ankles together. Bodies raced past, and then he was at the top of the stairs and bounding downward over the rumble of feet pounding the hollow steps.

Mosquitoes infiltrated the room above, their humming growing deafening. They filled the air like smoke, pouring through the gaps surrounding the windows. Phoenix could see them combing through the men's hair, covering their naked bodies.

They launched him through the open doorway into the basement and slammed the door.

He landed soundly on his back, ferocious pain blossoming from his shoulders and head when they pounded the concrete. The entirety of the house above him was buzzing, the walls and floor positively vibrating.

Screams pierced the darkness.

Phoenix scurried back to his bed of straw and buried himself in it.

The humming was everywhere around him, all of the insects swirling the air around in the room like a fan. They filtered through the straw and seethed over his skin in a living sheath. They crawled all over him, and then as one, speared him with their stingers. He screamed and bucked against the violent pain, his voice blending into the roar of agony from above.

III

Neither knew how long they'd been in there, but they weren't going to last much longer. Between the heat and humidity, they were starting to feel as though they were roasting, basting in their own fluids. Each wet breath brought with it a little more of the finite air. It was only a matter of time before they ran out. Mare could no longer tell whether he was soaked because of the wet blanket or the massive amounts of sweat, leeching the moisture from his dehydrating body. He'd resorted to licking the salty fluid from his upper lip to keep from passing out.

"I can't stay in her much longer," he whispered, eyelids fluttering.

Missy was able to open her eyes just enough to acknowledge him in the darkness beside her. At first, they'd huddled together, just so they didn't feel quite so alone in the pitch black, but as the temperature had risen inside of the closet, they'd moved farther and further apart until they were pressed against opposite walls, absorbing the last of the coolness from the drywall.

"What's the worst that could happen if we go back out?" she asked, her voice small, dry.

"We die."

"Oh," she said, falling momentarily silent. They could almost hear the condensation draining down the walls. "And what's the worst that could happen if we stay in here?"

"We could still die, but it would almost be more like falling asleep. They say it's one of the least painful ways to die."

Silence.

"Do you want to die?" she whispered.

"No," he said quickly.

"Well… we know what will eventually happen if we stay in here, right?"

"Yeah."

"Then I guess we have no choice but to take our chances out there."

"You've got a point."

Silence descended again, interrupted only by the sloughing of wet blankets.

"I think I might be able to open the door without breaking the seal," he said, "but if there's any radiation out there at all, it would come right through."

"And the door would hold it out?"

"Good point."

"Then let's just do it."

"Are you sure?"

She was quiet a moment.

"I'm so tired, Mare. I don't want to go to sleep in here and not wake up."

"Okay," he said, summoning his strength and tossing off his blanket. It hit the wall with a slap and slopped to the carpeted floor. Sweat drained down his shoulders when he stood, pooling against his lower back, soaking into his waistband. He felt his way along the wall until he reached the crumpled edges of the plastic tarp, then moved his hands inward until he felt the doorknob through the forgiving divider. Carefully, he gripped just the edges of the knob and turned. If he didn't try to twist too fast, he'd be able to open the door without breaking the plastic seal. With a click, the door popped open into the living room.

As soon as it fell away from him, Mare could hear it… a loud humming, like a million pagers vibrating. Mosquitoes hammered the plastic skin separating them from the outside world.

"Jesus!" Mare gasped, stumbling backward.

The entire surface of the plastic was alive with little black bodies.

"Help me hold them out!" he shouted, slapping the plastic to toss the bodies off long enough to clear his line of sight. The room beyond was thick with them. He stepped on the plastic bunched on the floor, pinning it there, hopefully hard enough to keep them from crawling under. He pressed his shoulder and hip against the sloppy seam on the right side of the doorway. Reaching up, he held the tarp tightly over the horizontal trim.

Missy stepped up and did the same, shrieking every time the plastic between them bowed inward with the amassed weight of the insects.

"What's happening?" she screamed, but Mare couldn't hear her over the humming.

They both felt as though their flesh was crawling with mosquitoes.

And as quickly as they had descended upon them, the mosquitoes vanished, rising as one from the tarp. They funneled back out the open front door like a cloud of pepper, sucked out on some unseen current. The humming faded until there was nothing left of it at all.

"Are they gone?" Mare whispered, finally allowing himself to breathe.

"I don't know."

"I've never seen anything like that before."

"Neither have I."

"What do you think would cause them to swarm like that?"

Missy just shook her head, swiping at the beading sweat that felt like miniature legs creeping all over her.

Condensation balled on the inside of the tarp, draining in rivulets toward their feet, distorting the room beyond. Time passed slowly as they listened intently for any sign of the humming returning, until finally neither could stand the heat or the tension any longer.

"What do you think?" Mare asked.

"I've got to get out of here."

"Then on three, we rip down the plastic. I'll shut the front door. You just run."

"Where?"

"Bathroom?"

"What about you?"

"I'll be right behind you. The hell if I'm going to mess around any longer than I have to!"

"On three?"

"Yeah," Mare said, sweat dropping from his lips. "One... two... three!"

Both jerked at the plastic, tearing it off the staples. Mare bounded over the crumpled tarp and grabbed the front doorknob. He felt the wind from Missy's passage behind him.

"Wait," he whispered, still holding the door ajar.

Missy stopped dead in her tracks and whirled.

Mare just stood in the doorway, framed against the roiling black sky. Lightning as blue as topaz flared furiously against the ebon clouds racing in from their right. The forks of electricity appeared sentient, striking first the roof of one house, then tearing free to stab the next.

There were no mosquitoes swarming in the streets as he had expected.

None at all.

Mr. Walton lie face down on his porch across the street, legs dangling onto the walk. His cane was on the lawn, his poodle sprawled out at the end of her red leash halfway to the Jernigans' house to the left. Its curly white hair tousled on the rising wind.

There was a car idling on the Petersons' lawn down the street, their mailbox uprooted in a pile of splinters on the curb. One of the wooden columns supporting the overhang was broken in half over the car's bumper, the awkwardly-leaning structure threatening to fall atop the old Mustang where it canted with its left front tire up on the porch. Smoke wafted along the breeze from the coughing engine.

"What's going on out there?" Missy whispered.

"I don't know…"

Mare stepped out through the front door, his flesh prickling. The air was electric, yet there was no movement along the street, save for the leaves blowing on the gusting wind and the rustling of the barren branches overhead. The sound of thunder grew louder, now almost like a background drum roll. It was the first time he truly recognized the stillness. Until that point, he'd never really noticed how everything around him was in a constant state of motion: cats scampering past; dogs barking and running the fence-lines; joggers on the sidewalks; cars driving by; a neighbor digging in her garden; children screaming playfully from some back yard. There was now nothing but the wind to ripple the grass and chase litter down the gutters.

He strode down the walk to the street.

"Where are you going?" Missy called, unable to bring herself to cross the threshold.

He looked back over his shoulder, but couldn't find the voice to answer. His stomach was flopping over and there was a tingling sensation in his lower abdomen. Something was definitely wrong. There had been the mosquitoes… and now there was nothing but the ugly black storm.

Feet scuffing the asphalt, Mare crossed to the other side of the street and hopped up onto the curb. He walked directly to where Mr. Walton was still sprawled across his stoop.

"Mr. Walton?" he asked, kneeling and tapping the old man on the shoulder.

The man's white hair flagged on the breeze, exposing the blackened skin beneath.

"Are you—?" Mare started, rolling the man onto his back.

He threw himself in reverse.

"Oh my God!" he gasped, clapping his hand over his mouth and turning away. He could still see the old man's face clearly in his mind no matter how hard he tried to force it out. Mr. Walton's cheeks and gizzard were swollen, his eyes sunken. His bulbous tongue forced his chipped teeth open from lips that looked like stomped worms. Every inch of his skin was mottled a rich blue and black, and the smell that billowed out from beneath him… he had never smelled anything even close to that repulsive.

Mare raised his head and looked down the street.

Everything was still.

"Help!" he screamed, shoving himself to his feet and staggering into the middle of the road. "Anyone!"

His legs finally gave out, dropping him to his knees on the asphalt.

"Please," he whispered beneath the rising thunder.

Missy sprinted out from the house and knelt at his side, throwing her arms tightly around him and burying her face in his neck.

IV

BARSTOW,
CALIFORNIA

Evelyn sat on the floor in the middle of her childhood bedroom, mesmerized by the swaying kelp waving in slow motion in the aquarium. The whole day felt like a dream, as though at any minute she would awaken and find the world normal again. After watching the mushroom cloud rise above Los Angeles in the distance, her body had tried to shut down, or maybe she'd simply hoped that it would. The smell of the burning pheasants was still fresh when the wave of destruction, riddled with the foul aromas of scorched rubber and vaporized humanity, washed across the desert. It was a tangible thing, like an oil coating her flesh, seeping into her follicles.

She needed to occupy her mind. If she could only switch her focus to something else—anything else—then at least she'd be fine for the moment, and right now, the moment was all she had. Who knew if there was even anything left to return to in San Diego? Granted, it was well down the coast from Los Angeles, but she knew little about radiation and fallout. And she could only imagine the poor sea creatures. What effect would an atomic detonation have on them?

She turned to the aquarium in the middle of the floor, allowing herself to be momentarily hypnotized by the swaying of the kelp at the whim of the manmade current. When she'd planted the hundreds of long leaves growing vertically from the spongy substrate, they'd been little more than sprouts. All it took was a clipping of roots from an adult plant buried in the foam and the right pH and nitrate levels, and they started to grow nearly overnight. Now, the largest leaves were close to a foot long and packed in there so tightly that within a week there wouldn't even be room left between them for the current to pass. Who knew what could happen in a week? Yesterday, the world had been normal. For all she knew, tomorrow could bring the end of it.

Evelyn pushed herself to her feet and went to the closet, opening the door. Sliding the clothes on hangers to the side, she revealed a large aquarium standing on its side at the back. It was only one-hundred twenty gallons, which would be enormous in her room, but she was used to working with tanks ten times that size at school. At least she'd had the foresight to bring it along. If the kelp started growing together and tangling, it was only a matter of time until it died anyway. At least now she'd have a couple of months of room for growth in the tank.

She tried not to think about the fact that she'd probably still be here.

At least switching out the tanks would keep her mind busy. She didn't want to wonder if the Hollywood sign was burning against the hillside or if Beverly Hills was now one enormous pile of rubble. The thought of the Sunset Strip reduced to smoldering coals would surely bring back the tears she had only recently forced down.

She was going to have to mix up some more saltwater. That would take a little time. She'd need to mix the synthetic sea salt with water at precisely seventy-two degrees. She'd need to gauge the salinity to ensure that it was exactly 1.22 and then she'd need to balance the pH. It would take some time, but it wasn't as though she was going to be able to sleep that night. She was simply happy that her father was able to use the painkillers for just that purpose.

There was a tapping at the window.

At first it had blended with the ticking of her clock on the nightstand, but the sound was irregular and now growing louder.

Evelyn dragged the tank into the middle of the room and balanced it against the side of the bed before walking over to the window. She threw back the light blue sashes and gasped.

A writhing layer of insects covered every inch of the glass.

She staggered backward, bumping into the enormous glass aquarium.

There was a humming sound behind her. She whirled to see the first couple of mosquitoes crawl from beneath her bedroom door. They flew directly at her.

Evelyn swatted at them, holding them momentarily at bay, but more still took flight into the room from that thin crack between the wood and carpet. They were even starting to funnel through the small gaps in the heating vent on the wall.

Spinning, she looked back at the window. There were so many that they blocked whatever weak light may have been out there. A few of the most ambitious creatures had managed to press themselves flat and squeeze around the seals.

"Daddy!" she screamed, swiping at the air. It felt like they were crawling all over her.

Before she even registered the thought, Evelyn grabbed the aquarium and ducked, closing herself beneath it against the floor. It squeezed her shoulders and pressed uncomfortably against her back, but at least it was heavy enough to seat itself firmly into the carpet. Eyes closed, she waited, the glass vibrating with the humming along with her fillings.

Her skin positively crawled with what felt like a million tiny legs, but she only felt one stick and slapped it reflexively, smashing the carcass on her forearm in front of her face. Blood smeared from the carcass as she brushed it off, but she'd killed it before it could have even begun to inject its anticoagulatory spew. The blood must have belonged to someone else.

Her eyes snapped open at the thought.

"Daddy," she whispered.

The glass surrounding her was covered with a moving sheath of mosquitoes, like so many grains of dirt had she been buried underground. With a scream, she clawed at the lip of the tank to ensure it was lodged firmly against the floor.

Her breath condensed against the glass, widening in arcs as she began to hyperventilate.

She couldn't even bring herself to blink watching all of the tiny pokers tapping at the glass, trying to skewer her from without. Like a cloud passing before the sun, they were everywhere, darkening the world around her, and then they disappeared as though they'd never been.

All she could hear were her rasping breaths, her eyes darting from one side to the next. There was nothing out there. Not a single mosquito buzzed anywhere as far as she could see. The glass no longer vibrated and the only sound she could hear was the gentle purring of the filters on the kelp tank.

Chest heaving, she placed her trembling hands on the carpet and pushed upward, lifting the tank from the ground. The flood of cool air felt divine against her already sweaty skin, and she didn't realize until then just how quickly she'd burned through what little air had been under the glass with her. It was an awkward process getting out from under the aquarium, but she finally toppled it onto its side and rose against the protests from her back.

The window was cracked where all of the mosquitoes had been trying to get in, but there weren't any tapping against the glass now. She spun to face the door, but there was nothing trying to crawl through the crack beneath.

What in the name of God could have caused those mosquitoes to swarm like that? Granted, her expertise was in aquatic species, but there were very few animals of any kind that ever congregated in such large numbers. It was completely unnatural.

Grabbing the doorknob, she tugged the door inward and was out in the hall before she even heard it bang into the wall behind. She nearly sprinted the short distance down the hallway, shouldering her father's door inward and dashing into—

"Daddy?" she whispered.

The sheets lie so still. Surely that would have awakened him. She slowed her pace, watching the sheet on his chest for the subtle rise and fall of his breathing as she had grown so accustomed to doing, but she couldn't see even the slightest hint of motion.

The blanket was tugged all the way over his head.

Often, the narcotics made him sleep so soundly that she feared he was dead, so as she always did, she slunk around to the side of the bed and gently peeled the covers back away from his face.

"God!" she sobbed, turning and slapping her hands over her mouth. The tears were already pouring down her cheeks.

All she could see, even as she raced down the hallway to the phone to call for help, was his black face, swollen and gorged, mottled with a deep blue. And his eyes… They were wide open, the lids sucked all the way back behind his eyeballs, which appeared precariously close to spilling out.

"Help me!" she screamed into the phone.

Only silence responded.

The line was dead.

V

EUGENE, OREGON

The power snapped off, the room now strobing in the lingering electric blue residue of the light from the bug zapper frying insects outside the shattered window.

Now only the flash of lightning marred the darkness.

"We have to get out of here!" Jill screamed.

"Calm down!" Rick shouted, grabbing her by the forearms and bringing her face to his. Anger flared in his eyes. "Panicking won't do a damned thing!"

"You don't understand!" she wailed, wrenching her arms free. "We're all going to die if we don't get out of here right now!"

The banging on the roof was nearly deafening as now much smaller hailstones flew through the broken windows and bounded around the room.

"We can't go out there!" April shrieked.

"We don't have a choice!"

"We're better off in here!" Darren shouted over the din. "Look at the cars!"

Tina whirled to the window. Hail bounced from hoods and roofs, but not before creating dents the size of quarters. Shattered glass was everywhere and headlights flashed as car alarms blared, though inaudible beneath the weather's barrage.

"We've got to get Tina to a hospital," Ray said.

"In what?" Rick shouted. "Look at what the hail's done to—"

"I don't care if I have to carry her on foot! We're going to the hospital right the fu—"

"Wait!" Jill screamed.

All eyes focused on her silhouetted form flickering with the blue stain.

She needed it to be quiet. She could almost see something, but everything around her was too chaotic for her to focus on it. All of the noise and the fear and her own throbbing pulse... The only recognizable image she could steal from her subconscious was of a—

"You have a hot tub, don't you?" she asked.

"Yeah, but what the hell good is that—?"

"Come on!" Jill railed, grabbing April by the wrist and yanking her into the kitchen. The window set in the door leading out into the back yard was obliterated, shards of glass scattered on the rain-drenched linoleum. Balls of ice littered the room. The furious wind blew straight through the flimsy curtains, gusting sheets of rain in their faces.

"I don't want to go out there!" April screamed, tugging against Jill's firm grip, but she was through the door before she knew it.

"Where is it?" Jill shouted, looking quickly from one side of the yard to the other, her bangs already drenched and sapped to her face. She swiped them away with the back of her hand and sprinted to her left toward the large wooden box set atop a slab of concrete.

The stones hammered them from all directions, battering them as though they were running a gauntlet. They splashed through the standing water, already nearly drowning the lawn. Arcs of mud flew from their heels.

"Get in!" Jill shouted, unfastening the lock and lifting the close half of the heavy lid.

April clambered up over the lip and plopped down into the scalding water, splashing a wave out onto Jill.

"What do you want me to do?" April sobbed.

"Scoot back and keep your head down!"

Jill could barely hold the lid up against the elements.

"Come on!" she screamed back to Darren who was already halfway across the yard to her. Ray had just passed through the kitchen door, carrying Tina against his chest. She was struggling to remain conscious with her eyes lolling upward.

Darren scampered past Jill and threw himself into the spa, sloshing water everywhere. He spat out a mouthful and scooted back next to April, ducking his head all the way to the surface of the water to squeeze beneath the closed half of the lid.

"You guys are out of your mind!" Rick yelled from where he stood in the doorway. "The last thing you want to do in a storm like this is get into water! Lightning can strike the water—" His voice was drowned out beneath the thunder and banging of hailstones on the hot tub cover.

"Help me!" Ray shouted right into Jill's face, but she was already helping to lift Tina out of his arms and guide her into the water. Her head sunk below the surface, but immediately came up as she violently coughed out the water she'd inhaled.

"Rick!" Jill screamed as Ray scrabbled up to the wooden ledge and dropped into water that felt boiling in contrast to the rain.

He shook his head and looked up to the sky. Lightning snapped from the belly of one black cloud to the next, every bit as blue as the crackling bug zapper.

"You guys are out of your minds!" he shouted back, but finally tucked his chin to his chest and sprinted toward her, splashing through the lawn. He pulled up in front of her and hefted the heavy lid. "Go on!"

Jill threw her left leg up and then splashed down, dragging her right in behind her.

Rick looked over the fence to the left. Past the side of the house he could see the Kappa Delta house across the street. All of the windows were dark, but he could still see the jagged outlines of shattered glass lining the sills. There was a pile of bodies beside the front walk, the yard appearing as though it was covered with half a foot of snow. A dozen girls packed into the open front doorway, screaming and reaching for their fallen friends without daring to step from beneath the safety of the overhang.

He looked back to Jill, who slid right up next to Ray to clear room for him to climb in.

His eyes snapped again to the left. He could barely make out Gina through the slanted storm on all fours, stretching from the porch toward her friends, recoiling every time her bruised arm was struck by one of the enormous chunks of ice.

"Hurry up, Rick!" Jill screamed.

He looked back to her with a wan smile adorning his face, water drenching his features. A line of fluid poured from his chin.

"No, Rick!" Jill screamed.

"I gotta go," he said, taking the edge of the lid in both hands.

"No!" Jill screamed. "You have to get in—"

He cut her off with the closed lid, patting it a couple of times before dashing to the fence and clambering over it.

Jill pressed the lid back open a couple of inches, which was all she could manage with the weight of it above her, but let it fall back into place when the night came to life with insects.

She remembered the vision clearly now. She hadn't seen Rick through a window like she had thought; she had seen his face as it was at that exact moment when he looked in at her with the hot tub lid above his head and the wooden edge below.

Heads tilted all the way back, they gasped at what little chlorine-riddled air was contained beneath the closed lid.

"What's going on?" Ray asked, doing his best to keep not just his chin above the water, but Tina's as well. Both had their eyes closed as the chemicals stung fiercely.

"I don't know," Jill said, swallowing a mouthful of water. "All I know is…" she coughed up the fluid, "…that I knew we were all going to die if we didn't find shelter in here."

"From what?" Ray shouted.

"Ray…" April said, hoping to assuage his tone.

"No! I want to know why the hell we're out here in this closed hot tub in the middle of a storm when we should be halfway to the hospital by now!"

"I'm fine," Tina whispered softly.

He couldn't see her in the absolute darkness—even trying to made his eyes burn—but he felt a swell of relief when her hand closed over his.

"Are you sure, baby? I don't know what I'd do if anything ever happened to—"

She silenced him with a soft kiss on the lips. He could taste her blood in his mouth, but he wasn't about to tear away for anything in the world.

"What aren't you telling us, Jill?" Darren asked. Until that moment he hadn't noticed that April's fingers were laced between his. He sucked in a deep breath to battle the swelling feeling of claustrophobia.

"I… I don't know." That was the honest truth. All she knew with any sort of surety was that when she had really strong feelings like she did right now, it was best to heed them.

The banging of the hail above them slowed like the last few popcorn kernels in a microwave while the rain still pattered the vinyl surface, the sound now almost soothing.

"I can't stay in here any longer," Ray said, though his voice sounded almost resigned.

Before Jill could stop him, Ray shoved open the lid and stood up, tossing it back onto the half above April and Darren.

"No!" she screamed, reaching to try to stop him.

"What?" Ray demanded, staring down at her as she tugged at his shirt.

All Jill could see past him was the driving rain sparkling with the electric glow of lightning.

"You can let go now," he said, offering his hand to Tina and helping her up. "Jill?"

Letting his wet shirt slip from her fingers, Jill leaned back with a confused look washing over her face. Maybe she'd been wrong about the whole thing. But there had been the girls strewn all over the lawn across the street…

She looked around, the rain massaging her scalp with miniature fingers.

The back yard was completely empty, save for the shadows that managed to cling to the shrubbery and ferns in spite of the lightshow overhead. The insects she thought she had seen swarming around the hot tub were obviously no longer there, which made complete sense considering bugs generally bedded down during heavy storms.

She rubbed her stinging eyes.

"Come on, Jill," April said softly, slipping out from beneath the back half of the lid and extending her free hand. "Let's go back inside."

"Okay," Jill whispered, allowing herself to be pulled to her feet. She plopped her rear end on the ledge and swung her legs over, dropping down into the grass with a splash. Ray and Tina were already ducking through the kitchen door. "I don't understand…"

April and Darren followed, neither wanting to break the seal formed by their hands.

Jill walked straight through the kitchen and into the living room, water pouring from her saturated form into the carpet, steam billowing from her shoulders and head. The heat was only now starting to dissipate, the cold slithering in beneath her clothing and prickling her flesh.

She stood there a moment, surveying the damage. Glass covered the floor in a million shards while enormous balls of ice melted into the carpet. The couch beneath the window was drenched and pocked with clumps of juniper torn from the hedge out front. Car alarms droned out in the night outside while somewhere in the distance a siren wailed.

"It's okay," April whispered, setting a hand on her shoulder. "It wasn't your fault."

Jill turned and looked her friend in the eyes, unable to make her mouth form words. She simply turned back to the front door and opened it, stepping out onto the porch. It looked like someone had taken a hammer to the wooden slab. Chunks of ice covered the porch from where the large stones had shattered on the concrete. The front lawn was white.

Feet slapping the wet pavement, she walked toward the street.

Across the street, the pile of bodies had grown beside the front door.

The rain softened, pattering away to nothingness.

Something blew down the center of the road beyond what remained of the parallel-parked cars, tumbling over shattered glass and the accumulation of hail. It wasn't until the wind allowed the object to lie still for a moment that she recognized what it was. The Seahawks logo graced the front of the hat, which headed back down the street at the wind's urging.

"Oh God," Jill gasped, staggering forward to the street. She passed between the bumpers of a pair of cars that now looked more like salvage, oblivious to the computerized epithets of the security system draining the battery, and crossed the street.

The bodies littering the lawn didn't move, and even from the distance, Jill could tell that their faces were beneath the level of the standing water on the grass. The hair trailing beside them in the mire looked like so many used mops. When she reached the curb and passed between another pair of cars, she was able to see eight different bodies lying prone in the yard. Not one of them moved, not even a slight elevation of the shoulders to draw in a breath.

"Are they alright?" someone called over her shoulder, but the words never permeated Jill's ears as she crept forward across the sidewalk to where the hill sloped upward to the yard beside the cracked trio of cement stairs.

A pair of feet dangled over the top step, one still wearing a muddy Nike while a sopping sock hung from the toes of the second. As she climbed the slope, she could see black legs running from the socks up into a pair of khaki shorts. The shirt was ripped to shreds, exposing the deep black back beneath. The man's arms were stretched straight out in front of him, the four fingers of his left hand curled into the soft earth and the bloodied tips torn from those on his right as though trying to drag him forward. His hair looked like a ravaged bird's nest.

Jill knelt beside him, tapping him gently on the shoulder.

"Rick?" she whispered, tears streaming from her eyes.

She couldn't steal her focus from his left ear, which looked like a burnt rind.

Marbled lines of deep blue rose to the surface of his flesh like worms seeking escape from within. Summoning her courage, Jill slid her hands into the mud beneath his chest, and with a heave, rolled him over. With eyes fading to yellow, he stared back at her from the grave. His flimsy mandible bounced, chattering his teeth.

He'd been screaming so hard when he died that he'd dislocated his own jaw.

VI

Near Cliffwood,
New Jersey

Samuels took the lead as they moved inland. Adam was certainly no ballistics expert, but judging by the size of the weapon Samuels pointed down the path ahead, it could have punched a hole through a concrete wall. These men had certainly undergone a different training regime than Adam had. The first thing all of them had done was smear the soil all over their faces, hands, and in their hair. While Adam had been elated to be back on American soil, these men were preparing for guerilla warfare. It seemed excessive to Adam, but the way things were going, he was content just to let them do their jobs and stay out of their way.

The forest crowded the small meandering path, the mighty vine-laden sycamores blocking out all but the occasional glimpse of the black sky above, the flickering lightning casting the shadows first one way, then ripping them in the opposite direction. Rounded stones marred the otherwise coarse dirt path, roots poking from the earth at precarious angles like tentacles feeling for their feet.

Samuels darted from one side of the path to the other, vanishing into the forest before reappearing a dozen paces down the path. His tread was silent, inaudible over even the rustling of the wind clattering branches together and shuffling the leaves on the ground. The desert camouflage didn't blend very well with this locale, but the soldiers disappeared all the same.

It was all Adam could do to keep up. His legs ached and his throat was parched, but beyond that he was finally beginning to feel like himself again. He tried not to think of the caves or anything that had transpired. It was now simply a dream. One thing still haunted him, though. He was sure he had seen the others emerging from the mountain into the sunlight, but it hadn't really been them. They'd been changed somehow. Yet he knew it was them. Not just because it had to be, but because he felt so certain…

Norman walked a stride ahead of him, occasionally looking back over his shoulder to verify that Adam was still there. He didn't speak, but Adam could see the man's nerves were on edge in the way his head jerked at even the slightest sound. Though he walked in plain view, his footfalls were silent, keeping far enough back from Samuels that he could only see the man at the furthest extent of his vision ahead.

Merton was somewhere in the wilderness to the left, keeping pace with Samuels from the thick cover, while Carter did the same thing off to the right. They never saw either man, only the occasional shivering of branches.

Peckham pulled up the rear, mostly walking backward down the path to ensure that nothing came at them from the rear.

No one knew what might be out there, but all agreed that the forest was too still. There were no crows cawing, no deer scampering through the scrub, no squirrels scurrying atop the detritus. It was as though every life form had vanished while they were over the Atlantic.

"Down!" Norman whispered.

Adam threw himself to the side into a tangle of thistle. He'd been so lost in thought that he hadn't seen Samuels stop and hold up his fist.

Looking through the bramble, Adam could see little more than tree trunks and shadows.

The wind scattered a gust of leaves across the path before the sky spat a handful of raindrops, sizzling on the leaves like grease in a frying pan.

"Okay," Norman said from somewhere to his left.

Adam rose slowly, peering through the gnarled forest for any sign of movement.

"Come on," Norman said, breaking into a jog down the center of the path. He kept his waist and knees bent so his head was no higher than the shrubbery surrounding them, but he still moved at a good click.

Adam kept his head down and followed, watching Norman's heels kicking up dirt. He didn't see the others until he was right upon them and nearly barreled right through them and sprinted out into the clearing. At the last second he caught himself on a trunk and hurriedly dropped to one knee. Merton and Carter had converged from the flanks, kneeling beside Samuels and talking so quietly that Adam was sure they had to be reading each other's lips.

The path opened up into a large pasture. A stone wall ran the length of the field to the right, little more than enormous rocks stacked atop one another. The weathered roof of a barn stood above the wall in the midst of a cluster of ancient elms. There was another structure past it, but he couldn't make out any details other than a slanted roof. A stag was crumpled directly across the field at the distant stand of trees marking the end of the clearing. Its antlers were staked in the ground; its front legs crumpled beneath it, rear legs holding the white patch of fur on its rump aloft as though it had been felled in stride. The wind ruffled the fur on the animal's back, but it didn't stir. The hind end of a doe poked out of the shrubbery, legs as stiff as rails.

At first Adam thought the other men must have been looking at the deer, but after a moment he finally saw what had drawn their attention.

A man sat against the wall, mostly concealed by the shadows. He wasn't moving. All Adam could clearly make out was a red and black flannel shirt hanging out from a pair of overalls. The man's hair flagged on the wind, his head lolling limply against his chest.

"You're a doctor, right?" Peckham whispered into his ear from behind. "Ever heard of anything that can drop a pair of deer without putting a hole through them?"

Adam shook his head. His experience with animals was limited to dissection.

"Awfully coincidental there's a dead man in the same field, don't you think?" Peckham whispered, then crawled silently over to the others.

Adam studied the man, waiting for some sign of movement, any little twitch or rise of the chest wall, but there was nothing.

He grabbed his own sleeve and gave it a jerk, tearing the seam and slipping it down over his hand. The other men looked at him as though he'd just blown a bull-horn. Bunching up the sleeve, Adam pinched it over his mouth and nose and stepped out of the forest into the open.

"What are you doing?" he heard someone gasp.

"Get down!" another shouted, but it was too late for that now.

Adam trotted out into the middle of the field, scouring the expanse of meadow as he went for any sign of what might have caused the deaths. The only thing he could think of that was powerful enough to kill anything without a bullet was a biological agent, especially one affecting the respiratory tract. If such an agent were still around, they'd have been dead already, but Adam wasn't prepared to take any chances.

There was something odd about the entire scene. The grass rippled on the wind like water, lightning crashing all around. The farther he got into the field, the faster he began to move. It felt like eyes were on him from every direction at once. He felt naked so far from cover, but there was only one way to figure out what was going on.

Racing right up to the man, Adam crouched in front of him. With his left hand he felt for a carotid pulse, while his right tipped the man's head back. He was prepared to look into the man's eyes to check his pupils, but there weren't any.

He glanced over his shoulder to the others, who were already halfway across the field.

Adam turned back to the man leaning against the rock wall. He'd seen hundreds of dead bodies through medical school and his residency. While it was a sight one never truly grew accustomed to, it was definitely easy enough to recognize after a while. The lips and nailbeds took on a bluish hue as the cells became hypoxic, followed by the other superficial layers of skin. Bruised rings circled the eyes and nostrils, the swelling tongue parting the lips. And there was the smell. There was always the smell. Adam likened it to the aroma that had crept out from beneath his dead cat when he peeled it from the roadside as a boy. The hint of ammonia, the stench of feces, and the indescribable gas that seeped past the body's lips as it slowly deflated.

The man before him now looked nothing like any dead man he'd ever seen.

There was no pulse, which he checked a second time to confirm.

It's not that the pupils had constricted to pinpricks as they occasionally did, but were completely absent. As were the irises. The only living thing that reminded him even remotely of this man's eyes were those of a Tokay gecko. The base color of the man's sclera was a uniform yellow from corner to corner and top to bottom, as though the eyeball had been removed and dunked in canary yellow dye. Amoeboid black shapes marred the surface of the eyes, swirling as though being stirred in liquid. They looked like sentient creatures skimming the surface.

The man's skin had turned as black as a diabetic's necrotic toe, but the texture was all wrong. Rather than the skin drying and losing elasticity, becoming scaly, it had plumped almost like a boiled hot dog. Instead of simply dimpling when he applied pressure to it, the fluids beneath the flesh flowed back into place. As he watched, streaks of a blue darker than the deepest depths of the ocean rose to the surface, marbling to black as though rather than dying, the body had turned into one enormous mess of bruises. It wasn't until he noticed the fingernails peeling away from the skin that he realized the body was still swelling from the inside. That meant there had to be some sort of cellular metabolism happening beneath the skin, but since the body was dead, there had to be something else growing or multiplying inside the man's husk.

"Good God A'mighty!" Samuels said. "What does that look like to you? We talking bio-terrorism here? Anthrax? What?"

"I've never seen anything like it," Adam said, pressing his finger into the man's cheek only to watch it spring back into place. "It's as though there's something infesting him."

"Like roaches?" Carter asked.

"Not like roaches, you idiot!" Peckham said. "He's talking about microscopic stuff."

Adam stood up and looked past the men to where the deer lie heaped at the edge of the field. He started walking toward the carcasses, but his curiosity urged him to a jog. When he reached the buck, he went right around to the head and lowered his face so that he was looking right into the creature's eyes. There was a milky haze over the wide brown eyes and they were bereft of moisture as they were supposed to be. Nothing unusual like the man now across the field. The stag's muzzle was lodged in the dirt, the nostrils packed clear up to the sinuses and the mouth unable to open. There was absolutely no way that it could have breathed if it wanted to.

He stared down at his hands, then carefully placed his right on its furry shoulder and pressed the coarse hairs back against the grain. The skin beneath wasn't black like the man's. Nor was it a healthy skin color. It was as gray as ashes and dotted with red as though it had been assaulted by millions of needles. No blood rose to the surface, only small puckers of flesh dotted with so many little red caps. His first thought was that they must have been caused by ticks, but no matter how he moved the fur, he didn't see a single insect. He traced the shoulder down to the middle of the back, toward the neck, and then stopped. Pressing with his fingertips, he followed the course of the spine all the way up to the base of the deer's skull.

"That can't be right," Adam said, a perplexed look washing over him.

"What is it?" Norman asked from behind him, but Adam was already hustling back across the field toward the dead man.

Winded, Adam dropped to his knees in front of the man's body, grabbing the man's shoulders and leaning him forward. The man's face fell over Adam's shoulder, but he didn't care as he was already palpating the swelling on the back of the man's neck leading up to his head.

"Encephalitis," he said, lowering the man to his side and rolling him onto his chest. He pushed at two barely noticeable lines of swelling paralleling the corpse's spinal column.

"What does that mean?" Peckham asked.

"See all of this swollen tissue to either side of his cervical spine? Those are layers of the sheath that covers his spinal cord to protect it from damage within the vertebral column. When these layers get irritated or filled with fluid, the spine can no longer contain them, and they end up increasing in pressure until they finally rupture through the gaps between bones."

"What causes something like that?" Norman asked. "I've seen a couple cases of encephalitis, but this looks nothing like those."

"It more closely resembles a meningocele, which is a birth defect where spinal fluid accumulates between the layers of the sheath."

"So you think this guy's got a meningocele?"

"No... not specifically, but both this guy and the deer have an abnormal amount of fluid collected in their spinal cords, which would lead me to believe that either there was some sort of organism inside them capable of stimulating the production of cerebrospinal fluid or some other kind of fluid has been injected into that space."

"And that would have killed him?" Peckham asked.

"A large amount of pressure on the spinal cord or brain could definitely kill someone…"

"You don't sound so sure," Samuels said.

"I've never seen anything quite like this, it's as if—"

"Down!" Samuels shouted, slamming Adam in the middle of the back. His chin bounced off the ground before he even felt himself falling. He scrabbled forward until he felt the cold stone wall in front of him and blinked frantically to try to chase the stars from his vision.

"What happened?" he asked, wiping a smear of blood from his lips. He'd nipped his tongue when he landed.

Samuels leaned into his face and held a single finger in front of his lips to shush him.

Adam nodded weakly and rose to his knees so he could see through a gap in the wall.

Past the barn, the field sloped upward toward the tree line. It was hard to discern the shape from the shadows beneath the trees, but Adam could certainly feel its eyes upon him.

There was a series of faint clicks as safeties were disengaged from weapons.

Adam couldn't seem to tear his gaze away. It was as though whatever was up there held some sort of power over him. Faint contrast finally drew its silhouette against the darkness with each ferocious explosion of lightning overhead.

A man sat atop a steed, his pallid skin reflecting the shifting glare as though his skin were made of polished pearl. Electricity stabbed the ground all around him, making the horse appear to be constructed only of bones. The forest behind the rider cringed, the trees bowing away from him as though blown by a ferocious gale. Though it couldn't have been possible, Adam was certain that the rider stared directly at him through the small gap in the stone wall.

"What the hell is that?" Norman gasped. "That horse has no skin!"

The horse rose to its full height, punching at the air with its front hooves. The man astride the beast knotted his fists into a mane that looked like a tangle of briars, his head buckling backward against his shoulders. Lightning tore up the ground all around him, his opaque skin not just reflecting the attacking bolts, but absorbing them until he was the same shade of electric blue. Darkness erupted from his open mouth, as though the tail of a tornado was trapped in his throat, swirling, trying to tear free. The conical whirlwind rose above the man, funneling up into the sky until it connected the rider directly to the storm, and then raced outward like a flood.

"Jesus Christ!" one of the men shouted.

By the time Adam spun to face the sound of the voice, all he could see was the man's back as he sprinted away. Darkness blotted out the sky, smothering even the lightning, which barely passed through in shimmering arcs like the evening light through rustling leaves.

It sounded as though a jet engine had been turned on them from the other side of the wall, but it wasn't just the nearly deafening drone of the buzzing, but the tremendous wind that blew hard enough to topple some of the loose rocks from atop the wall.

A tsunami of seething blackness hammered whoever had decided to run squarely in the middle of the back, cleaving him from his feet and tossing him forward into the air before engulfing him whole. A bolt of lightning crashed right down where he fell.

Adam spun back to the safety of the stone wall, which felt as though it was being rammed by a tank from the other side. A solid stream of darkness blasted over his head above the wall, but it wasn't until he stared directly up into its heart that he was able to discern what it was.

Locusts. Millions of them, flowing like shotgun pellets fired from so many guns. The buzzing wasn't a single sound, but the cacophonous roar of an infinite number of wings.

Throwing himself to the ground, Adam scurried along his belly toward where he assumed the other men to be, ramming headfirst into something soft and forgiving. He looked up and found himself staring into the open eyes of the dead man. Locusts crawled across his face, darting in and out of every available orifice, before arising as one and merging back into the impossible swarm racing past overhead.

As quickly as they had descended upon them, the locusts were gone, their buzzing fading like a trucker's horn on the interstate. It was only a moment before the sound was gone entirely.

A soldier lie face down in the field a dozen strides away.

Adam scurried toward him on all fours, grabbed the man by the shoulder as soon as he was within reach, and flopped him over onto his back.

Merton's rag doll arms flopped uselessly to his sides.

"Talk to me, soldier!" Adam shouted, but he could already tell from his vacuous eyes that the man was dead. His mouth hung askew with triangular chips missing from his front teeth.

"What's his status?" Peckham asked just loud enough to be heard.

When Adam turned to face him, the lieutenant could read his answer in the doctor's face.

The crest of the hill behind Peckham was now abandoned. Only the fragmented trunks of trees remained around a ring of scorched earth, the lightning now stabbing farther in the distance beyond the forest.

Adam grabbed Merton's legs and dragged him back to the relative security behind the wall. What wasn't burned was broken, the body flopping behind him as he pulled it through the tall grass.

Adam felt as though his skin was covered with locusts, crawling beneath his clothing and setting every nerve ending to tingling. He'd never seen so many insects in all of his life combined, let alone all at one time... and so many moving at such great velocity... Nothing made any sort of coherent sense as his mind flashed images past at blinding speed. The plane crash. The dead soldiers smashed flat in their seats. The deer. The locusts. Encephalitis. The man.

Adam scrambled up against the wall, his heart beating fit to burst. Pressing himself uncomfortably against the stacks of stones, feeling as though his life were in dire danger, he looked to his right.

Yellow eyes with a skein of swirling black oil stared back at him from the corpse.

And blinked.

CHAPTER 6

I

Secretary of Defense Jack Remington lie on the floor at the head of the table in the War Room, his feet tangled in the legs of the toppled chair. A dozen other bodies littered the floor like a child's forgotten plastic soldiers. Bottles of champagne sat in the middle of the table, the foil wrappers over the corks perfectly intact.

Dim red and blue light lit the room like the stilled sirens of a police cruiser from the large screen in the wall past the foot of the table, where a map of the United States was prominently displayed.

The Star Wars defenses had been ninety-eight point six percent effective in destroying the surface-to-air nuclear warheads launched from nearly a hundred different sites across China. Only three missiles reached their desired targets, leaving little more than smoldering craters where Tucson, Albuquerque, and Amarillo once were. The other two-hundred and thirteen warheads were now sifting into the silt on the bottom of the ocean.

Rows of high-definition monitors lined the walls behind the overturned chairs, featuring live satellite reconnaissance feeds of various important international sites. There were no signs of movement on an aerial view of Buckingham Palace. Tanks and military vehicles ringed the outer gates, the inner courtyard packed with the corpses of fallen soldiers. The outer expanses were filled with the corpses of the citizenry who had erroneously sought protection by the Crown, piled one atop the other throughout the entire frame, a cemetery of the unburied lorded over by the golden angel with trumpet in hand atop a fountain covered with corpses, heralding the rebirth of the scurrying black things that swarmed over the fields of the dead like ants.

Smoke shrouded the Kremlin, the wind alternately exposing vast fields of carcasses under a settling mat of gray snow and ash, and the ornate golden parapets atop buildings and cathedrals violated by black shapes slithering in and out of the shattered windows.

The streets surrounding the Brandenburg Gate in Berlin were packed with the bodies of the picketers who had been protesting the war from afar, their signs blowing across their bloated remains. Atop the stone gate itself, someone had spray-painted the words "More Man Tea" and punctuated them with a wash of blood several dark things now fought over.

There was nothing left of Tiananmen Square but the gray and red rubble atop charred bodies fueling the nuclear fires.

Jack had been preparing to pop the champagne when the buzzing had begun in the ductwork leading up to surface above the subterranean compound. Mosquitoes had poured through the grates before anyone was even able to identify the sound.

The war had been over before the United States' retaliatory nuclear strike ever reached its target. The dogs lie still, felled before they could celebrate that the eight hundred thousand in Tucson, five hundred fifty thousand in Albuquerque, and one hundred ninety thousand in Amarillo were the only casualties. Though compared to what was soon to come for Jack Remington and his mongering compatriots, their deaths were merciful and swift.

The bodies had already plumped and bruised, threatening to tear through the confining clothes when the locusts funneled down through the ductwork and covered their corpses, scuttling in and out of every orifice unnoticed until they were finally called away by their master to continue the westward infestation.

Now, the toils of their labor began to bear fruit.

A knot of flesh rose on Jack's bloated black neck over his spine, followed by another, and then another like an unborn child's hands through a mother's belly. The flesh stretched taut until it looked as though pyramids were growing all up and down his neck. With a tearing sound, his flimsy flesh ripped right down the center, peeling back to either side. A series of long black spines rose to their full height from the middle of the chasm of flesh.

The skin tore away from the opening like lightning bolts through the tissue, the clothes holding the halves together only momentarily before tearing from the collar all the way to the waist, where the belt strained against the inner revolt. With a scream like a hiss of air through a hole in an oxygen tank, the body buckled, folding sickly forward. Both hands slapped the floor, pressing the body up to all fours. The skin covering the fingers popped open and was shed away from the knobby lengths of bone formerly sheathed within; chunks of adipose tissue rode a wave of pus out of the body through the skin, now sloughing off in chunks. As he arose, Jack's humanity fell from what he had become like placental remains following his rebirth.

The creature that had been the Secretary of Defense rose to its full height, sinewy spine popping loudly.

Tightly-meshed scales like those of a salmon covered his bare body from head to toe, a shade of black deeper than midnight. Sharp spines protruded from his jawbone beneath either ear, a series of them running along the slant of his mandible to his chin, growing smaller until they were little more than nubs. A tatter of scaly flesh hung beneath his chin, flattened to his scrawny neck like a dewlap, red as a widow's hourglass, as though he'd been slit straight up the neck. What had once been lips were now twin rows of matching scales following the course of the torn corners of the mouth halfway back through the cheeks. There was no cartilage to blunt the nose, but rather a small spike which formed the peak of a triangle of stretched reptilian skin, the nostrils oblong diagonal slashes. He scoured the room with eyes so yellow that they created a phosphorescence of their own, marred by amoeboid black shapes like a leopard's coat had it taken on life, watching as the others slowly began to draw their first breaths of the afterlife.

Limp spines cascaded from his head and the sides of his neck like so many dreadlocks, draping down over pectoral muscles resplendent with small pointed peaks like chocolate chips, his smoothly scaled abdomen leading to a cloacal vent surrounded by an assortment of spikes like a mountain range encircling his waist before trailing down the backs of his thighs to his calves where they again rose as sharp lances like miniature yucca plants. Where the flesh had been stripped away from the bones of the feet, the toes had been replaced with scales clear back to the bases of the metatarsals so their feet looked like a bird's, were it to have five long toes rather than three, and a stunted calcaneal hook.

The creature rocked back onto its heels and screamed up into the ceiling, causing the very earth between it and the surface to tremble. The formerly limp spines adorning its neck straightened to attention, giving it the appearance of a pine tree for a neck, while the great flap of skin under its chin snapped wide into a tattered arc, flaring as red as a matador's cape. The whole head shivered with bestial rage, shivering loose the last droplets of humanity to pattern the floor of the War Room.

It leapt effortlessly atop the table and sped across it, sharpened protrusions of bone like talons tearing ribbons of wood from the oak table. Bottles of champagne were launched across the room to shatter into a foaming mess that spread toward the discarded refuse of humanity littering the tiled floor in piles. Tendons flinched under the black skin, and the creature was airborne, driving its claws through the metal grate and wrenching it aside, sharpened heels boring straight into the concrete wall. As if lacking any substantive structure, the creature flattened first its head and then its shoulders, and shimmied right into the duct in the wall. Sparks flew from its talons as it disappeared into the darkness, following the air to its source a hundred feet up.

The others followed, bellowing shrieking hisses and scurrying up the walls as though gravity were only a mild inconvenience, ducking through the far too small vent and slithering upward to the world. Their world.

Cry havoc...

II

Adam threw himself backward, slamming his head against one of the smooth stones fallen from the wall, but he didn't even feel it. He was completely enraptured by the yellow and black eyes locked on his, on the groaning sounds the corpse was making as it tried to rise from the ground.

Claws split through the bratwurst-like fingers of the body, the flesh curling back like petals from a blooming stamen. With a tearing sound, long black spines arose from the back of the man's head, trailing all the way down past his shoulders. A seam ripped down the center of his forehead, and before Adam could even catch his breath, those clawed fingers were hooked beneath the rent flesh, skinning himself.

Adam scrabbled in reverse, unable to steer his gaze from the scene playing out before him. The flesh peeled away to reveal a misshapen head wider than the cranium that had formerly contained it. It was flat along the top, the spikes rising from the center of it like a series of daggers. The eyes were set into deep gouges, surrounded with heavily ridged scales like the twin mouths of so many caves. It shivered, the fleshy chunks of the face and shoulders slopping to either side. With a loud hiss like water tossed on boiling oil, the creature reared back, opening a mouth so wide it extended nearly all the way across its cheeks to its ears. Hooked reptilian teeth rimmed the black maw, the bulbous tongue merely tipped by the formation of a fork.

"What the hell?" Samuels gasped, and the next thing Adam knew, the grunt had the barrel of his weapon against the side of the creature's head.

Before Adam could close his eyes, hot fluids spattered up his chest and across his face, the headless creature swaying momentarily as it tried to continue the motion of rising to its feet, before finally dropping back to its knees and falling forward. A rush of pasty fluids washed out across the grass from the thing's stunted head.

"Jesus," Peckham spat, unable to comprehend what he was seeing. "Stand down!"

Samuels didn't even hear him over the whirring expulsion of another round, which pounded a hole through the dead thing's back, leaving a crater in the dirt below.

"Did you see that?" Carter shrieked. "Did you guys freaking see that? He was dead. You all saw him. The guy was freaking dead and then he was trying to get back up... His head just split open like—"

Norman placed a hand on the soldier's shoulder and he flinched like the medic had been holding an iron to his flesh.

"Time to move out," Samuels said firmly, his wild eyes unblinking. Something had tripped inside of him and he was now strung as tight as a power line.

"I'm in charge here," Peckham said, but when the other man turned and Peckham saw the look on his face, he gave up his pretensions.

Adam dared to scoot closer to the body, staring straight down the neck. The head hadn't been cleanly removed, but he could clearly decipher the anatomy. His cross-sectional understanding was limited to CT and MRI scans, but he could clearly see the severed trachea burbling little white bubbles in front of an esophageal tatter. The cervical spine looked as he had expected it to, with one small exception. The spinous processes had grown nearly a foot long, terminating in the spikes he had watched tear through the back of the dead man's neck. The canal that carried the spinal nerves to the brain had expanded so much that it had ruptured through the weakened pedicles of the vertebrae, the spinal fluid no longer a light amber, but rather a rich rusted orange like an aged railroad spike.

Before he could even begin to examine what remained of the man's back, Samuels was jerking him to his feet by the back of his shirt and shoving him forward across the field. The other men were already sprinting low along the wall to the far side of the field, disappearing into the thick forest again.

Adam glanced to his left before he crashed into the underbrush. The buck's carcass no longer stood from the ground as it had only moments prior, its antlers stabbing the earth. All that remained was a long patch of blood atop a spread of fur as though it had been removed from the meat and stretched to tan. A flash of gold caught his eye as something bounded away from him, its hind quarters as red as the setting sun, and then he was slapping branches from his face.

He tripped and scrabbled on all fours, forcing himself to his feet to keep pace with the other men. Without a path, they threw themselves heedlessly forward through the brush, the scrub slashing nasty scrapes into their forearms and cheeks, the rapidly approaching trunks of the sycamores giving just a heartbeat's notice for them to swerve to the side.

Adam couldn't even begin to comprehend what was going on. He had witnessed whatever that thing was crawling out from the dead man's skin. There was no rationalizing that thought away. He'd peeled his own skin like he was tearing off a bandage.

"There!" one of them shouted ahead of him, though by the time Adam looked up from making sure that he didn't trip and lose his footing, they were already upon it. Carter stood at the back door of a small farmhouse with some sort of warehouse abutting it. He was banging on the door with his fist so hard that the trim around it was starting to crack.

"Open the door!" he shouted, looking back over his shoulder and doing a head count.

"Stand aside," Samuels said calmly, walking up the pair of cement steps and raising one of his enormous boots. With a grunt, he kicked the door inward so hard that the knob was driven into the waiting wall behind.

Samuels disappeared into the darkened kitchen as the storm grumbled overhead.

The others hurried into the house behind. They were through the kitchen and into the living room before they noticed the absolute silence. The smell intensified with each advancing step.

Down the hallway to the right, a bloated woman with diseased-looking black skin lie on her side under the blankets in the bedroom to the left, her child in the room across the hall. Neither so much moved enough to suggest any semblance of life, though the stench was nearly proof-positive to the contrary.

"No one back here," Carter said.

"You think?" Peckham snapped.

Carter's stare flashed with rage, barely contained by twisting his grip on his rifle.

"There's no time for this," Norman said, wrapping his arm across Carter's chest and guiding him toward the front door, which stood wide, revealing twin Hummers sitting right in front of the house.

Samuels was nowhere in sight.

"Where did he go?" Norman asked, the last across the front porch and onto the withered lawn, but his question was answered by a large bang from off to the right.

They followed the sound, rushing to the front of a large steel building that almost looked like an old airplane hanger. The wide front door stood ajar.

"Samuels," Peckham called, charging through the open door.

The larger man was at the back of a room filled with farming implements, from a tractor that looked like its prime was well behind it to a claw-toothed tiller that was dented and broken from trying to turn the rocky earth.

"Tell me," Samuels shouted from the back of the room, where he was grabbing large steel racks covered with paint cans and bags of seed, prying them from against the back wall and toppling them face-first to the concrete floor. "How does a small farmer with little cash crop afford a Hummer, let alone two?"

Peckham didn't know where Samuels was going with that question, but Carter picked up on the cue.

"Come to think of it, I didn't see much of anything at all growing on that back acreage."

He joined Samuels against the back wall, banging against it to hear the hollow intonation like a bass drum.

"Stand back!" Samuels finally yelled in frustration. He raised the assault rifle and punched a hole through the drywall. Pounding the edges of the freshly-opened wound, he widened it until he could crawl through, slipping one leg through before following with his upper body and finally the remaining leg.

He whistled from beyond.

"What'd you find, Sam?" Carter called, ducking in behind him.

After a moment, he stuck his head back out. "You guys aren't going to believe this."

◉   ◉   ◉

Adam had never seen that much money in his life. Each of the steel cases lining the wall to the left were packed with hundred dollar bills stuffed so tightly that he couldn't even slip his fingertips in to pry any of the stacks out. There had to be multiple millions of dollars in that one room alone and God only knew how many more were stashed around the place.

Samuels stared up at the retractable roof, following the steel cords down to the wenches mounted on the walls to either side. Large wooden crates were stacked atop palettes in the center of the room. Lengths of thick chain ran beneath the palettes before wrapping back over the top where they were bound together by a large rusted hook.

Carter broke open one of the crates, hauled out a large bundle and tossed it into the middle of the floor. It was about the size of a concrete block, wrapped tightly in duct tape. He set down his rifle long enough to grab his knife from the hilt and stabbed it into the brick. Withdrawing it, a cloud of white powder blossomed from the wound.

"Well, now what do you think about that?" he mused.

"Any luck?" Norman called to Peckham, who was clear back in the outer room trying to raise anyone on the com-link. So far all they'd been able to find was static, but Peck looked bound and determined that he was going to find something regardless. As he had one hand pressed over his free ear, and the other mashed by the receiver on the device, he was oblivious to anything but. There had been no dial tone in the house, nor any other means of outside contact.

"A real entrepreneur," Adam said, finally turning away from the massive stockpile of cash, "but what does this have to do with getting out of here?"

Samuels smiled and walked over to one of the chained palettes. He closed the enormous hook in his hand and gave it a solid tug, looking up at the peak of the corrugated metal roof.

"It's got to be close," was his only response, though a smile crossed his lips.

Grabbing his rifle, he walked back toward the impromptu entrance they had created not five feet from where the real door was hidden behind a cabinet filled with camouflaged jackets and hats for all of the various seasons, and climbed through the hole. He passed Peckham without a second glance and walked just out beneath the slight overhang of the building.

To the right was a thick copse of trees bordering the driveway leading off into the forest. He ran for it without a word or a look back over his shoulder.

Carter followed while the others hung back with their commanding officer, who was now shouting obscenities into the crackling static, watching as Samuels disappeared into the woods.

"I don't know what in the world that jackass thinks he's possibly going to find that will be of any kind of use—" Peckham cursed, the words dying the moment Samuels staggered backward toward the road, dragging what looked to be a mess of vines out onto the gravel.

The whole wall of trees seemed to be following him, trailing what appeared to be large branches as though cascading down a waterfall behind until they revealed—

"Sweet mother of Pearl," Norman said reverently, chasing the words with a whistle.

Four long blades were the first to reveal themselves, followed by a camouflaged body that nearly matched the forest identically. A smaller rotor adorned the tail of the thing.

Carter whooped and threw back the sliding cargo door and hopped up into the cabin beside what appeared to be a bucket seat.

"What?" Samuels called, beaming. "You ladies need an invitation?"

III

Missy sat on the living room floor in front of the couch, repeatedly dialing 911. Each time a busy signal replied, she switched off the cordless phone and dialed it again. Over and over and over until, with a scream, she hurled it across the room against the wall. A piece of plastic fractured off, letting the battery dangle out by little red and black cords onto the carpet.

They'd gone house to house, ringing doorbells at first, and then finally just walking through the front doors with a cursory knock. Everyone they came across was not only already dead, but swollen up like so many hammer-smashed thumbs. Mrs. Perkins had stared back at them from beneath the dissipating bubbles in her bathtub. Mr. Houghton had been propped up in the corner of his brand new theater room with a flyswatter in his hand, his corpse framed by Rorschach smears of insect guts on the freshly painted wall. Kelly Weston, who Missy had babysat until the year before, had made it halfway from the swing set in the backyard to the screen door, propped open by her mother's bloated form, before being overtaken. There had been plenty of other people whom they couldn't recognize sitting behind the wheels of their cars where they'd crashed into lampposts, or heaped in front of their open mailboxes, or scattered around their television sets that hummed the emergency broadcast signal tone. How many had died with the 911 recording playing in their now deafened ears. It even looked like there was a whole football team lying in the field beyond the high school amidst toppled orange cones.

The endless droning of car horns was the only semblance of life to be either seen or heard. Squirrels encircled the trunks of the trees where they'd fallen; lifeless lumps of fur lie behind fences and in windowsills; birds littered the streets. No matter how loud either screamed or how fast or far they ran, there was nothing left alive to answer them. No one running panicked through the streets like they were. No one cowering in their homes waiting for whatever fate had slipped through town like the spectral cloud of death to return. Everyone. Everything. Dead.

Mare had receded into himself, leaving Missy as the only one still even remotely attached to her senses. She knew it had fallen to her to come up with a plan, but what could they possibly do? They couldn't walk endlessly through the streets looking for signs of life that were nowhere to be found. With each passing cadaver, hope seemed to slip just a little further away like air through a leaking balloon. She feared that if they set out again, they'd simply continue walking until they either found something, someone, or walked themselves into the grave.

Right now she could only imagine what her little brother was doing upstairs. He hadn't said a word on the way back and had walked right to the staircase and ascended without pause.

She was scared to death and the entire world felt as though it was swimming in circles around her, but if she didn't force herself to her feet and start figuring out what the hell they were going to do, who was going to?

"Mare?" she called, her voice a weak rasp.

Clearing her throat, she rose and stumbled toward the stairs on feet under assault from pins and needles. It felt as though she was in slow motion, every movement labored and deliberate, winding down like a clock. The groaning of the banister, the moaning from the steps, even the most minuscule sound of her heel squishing in her shoes was comforting. Anything that reminded her of normalcy right now was worth its weight in gold. What she wouldn't give for the doorbell to ring or for the dog to yap endlessly next door.

"Mare?" she said from the landing, interrupting the otherwise oppressive silence.

The door to her father's bedroom stood ajar.

Please don't let him be in there, she thought, momentarily closing her eyes to summon her strength before taking the first step toward the last place in the world she wanted to go. She didn't realize her hand was shaking until she saw it reaching for the door and pushing it inward.

Mare sat on the floor with his back to her, resting his head on his father's hand, dangling over the side of the bed, which he held tightly in his own.

"I'll be good. I promise," he whispered.

Missy couldn't bring herself to take her eyes from her brother for fear she'd register the dried blood on the walls and ceiling or reconcile the stench with its origin.

"Come on, Mare," she whispered, gently placing a hand on his shoulder and trying to coax him from the bedside.

"Just a minute," he whispered, planting a kiss on the back of his father's now blackened hand, which she hadn't noticed until now was swollen so much that his wedding band looked like it was about to cost him a finger. "He didn't mean to do it."

"I know," she said, still trying to ease him up from his knees.

"It was the whiskey."

"I know, Mare."

"He wouldn't have ever thought of hurting us without it."

"Come on, little brother."

"We can't just leave him here like this, Missy," Mare said, allowing himself to be guided to his feet but no farther.

"There's nothing we can do for him now."

"I know. I just… I can't stand the thought of him just lying here for… for God to see."

The last four words trailed into nothingness.

A tear swelled from her eye and crept tentatively down her cheek. She fought the urge to swipe it away as the sensation was the only thing she'd actually felt besides fear in far too long.

"God knows he was sorry," she said, though the last image she would carry of her father was a snapshot of the look of rage on his face when he had belted her.

"But does God forgive him?"

Missy averted her eyes from her brother's. All she could see within was the little boy whose stare she'd locked onto as they'd lowered her mother into the ground.

"Mare," she started, but never even formulated the rest of the thought.

A shadow passed over the window as though God Himself had flipped off a light switch. Suddenly, there was no flash of blue lightning through the windows. No light at all, save for dazzling dots of light that managed to permeate whatever had crossed over the sky, swirling all around them like fairies.

A roaring sound enveloped them, like speeding into a long tunnel with the windows down. It felt as though the sky itself had collapsed down upon them and was preparing to smother them.

Missy screamed for Mare to get down, but the sound easily swallowed her voice.

Black dots hammered the window like pebbles. Cracks splintered sideways all the way to the frame, the glass dropping free in jagged triangles from the shattering pane. Her only thought was of her brother as she threw herself at him, tackling him to the ground beside the bed where their father's corpse rested. It sounded like a tornado had been set loose within the room, the wind roaring. A heavy weight dropped down upon her, knocking the wind out of her.

She felt thousands of small legs scurrying all over her flesh in time to bite down on her lip to keep herself from gasping for air. They seethed all over her, scuttling through her hair and scratching their way into her ears with a sound like a mouse chewing wood behind drywall. Every nerve ending in her body screamed for her to slap whatever they were off of her, but she had no choice but to fight the urge and keep both hands pressed firmly over her face so that nothing could scurry up her nose or burrow into the corners of her teary eyes.

With a great whistling sound, the sky drew a deep inhalation and sucked all of the insects out through the window they had shattered only moments prior.

"Get 'em off me!" Missy trilled with her first breath, flopping over onto her back and clawing at her own arms.

A dozen crushed carcasses that reminded her of enormous grasshoppers crunched beneath her as she struggled to her feet, still shivering against the crawling sensation.

Mare just stared up at her from the ground, his eyes wide, pupils dilated. His face was covered with a thin layer of brown sludge like tobacco spit, save for the white rings around his eyes and mouth. His hair was slick with it and even his clothes were damp. It looked like he'd been splashed with a couple buckets of swamp water.

"Are you okay?" he gasped, still lying perfectly motionless as though the slightest movement would prove fatal.

"They're all over me!" she shrieked, clawing red scratches into her snow-white legs.

"No they aren't," he said, finally forcing himself to his feet. "They're gone."

He clasped his hands to either side of her face and lowered his voice.

"They're gone, Miss. They're gone."

She still stomped in place, but collapsed forward into his arms, allowing herself to be overcome by sobbing.

"We'll get through this," he whispered into her ear.

She balled her hands to fists and squeezed his back.

"You've just got to promise me one thing, okay?"

She took a step back and dropped her eyes to the floor, forcing herself to only rub at her skin instead of ferociously scratching it like she really wanted to.

"Name it," she whispered, sniffing and dragging her forearm beneath her nose.

"Promise me you'll take a shower."

She snorted back what felt like laughter and looked up in time to see a flash of the Mare she knew and loved in his eyes.

"You look like you've been rolling in crap," he said, the corner of his mouth curling upward.

"So do you," she said, pawing the tears from her eyes. "You've got it all over your fa—"

The word died on her tongue, her eyes snapping wide.

Mare spun around as Missy caught her breath and screamed.

Their father was standing on the bed, though it looked like someone else was standing behind him, holding his body aloft. His head lolled forward, but rather than stopping when his chin touched his chest, he just continued tumbling over the side of the bed and into a heap of gushy black flesh. What now stood in his stead was something stolen straight from a nightmare.

Its head was broad and flat with a chunk missing from the middle as though someone had taken a giant bite out of it. Rich white fluid burbled from the opening, spilling from its head like lava down the sides of a volcano. It swayed back and forth, gaining momentum until it stumbled off the back of the bed and slammed into the wall beneath the window, what looked like spikes on the back of its black head stabbing straight through the plaster and tearing twin gouges all the way down to the floor, chalky powder floating around it like snow.

Mare looked quickly down to where the creature had deposited his father's remains, but there wasn't enough mass there for it to have been a human form. It was as though all that was left of his father was a puddle of skin atop a mess of gelatinous fat, seeping out from the sleeves and pant legs of the clothes he'd been wearing when he died.

"What in God's name was that?" he shouted, whirling to face his sister, who'd backed against the wall beside the doorway and appeared to be trying to retreat straight through it.

He cautiously leaned forward over the edge of the bed, bracing himself on his hands and rising to his tiptoes to see past the far side.

Whatever it was, it was folded in half between the bed and the wall, legs pointing to the ceiling like a dead canary at the bottom of a cage, knees crammed against its shoulders. Its skin was black and shiny like some of the marsh snakes he'd caught as a child, only it had a texture more like that of a trout, smooth, seamless. Long spikes protruded from the thing's shoulders, while shorter nubs lined its neck. A scaly black beard hung from a chin that looked like a jagged rock formation, the mouth formed of smooth stones lining the lips halfway across the cheeks to a larger oblong scale right in front of ears that looked as though they'd been turned inside out. Clear eyelids snapped open and closed over eyeballs as bright as the sun, swirling with black sunspots as it clawed at the enormous wound atop its head with reptilian digits. More of the fluid poured from its fractured skull before it finally shuddered violently and stilled with a long hiss.

Its left hand fell limply to its side, spattering ivory goo onto the carpet, but that wasn't what held Mare's attention. He was enraptured with the creature's gnarled finger, where between grotesquely knobbed knuckles, it wore his father's wedding band.

IV

Phoenix awoke with his own screams echoing back to him in the confines of the small room. It felt as though his skin was covered with tiny legs. Slapping madly at his arms and legs, grinding his fists into his eyes, he leapt to his feet, throwing the straw he had burrowed beneath all around. It wasn't until he'd swiped his palms across every inch of himself that he was able to comprehend that all he felt was the straw.

He could clearly remember the mosquitoes. How could anyone possibly have forgotten the excruciating pain of having every available inch of flesh stabbed by so many insects? His mind must have spared him from the pain by simply shutting down and leaving him in the darkness of his unconscious until he was able to finally awaken remarkably… unscathed.

Grazing his fingertips across his face, he couldn't feel any sort of noticeable swelling or pocks anywhere. He could very vividly remember the moment when he'd been stung, but absolutely nothing after that.

"My friends must have spared me," he whispered, turning round and round in the darkness.

As if in response, the sounds of scuttling filled the room, from the rafters, the walls; the basement came to life all around him.

Chitinous bodies dropped from above onto his shoulders and scurried up his legs, speaking to him in tones so silent he couldn't comprehend their words, only the scratching sounds of their feet on concrete and each other, a choir of clicking. They swarmed the entirety of his form, wrapping around him like a blanket that felt not frightening or repulsive, but warm, almost like the woman's embrace. He was filled with a sense of security, of belonging, and for the first time in his life felt a sense of completeness.

The house moaned above as a great wind arose to make it tremble, the thundering sound vibrating the very foundation beneath his feet. Faster and faster the roaches moved, covering every inch of him like living armor. He could feel them on the sensitive skin of his eyelids, plugging his nose and ears.

"More man tears," he whispered before closing his mouth and allowing the roaches to cover his lips.

As the first of the locusts pressed under the seal of the door and forced themselves through every possible fissure and crack, Phoenix was transported into a dream to leave his guarded body to stand against the plague of insects.

He remembered it now, for he had dreamed the same dream hundreds of times before, the kind of elusive visions that dissipated upon the dawn. Water as cold as ice lapped at his bare heels, snow white sand clotting between his toes. Steam rolled in banks of clouds from an interminable body of water to his left, water so deep blue it was nearly black faded in and out of the fog, choppy with waves. His eyes dropped to his right hand to find smaller fingers laced between his, beyond another pair of bare feet covered in white silt. He looked to her face, but all he saw was a hint of a smile before the sun beyond washed out her features. She was familiar. He'd seen her so many times that her visage was more recognizable than his own, and yet even in the dream he couldn't reassemble her features into a tangible image.

A tornado of locusts swirled around his body in the dank basement, filling every inch of airspace while almost imperceptible roach feet poked through his outer layer of skin.

In his mind, Phoenix strode forward with foaming brine rising over his ankles. Shapes appeared through the mist, no more substantial than ghosts. If it were possible, they appeared even lighter than the sand, as though formed of the same substance and glazed in the heart of a celestial body. As he drew near, features formed from the smooth granite: a woman knelt with her hands clasped before her, head covered by a long shawl which flowed around the rest of her like a gown; a cherubic child with wings coming from his shoulders stood on one foot atop a tall pedestal, a horn in his right hand eternally raised to the heavens; a man stood with his arms stretched out to either side as though welcoming Phoenix to enter his embrace. There were dozens more, simply standing there, motionless, awaiting his approach. It wasn't until he was nearly upon them that he noticed the earth standing before them was mounded, as though the unmoving people guarded whatever was buried beneath the long lumps of white sand. He walked carefully so as not to step on any of the mounds, weaving between them. Thick black smoke eclipsed his vision, swallowing him into darkness.

The locusts pounded his body, trying to force their way through the shield of roaches, until finally they were sucked back through the holes they had entered through, leaving him standing alone in the cellar.

The vision was ripped away from him like a receding tide, carrying with it the deep black smoke he could still feel in his lungs and the taste of salt on his lips.

Emerging from his ears and his nasal canals, the roaches began scuttling back down his body. They descended his face, their little legs twitching spastically before simply falling off. Hundreds of bodies dropped from his shoulders and bare arms, from his chest and suddenly trembling legs. There was no longer the sound of scratching or the clicking of so many feet on the concrete. The entire room was still around him, save for the last of the current from the locusts' passage winding down into the silence.

He feared to move, for the thought of crushing even a single one of those insects, his friends, was more than he could bear. Sweeping his feet from side to side, he cleared a swatch in the middle of the bodies, just enough to allow him to drop to his knees. His fingers crossed the cold cement floor until they encountered the mess of exoskeletons, slipping beneath and lifting handfuls of the motionless creatures. With his thumbs, he traced the backs of their shells in his palms. Each and every one of them bore a large puncture wound as though a nail had been driven straight through. A viscous fluid poured from those openings as he shifted them in his hands, already the first patter of droplets tapping on his knees.

"Please forgive me," he whispered, gently easing the handfuls to the right where he set the bodies neatly atop the straw. "I am not worthy of your sacrifice."

He swept up two more mounds of roaches, again finding each diminutive shell to have been drilled through by the other insects that these wonderful creatures had protected him from. They must have had fierce claws or mandibles sharp enough to drive through even the roaches' venerable shells, or perhaps whatever fluid had been injected into them had been corrosive enough to melt right through the chitin. Either way, there was nothing left of his friends inside of those hollow exoskeletons. They were nearly as light as the air itself.

Gently, he dropped those from his hands beside their brethren on the straw bed and began the arduous process of gathering the remainder to lay them to rest. They had given their lives for him in exchange for a bowl of soggy oats. To Phoenix, their lives were worth more than the single oat they each must have consumed. He would have gladly spilled a drop of his blood for each of them if it were able to fill their voided shells and again make them whole.

With tears streaming down his face, he continued moving them, one handful after another, until he reached the point where he would have to begin collecting them singly, pinching them carefully between his thumbs and forefingers so as not to damage what little physically remained of his saviors.

There was a loud thud on the floor above, a sound he recognized immediately, for he had heard it countless times before. It was the sound of a body falling to the floor, though until that moment he hadn't realized precisely how silent the house had been around him.

When unconsciousness had claimed him, his ears had been filled with the screams of The Swarm above and the mosquitoes descending upon him. Outside of the scurrying of the roaches and the roar of the wind assaulting him with the plague of locusts, he couldn't remember hearing any sound at all.

There was another thud.

He was accustomed to the sound beneath the wailing of the people above in tongues as the spirit took them. But there were no such cries now. There were no voices at all. No sound. Just the loud thumping of a pair of bodies hitting the floor.

As he carefully exhumed his quarry from the cold cement floor, he listened attentively for the sounds that usually followed: the scraping of hands and knees on the floor as the people tried to rise again to their feet; the shifting of the floorboards; the footsteps to follow.

Nothing.

Depositing the last of his fallen friends onto the only suitable surface in the room, he crawled slowly forward toward the door. The concrete beneath him was painfully cold; his hands, knees, and toes recoiling against the bitter sting.

Another thump overhead.

Then another.

"Is anyone out there?" he whispered.

The crack in the floor had widened like a vein filled with nothingness, emanating that same cold that permeated his shivering flesh.

He couldn't see the thin gap beneath the door, but he could tell by the slight breeze of warm air crossing the floor that he had to be getting close.

He flinched at the sound of a flurry of heavy banging above his head, releasing a dusting of rust from the overhead pipes.

Reaching forward, he placed his right palm flat against the door, gently pressing the wood for even the slightest hint of movement. It allowed him to push it almost imperceptibly away before the bolts wouldn't allow any more.

"Is anyone out there?" he whispered again, cocking his head to bring his left eye to the crack beneath the door.

The darkness in the stairwell beyond was nearly as black as that surrounding him, though he was immediately accosted by a horrible stench. Recoiling, he pinched his nose and took several deep breaths before again lowering his head to try to see.

"Anyone?" he whispered.

He knew that the woman wasn't out there, for he had surely witnessed her painful demise. Though she was his only ally, what he wouldn't have given for the sound of another human voi—

A loud hissing erupted from somewhere toward the top of the staircase, joined in short measure by another.

Footsteps scampered overhead, fast and furious, across the floorboards.

Phoenix fell back from the door, his heart pounding in his chest. Though he knew not what was happening in the room above, the sounds frightened him far more than he had ever been in his life. His skin was cool with sweat budding from his pores, every hair on his body standing electrically. The overwhelming desire to get out of that basement was nearly crippling.

Faster and faster they raced above, until finally the frenzied activity slowed to the dwindling patter of footsteps, and then finally disappeared into the silence.

The cement beneath him was so cold that it positively hurt his rear end, though the woman's smock dulled some of the sensation. Much as he wanted to just sit there with his knees pulled to his chest, rocking himself nervously in the darkness, he had no choice but to move. Rolling back to all fours, he crept noiselessly forward toward the door, his ears focusing on the silence for even the slightest sound of pressure applied to the rickety stairs beyond.

Something scraped the door, like the tines of a rake carving into the wood.

Phoenix cringed, holding his breath.

There was another loud scratching. The door wiggled in the frame.

He hadn't heard anything on the landing outside the doorway. He knew that sound as well as his own breathing. There was no way anyone could have stepped from the bottom stair to the landing without him hear—

The scratching resumed, though this time it wasn't a single sound, but a multitude.

He could smell the freshly carved wood falling from the door to alight just on the other side of the thin crack, which he hurriedly pressed his face to in order to prove to himself that there were no feet on the other side.

The door started banging as though being bludgeoned from beyond. Phoenix threw himself backward and scuttled away.

He could hear the wood splitting, the aged trim wrenching away from the jamb with the moans of rusted nails. Footsteps pounded on the landing as though they had leapt from the top stair without touching another between, though with the bend, he knew that to be impossible.

The hissing arose once again, a sound like voiceless screaming, an army of startled cats.

"Who's out there?" he shouted, retreating until he was against the roach-covered straw.

The sound of his voice silenced whatever was on the other side, though only momentarily.

The banging and hissing resumed in earnest, the door cracking, the jamb splintering, and the deadbolt threatening to tear right through the wall. It grew so loud that Phoenix had to clap his hands over his ears and even then his screams were drowned out by the ruckus.

Chunks of fractured wood skittered across the cement floor. Dust shivered from the walls while flakes of rust and dust rained from the cobweb-riddled ceiling. The door flew inward, half of it falling away with a clatter while the remaining half slammed into the wall.

All Phoenix saw were orbs of sickly yellow in the darkness.

He screamed, and the hissing intensified.

Suddenly, those glowing eyes shot skyward and were racing toward him along the ceiling. Hooked claws stabbed into the wooden joists with a sound like darts hitting a dartboard. And before he knew it, Phoenix was lying flat on his back staring up into half a dozen golden eyes, marbled with darkness like storm clouds passing over the midnight moon. They lowered toward him as though dangling from the rafters by their feet and hissed down at him, spattering his face with strands of saliva flung by rancid breath that reeked of carrion. Clawed hands slashed inches from his face, so close he had to close his eyes against the wind created by their frenetic passage.

He jerked his head to the left in time to see another half dozen of whatever these creatures were leap up from the landing to the basement ceiling and scuttle across toward him. Their skin was so dark they were simply shadows passing through the darkness, their frantic movement marked only by their glowing eyes.

Phoenix looked straight up into their fierce stares as they hung above him like bats from a cavern roof, hissing as they tasted the fear that grew with each panicked exhalation.

V

BARSTOW,
CALIFORNIA

Evelyn pulled the old Ford up in front of the house, slumping over the wheel while the engine idled noisily. Dust filled the sky, leaving a grainy haze on the windshield that only turned to mud when she tried to use the wipers to smear it away. She'd tried the phone repeatedly to dial for help, but the line was dead. Even when she was finally able to get a weak signal on her cell phone, the ringing was so soft that she couldn't tell whether or not someone on the other end had even picked up or if she was screaming at nobody.

Her father was dead, of that she was absolutely certain, but she hadn't been prepared to deal with it. Instead, she had swiped the keys to the truck from the hook by the front door and sped down the driveway toward the main road. She had tried the Jenkins Ranch first, rocketing down their washboard dirt drive before finding all of the lights still out. The doors had been locked and no matter how many times she beat on them or how loud she screamed, no one ever answered. All of the cars were still in the circular drive, from the rusted out Buick to the new F-150. None of the dogs even barked from inside that old weathered house to announce her arrival.

Farther down the road she'd found the Millers' trailer deserted, the front door banging against the flimsy siding on the dust-clogged wind. She was already turning around to leave when the headlights flashed across a lump off in the weeds. A lump wearing a tattered nightgown.

June Miller had been face down in the dirt, gravel pressed into her forehead, body swollen and black just as Evelyn's father's had been. Elmer Miller was another twenty yards deeper into the field with his finger still curled beneath the trigger guard of his twelve gauge, his lifeless black body strewn across a clump of sage like refuse. There was no sound from the chicken coops deeper in the field, yet coyotes lie dead in rings surrounding them.

She could remember screaming at the sight and sprinting for her truck, but everything after that was hazy. There were random flashes of town, where she'd found the streets deserted save for the few cars idling at the side of the road with their drivers crumpled over the wheels, front tires up on curbs, wrapped around other parked cars, or stalled in the middle of lawns. The lights had been on at the police station, but the man behind the bullet-proof glass shield lie face down on his desk with his bald pate black against his wiry gray hair. The in-house phones in the lobby had produced no answer, though she could hear them ringing beyond the glass.

There had been a couple sprawled out on the front porch of one of the houses she'd passed, still dressed to the nines from their evening out. Perhaps they'd been preparing for their goodnight kiss before they'd been besieged, their bodies corrupted by whatever festered within to cause the skin to become necrotic. Through the windows of a Laundromat, she'd seen three or four bodies on the floor amidst scatterings of their unfolded clothes, one dryer still turning despite the black bodies that would never unload it. The overhead lights flickered before darkening the scene in her rear view mirror.

On the way out of town, there had been a police cruiser sitting beside Meadows Park, but she wasn't even within a block when she noticed the driver's side door standing open, spilling muted light out across the body of the officer lying face down in the middle of the road. His plump black fingers pointed to his gun, lying spent well out of his reach. The windshield was spotted with insects, blood spattering in small firecrackers of crimson.

There had even been a point where she was sure that an endless swarm of locusts had descended upon the entire town, wings buzzing so loud she thought her head was stuffed inside a bee hive. They'd crawled all over the glass while she'd been at a stoplight, but by the time the light turned green, they were just a distant hum. She even questioned whether or not it had really happened, as she felt so loosely bound to her sanity.

By the time she returned home, Evelyn could neither remember driving there, nor how she'd come to find her head aching from the pressure on the wheel, staring down at the fuel light burning bright orange in the dash. She killed the engine to save what little gas remained, and raised her head so she could look back out the window toward her house. The lights were still on in the bedrooms as she had left them, now barely apparent against the intensifying dawn. The front door still stood ajar, though it had welcomed in a fair share of the desert sand to spread across the linoleum, and within it appeared as though everything was as she had left it.

She knew what she needed to do. Perhaps that was why she'd been sitting in the car so long. She just didn't know if she had the strength to do it.

"What's happening to me?" she whispered, steeling her chin before the emotions could pour out. Why hadn't she been able to find anyone in town? She hadn't even come across another vehicle heading down the road. It was as though the entire world had taken in one final breath, and then shuddered its death rattle.

She looked up to the rear view mirror.

A stranger stared back at her. Her eyes were bloodshot, ringed with puffy red tissue as though she'd been punched repeatedly in the face. Dirt was crusted into the dampness on her cheeks, the dust congealing in a mask over her features, forming rings around her nostrils.

She'd never been this scared in her life. Her body felt as though it were slowing down with the onset of shock, the entire universe moving in slow motion around her, and as much as she wished she could just awaken from this nightmare, she knew that this was real. Deep down she'd already accepted the fact that everyone around her was dead, but the events of the night before now seemed completely surreal as though she was remembering the events from a distant past life. She wanted nothing more than to crawl into her bed and curl up like a little girl and wait for her daddy to come in and let her know that everything would be fine, but he wasn't going to. He was dead. They were all dead. Only she remained.

If she had survived, then surely others must have as well. Maybe not this close to the epicenter of the L.A. detonation, especially with all of the mosquitoes that had descended upon them, but surely there would be more people who lived through it to the east. Whole cities unscathed. Surely Las Vegas and Reno would have been unaffected, maybe even Portland or Seattle up the coast.

They all sounded so far away. She'd been stuck on this little ranch for so long that it felt as though the world beyond had simply ceased to exist. She would find out soon enough though. Of that she was sure. She could feel something calling to her, drawing her away from the house.

Past her image in the mirror, she could see the line of the eastern horizon beneath the rising sun. That was where she needed to go, she was certain of it, but first... but first she needed to take care of something important.

Looking to her left hand, she opened the door and threw it outward. The dust scuffed under her feet as she alighted on the earth, her numbed legs bearing her weight and seemingly guiding her of their own accord. Up the front steps. Through the doorway and into the living room. She didn't even pause as her sole focus was directed toward the hallway leading back to the bedrooms. Passing couches covered with a layer of dust, hovering all around her in the slanted sunlight coming through the windows, she strode right through the doorway into her father's room and stripped the covers away. He lie there on the bed, the middle two buttons of his pajama top torn away by the swelling of his ebon belly beneath, the skin marbled with blue.

Unable to look at his face for fear she would simply fall blubbering to her knees, Evelyn wrapped her arms around her father's chest and groaned as she pulled his torso up from the bed.

He was so cold. Even the sheets beneath him were bereft of any heat. His joints were beginning to stiffen, his head propping itself up of its own accord before finally falling onto her right shoulder as she heaved him to sitting.

"More man tears," he whispered into her ear.

She jumped back.

His corpse lolled forward, and then crumpled off the bed onto the floor, neck bent back awkwardly with his face in the carpet, his rear end standing high as his knees were beneath him.

"Daddy?" she whispered. "Daddy!"

She dropped beside him on the floor, shoving him roughly onto his right side so she could look directly into his face. His eyelids were only partly closed, the deteriorating eyes beneath a putrid white. His plumped blue lips sagged from his exposed teeth, propped apart by the swollen tongue. Pressing her first two fingers into the side of his bulging neck, she felt around for a pulse that she knew wouldn't be there.

Had he really said 'More man tears,' or had it just been the last of his gasses escaping from his chest as she folded him forward like a billows?

She was losing her mind.

There was one thing she knew would bind her to reality and solidify her senses. One thing that would scrape away whatever cobwebs were forming in her head.

Evelyn knelt and rolled her father onto his back. Slipping her hands beneath his armpits, she stood as well as she could and started dragging him toward the hallway.

Evelyn wiped the splashed gas from her hands onto her jeans, kicking the now empty can off into the vacant desert. The lighter fell from her hand, clattering to the hard terra. She leaned unconsciously down and jammed it into her pocket.

Black smoke coughed sideways from her father's body, consuming his clothing first. She kept waiting for him to open an eye or cry out in pain, but instead he lie still like a log on the fire while the flames rose higher and higher from his supine form, snapping like red and gold capes on the rising wind.

"Goodbye, Daddy," Evelyn whispered, turning from the impromptu pyre. Tears rolled down her cheeks through the dust, but she was oblivious. She couldn't feel anything. As far as she was concerned, she had ripped her own heart through her ribs and set it ablaze with what remained of the only man she had ever truly loved. She was a hollow shell, an empty soul with only thought in mind, one imperative urging her from her home into the unknown.

"More man tears," she said aloud, throwing open the door of the idling pickup and shoving her backpack onto the passenger seat. Within was a single change of clothes, a sweatshirt and jacket, cans of Speghetti-O's, beans, and the requisite opener. She'd also removed the revolver from her father's closet along with a small box of bullets from the top shelf where he assumed she'd never find it. There was a lone teddy bear from her bed, missing the little black nose and the ears were crusted from where she'd chewed it as a child. She also wrapped a dozen leaves of kelp, roots and all, in newspaper to hold the moisture before sealing them in a plastic bag. She didn't know why she grabbed the bear, but the kelp she would need. It was the only thing left of her former life, a life that was never meant to be. Bound inside with those salty plants was the glue to hold her shattered mind together.

Revving the engine, the dropped the truck into first and lurched down the driveway.

She was going to need to fill the tank if she had any hope of making it to Nevada. She could feel her body being summoned east as though by a string sewn right through her chest. And the only thing she could imagine out in the desert was Las Vegas, where she assumed many a man had shed a tear over lost fortunes. That, combined with the undeniable urge to head east, made perfect sense to her while absolutely nothing else did.

It was a plan. Or at least it was the start of one.

She couldn't bring herself to look back in any of the mirrors as the flames lapped the side of the barn from her father's charcoaled corpse, rising upward along the wood while blowing embers took root on the roof.

VI

EUGENE, OREGON

Jill couldn't get the image of the sorority house out of her head. It had come to pass exactly as her vision had foretold. The bodies... tortured and bleeding... heaped in massive piles of humanity... all of the death... how could she possibly have known?

She stood before the emergency room entrance to the hospital, the automatic doors opening and closing on the bloated body lying facedown on the sensor pad. The swollen sides were already starting to leak a pus-like fluid where the door continually bit at the flesh.

The others were somewhere inside, yet for the life of her, Jill couldn't bring herself to step over that corpse. She had the most overwhelming sense of impending dread, as though within lurked something unfathomably evil, something that stilled her chest even outside the building as though something vile crept out from the opening and closing mouth.

Getting there had been a chore in itself. The streets had been clogged with stalled cars, the occupants sitting lifeless amidst the shattered balls of glass from the windows and windshields. Turn signals flashed uselessly. Hoods were crumpled around trees and hydrants firing fountains of water into the air. Bodies littered the streets like so much garbage left out on the curb. No faces arose from the vacant demolished eyes of the houses, staring lifelessly down upon them as they drove across the lawns. Only sirens and alarms raised their voices in defiance, but even they fell eventually silent.

Ray had repeatedly dialed 911 on his cell phone as Darren had driven them in his black, hail-bludgeoned Blazer through the mess of cars, climbing over curbs, knocking down mailboxes and shoving parked cars aside with the bumper so they could pass, yet the only response he seemed capable of receiving was that same hiss of static he reached from the home phone.

Tina had insisted that she was okay, though the wound looked like an infection waiting to happen. The sides of the ragged laceration were nearly closed, congealing around a tangle of hair, scabbing over in a rough mass. Ray insisted that she go to the hospital regardless. Perhaps it was because that was the only thing resembling a plan that he could concoct, or maybe he just couldn't have stood in the house staring across the street at Rick's body as it swelled from within even a moment longer. He'd resigned to the fact that everyone across the street was dead and his mother more than likely was as well, but everyone couldn't be dead. He was sure of it. In his mind, he was convinced that once they made it to the hospital they'd find a team of doctors and nurses triaging thousands of injured people in every available room and the lobby, expanding into haphazardly-assembled tents and lean-to's in the lot and along the lawn.

He'd still been clinging to that hope when he led the others across the corpse in the threshold into the ER.

Thuck.

Thuck.

Thuck.

The door continued to try to gnaw through the body.

Turning, Jill stared across the parking lot through the drizzle of sizzling rain. There was no sign of life out there. The lights flashed atop the idling ambulance in the intersection in contrast to the nearly purple lightning strobing the sky, but the siren had already died. The driver looked as though he'd tried to leap from the vehicle, but succeeded in only making it as far as the asphalt, where the car that crashed into the side of the ambulance was parked atop his legs. There were no birds flitting by beyond or bedded down in the trees freshly beaten of their leaves. No chirping or twitting or cawing. No engines roared and no tires squealed over the constant din of engines all over the roads idling themselves into oblivion. There was no music, no laughter, no yelling or screaming, nothing. Only the hissing of the smoldering rain raising accusatory fingers of smoke to the sky, the patter on the long awning over her head, and the door's ceaseless chewing on the body.

"Jill," April whispered from the other side of the doorway.

Jill turned, already able to read the sadness on her best friend's face. Her eyes were sunken into pits of darkness, her cheeks swollen and red from the deluge of tears. Her lips trembled, but she'd already cried herself out. Nothing was left now but futility and despair.

"There's no one here, is there?" Jill asked softly, already knowing the answer.

April only shook her head.

"Please come in with the rest of us," April said, closing her eyes to try to reinforce her courage.

Jill looked at the corpse between them, the sickly white fluid expanding in the fine grooves of the rubber plate. She couldn't envision it like she could her sorority sisters dying on the lawn, but there was just something about this hospital that made her feel every bit as sure that something terrible was about to happen within.

"April…"

"Please, Jill," she whispered. "We all need to stay together."

Jill raised her eyes to meet her friend's; they were so wide, the tears spilling in rivers.

"Okay," she finally acquiesced, scooting her sluggish feet as close to the body as she could manage, then raised her right foot, bracing herself on the door frame, and lunged across. The intense feelings of fear amplified exponentially as she took her first steps into the lobby and was accosted by the horrific stench of death. She couldn't imagine that a worse smell existed anywhere else in the entire world. Retching, she pulled her shirt up over her mouth and nose.

"Where are the others?" Jill asked.

"We can't get through the door to the emergency room, so they're trying to find a way around," April said through the sleeve she held over the bottom portion of her face.

Jill walked over to the door beside the plexiglass-enclosed reception desk and jerked on the handle, but it didn't even budge. Holding down the call button beside the door produced little more than a buzzing sound that droned on somewhere beyond.

"It's magnetically sealed," April said. "We already tried it. There's a lady behind the desk back there, but she's… um… not going to be able to help."

Jill peered through the glass beyond a desk riddled with paperwork. The chair had been overturned; the nurse sprawled on the floor in the doorway leading back into the unseen facility.

Bug carcasses marred the clear divider in bloody smears.

"Nothing down there either," Darren said as he emerged from the hallway behind them, startling Jill so badly she nearly left her feet. "There's the same kind of locked door in the main lobby and all of the people at the admissions desk are dead."

"We should leave," Jill whispered.

"You're going to be a doctor, Darren. You could stitch up Tina's head," April said, her right eye was starting to develop a twitch.

"Yeah, but that isn't the kind of thing you learn until medical school. I'm still trying to get through microbiology and chemistry."

"I can sew," Jill whispered, so quietly that the others questioned whether she had said anything at all.

Ray limped into the room, supporting the majority of Tina's weight against his side. She still looked pale, but at least she was able to hold her head up without assistance.

"They're all dead," Ray said plainly, his face lacking emotion.

He lowered Tina into one of the chairs against the far wall by a row of vending machines and plopped into the seat beside her, burying his face in his hands.

"I'll be alright," Tina said, gently stroking his back. "It isn't even bleeding any more. See?"

He looked up at her, eyes welling with tears, then leaned his head on her shoulder.

"What are we going to do?" he asked, eyes dropping to the floor, loosing the tears he'd until then held at bay.

"We need to get out of here," Jill said, looking back to the front doorway. "Something bad is going to happen he—"

"And go where, Jill?" Ray shouted, jumping to his feet. "Look around you! Everyone's dead! Where in the world could we possibly go?"

"I'm afraid—"

"This is about more man tears, Jill! This is about what in the hell—"

"What did you say?"

"I said this is about more than fear, Jill! This is about what we're going to do to survive! What if whatever germ or disease or who-knows-what killed these people is still floating around in the air? These bodies are just breeding bacteria and waiting to explode! What are we going to do then, Jill, huh? What the hell are we going to do then?!"

"Shh." Tina took him by the hand and easing him toward her. "It's not Jill's fault."

"I know," he whispered, sitting back down and bringing her hand to his cheek. The contact was about the only thing binding him to reality. "I'm sorry, Jill."

She just nodded, still on guard after the verbal thrashing.

"How did you know to get us in the hot tub?" Darren asked softly. "What would have happened if we hadn't?"

"I don't know," Jill said. "Sometimes I… sometimes I have déjà vu. Not premonitions per se, but sometimes I… see things."

"Is that what happened earlier?" April asked. "Back at the house, when you… you know… when you freaked out?"

Jill nodded and turned away from them.

"What did you see?"

"Bodies," she said, her voice barely audible. "All over the lawn… Broken…Bleeding. Heaped in front of the house. Just like they are now. Only… Do you hear something?"

There was a low buzzing sound that she could feel vibrating the air around her as much as hear.

"Only what?" Ray interrupted.

Jill held up a finger and cocked her head.

The buzzing was steadily growing louder, as though the bowels of the earth beneath her feet rumbled with hunger.

"What, Jill?" Tina asked.

"Only… they were covered with mosquitoes."

She walked up to the smooth glass pane and traced her hand across it, knocking crusted insect bodies to the floor while she stared at the nurse lying black and bloated on the ground.

"More man tears," she whispered, but the words were consumed by the buzzing.

She whirled in time to see them explode through the open front door; locusts, tens of thousands of them, filling the air like smoke.

266

Closing her eyes, she threw herself to the floor and wrapped her arms over her head. They pelted her body like buckshot, lodging in her hair and scurrying all across her, tiny sharp feet poking and prodding like needles. Her skin grew damp as tacky fluid was spewed from tiny mouths, clinging to her.

Jill screamed, but only succeeded in drawing a pair of the creatures into her mouth. They scurried onto her tongue before her instincts snapped her teeth together, crunching their exoskeletons and leaving her spitting chunks to the floor.

It sounded as though there was a jet engine directed right through the open doorway, the buzzing rising to a furious roar. She couldn't even bring herself to try to look for the others, as even the slightest movement brought an assault of insects slamming into her face.

And then, like a dream, they were gone.

The silence was painful, interrupted only by choked sobs.

Jill slowly raised her head from the floor, looking to the others. Ray lay atop Tina on the floor, trying to shield her head with his elbows while blocking the entrance to his ear canals with his palms. He looked tentatively toward the door past her, dripping with what looked like tobacco juice, a sheen of it shimmering on his exposed skin and clothing.

"Is everyone okay?" Darren asked. He was flat on his stomach on the floor, unlacing his fingers from atop his sapped hair.

April whimpered beside him, nodding hard enough to loose the tears drawing clear tracks through the brown crud on her face.

"We should get out of here," Tina gasped, sliding out from beneath her boyfriend and spitting a mouthful of ochre fluid onto the white tile.

"Where are we supposed to go, huh?" Ray snapped, immediately regretting his tone. "Sorry… it's just that… I don't know. Even if we go home, what are we supposed to do then? And if we don't go home… where would we go?"

"More man tears," Jill said, looking to the others from beneath lowered brows.

"What in the hell would Mormons have to do with this?" Ray spat.

"I said, more man…" Jill stopped. Her lower lip slipped between her teeth to be gnawed contemplatively. Her face wrinkled as she tried to work it out in her head. "Mormon tears."

"You're starting to scare me, Jill," April said, swiping her palms across her sticky face and slinging the fluid to her sides.

"Could it really be that simple?" Jill asked, closing her eyes.

None of the others knew what to say. All eyes were fixed upon her; the room silent.

"I know where we need to go," Jill said, looking to each of them in turn. The sight of the sparkle in her eyes against the otherwise glimmering brown skin was positively unsettling.

Bang!

Jill flinched and slapped her hands to her ears as April let out a scream. Spinning, she locked stares with it before it could raise another heavily scaled fist to pound at the plexiglass. It had eyes as bright as the sun reflecting on a placid pond, seething with black globs like a fresh hatch of larvae. A large flap of skin trilled beneath its broad black chin, streaked with orange like a cutthroat's gills, shivering like a matador's cape. Black skin glistened as though the body was recently dipped in crude oil, long black spines standing erect like a Mohawk of blades over the top of its head and down its back, curling from its shoulders as it stood atop the nurse's desk.

Bang!

It struck at the glass again, the entire pane shuddering in the frame. Enraged, the thing buckled its head back and opened a mouth full of way too many sharp little triangular teeth, letting out some sort of scream that spattered the glass with saliva.

In one swift motion, it raised that same arm, curling long clawed digits toward the ceiling, and slashed through the flimsy paneling. Sparks flew from the overhead light as shards of glass and powdered tiles fell down all around the thing's head. Crouching, legs tensed beneath it like powerful springs, it leapt straight up, disappearing into the ceiling.

"What in the—?" Darren sputtered, but April already had him by the hand and was sprinting toward the doorway.

Another black, now only vaguely humanoid shape slammed into the clear divider with a thud, stumbling backward and shaking its head to clear it. It quickly leapt up behind the first.

"Go! Go! Go!" Ray yelled, jerking Tina all the way to her feet and sprinting for the door.

Jill stared straight up in paralyzed terror at the scraping and scrabbling sounds coming toward her. Ceiling tiles bowed downward, cracking and falling away. Long lighting fixtures exploded with sparks, dropping from their moorings to dangle by their exposed cords, the bulbs shattering all around them with loud popping sounds.

"Jill!" Tina shrieked as she raced past, managing to grab her friend's hand just long enough to whirl her around.

"There's no time!" Jill screamed, forcing her trembling legs to a sprint to try to keep up. She didn't even look down at the body propping the door open as she raced right over it, her weight squishing out white ooze like canned cheese.

Something thumped to the ground behind her a heartbeat before she heard the clatter of nails like a dog chasing her.

"Get in," Darren said, his voice cracking. He brought the Blazer's engine to life with a roar, the tires squealing as they kicked pebbles across the parking lot. April was only halfway in the car when it started to move. She barely managed to scamper over the passenger seat and throw herself into the back before Ray was shoving Tina up behind her, shouldering her rear end to force her back enough to allow him to follow.

"Wait!" Jill called.

The automatic door shattered behind her, sending shards of glass skittering past her and across the parking lot. She let out a shrill scream, but managed not to look back over her shoulder. She could see in the terrified looks in both Ray's and Darren's eyes that she really didn't want to know how close they were.

Nails clattered from the asphalt as fast as a horse's hooves behind her.

She lunged for the side of the Blazer. Ray managed to get an arm around her chest while shouting for Darren to hit it. Jill could only loop her arm around the frame of the window in the passenger door, holding on as the open door swung outward away from the vehicle, nearly pulling Ray right out behind her as the car rocketed forward.

The rear end kicked to the left with a bang.

Screams echoed within the cab as Ray tugged Jill onto his lap on the passenger seat with a groan, the door slamming shut behind her.

Darren glanced at the rear view mirror to see what looked like a snake made human trying to wrench its claws out of the rear quarter panel of his Blazer, those long talons standing out from it like so many hooks. Black shadows swept down the front of the building from the shattered windows on the upper floors, sliding effortlessly down the sheer face until they reached the ground with the others, now growing rapidly smaller behind them.

CHAPTER 7

I

Phoenix had grown accustomed to the horrific stench, but the eyes were something else entirely. Staring at him from the darkness, carefully scrutinizing him, waiting for him to give them even the most remote opportunity to snatch him and carry him off into the darkness. He imagined them to be light bulbs set into the recessed ceiling, crawling with fat spiders. While that in itself wasn't especially comforting, it was vastly preferable to the truth.

For some reason, they wouldn't set foot on the basement floor. They'd come down the staircase from above, but had only been able to enter his cellar prison by leaping and climbing up into the cobweb-rife rafters. At first they'd dangled from clawed feet, trying desperately to slash him, but had given up as they realized that so long as he was flush with the ground, they wouldn't be able to reach him. He wondered if they were aware that he could see them up there, bodies flattened between the long wooden slats, absorbed by the darkness, only their glowing eyes tracing the outline of the reptilian forms. Or if they even cared.

Each time he so much as flexed a muscle in preparation of making even the slightest movement, he heard the clatter of claws above, the inhalation of sharp breaths reissued as hissing. There was nothing to eat. Nothing to drink. Even crawling to the end of the room to slurp the condensation from the mildewed walls was out of the question, for he had no idea whether or not those creatures could scurry down the walls or if they just hadn't yet. Either way, he didn't want to have to find out.

He could last a while, he was certain, so long as he just receded into the darkness in his mind and imagined himself at the edge of the beautiful pond where he now pictured the woman sitting with her feet in the cool water, letting the sun bathe her face while the doe and her fawn drank from their mirrored reflections. The girl with the snow white legs was there beside him, her cool fingers interlaced between his, her sweet breath warm on his cheek. Nuzzling his head to the right, even in that dank basement he could feel her skin against his, the gentle touch of the downy hairs on her forehead against his chin, the—

"Help me!" she screamed into his ear.

Phoenix's eyes snapped open, but he was able to resist the urge to quickly sit up.

Had he really heard that?

"Help!" she screamed again.

The monsters slithering through the darkness above hissed at the sound.

"Where are you?" he shouted, having to close his eyes against the sudden genesis of saliva dripping onto his face from the ceiling.

"I can't find you!" she screamed, her voice so frightened that the hairs on his arms and neck stood erect.

"More man tears!" he bellowed into the darkness.

"I don't know what that means!"

"You have to find more man tears!"

"Help me!" she called again, this time her voice much weaker as though moving down a long hallway away from him.

"White sand!" he screamed so loud it felt as though his throat had torn, remembering his dream. "Black smoke! White sand! More man tears!"

And then her voice was gone, leaving him alone in the cold darkness, surrounded by a constant excited hissing. He could tell that they were tasting his fear.

"No!" he roared, slamming his fists into the ground.

Flailing claws dropped from the ceiling, slashing inches above his chest, but right then he didn't care. He needed to find the girl and he needed to help her.

"Leave me alone!" he railed, grabbing onto one of the slashing wrists and yanking it.

With the sound of a saw tearing through wood, he felt the thing's weight slam down upon him before he even knew it was falling. Razor-honed nails cut easily through the smock into his skin, releasing a swell of warmth long before he felt the pain. His breath exploded past his lips and he rolled quickly to the side to try to knock the thing off of his chest.

There was a flash of blinding light and the smell of burning rubber when it hit the floor.

Phoenix averted his eyes, shielding them with his hands as he could hear the crackle of fire consuming flesh, snapping like bacon grease. When he finally forced himself to look, the creature was little more than a charcoal sculpture coated with the yellow and orange glow of the dwindling fire, its clawed hands reaching back up toward the roof, before spontaneously dissociating into piles of black carbon. Its brethren hissed and snapped their jaws above him, carving grooves into the wooden joists and clattering from the pipes and ductwork.

"I know you can hear me!" Phoenix screamed, closing his eyes and nipping his tongue to focus his concentration. A spurt of blood slapped the back of his teeth. "We have to help her!"

He thrashed on the floor as his eyes fluttered beneath flagging lids, preparing to seize.

"We're out of time!"

His head banged up and down on the cement.

"Find me now!"

II

Neither of them had spoken since they left the house for what they could both feel would be the last time. The entire situation seemed surreal, as though rather than living their lives, they were dreaming their way through them. No matter how many times they'd tried the phone, they were never able to raise anyone. The only plan they could come up with was to get in the car and drive until they found more survivors. That was all they had. Everyone in town was dead. It had taken a while for the grim reality of that thought to sink in, but now there was no denying it.

"We're not going any farther in this," Missy said, turning off the idling car with a click.

They'd sat in the lane behind the snarl of wrecked cars, smoke wafting from beneath hoods, hazard lights blinking slower and slower as they drained the batteries. From their vantage, they could clearly see several of the occupants lying on the side of the road, already beginning to rot into the earth like so much road kill. Others were tangled in the barbed wire fence lining the pasture to the right; those fortunate enough to have cleared it or crawled beneath it littering the coarse grass like the piles of manure surrounding them. A small farmhouse sat at the far side of the pasture with its back to them, turned away from the close-cropped rows of dead cornstalks. A mass of trees lined up on the other side of it, tracing the progress of the river along the eastern horizon. A large aluminum construct, more like a warehouse than a barn, sat beside it, three times the size of the adjacent house. Huge letters adorned the face of the building above large corrugated sliding doors reading in bold red letters:

AUCTION HOUSE
JONATHON
MIRAMONT
STEERS

The building was surrounded by a split-rail fence that had to encompass an acre by itself, with wooden ramps along the north side where cattle could be loaded into the awaiting trucks.

The embankment to the left, across the opposite lane filled with cars that had tried to circumvent the pileup only to run headlong into oncoming traffic, sloped steeply upward to a tufted lip of bluegrass, marking the edge of the forest beyond.

Neither knew how long they'd been sitting there. The prospect of turning back toward town, which they already knew was filled with nothing but corpses, was demoralizing. So long as they were moving forward, there was at least the elusive promise of hope somewhere beyond the approaching horizon, while behind lie nothing but death.

Without the rumble of the engine, the car seemed far too still.

"Where can we possibly go?" Mare asked. His voice was hoarse from screaming, his face stoic, as the tears had washed away all feeling and left him numb.

"I don't know," she whispered, "but I can't sit in this car any longer. I need to keep moving or I'm going to lose my mind."

Mare nodded. He couldn't think of anything better. If the options were narrowed to sitting in the car and pretending not to see all of the corpses slumped over the wheels and felled on the roadside and simply getting out and walking, then the choice wasn't that difficult. After what had become of their father, neither wanted to be close to any of the bodies. The car provided a little security, but the windows were only made of glass after all.

He opened the door without looking at his sister, slinking from the car on legs that felt like rubber. The powerful smell of exhaust barraged him, but was ripped away on the wind, which rose and fell as though unsure of which direction to blow. It almost looked as though if he jumped he could touch the black stormclouds that grumbled past overhead.

Hauling open the rear door, he pulled out his backpack and slung it over his right shoulder, straining to bring his left through the strap on the other side. Missy's clanked as she did the same, the collision of the cans within almost a reassuring sound against the purring of engines and the thunder.

Mare looked back over his shoulder to make sure that she was behind him, but said nothing. He knew that Missy wouldn't know which direction to head any better than he, and broaching the subject could only lead to more time wasted in discussion. It was best to just put one foot in front of the other and start walking. So long as he maintained some form of inertia, then at least he would feel as though he was doing something productive. There was still the flicker of hope that the next town they came across would have been unaffected by whatever had happened in Dover, but the rational part of him knew otherwise. He could accept the deaths back in town, for they had been impossible to miss. He could even somehow fathom that after his father had died, he had become something else entirely, but if he were to accept the notion that there was no one else alive beyond the next turn, or the one past that, then he would be forced to accept that even hope had abandoned him.

He walked beside the yellow line, paralleling the highway, skirting angled cars knocked onto the shoulder, covering his mouth through the thick black smoke coughing from the dying engines, stepping carefully around the dead bodies of children within arm's reach of the teddy bear that would forever elude them; past men and women holding hands with their final efforts; past faceless bodies just sprawled prone on the asphalt. And some he couldn't bring himself to think about, or wouldn't allow himself to ponder more precisely. There were melting puddles of shed flesh, minus the skeleton that had once been beneath, as though like snakes they had merely slipped out of the last layer of their existence and hurried away. He couldn't stand the smell. The inside out flesh, thick with yellow clusters of adipose tissue, made him want to vomit. But worse still was the thought he fought most to keep from pondering... Where had whatever had once been in those bodies gone?

He imagined one of those black-skinned creatures leaping up from behind every parked car or slithering out from the shadows beneath. He pictured them smashing through the windows and lunging for him, wanting nothing more than to drag him back through that shattered maw to rip him to ribbons in the back seat.

Yet there was nothing. No movement. No flies buzzing around the bloating corpses or abandoned children like themselves crying where they hid.

Ahead, a Greyhound bus had been knocked sideways, crossing the entire shoulder and dipping from the road to the right, the bumper tangled in the barbed wire. There were dozens of black shapes slumped forward against the seats, while more disturbing still were the vacant seats with the shattered windows beside them, balled glass mixing with the gravel on the shoulder.

He was prepared to ask whether Missy wanted to walk between all of the parked cars to get past the obstruction or avoid the whole mess by detouring through the field when he heard the crumple of gravel as she slid down the shoulder and then stomped forward with a crash into the tall brown weeds lining the fence.

"Wait up," he called, jogging to catch up. He grabbed the top wire between a pair of rusted spines and pulled it upward while standing on the middle line to create a gap for his sister.

A body a dozen yards up slipped free from the top wire and made a horrendous tearing sound as it fell forward into the grass. It released a wet smell that assaulted him like an uppercut from the spread of innards that splashed out onto the earth.

Missy ducked beneath and stepped out into the field, turning to hold it for her brother.

"Which way—?" Missy started, but was cut off by a loud thump of metal, like something jumping on the hood of a car, and the sound of smashing glass.

They stared at each other a moment, listening.

Silence.

"I'll bet once we get around this traffic jam there'll be some open road ahead," Mare whispered. His eyes darted everywhere at once, making him look as skittish as a prairie dog poking its head out of its hole. "Maybe we could just take one of those—"

Another bang of buckling metal somewhere on the other side of the bus.

Missy found her brother's stare and latched onto it. She jerked her head in the direction of the house and then pointed in a looping half-circle around the edge of the field.

Mare nodded.

Without further conversation, they struck out into the field, looking back behind them every few strides as the chaotic sounds of something thrashing around in the midst of the stalled traffic grew more frequent. Neither looked at the bodies spotting the pasture around them in the knee-high grasses, silently giving them a wide berth.

They reached a point where the thrum of engines blended with the chuckle of the Cumberland, only to be drowned beneath with each subsequent step. While they could no longer hear whatever was raising such a ruckus in the pileup, they still glanced back every few seconds, half expecting something to be racing through the field toward them. The crisp stalks and fallen husks crunched uncomfortably loudly beneath as they passed from the comparatively posh meadow into the decapitated rows. They weren't even fifty yards from the back of the farm when they saw the woman on the ground next to her basket of sheets and quilts that were now trying to flap away on the breeze. Several more snapped and flagged from the clothesline like ghosts.

"I think we're far enough away to start heading back around them," Mare panted.

"What do you think was causing all the commotion back there?" Missy whispered.

The wind howled its response, the grasses in the field rippling toward them like waves on a lake.

"I don't know, but I don't like the idea of finding out."

She nodded and turned north, the gale now battering her from the side, tossing the dirty tangles of her hair across her face, heading for the edge of the field where the stands of mixed deciduous and evergreen trees waited with open arms. The barn rose to their right, the scent of manure creeping off of the dirt pen and through the fence toward them. Compared to the now-familiar reek of death, such a banal, commonplace smell was a welcomed change.

"Where are we really going?" Mare finally asked. It had been gnawing at him since they'd left.

"I thought we were going to drive until we ran into someone else," she said.

"The most logical route would have been heading to the west away from Atlanta. We're heading north."

She looked quizzically at him a minute, and then turned and started walking again.

"I…" she said, pausing to rub the dust from her eyes. "I don't know why we came this direction. I guess I wasn't thinking. You could have said something, you know."

"I—" he started, but was cut off by a loud bang.

Both looked at the auction house to their right.

"What the—?"

Another bang.

The closed barn door shivered in place.

The words gracing the façade were made of carved wooden letters painted cherry red and glued to the aluminum. There was another loud bang, this time the closed sliding door bending outward as though rammed by a truck from the inside. The letters A and U shook free from AUCTION and fell to the ground in front of them.

"Something's in there," Mare gasped.

There was another deafening collision and the left side of the door bowed upward with an awkward wrenching of metal. Beneath they could see four wide feet capped with thick hooves swirling through the dust seeping out from the building. The legs vanished, only this time they heard the thundering charge of the beast before it slammed into the door and sent it flying out into the pen.

Missy screamed, but she couldn't look away.

Dirt showered them where they stood just beyond the fence, thrown up from the ground when the bent metal sheet hit.

The thing that stood before them was like nothing they had ever seen in their lives. The general shape was reminiscent of a bull, but that was about where the similarities ended. It had a short broad head from which two long golden horns originated, framing a pair of flaming red eyes that stood out like beacons against the yellow fur. A shaggy beard hung all the way from its chin to the ground, matching the thick mane of rust-colored fur that arose from its shoulders. The rest of the body was more straw-colored, save for the end of the short tail that was capped with a tuft of orange hair. It snorted furiously, blowing up clouds of dirt from the pen. It looked as though they'd bred a bull to a lion and highlighted the coloring.

"What's in the world is that?" Mare gasped.

"I… I don't know."

As they watched, several more animals appeared through the stirred dust like ships through a fog. Only a couple bore horns like the first, though theirs were much smaller and lacking the sharp curvature.

Several smaller animals stayed behind the females, trying to both keep out of sight and see what was happening at the same time.

"They're beautiful," Missy said.

"Those can't be cows, can they?"

Before he could even think about stopping her, Missy was up on top of the fence, her legs dangling down into the pen. She brought her backpack around into her lap and unzipped the pocket. She removed a box of Triscuits and tore it open, palming a handful in her left hand and extending one of the crackers in her right.

The bull snorted again, lowering its head until its beard was folded atop the dirt.

"Come on."

"Are you out of your mind?" Mare snapped. "Lord only knows what those things are!"

She made a clicking sound with her tongue and the bull took a couple of heavy steps toward her, watching her with eyes like fireballs.

Missy tossed the cracker in front of the bull, its nostrils flaring.

Mare grabbed her by the back of the pants and prepared to haul her backward the moment that thing even looked like it was thinking about charging.

"It's okay," she said, tossing another cracker in front of it, only this one a little closer.

It snorted again, grunting, but made no advance.

"We should keep mov—" Mare started, but she cut him off with a look and her finger pressed to her lips. "We don't have ti—" Again, the look.

The bull raised its head, unblinking eyes studying Missy. It stepped forward, first with its right, then with its left, drawing in another deep inhalation and blowing it forcefully out. It lowered its stare to the cracker, cocking its head to the left and studying it curiously. Slowly, it righted its head and lowered its chin, looking alternately to the cracker and then back up to Missy until its snout was within inches, its jaws already parting for the tip of a bulbous blue tongue.

One of the calves raced around from the back of the small herd and darted in front of the enormous bull, snatching the cracker from the dirt and then galloping to the edge of the pen.

Missy laughed.

The big bull looked at her, then took another step forward and slopped its long purple tongue onto the remaining cracker, jerking it back into its mouth. Its jaws ground from side to side, the only remaining thing familiar about the cow.

Missy pulled out more crackers and scattered them across the dirt in front of her. The unusual bovines crowded around her from all sides, mobbing her as she tossed handful after handful into their midst.

Mare allowed himself a smile.

"Look at them," Missy giggled. "Aren't they the most amazing things you've ever seen?"

The largest bull stiffened then raised its head, cocking its ear to the sky with a snap. Another bull followed suit, then another. Despite the crackers still sitting on the ground around their feet, all of the cows stood perfectly still, noses raised to the wind.

Thunder grumbled above like explosions crossing the sky.

The calves all scurried away from the group, dashing so quickly toward the open barn door that dirt flew from their heels. The females hurried behind, far more lithe and coordinated than any cows they'd ever seen. The ground rumbled beneath their weight, nearly knocking Missy from the fence.

Mare grabbed her hips and braced her before she could topple backward.

"I don't like this!" he shouted, but between the thunder and the stampede, the words didn't even reach his own ears.

The bulls inside the pen lined up side to side, horns lowered toward Missy and Mare, their shoulders forming what appeared to be an impregnable barrier between them and the females and calves whose eyes burned brightly inside the darkness behind the mangled door.

The largest bull snorted, blasting steam from its nostrils. Its eyes now resembled molten lava.

Mare looked back over his shoulder.

The long grasses in the field between the barn and the highway shimmered like waves rolling to shore. Had the grass grown even longer since they'd passed through?

In the distance, smoke drifted from the stalled cars lining the horizon.

A dozen long V shapes parted the grasses, firing straight toward them.

Before whatever was out there reached the end of the pasture and emerged into the cornrows, Mare was already leaping over the fence behind Missy, sprinting past the formidable line of bulls toward the barn.

A series of loud hisses filled the air, like so many kettles spontaneously come to boil.

The ground trembled beneath their feet as Missy disappeared into the darkness, followed by her brother. The red eyes fell away from them, receding into the shadows before closing gently and all but disappearing.

Missy slammed into the side of one of the beasts, which bucked up from the ground nervously, before darting around it and looking back out through the doorway into the lightning-strobed pen. Clouds of dust clogged the air, ripped side to side by the rising wind, thrown from the ground behind the advance of the bulls. Black shapes like human shadows slithered up atop the tall fence before the much larger beasts slammed into it. Wood splintered in all directions, the fence exploding with a furious crash.

The shadows leapt into the air, skin shimmering with the lightning like so many fish leaping from a pond at sunset, and then knifed back down into the herd. Braying screams erupted over a chorus of hissing.

"We've got to get out of here!" Mare screamed, grabbing Missy by the hand and sprinting deeper into the darkness. Surely there had to be some sort of entrance on the street side.

Sounds only vaguely reminiscent of mooing arose, more like the horns of semis.

"Hurry!" he yelled, pressing his palm into his sister's lower back to urge her faster.

All of the windows on the front side of the building had been painted over; the only light permeating was a muted grayness that hovered like a mist rather than expanding outward. Missy hit the bank of doors first, lowering her shoulder and slamming her hip into the long metal release bar. The door bowed outward just enough to give a glimpse of the rusting chain locked between the handles from the outside, before knocking her back into her brother, who smashed her again into the unflinching door.

"They're locked!" she screamed, grabbing for her sore right shoulder.

"They can't be!" Mare raged, throwing himself over and over into the door, kicking at the metal bar as hard as he could. He whirled around in time to see one of those tall black creatures, its movements sinewy and serpentine, framed in the middle of the distant doorway, arms extended to either side with fingers curled into hooks. Spikes rose from the top of its head, jutting out from its shoulders. There was a flash of auburn from beneath its chin as it released a hiss. Hooves pounded a retreat toward them in the darkness.

The creature rose to its full height, cocking its head back and flashing the colored strap of scales hanging from its chin, and then bent sickly in half from the right. A pair of long golden horns framed its waist, its torso flopping awkwardly onto the bull's skull. There was only a flash of orange and gold like the sun emerging from the clouds before the creature was pounded into the side of the door, the entire building shuddering around them. White sludge exploded from the impact, spattering the bull's mane, the door frame bending outward. Several of the wooden letters adorning the front of the building snapped free and fell down onto the bull's back.

It took a step back, shook the fluid from its shoulders like a dog, and then turned its blazing red eyes toward them. Snorting loudly, it stamped its right foot on the ground.

The cows and calves slowly separated themselves from the darkness, first by opening their blazing eyes, then by emerging into the wan light stretching into the barn from where the door had once been. One of the females nudged first Missy and then Mare, herding them over with the calves. She trotted around them and stood sideways to the barn door, as though shielding them with her body like the other mothers had done with their offspring. Two more bulls appeared behind the first, one shaking the tattered torso of one of those black creatures from its horns.

Missy and Mare dared to follow the advance of the other animals as they skirted piles of sloughed hides, still slick with a film of blood and connective tissue, where whatever these things were had simply arisen and stepped out of their former bodies.

The herd parted for the largest bull to step through, falling back into rank behind him to shield him from the rear. He stomped all the way over to Missy, then lowered his nose to the ground between her feet, its front limbs bending as though kneeling before her.

Missy reached tentatively toward the bull, her fingertips touching the smooth horns that felt like polished gold, then quickly recoiled.

"What are you doing?" Mare whispered.

Gently shaking her head, Missy reached back out and stroked the long horn from the tip all the way down to the shaggy mane, combing her fingers through it.

The beast snorted impatiently.

Missy stepped around the side of it, fingers still working through the coarse hairs, finally summoning the courage to slide her other hand into the scruffy mane as well.

One of the other males let out a bellow, its footsteps charging away from them over a rising swell of hissing.

Mare turned his head at the sound, but couldn't see where it had gone. By the time he looked back, Missy was already on top of the bull, legs clasped firmly to its sides, hands knotted in the mane. The beast turned away from him, Missy's hips silhouetted atop its rump.

"Come on, Mare!" she called over her shoulder.

By the time he spun around, one of the smaller bulls was kneeling beside him.

He looked again to Missy, who was already through the door and into the pen, and all he could see beyond her was a rising tide of those black creatures swelling up over the fence.

"Come on!" she screamed.

Mare threw his right leg over the bull's back and wrapped his legs as tightly as he could around the massive belly. He feared pulling too hard on the mane, but as soon as the creature started to move, he had no choice but to clasp those handfuls as tightly as he could and wrap his wrists several times. Powerful muscles flexed and relaxed beneath him, nearly bucking him. It was all he could do to turn his face to the side so he could see anything, as he feared raising his head even an inch. Dust filled the air all around him now, thrown up from the charge of the cattle. Black creatures with faces like lizards flew past, arms striking at him, tearing bloody chunks from the thing beneath him. It let out a piteous roar and almost collapsed forward into the dirt, nearly launching Mare from its back.

"Help me!" Missy screamed from ahead of him.

Mare raised his head and looked in time to see one of those black creatures with its fist entangled in her bull's mane, dragging its heels in the dirt as it clawed furiously at her. The bull beneath him righted itself and charged forward into the cornrows, leaving the black monster, claws dipping with blood, to be run down and trampled beneath the stampede of cattle behind.

"Help!" Missy screamed again.

Where are you? a barely audible voice whispered inside of her head.

"I can't find you!" she screamed.

More man tears, the voice whispered.

"Hold on!" Mare shouted, ducking his head as soon as he realized his bull's intentions. It canted its head to the left and gored a horn through the creature's back, rearing up and tossing it over its shoulder and away from his sister.

"I don't know what that means!" she wailed.

You have to find more man tears.

"Help me!" she called again as the raging behemoth beneath her barreled straight into another reptilian person, launching it up and over her with a slap of warm fluids.

White sand. The voice was growing smaller in the recesses of her mind. *Black smoke. White sand. More man tears.*

Missy craned her head back from atop the lead bull's back, listening for the voice, but all she could hear now was the pounding of hooves. She could vaguely see the shape of her brother on a bull's back behind her before the herd closed in tighter, bodies blending together into masses of pounding legs, rising and falling heads, and flaring manes.

Those black creatures were faded into the distance, racing out into the field behind them.

The last thing she saw before bringing her face back down into the thing's wild mane was the front of the building. Several of the letters had fallen from where they had once formed words, knocking down others beneath and lodging in their stead to form an entirely new arrangement.

CTION HO SE

J NATHON

MOR MON

TEARS

"Mormon tears," Missy whispered, hugging tightly to the bull's back. "White sands."

She closed her eyes and, for the first time in what felt like forever, thought she just might know where she was going.

III

WEST OF EASTON,
PENNSYLVANIA

Patchwork fields passed below, spotted by the occasional farmhouse, bordered irregularly by the forests separating the black rivers from the quilt of wheat and grains. The fields themselves were divided by channels carved away from the rivers, the crops marred with semicircular grooves from the large wheels of the sprinkler systems mounted between like metal rainbows. The highway bisecting the farmland was barren, save for the random car parked askew across the twin lanes or dead in the fields torn by its passage. New Jersey had faded and fallen away beneath them without event. The cities had been clogged with stalled cars, the streets littered with human remains. None of them had wanted to set down for fear that once they were on the ground, they wouldn't be able to return to the air. There were no signs of life besides, though every now and then it looked as though shadows raced from one darkened recess to another. The clouds were so low overhead that they flew only several hundred feet from the wavering fields, fearing the roiling heart of lightning flaring above them should they dare to rise any higher.

I know you can hear me! a voice screamed inside Adam's mind, piercing his temples like knitting needles. We have to help her!

Adam slapped his hands to the sides of his head to keep it from exploding.

"Doc!" Norman shouted from the seat beside him, grabbing Adam by the back of his fatigues and jerking him away from the open door before he could topple forward. "You okay?"

"I don't—" Adam started, only to again be cut off by the voice inside of his head like a razor blade slashing through his gray matter.

We're out of time!

Adam screamed at the pain, though he didn't even hear it over the bullhorn assault of the voice in the confines of his skull.

Find me now!

Adam eased farther onto the seat, grateful for the hand tangled in the cloth on his back. His head lolled back over the headrest and he realized he was panting. He wiped the back of his hand beneath his nose and dragged it away with a long crimson smear.

"Holy crap," Norman gasped, eyeing the bloody spatters down the front of Newman's uniform. "What in the name of God was that?"

Adam lowered his head, pinching his nostrils tightly shut. He looked up in time to see a bolt of lightning tear the air in front of them, striking a stalled pickup on the road beneath, whipping back and forth before lifting the truck from the asphalt and throwing it off into the cornfield. It receded back into the clouds with an electric crackle and a bang of thunder that sounded like the chopper had been rammed from the side. The helicopter lurched, the nose tilting upward as the air around them became electric, causing all of their hairs to stand on end.

"Whoa!" Samuels shouted, fighting with the control stick.

The floor bucked up and down beneath them, the tail swinging in rapidly changing directions like rear tires on ice. The overhead rotor let out a loud whine to replace the thrum of the blades and the floor dropped from beneath them, the ground rising and reaching for them with wavering arms. What had looked like wheat from so far above came into focus as nothing Adam had ever seen before. Rather than the wispy grains fringed with feather-like tendrils, the field appeared to be a snarl of grayish-brown bramble.

The blades resumed with a whoosh, jerking them back upward, before ceasing altogether with a pitiful whine.

"What's going on?" Peckham shouted from the front passenger seat. As he watched, all of the instrumentation lights on the control console snapped off, the needles on all of the gauges dying flat to the left. In that moment, it sounded as though the very air keeping them aloft took a deep, whistling inhalation, sucking them toward the ground.

"Hold on!" Samuels yelled, baring his teeth and gripping the stick with both hands.

Carter whimpered something from Adam's right, beyond Norman, then brought his head down between his knees, clasping his hands over his helmet. He disappeared behind Norman, who gritted his teeth and pinched his eyes shut before assuming the same crash position.

Samuels roared in defiance, urging the stick to keep them airborne, while Peckham braced his hands and legs against the console, watching the horizon rising quickly ahead.

The nose tipped up just enough to show them the fiery underside of the storm as the runners beneath made first contact with the tops of the crops. It skipped like a stone across a pond before one again dropping down into the field. Tall plants pounded at the front windshield before being turned to straw and thrown in their wake, reaching in through the open doors to either side of the cabin.

A scream was silenced by the loud growl of the runners striking the earth and the screeching of bramble tearing through the exterior paint.

They stopped abruptly, launching the men in the rear against the seats in front of them while Peckham had his breath knocked out by his seatbelt.

The cloud of dirt and dust thrown up from the impact closed around them.

"Everyone okay?" Samuels asked, tearing off his seatbelt and leaning first to Peckham, who finally caught his breath with a loud wheeze, and then turning back to check on the men tangled together in the back.

"What in the hell was that?" Peckam asked, his voice an octave too high.

"I don't know for sure," Samuels said, already gathering his pack from the floorboard in front of Peckham. "All of the instruments shut down at the same time, almost as though there had been an EMP."

"An electromagnetic pulse?" Carter said, pulling himself from atop Norman and settling back into his seat long enough to find his own pack. He slung it over his shoulder and leapt down to the ground in one fluid motion. "What would you know about EMPs?"

"You have a better idea? I'd love to hear it," Samuels growled, shouldering his door open and launching himself to the dirt.

"I'll bet you just ran the damned thing out of gas."

"You think I'm that stupid, man?" Samuels rushed around the damaged front of the chopper and shoved Carter right in the middle of the chest. The much smaller man left his feet and slammed backward into tangles of foreign shrubbery nearly as tall as he was.

He screamed.

Samuels was a furious step from grabbing the soldier again to rip him to his feet when he stopped, his breath hitching in his chest.

Long lacerations opened along Carter's cheeks, tearing through even the thick fabric of his jacket to summon fresh blood into the material. At first they had been simple red lines, but had opened like mouths, spilling out Carter's warm fluids. Jesus," Norman gasped, hopping out onto the mangled ground. The dirt was mounded to either side of the twisted runners, the angled fronts staked into the ground. He was already on his knees and tearing into the medical kit when Carter screamed again.

These weren't crops of anything he could recognize. They had long thin stalks somewhere between the thickness of corn and wheat, but there were what looked to be coiled vines spiraling up toward the top, the outer edge serrated like the lip of an aluminum foil box. Long gray leaves reached out to either side, grabbing hold of their opposite number on the adjacent plant and tangling into a twist, their sharpened ends standing up like twin barbs on a fish hook. From the top of the plants grew large cones shaped like spades, the outer layers peeled back like an onion blossom, only the edges so sharp they glinted with the flashing lightning.

"Hold still," Norman said, easing his way closer to Carter. "Someone give me a hand!"

Adam walked around the rear of the copter from the far side, ducking beneath the remaining half of the tail. A trail of gouged earth led away from the wreckage like a meteor strike.

Samuels reached for Carter, grabbing him right in the center of the chest, his fists tangled in the man's jacket, and jerked him back out and to his feet. Carter's legs buckled beneath him and he crumpled to the ground. Norman eased over the top of him, staring at all of the bleeding slashes as though he hadn't the faintest idea of where to begin. He pulled a small bottle of betadine from his pack and simply squirted it all over the man's skin, turning the flesh a rust color. Carter screamed as the antiseptic worked its magic, thrashing around on his back as Norman pulled rolls of bandages out and tossed them to the ground beside him.

Adam hurried to the other side of the man and tore off the tattered sleeve, tossing it over his shoulder. Carter's arms were smeared with blood, but none of the wounds were more than superficial. He would wrap the man's arms after he tended to the more serious lacerations.

"I need steri-strips and butterflies," Adam said, raising his right hand without stealing his eyes from Carter's face. The cuts across his face were much deeper as they hadn't had the benefit of the layers of clothing to absorb the worst of the injuries. His hands were already covered with blood and dirt so the dressings would be far from sterile, but he would have to worry about that later. Right now, the betadine solution would be enough to at least stall any potential infection. Norman slapped the line of steri-strips into Adam's hand, which he peeled off one at a time, sticking the bottom edge of the length of tape to the lower lip of the wound, and then drawing it upward and taping it to the skin above. As soon as all of the facial wounds were sealed with the thin strips of tape, he applied the butterfly bandages, closing those formerly screaming mouths until only swelling droplets of blood blossomed from the seams.

Norman gave Carter a solid bolus push of what Adam assumed to be a morphine derivative and then loaded a tiny needle to begin numbing the surface of the soldier's face with a local anesthetic. The tension in Carter's face faded with his consciousness as Adam wrapped one of the bloody arms with several rolls of gauze, while Norman did the same on opposite side.

"Good thing he was wearing his helmet and backpack," Norman said, gently rolling the unconscious man up onto his side so that he could survey the posterior surface of his head and back. Neither of the legs seemed to have sustained more than rips in the fabric and a few small gashes easily rectified with gauze squares and tape.

Samuels's eyes had grown hollow and distant as he simply stared forward into the weeds, cocking his head side to side like a bird as he inspected them. Slowly, he reached forward and placed just the tip of his right index finger on one of the thorns. He recoiled at the sight of the blood, his hand already cradled to his chest before he felt the sting.

"They're as sharp as razor blades," he said, pinching his fingertip against his jacket to staunch the bleeding. "How the hell are we supposed to get out of here?"

"We crawl," Peckham said from what sounded like a dozen paces away.

"Where are you, Peck?" Norman asked, shoving the last of the unused bandages into his pack and snapping it shut.

"The road's to the northwest," he called back. "I saw it as we were going down."

Samuels dropped to his hands and knees and lowered his head. There was a good eighteen to twenty-four inch gap between the ground and the lowest row of those astoundingly-sharp tangles of leaves and three to four feet between the stalks. He looked back to the grooved earth behind the chopper, the foliage lining the earthen wound like a trench. The prospect of crawling under those knife-like brambles was mortifying, but what else were they going to do?

"I've got Carter," he said firmly, unfastening his belt and tugging it loose from his pants. Crawling over to the unconscious man, he looped it around Carter's chest beneath his arms and tugged it tight. "I need your belts."

Norman already had his off by the time Samuels asked, passing it to the larger man, who this time wrapped it around Carter's chest on top of the other belt, but outside of the arms, pinning them to his sides.

"Now yours," Samuel's said, taking Adam's belt. He slid the end of the belt beneath the others and pulled it through, sliding the end through the buckle and pulling it tight.

Before either Norman or Adam was sure of Samuels's plan, he was out of his backpack and lying on his back with the end of the belt knotted in both fists.

"Grab my pack," he said, then dug his heels into the soft ground and pushed himself in reverse. No sooner had Carter's legs disappeared beneath the crops than Peckham called out.

"There's a thin stream down here!" Loud splashes signaled he was thrashing forward through knee-deep water. "And I think I can see the road!"

"Wait up!" Norman called, throwing himself to his belly and shimmying forward, using his elbows and the insides of his feet for propulsion.

Adam looped his foot through one of the straps on Samuels's pack, twisted it again to make it tighter and then began crawling through the darkness following the sounds of Norman's harried scrabbling.

Adam splashed down into the stream before he even knew it was coming, sputtering water that must have serviced cattle somewhere upstream. He managed to catch himself with his hands in the soft silt, keeping his head and backpack barely above the water. Pulling the other backpack from his right foot, he cradled it against his chest and dropped to his knees in the cold water.

The bramble to either side of the stream grew together above him like a natural ceiling, just high enough that he could walk if he ducked. The water barely moved at a trickle around his legs, leading him toward a corrugated pipe that passed beneath a steep embankment that stood ahead of him like a wall.

"You coming, Newman?" one of the men called from out of sight somewhere above him.

A wet trail of mud and sludge led upward from atop the round pipe and out of sight.

"Yeah," Adam coughed, his lower back protesting the weight he carried at a stoop, but he sloshed forward until he reached the duct, balancing his right boot on the slick top and propelling himself upward. Hands grabbed his backpack and tugged him, nearly lifting him from his feet and out of the vegetative enclosure onto an elevated, single-lane dirt road.

With Carter slung over his back, Samuels was already fifty yards down the washboard road toward a distant house.

"Are you okay?" Norman asked, already striking off after Samuels.

"With the exception of a bunch of cuts on my palms, I'm none the worse for wear," Adam said, wiping his hands on his pants.

"Good," Peckham said, wincing as he applied pressure to a laceration on his cheek.

They walked along the road in silence marred only by the scuffing of their boots on the loose gravel. Adam watched the house growing larger as they approached. A chain link fence surrounded the front yard, enclosing even the detached garage to the right. Faded paint, as light blue as the sky had once been, peeled from the weathered siding, the front screen door hanging askew. The closer he got, the more it began to look familiar. Weeds grew from the wide cracks in the disintegrating driveway, the front porch framed by walls of browning junipers. A stripe was worn into the lawn from the front gate up to the crumbling steps and the windows were painted over, but it wasn't until he was nearly to the gate, watching Samuels crossing the yard with Carter, that he saw the basement window wells had been filled with concrete.

It was exactly as it had been in his dream before the plane went down.

Samuels banged his meaty fist into the door several times.

"Wait," Adam called, dropping the other man's backpack, shouldering aside Norman and Peckham and sprinting through the gate.

The force of the big man's knocking loosed the front door, which shuddered slowly open to reveal a darkened room beyond.

"What's the deal, doc?" Samuels asked, turning to face him. "I'm guessing that whoever lives here is dead already. Just like everyone else."

Yellow eyes snapped open in the darkness. There was a tearing sound and Samuels was on his back on the porch with Carter's legs vanishing into the darkness. Sounds like threshing erupted from the doorway as Carter's bloody helmet bounced back down to the porch beside Samuels, who was already rising to his feet and unholstering his service pistol.

He fired into the darkness with a flash of muzzle flare and strode directly through the open doorway to be swallowed by the shadows.

"Don't go in there!" Adam shouted, knowing full well he was too late.

He pried the assault rifle from where it was clipped to the pack he'd inherited from Merton and brought it out in front of him.

More flashes in the darkness coupled with a bellow of challenge.

Eyes flashed through the darkness like bats at dusk. Before Samuels could even finish his war cry, he was abruptly silenced, followed by a thud and the subsequent scramble.

"Jesus," Adam whispered, easing toward the doorway with his heart beating a million miles a second. "Jesus Christ."

He clicked off the safety and inched past Carter's helmet. He couldn't see a thing. There were no flashes of gunfire, no eyes watching him. The room was completely black, save for the wan strip of gray that crossed the entryway from the open door and reached into the room.

There was a series of clicks from behind him as bullets were chambered and safeties were disengaged.

"We go in on three." Peckham's voice even quivered in a whisper. "Norman, flank left. Doc, you flank right. On my count. One."

All Adam could hear was his own panicked breathing. He had to take the gun in both hands to make it even remotely steady.

"Two."

Eyes like flashlights poured into the room from the left, leaping over the banister and scurrying up the stairs. A dozen more snapped open on the ceiling where they hung in suspension with fingers and toes embedded in the plaster.

Adam screamed and tugged on the trigger, spraying a barrage of bullets into the room, strobing like a disco with the flaring of gunpowder.

III

BETHLEHEM,
PENNSYLVANIA

The creatures now pressed themselves into the shadows between the horizontal joists above, owl eyes staring down at Phoenix as he lie on his back, merely breathing. Reaching out to the others had taken all of his energy, leaving him feeling a shade this side of death. His skin was cool, clammy, each breath like trying to catch a rattlesnake by the tail. Mind swimming in and out of consciousness, it was all he could do to focus on the eyes leering down at him, gauging their size to ensure that they weren't advancing on him. Though after what had happened to the pile of ashes on the concrete next to him, Phoenix couldn't imagine that they would take that chance again. They may have looked like reptilian monsters, but there was an unquestionable sentience behind those eyes, as though even now they were formulating how they would get him. And perhaps the most disturbing thing of all was that they didn't blink, but rather a clear crescent of skin would rise from beneath the lower lid to wet the surface and then zip back almost invisibly.

Those eyes stayed glued upon him right up until the moment that he heard a muffled knock from the front door above, followed by but the most insignificant sound of the hinges allowing the door to swing in.

Their eyes darted to the doorway, followed by their bodies, and then they were gone, scurrying upside down past the doorway and into the thick shadows of the hallway. There had been even more of them up there than he had originally thought as some of them must have had the presence of mind to keep their lantern eyes closed. He hadn't known they were there at all.

"Don't come in," he tried to shout, but all that came out was a hoarse whisper.

There was a loud thud from above that shook the ceiling.

"No," Phoenix rasped, rolling over onto all fours. He expected claws to immediately slash through the skin on his back, though at that point he didn't care. They needed to be warned. He needed them to get him out of there; they were no good to him dead and certainly the guilt would have been more than he could bear after having called them to their deaths. The girl was in trouble. The men upstairs were as well. If they were unable to survive then there would be no reason left for him to either. Nothing else mattered now.

Phoenix reached the stairs at the end of the room and used them to rise to his knees, crawling around the landing until he was able to grab hold of the railing and haul himself to his feet. His legs trembled, but he willed himself to walk, taking one stiff-legged step at a time—

Bang!

The first gunshot had been so loud that he thought something inside of his head must have popped. By the time he recovered enough to drag himself onward, there was a man yelling at the top of his lungs and firing blast after blast into the room. Light flashed above at the top of the staircase, illuminating clouds of powder that exploded from the plaster walls. Phoenix shielded his head, barely able to see anything besides his arms, and advanced at a crouch. The creatures moved like shadows, darting out of the illumination from the discharge, not running on both legs, but flattening themselves to the floor and then scurrying up the nearest wall. By the time they opened their eyes and betrayed their location, the ceiling was thick with them.

The scream was cut off abruptly, followed by a thunderous crash that shook the floor.

All of the eyes rained down from the ceiling, a black tangle of darkness scrabbling in the middle of the room like so many roosters in a cockfight. Blood splashed the walls all around, even slapping down on Phoenix as he neared the top of the stairs. The warm fluid caught him by surprise, startling him just enough to cause a moment of hesitation.

A pair of the beasts had crept over the ceiling and gotten behind him, his stall throwing off their attacks as they flew past and over his head.

Light flashed from the room above, flickering like an 8mm reel. It sounded as though a wind had spontaneously risen and was blowing straight into the house, but he knew otherwise as soon as the bullets slammed into the walls, taking chunks from the railing beside him.

Hissing tore through the darkness as the shadows came to life, scurrying up the walls and to the ceiling again, where they immediately closed their eyes, though in the flashes of gunfire he could still see them advancing toward the front door from above.

"Shoot at the ceiling!" Phoenix railed, his voice finally returning in a scream.

He dared to peer up over the edge of the floor, through the railings into the main room. A shadowed man stood in the doorway, framed against the gray sky outside. Phoenix was sure that the man looked directly into his eyes before raising his weapon and directing it up to the roof.

This was his chance!

Phoenix dashed around the top of the staircase into the living room, his eyes fixed firmly on the outside world behind the silhouette.

Manmade lightning crackled in the close confines before being overwhelmed by a furious hissing. Warm fluids rained down on him from above as straps of flesh and chunks of bone pounded the ground all around him. He couldn't think. He was functioning on pure instinct as all he could do was watch the strobe of the discharge as he sprinted toward the man with his arms over his head, already soaked with a thick fluid.

The whir of gunfire died and the man backed out of the house, swinging the butt of the gun as the wounded leapt down from the ceiling and raced at him as fluid as living darkness.

Phoenix dove forward, grabbing the lip of the threshold and pulling himself out into air that felt alive with static energy—

A clawed hand seized his ankle; so intensely painful it felt as though it had grabbed bone beneath the skin. He screamed as he was pulled back into the darkness with hissing and the clattering of eager talons all around.

The man jumped to his aid, slamming the butt of the assault rifle down squarely in the middle of the thing's head. The pressure abating,

Phoenix scrambled forward and tumbled out onto the cement porch, tearing the skin from his knees, but he didn't even feel it. All he could think was how amazing the outdoor air felt passing his lips and rushing down his trachea into his lungs. It was as though he were a rag doll tasting its first breaths of life.

Two other men rushed toward him, each grabbing him beneath an arm and hauling him off toward an open gate in the middle of a chain link fence and onto the dirt road beyond.

"Stay with him," the larger of the two men said, sprinting back toward the house.

"Are you hurt?" the remaining man shouted into his face. He held a weapon extended in his right hand while he yanked the contents of his camouflaged sack out with his left.

Phoenix shook his head, though he was sure that the man was otherwise occupied as he jerked the smock off over Phoenix's head and forced his arms through the sleeves of a shirt matching those of the other men, all the while watching the front door, his nervous finger tapping on the trigger.

"Put these on and stay down!" the man commanded, thrusting a pair of pants into Phoenix's chest and then placing his body between Phoenix and the open doorway.

The purr of automatic gunfire summoned a frenzy of hissing and a chorus of thack, thack, thack as the bullets tore into the walls and ceiling.

"Fall back!" a voice shouted.

As Phoenix tried to force his feet through the awkward holes, he tried to see around the man crouching in front of him with his rifle trained on the doorway. One man sprinted at them, his rifle dripping with white sludge, the barrel still smoldering, while the other backed down the beaten path, releasing clouds of bullets back into the house until the chamber spun dry.

"Cover fire!" he bellowed, dropping his weapon to his side and running toward the gate.

The man who clothed Phoenix rose to his feet and stepped forward, the men dashing toward him throwing themselves to all fours and crawling past him.

No further gunfire ensued as a dust of plaster and smoke wavered in the blackened doorway like a mist. Nothing moved beyond. No shadows stirred. Only the thinning mist as it slowly dissipated.

"Carter and Samuels?" the man holding the rifle in his shaking hands asked without looking back.

"Neither made it," a voice said from right behind Phoenix.

"What in the name of God are those things?" the other man asked, tossing aside his spent cartridge and chambering another with a loud click.

"The Swarm," Phoenix whispered.

The man in front of him turned around at the sound of Phoenix's voice.

"The what?"

"The Swarm," Phoenix whispered again, watching through the gap between the man's legs as a dark form slithered into the open doorway. A crimson flap unfolded from beneath its broad chin, flapping like a cape and shivering with the exertion of a massive hiss. A long red scar drew a diagonal across its right eye to a star-shaped gash on its cheek.

Phoenix knew The Man, no matter which form he took.

The scarred creature took a single step back and blended again with the shadows, that same insane look fading from his eyes as he closed them and become one with the blackness.

"We have a long journey ahead," Phoenix whispered, rising to his bare feet on the dirt road. He started walking away from the house for the first time in his life with the men simply staring after him. Phoenix suspected their head start would only last until what remained of the sun drained from the sky, and that even in death The Man would be unable to let him go.

CHAPTER 8

I

AURORA,
COLORADO

Death sat high atop Harbinger, the proud steed wearing a new suit of shiny black human flesh stripped from the corpses littering their path, drawn tight and stitched over its skeletal form. The patchwork skin suited the nature of the beast, a haphazard creation of both the living and the dead. Death wore a matching cloak to hide his black, scaled flesh, only his had been stitched together from the skins of the living while they endured the torment of their screaming nerve endings, praising God, praising Death, when their suffering was finally ended. Only he wore the browning skins that shrouded his form, the long hood shielding his face. The others wore the black, rubbery skins of the dead like their horses, for to wear the skins of the living, one must truly be able to appreciate life, and who would be able to more than Death? The others were simply ravagers, serving their one function and no other. For Famine, his seeds had been sewn and fertilized, it was only a matter of time until they transformed the entire landscape as they had the humans unfortunate enough to have had weighted souls that couldn't rise to Heaven, their eternal sins and wickedness trapped in the realm of the living dead, boiling in the fire that coursed through their veins. They were Death's minions at War's command. They would kill for him. Die for him. And only then would their souls be set free, their penance complete. Pestilence's day had come and gone as well. It was her mosquito swarms that had sucked the lifeblood from the survivors, releasing the souls of the righteous to take their ethereal journey, while leaving the souls of the sinners in their bodies to be fertilized by Famine's locust-borne seed. The animals though, their souls were untainted by the seven sins of man. They knew only instinct, be it grazing or killing, and aspired to nothing more. They were essentially turned inside out to wear their souls on the outside after shedding their prisons of flesh. It was only man who remained to be taught the lesson that must be learned, man who must bear the weight of the sins the Son of God had tried to bear for them. How soon they forget.

That was the problem with man: he could see no further back than yesterday and no further ahead than tomorrow. It was a species born unto the grave.

Harbinger snorted a gust of flame and smoke, dancing eagerly from one foot to the other as its master stared through eyes that varied in color as the leaves of fall to match his mood, now as red as the heart of the earth, toward the horizon from atop that scorched knoll. Pestilence and Famine flanked him, though several paces behind, their steeds yet to crest the hill, faces swallowed by shadows within their cowls. War stayed behind them, Thunder treading the same path as that of the master, the red rider cloaked in the festering remains of the dead. Behind him, trailing all the way to the horizon in a triangular formation to shame the largest battalions to set foot on the earth, was his army of black-skinned abominations, their glowing eyes lighting the way like so many torches.

The sun had only recently set. The night was theirs.

Death studied the jagged crests of the Rocky Mountains standing like broken glass against the western horizon, fading in and out of the dust that was only now beginning to settle. The grasslands of the eastern slope surrounding him were flattened and dead, what remained of the houses now little more than random walls standing guard over their rubble, chimneys lording over the destruction. If there had been any saved by the thumbprint of God, then they were not out this night, as the only movement belonged to the reptilian denizens of the night as they joined the ranks of the army of the damned from all directions, as they became one with The Swarm.

The suburbs stood in a ring around the crater and wasteland that had only the day before been Denver, Colorado, missing roofs and walls, some still burning for lack of anyone to put them out. The sky tasted of ashes, both formerly living and non, the powder of death drizzling like rain beneath the blue lightning ripping seams in the grumbling thunderheads. The entire area had taken on the smell of scorched rubber, a liquid scent that seeped in through the pores.

Where downtown had once stood, at the epicenter of the enormous crater, skyscrapers had toppled into one another to create a spire of destruction into the heavens, leaving a moat of black earth around the fallen structures. Partially demolished buildings and houses lined the rim of the crater, broken and burning walls standing like tombstones.

The tangle of crumbled and bowed metal that had once been the city skyline of Colorado's largest city now appeared to be one ungodly structure with portions of felled buildings looming over the rubble like leaning parapets of exposed girders and steel. A central tower rose from the midst of the wreckage, pinched in place from either side by other fallen skyscrapers like a middle finger raised to the sky. The ground surrounding shimmered with violet from the constant assault of lightning reflecting up from the fields of shattered glass melted into a continuous sheet by the blast, covering everything from mounds of powdered brick and mortar to the crumpled and abused remains of cars.

It looked like a giant castle in the middle of a lake of electrical fire.

This was the seat of power, the staging grounds from which they would wipe out what remained of humanity and prepare the world for its next evolutionary leap. The human race had been a mistake, a mistake easily enough rectified.

He kicked Harbinger in the sides with his spurred heels, startling the beast to gallop forward, the long train of sewn flesh flagging like a cape.

Famine and Pestilence rode behind.

As War took to gallop, Heaven and Hell alike trembled beneath the advance of The Swarm.

CHAPTER 9

I

They'd only been able to make it to the suburbs of Eugene before Darren's Blazer could take them no farther. The interstates were clogged with stalled vehicles and long pileups of crumpled metal and taillights dying like red eyes through the smoke. Half of the city looked to be on fire, but there wasn't a single siren to respond. The base of the cloud of black smoke just seemed to grow wider and wider as it enveloped the city, and with the way the wind had been picking up, it was only a matter of time until it consumed everything. The only good thing about the thick smoke was that it was so overwhelming they weren't even able to smell the carnage anymore.

The majority of the occupants were still in their cars, visible through insect marred windows and shattered windshields, their bloated black bodies only now beginning the process of deterioration. Still other cars were empty, save for the straps of flesh torn from whatever had crawled across the jaggedly fractured window into the night, shedding its former humanity in a puddle on the road. There was no sign of them, though as the sky grew increasingly darker, the shadows beneath the bridges and under the wrecked cars seemed to come to life.

April had whispered something about her parents being wrong; this couldn't have been the way The Rapture was supposed to happen. When God called his faithful children again to his side, they were supposed to simply vanish, flesh and all, leaving only the sinners to stand against what the world would soon become. None of these bodies showed any signs of even the souls departing gracefully. Every face they passed was a frozen mask of agony. Had their eternal life force indeed risen from their flesh, then why had it not done so sooner? Why had everyone been forced to endure what must have been an excruciating death so that their souls could be free? She wondered what kind of sick God would force his own children to endure such an awful and violent death when He could have done as the Bible promised and made the righteous disappear and reappear at the side of His eternal throne. The prospect of the Bible being wrong led her down the thought path that inevitably led to the dilemma of if there even was a God, and if so, how could He possibly justify being so cruel? She hadn't spoken since, at least not to Jill, who was beginning to wonder if she really should share the blame for everything going on. Perhaps they would have been better off had they been claimed by the insects like everyone else.

It seemed as though Darren was the only one still in touch with his wits. He didn't have a plan per se, but he seemed capable of making a decision. Had it been left up to the rest of them, they would have still been sitting in that Blazer waiting for the permanently snarled traffic to move. He'd been the one to spot the Yamaha Cycle dealership a half mile off the highway, and his idea to change their mode of transportation to allow them the ability to either weave through the mess of cars or completely avoid them by heading off-road.

Of the five of them, only Ray had ridden a dirt bike before, but once the others managed to figure out how to manipulate the handheld gear shift and toe clutch, it hadn't taken long for them to be able to keep up. The shoulders on the sides of the highways had been relatively clear, the headlamps adorning the front of the cycles just long enough to warn them of impending danger before they slammed right into it.

After leaving Eugene, they'd kept to the back highways where they knew the traffic couldn't possibly be as bad, cutting through the northeast corner of California into Nevada, skirting Reno as, even from a hundred miles away, the sky was charcoal-colored with the smoke from that burning city, the horizon a solid glow like the rising sun. They'd passed through a small town called Virginia City, which had been a ghost town, before heading to the east.

The best part of this new traveling arrangement was that none of them had to talk to each another. For as long as they rode with the buzzing of the engine and the vibrating motor between their legs they were alone inside their heads. Tina rested her cheek against Ray's back, her arms wrapped around his chest and thighs pinched tightly around his hips. Every time Jill thought Tina had fallen asleep, she'd raise her head just enough to betray her consciousness, generally looking past Ray's shoulder down the road toward Lord only knew what.

Darren and April rode behind, though April didn't look half as comfortable. She had the entire front of her body pressed so firmly into Darren's back that it was a wonder he could even breathe. Each time the tires so much as threatened to kick out on the gravel, she bolted straight and held on for dear life.

Jill envied them as she followed from the rear, pushing the bike uncomfortably fast to try to keep up. Much as she would have rather just been riding behind someone like Rick, hands locked over his chest, feeling the reassurance of his heartbeat, she didn't think she'd be much good to anyone. All she knew was that they needed to head southeast and even that wasn't something she could articulate. She felt no more in control than the needle on a compass being drawn toward magnetic north. Her mind kept repeating the phrase More man tears over and over until it became the only thought in her head. She was a ghost residing in her own form, watching the headlight bounce up and down on the uneven shoulder, merely making sure that she followed the red taillight in front of her whenever it swerved to avoid something, sputtering out the dust from its passage. Her mind rehearsed those three words over and over. What was that supposed to mean? She just wanted to be left alone. To sleep a dreamless sleep. To lose herself in the void if only for a little while. The world around her had become something out of a nightmare. The Joshua trees and pitchfork cactuses appeared to be metamorphosing into something different altogether. Granted, she could only see them as silhouettes against the distant lightning slashing the sky, but they almost appeared to be growing more appendages, creeping toward the road from the desolate desert. She was even starting to think that there were other things out there as well, other black things that held to the shadows, dashing across the sand on their bellies to hide behind the next stand of wildly branching sage like so many birds flying past in the trees.

She tried not to look, tried to focus solely on her own headlight, watching the relatively flat shoulder of the bubble-gum pink highway to ensure that she didn't run her front tire into a large rock or drag her legs through a tangle of yuccas, which were by now starting to look more like collections of javelins. Every time she wanted to look at the spotted abandoned cars or the living desert to her right, she forced herself to look down instead. It was impossible not to read the gas gauge, the needle flirting passionately with the thin red line before the E, the little orange light flashing on and off as it tried to make up its mind about warning her of its impending threat to stall out there in the middle of nowhere. All three of the Yamahas had been full when they found them, the keys still in the ignition as she could only imagine the dead people surrounding the bikes in a ring had been in the process of test-riding them.

Jill looked back up in time to see the taillight in front of her rapidly growing larger through a swirling cloud of dust. She gasped and hit the brakes, her bike wanting nothing more than to start sliding on its side, but with a lurch she regained control, slowing just enough that when she hit the rear tire of Darren's cycle, it only made theirs torsos buckle forward.

"Jesus, Jill," April whined. Her tear-soaked eyes shimmered in the bike's headlight, highlighting the streaks where the saline had dragged the mascara to her temples.

"How was I supposed to know you were stopping?" she blurted. She winced and took a deep breath. The last thing that any of them needed now was an argument. Things were bad enough without turning on each other.

"It's okay," Darren said, forcing a smile. "I don't even think I know where the turn signals are on this thing." He patted April reassuringly on the thigh and waited for Ray to turn his bike around and let him know why they had stopped so quickly.

Ray rolled the bike up beside Darren, the headlight pointing right into Jill's face. Their forms were shadowed and often eclipsed by the bright glare, but she could see Ray lean close to Darren so that he was speaking almost directly into his friend's ear. She could see their mouths moving, but couldn't hear a word over even the gentle purring of the beasts between their legs. Both of the guys turned as one and looked straight down the highway, past the lone pair of crimson taillights watching them vacuously from the middle of the deserted road.

She hadn't seen it at first, but there was a small halogen glow in front of the all-but-invisible foothills along the horizon. Had it not been for the hills beyond, it could have been easily mistaken for a distant star sitting low in the night sky.

With considerable effort, Jill found the kickstand with her heel and forced it down, leaning the bike to the side until it balanced and climbed off. The others didn't even notice her until she was right there between them.

"I don't know," Darren said, "but it could be more people out here on the road like us."

"Or it could be those things we saw back at the hospital," Ray said.

"I don't think so," Jill said, still scrutinizing the small light. "It almost looks to me like a truck stop or something."

"There's no way to tell from this distance," Darren said. "With how flat this desert is, we could be fifty miles from it for all we know. It could just as easily be Vegas."

"It's not Vegas," Ray said.

"I know, I was just exaggerating, man. No need to take everything so literally."

Ray's eyes narrowed, his frayed nerves playing like worn guitar strings, but his pursed lips slowly relaxed and he just nodded.

"The only way we'll know for sure is if we get close enough to check it out," Jill said, looking off into the darkness to her right where she could have sworn she saw a shadow run past.

"Are you volunteering?" Ray asked.

"Leave her alone, Ray," Tina said, leaning forward to softly kiss his neck.

"I didn't mean…" he started, but fell silent. He felt as though simple conversation was now more like trying to cross a minefield. "Look. We're all scared, and who in the world knows what's up there. All I'm saying is that we need to come up with some sort of cautious plan so we don't get ourselves into even more trouble."

April nodded against Darren's shoulder, dragging her runny nose up and down the back of his sweatshirt.

"Don't you, you know, see anything about this?" Darren asked, turning to Jill, who shook her head.

"All I know is that we're heading in the right direction and it's important that we find 'More man tears.'"

"Whatever that means," Ray groaned.

"I wish I knew," Jill said. "I just keep hearing those words over and over like some kind of recording or something. That's all I know."

Ray opened his mouth to say something, but was silenced before he could by a squeeze around his ribs from Tina, who looked back into the field to her left.

Jill looked out into the desert as well. There was no movement as she thought she had seen earlier, but she could have sworn that the sage had been shorter a moment ago, the cactuses farther from the road.

"We're just wasting time," Darren finally said. "The way I see it, we only have two options. Either we keep going forward or we turn around and head back. It's that easy."

"We could head out into the desert and swing wide around whatever it is," Ray offered.

"No," Jill and Tina said at once, looking curiously at each other.

"I'll go," Jill said softly, lowering her eyes. Without another word, she scuffed back to her motorcycle and climbed atop it. It took several tries, but she finally knocked the kickstand back into place and revved the engine. She guided the bike around the others on tiptoes before bringing her feet back to the pedals and taking a deep breath. When the nerve finally hit, she launched the cycle into gear, unintentionally showering her friends with gravel, and rocketed as fast as she dare go down the side of the road.

As soon as she passed the lone stalled car, she looked back over her shoulder.

Two headlights were gaining on her from behind, one brighter than the other.

She allowed the stale air in her chest escape, easing her thrumming heart just a touch, and returned her attention to the weathered interstate and the distant glow at the edge of the desert.

II

THE OUTSKIRTS
OF FALLON,
NEVADA

Evelyn leaned against the side of her dusty pickup, unconsciously scraping rust from the wheel-well with her fingernail while gas coursed through the black hose into her nearly bone-dry tank. This was one of the few things that she could be thankful for. She'd been driving down some two-lane highway she couldn't even find on the map through the Anargosa Mountain Range bordering Death Valley into Nevada for the last three and a half hours before she'd seen the glow from the overhead lights of the gas station. Wonder of wonders, the pump even took her credit card. It was obvious the attendant was dead as she could see him through the bug-pocked front window of the place on the floor in front of the register in his bright red vest. She had no idea what they did behind the counter to make the gas flow, so she considered herself fortunate enough to have found a pump without a balance on it.

The store shared space with a diner servicing the lines of interstate trucks parked in the dirt lot to the east past the building, though she tried not to look at them. A mesh baseball cap tumbled across the gravel, presumably from the lump of black flesh sprawled in front of an International Harvester, the man's flannel flagging on the breeze. A pair of headlights stared past him over the rumbling engine, but from the looks of the people inside the restaurant, it wouldn't be going anywhere any time soon.

The lights above the counter inside Linden's Corner blinked every couple of seconds, alternately exposing the bodies littering the floor surrounding the red vinyl stools and then hiding them. Unfilled tickets still hung from the wheel for the short-order cook who she guessed was back there somewhere in the rich black smoke from what remained of the burgers and eggs that had been on the skillet.

Gas squirted over the back of Evelyn's hand when the tank filled. Shaking her fuming hand, she hung the nozzle back on its perch and looked over the bed of the truck into the convenience store, separated from the diner by a wall displaying rims and tires. Past the register she could see a wall of refrigerators holding all kinds of cold drinks. Her gaze dropped again to the clerk lying facedown in the middle of the main aisle between her and her destination.

She tried to swallow, but her tongue stuck to the roof of her mouth.

There was no choice. Much as she detested the prospect, she was going to have to step over that attendant and get something to drink or she was going to die out here. It couldn't have been more than forty-some degrees now, but when the sun rose—assuming that it would indeed do so again—it was going to get hot in a hurry.

She spun the gas cap back into place and closed the hatch.

Trying not to think about all of the bodies in the diner or the one in the adjoining convenience store she would soon have to come way too close to, Evelyn hurried across the parking lot, slipping between two cars she knew would never move again, and stopped as soon as she reached the door. Tugging her shirt up over her mouth and nose, she held it there with her teeth and threw open the door. Even through the fabric the smell was atrocious, but she didn't intend to linger. She went straight to the back of the store, pressing her right hip against the counter and sliding along, doing everything in her power to keep from looking down. Her left foot knocked aside the clerk's Nike-clad foot, but that was the worst of it. Pocketing handfuls of candy and gum, she went directly to the nearest glass case and slid the door to the side. She grabbed a twelve pack of Pepsi in one hand and a twelve of Diet in the other. She could almost feel the burn of the carbonation in her ragged throat already. Stacking both onto her left arm and leaning back to brace the weight against her chest, she went straight for the energy drinks. The last thing in the world that she wanted right now was to have to sleep. Not that she felt the urge now, but it was only a matter of time.

She grabbed a Red Bull, but put it right back. It was too small and she was only making one trip. She reached instead for the energy drinks in the largest cans, pulling down the front can from each row until she had all she could hope to carry.

The shirt slipped from between her teeth, but there was nothing she could do now but hold her breath. Walking as quickly as she could, eyes focused solely on the front door, she passed the corpse on the floor and burst back out into the night, allowing her pent-up breath to explode out. Part of her felt guilty for taking the food and drinks without paying for them, but the majority of her was counting down the seconds until she could crack open one of those cans.

Leaning against the side of the truck, she opened the passenger door and shoved the stack of drinks onto the seat, knocking her backpack onto the floor. At the moment, she didn't even care. All she could think of was pouring something cold down her throat. Seizing one of the energy drinks, she popped the tab with a hiss and brought it to her lips so quickly that she smashed her upper lip against her tooth. Inhaling it, she fought the pain in her throat to force it down, gulping until she had to come back up for air. Lowering the can from her face, she panted heavily, trying to resume normal breathing while enjoying the wet feel of her esophagus, no matter how much the carbonation felt as though it were burning holes through the tissue.

"Ahh," she said aloud, the sound even startling her.

She rotated the can in her hand until she could see the label. She hadn't looked at what she was grabbing any more than she had tasted it going down. It was a black can with lime green writing, taller even than a can of soda.

"Monster," she read, tipping it back again.

She stopped, a wash of the amber fluid passing her lips, but that was all. Her brows formed a thick ridge over her eyes. Slowly, she brought the can away from her face, trying to keep the same arc she'd used to raise it in the first place. She'd seen something, but it had taken her brain a moment to rationalize it. The can. The way she was holding it, her thumb covered all but the first three letters of the brand name.

Mon.

She looked out at the highway. There was a large reflective sign right at the eastern edge of the gas station's property:

Austin	38 miles
Battle Mountain	80 miles
Salt Lake City	246 miles.

Tears streamed from her eyes, racing down through the dust on her cheeks.

"It isn't 'more man,' it's Mormon," she said, the can falling from her trembling hand and spilling out onto the asphalt. "Salt Lake. Saltwater. Saline. Tears."

Evelyn mewled with joy, darting toward the driver's side of the truck, before dashing back around to close the passenger door. She was nearly around to the driver's side again, when she looked back to the building. There were a couple of things she was going to need, she thought as she sprinted back across the parking lot. She didn't think about the man on the floor or the corpses in the diner as she nearly threw the door off its hinges in her hurry to get in.

Dashing straight toward the automotive aisle, she grabbed a folded map of Utah and another of Salt Lake City itself, and was nearly back out the door when she saw a can of spray-paint. Snatching it up, she ran out into the fresh air, the thunder grumbling so loud now it sounded like a gang of motorcycles, past her car and the parked semi-trailers to the sign. She tucked the maps beneath her left arm and shook the can, the metal ball inside clanking loudly, and then ripped off the cap.

At the bottom of the sign, she spray-painted two words right over the top of the reflective white lettering of Salt Lake City.

"Mormon tears," she said, inspecting her work only long enough to watch the lines of paint start to roll down from the words toward the bottom of the sign.

Beaming, she whirled and was about to run excitedly to her car when the first of the lights hit her directly in the face and she screamed.

III

The boy had been able to run for the first half mile or so before he just fell flat on his face on the dirt road. He had absolutely no stamina, as though he hadn't exercised a day in his life. With his pasty white skin and dark rings like Goodyears around his eyes, Adam wondered if he'd ever actually left the house. He was little more than skin draped on bones.

Peckham turned around at the sound of the boy slamming into the gravel and dashed back to where he had fallen, scooping him up and carrying him in his arms.

Adam nearly ran right into them in his mad dash away from the house. The fear was so intense that he couldn't even bring himself to look back over his shoulder. What good was running, anyway? How far could they possibly get? Where could they go? They were in the middle of nowhere in eastern Pennsylvania to his best assumption. The nearest Army installation would be either the Tobyhanna Army Depot to the north or Willow Grove to the south, but that had to be at least a hundred miles away and they were on foot. The chopper was in ruins and he hadn't the slightest clue how to hotwire a car. They were just delaying the inevitable if whatever those things were inside that house came after them. Samuels had been about as big and strong a soldier as Adam had ever seen, and no doubt a world-class marksman, but he'd been ripped to shreds before he could even get any of those nearly invisible creatures in his sights.

Peckham tripped, managed a few move

stumbling strides, and then collapsed onto the dirt road, rolling onto his right shoulder to absorb the brunt of the impact and keep from smashing the boy.

Adam stopped and turned at Peckham's cry.

Norman, who was already fifty yards up the road, stopped as well, his fidgeting legs seeming unable to decide whether he should turn around to help or not. It was only a matter of seconds before he joined Adam at Peckham's side. The older man had managed to roll the boy off of his chest and onto the ground, freeing a hand to grab at his right shoulder, the arm hanging limply at his side.

"It's dislocated," Adam said, taking Peckham by the arm while Norman helped him to his feet from behind.

"Ya think?" Peckham said, wincing at the pain caused by even the slightest movement.

"I can reduce it for you right now," Adam said, taking the sergeant's left arm by the biceps and bracing the top of the shoulder.

"Wait! Wait!"

Adam took a step back.

"Okay," Peckham said, blowing out a deep breath and biting down on his lower lip.

Adam nodded to Norman, who matched Adam's hands from the opposite side. With a sickly crunch, they forced the shoulder back into the socket. Even though he thought himself prepared, Peckham screamed like he'd been shot.

"Holy Mary Mother of God!" he shouted, turning in a circle and grabbing his arm.

"Show me your palm," Adam said.

Peckham rolled his wrist and flashed the underside of his hand at Adam.

"Bend your elbow."

He did, though tears pinched from his eyes with the exertion.

"Good to go," Adam said, turning and offering his hand to the boy.

"What's your name?" he asked as the boy grasped his hand with long, delicate fingers.

"Phoenix," he said, his eyes meeting Adam's. The boy's irises were reddish-pink like an albino's.

"What's the best way out of here?"

"I don't know. I've never... never been out here before." Phoenix's stare moved from one side of the road to the other, absorbing the sights for the very first time.

On the left side of the road were endless fields of what had once been corn, with tangled and sharpened leaves, the stalks capped by pinecone spades. Even in his imagination he'd never seen anything like it. Tufts of weeds sprouted from the rut running down the middle of the gravel lane. He hadn't seen those before. Not until just now. The road terminated in a bend about a hundred yards west, the trees closing around it like a mouth, leaving the blackened impression of a tunnel. To the right, he could hear a faint trickle of running water beyond a wall of what had formerly been cottonwoods and willows. Rather than broad, flat leaves, vines now grew from the red stems of the cottonwoods, bowing the branches so low that it almost looked like a wig. Small red thorns lined the vines, which terminated in tiny spirals like a pig's tail. The trunk was invisible somewhere in the shadows contained beneath. The long, sharp willow leaves had grown even more so, taking on an olive gray color and an exaggerated weight that made them point straight down from the buckling branches. A gust of wind made the tree shiver, dropping handfuls of those spiked leaves straight into the ground where they stuck like lawn darts.

Adam watched it too.

"What's happening?" he whispered.

"I don't care," Norman said, grabbing Adam by the shirt. "Nothing matters right now but getting out of here and finding—"

"Finding what?" Peckham interrupted.

"I don't know... other people, other soldiers, what the hell do you think?"

"Have we seen any other people?"

"This isn't the time, guys," Adam interceded, stepping between the men before Peckham could take a step forward with that bright red face.

"Tell that to Samuels and Carter," Norman said.

"Please stop," Phoenix whispered.

"Oh, I see. You can't, because they were torn to pieces back there!"

"Please," Phoenix said, unaccustomed to the sound of his own voice.

The others looked at him, this thin boy in fatigues a dozen sizes too large, his pants barely staying up by the bundle of fabric in his fist, the shirt coming nearly to his knees.

"More man tears," he said, watching each of their eyes in turn for any sign of recognition.

"What did you say?" Adam asked, all of the blood draining from his face.

"More man tears," he repeated.

"I've heard that before," Adam whispered. "What does it mean?"

Phoenix turned and locked his eyes on Adam's, no longer even aware of the others.

"It's where we need to go," he said. "It's where the others will be."

"There are other survivors?" Peckham asked.

"Not many," Phoenix said. "At least that I know of, but I do know that there is a plan for us. I'm not sure what, but we'll find out when we find more man tears."

"None of this makes any sense," Peckham said. "What were those things back at the house? What happened to all of the people? Where is everyone?"

"Those… things… they were The Swarm. And the people…" Phoenix's eyes grew distant. "So much death… so much pain."

He closed his eyes, loosing the burgeoning tears from his lashes to stream down toward the corners of his thin mouth.

None of them knew what to say to this… child.

Phoenix cocked his head suddenly, his gaze shooting through the now feral trees.

"What is it?" Norman asked, his hand finding his assault rifle.

"I don't know," Phoenix whispered. "Can't you hear it?"

"I don't hear anything," Adam said, but by the time he finished the sentence, Phoenix was already stepping off the right side of the raised road toward a gap in the trees. "Where are you going?"

"This way," the boy said, as if the answer had been self-evident.

He passed between a pair of cottonwoods, and if Adam hadn't known it was just the wind, he would have sworn that those long vines had been trying to reach out and grab the boy.

"Wait up," Adam called, jogging between the trees after Phoenix.

The boy was already a dozen paces into the middle of a field of knee high grasses as yellow as spun gold. They swayed back and forth in a rhythmic pattern, lapping at the boy's knees, almost appearing to caress his thin legs as he swept through. It reminded Adam of the motion of underwater plants on the current, the whole field moving in time.

"Phoenix!"

The boy stopped and dropped to his knees in the middle of the meadow, the grass now hiding everything below his ribs. He looked back at Adam and smiled, then looked back down into the grass.

At first Adam thought the boy was crouching in a pile of manure, but the closer he got, the clearer the picture became. The boy stroked a thin layer of brown fur, the hair cropped closer than a dog's. The opposite side of the fur was clearly made of flesh in the process of drying to hide as evidenced by the thin web of purple veins and red blotches of burst capillaries. It wasn't until he saw the long black tail tangled in the weeds that Adam knew exactly what it was.

"Don't touch that," he said.

"Why not?" Phoenix asked, looking up to him with dewy eyes. "It's beautiful."

"It's dead."

"Only the outside."

Adam reached down and took the boy beneath the armpits, coaxing him carefully to his feet. It almost looked like the long blades of grass tried to hold onto his legs.

"We need to keep moving."

He set Phoenix back on his feet and looked over his shoulder. Norman and Peckham were through the wall of trees and crossing the fluid weeds toward them.

"I think—" Adam started to say, but turned around to see Phoenix running deeper into the field toward a clump of trees that looked almost like an island in the middle of a glimmering sea. The leaves were the most perfect shade of green, the tree so wide and tall it looked like an emerald cloud had settled on the earth.

"Phoenix!" Adam called, running after the boy.

All he could see were flashes from the boy's light blonde hair and his alternating heels kicking up behind him. The desert camouflage of his outfit blended with the golden straw.

Phoenix ran straight into the tree. There one moment and gone the next.

Adam stopped within feet of the closest branches, marveling at the fact that while they had looked like wide leathery leaves from a distance, they were actually long needles only vaguely resembling those of a pine. He reached out and felt them, expecting the sharp-looking tips to poke his skin, but instead they felt like velvet. Walking into it was like he imagined it must have been to walk through a hippy's doorway, though rather than beads hanging down in the stead of the door, they were like warm noodles that licked him as he passed beneath.

The ground was soft and spongy, giving just enough to remind him of Nerf. He hadn't noticed that the sounds were absent until he heard them. There was a twittering of birds all around him, though he couldn't see anything through the fern-like fronds of the pine. It was how he imagined a tropical rainforest, the lush vegetation closing in all around him in an earthen embrace while animals of all color combinations called merrily out of sight.

He passed through to the other side, brushing aside the branches like drapes.

Phoenix was only a few feet in front of him, but that wasn't what caught his attention. It was the enormous thing that towered over the boy that held him enrapt. It had a vaguely equine shape, though rather than smooth curves, it was composed of sharp angles as though chiseled from stone. Its eyes were jet black, spheres of tar swirling in its sockets, contrasted against leathery skin a shade of blue darker than the midnight sky. The creature appeared to have an exoskeleton, but as Adam drew closer, he could see that the sharp angles were underneath the taut flesh. It looked more like a seahorse than the sloppy shell of the land animal it had shed on the ground, though it stood on four sturdy legs and a tail that curled concentrically, stretching as it clopped toward them like a separate appendage. Phoenix reached toward its muzzle, causing it to shake its head and blast steam from its nostrils.

Adam wanted to tell him to stop, to move away from that thing, but no words would form. His mouth merely hung slack as he watched the boy gently place his palm of the thing's elongated snout and stroke it carefully.

It raised its front hooves alternately, stamping them back down into the tall weeds, shifting its weight from side to side as the muscles in its chest bulged.

Phoenix turned back to Adam with a smile lighting his face, then quickly returned his attention to the animal.

"What is it?" Phoenix asked.

"I…" Adam started. "I don't know."

Peckham and Norman burst from the foliage and nearly slammed into them.

"What in the name of God is that?" Peckham gasped.

"Transportation," Phoenix whispered, stroking the long face all the way what looked like a chitinous ridge ringing the eye like a crown.

With what could only be described as a whinny, two long appendages like the pincers of a praying mantis arose from the thing's sides, standing straight up from the shoulders. With a snap, they fell to the sides, a long flap of skin stretching from one end to the other, divided into smaller triangles by hooked extensions that grew from the joint in the middle of the long arms like bat wings.

It continued to stomp its front hooves and buck, feigning away from Phoenix before nervously edging toward him again. Phoenix stroked its coarse neck whenever it was close enough, speaking to it in a hushed tone the whole while. After a moment, the strange beast seemed to gain a measure of comfort with the boy, leaning its neck into his hand to allow him to stroke it in earnest. Phoenix stepped to the side and grabbed onto the stiff spines rising from its neck, giving them a solid tug as he leapt up onto the thing's back, straddling its midsection.

Adam took a step forward and placed his hand on what had surely once been a horse's head as it adjusted to the boy's weight on its back. It looked as though it should have been smooth like vinyl, but it was more coarse like stretched and tanned animal hide.

"They're migrating to the inland sea," Phoenix said. "They'll take us that far."

The other soldiers walked up behind him and he watched their trembling hands reach out to the animal. It snuffed a gust of visible steam and shook its head, but allowed them to touch it.

"What's happening here?" Peckham whimpered, tears streaking his red cheeks.

IV

FALLON, NEVADA

●

Jill was the first to reach Linden's Corner. From a distance, it had looked as though everything there was normal, with cars parked at the pumps and the lights on in the store, but they'd already seen that same image so many times on their travels, each time reaching the station with a newfound sense of hope only to have it dashed as they drew close enough to smell the bodies. This one was no different. With each town they passed through and every highway clogged with cars they skirted, the chances of finding anyone appeared more remote.

At least they'd be able to fill their tanks.

She pulled in beneath the well-lit overhang and parked at pump number six. On the other side was a dirty old pickup truck with the driver's side door standing wide, but she'd grown accustomed to such sights. Where there was an unclosed door, chances were there was a body within a few paces. She didn't even try to look anymore. She unscrewed the gas cap on the bike, removed the handle, and shoved it into the tank. She didn't know how Ray did it, but he knew how to activate the pumps from behind the counter from the handful of months he spent working graveyard at a 7-11 to save money for school.

Jill was sitting on the seat, facing backward at them when the others caught up.

Ray revved the engine as Tina climbed off, pinching her knees together with a look of extreme discomfort. The dried blood looked brown from the accumulation of dust.

"It's about time you guys—" Jill started,

but stopped at the sound of a loud bang from the convenience store. Tina had been just about to pass by the tailgate of the adjacent truck when she heard the sound and froze.

Footsteps pounded across the asphalt, changing to scuffing on the dirt lot to the north.

Ray looked to Tina and then to Jill.

"You get her out of here," he said, revving the engine again and lifting his feet. The tires caught with a squeal and Ray rocketed straight across the parking lot.

A shadowed figure passed through the glare of a semi's headlights and raced to a sign by the side of the road, merging with the shadows.

"Ray!" Tina screamed. "No!"

She blew past Jill at a sprint, but April was quick enough to hop off the back of Darren's bike and catch her by the arm. Both went down on the cement, April using her size advantage to keep Tina pinned beneath her.

With a roar, Darren's bike rocketed forward after Ray's and April realized she'd just made the same mistake as April.

Ray gritted his teeth and clenched the handlebars so tightly he cut off circulation to his fingertips. He had no idea what he was going to do. The only thing he could come up with was that he was just going to have to ram that creature and hope he did enough damage that he could finish it off from there.

The headlight illuminated the shape in front of him, casting a shadow that reached clear up and over the highway sign, focusing in like a microscope as he sped closer. Details grew from the wash of light. He recognized a pair of jeans and a sweatshirt, long hair tied in a pony tail. Whoever it was whirled to face him. He was about ten yards from laying the bike on its side and hoping to break the thing's legs when eyes flashed in the headlights and a mouth opened into a scream. It was a girl. Still human. She held up something in her right hand that he couldn't immediately identify, but he was sure whatever it was, she was aiming it at him.

He slammed on the brakes and skidded to a stop on the gravel, the rear tire kicking out to the side and covering whoever it was with a spray of pebbles.

"Drop it!" he shouted.

The woman looked at him strangely and then looked to her right hand.

"I said drop it, lady!"

Ray hadn't the foggiest notion of what he might do if she didn't. She looked back at him, through loosened strands of bangs that fell across her face.

"Stay back!" she screamed, pointing the thing in her hand at him and spraying out a cloud that looked a lot like glitter.

"You think I'm going to hurt you?!"

"I'm warning you!"

"Guys," Ray called back over his shoulder. Darren stopped the motorcycle right beside his friend. "She's one of us!"

He looked back at the woman with a beaming grin on his face.

"You're alive," she gasped, dropping the can, which clattered to the ground with a ping of the steel ball inside. "I thought I was the only one."

Tears shimmered on her eyes in the headlight's glare.

"I'm Ray," he said, taking a step toward her and offering his hand. "Ray Gorman."

She just looked at it for a moment like she was uncertain exactly what she was supposed to do with it. With a quick glance at his face, she sighed and walked toward him.

"Evelyn Hartman," she said, shaking his hand and taking a step back.

"And I'm his girlfriend," Tina said, stepping out from behind the headlight that was still trained on Evelyn. She strode up beside Ray and wrapped her arm around his waist, leaning into him. "Tina."

Evelyn nodded and forced a smile.

"Evelyn," she said, uncomfortable under the younger girl's glare.

She offered a hand, but it stayed empty until the other guy stepped to his right and shook it.

"Darren," he said, looking as though he was trying to smile but not succeeding, his lips twitching awkwardly. "And this is April." He released Evelyn's hand and reached back for April's. She was cute in a kid kind of way, with just the touch of her baby fat remaining on her belly and in her cheeks.

"We haven't seen anyone else alive since we left," April gushed, extending her hand and shaking Evelyn's. "We didn't think that we ever would."

"Neither did I," Evelyn said, unable to control the tears and the tremor in her voice. "I've been driving for hours and my dad's dead and—"

"What's that?" another girl asked, this one all arms and legs. She had shoulder-length blonde hair and eyes so blue they could even pierce the darkness.

"What?" Evelyn asked, looking over her shoulder to follow the girl's wide eyes.

"Mormon tears?" the girl whispered. "Did you write that?"

"Yeah." She drew out the word until it sounded more like a question.

"This is Jill, by the way," Darren said, but neither looked at him as they appeared to now be communicating with their eyes.

"You've heard it, too, haven't you?" Evelyn asked.

Jill nodded her head slowly, never allowing her eyes to stray from the other woman's.

"I was starting to think I was losing my mind," Jill finally sobbed, lunging forward and wrapping her arms around Evelyn. The two embraced there beside the dead road, sharing a familiarity that neither could explain.

"Ray!" Tina whispered, giving him a playful pinch.

"Okay, okay," he said, rolling his eyes. "I've got to take Tina to use the can, do you think you guys can start filling up the bikes?"

"Sure," Darren said.

Ray climbed back on his motorcycle and Tina hopped up behind, wrapping her arms protectively around him. They walked the bike in a half circle before kicking it into gear and driving right up onto the sidewalk in front of the restaurant.

"Not in here," Tina said. She could see the bathrooms at the far left side of the diner, but to get there, she would have to navigate the slalom of black corpses.

"You want to go back behind the building?"

"No!" she shrieked.

"Fine. No sweat. What would you propose then?"

She studied Ray, who was looking back at the others.

"She's pretty, isn't she?" Tina whispered.

"Are you getting jealous?" he asked with a lilt in his voice.

"No, I just… I don't know. Maybe."

Ray booted the kickstand and climbed down. He looked at her face, waiting for Tina to raise her eyes to meet his. Finally, with a sigh, she relented.

"You know you're the only girl for me," he said, smirking. "I love you."

He lowered his chin and looked up to her with puppy dog eyes.

She shook her head and smiled.

"Of course, and you know I love you too."

"Forever and a day," he said, pressing his lips to hers.

"Forever and a day," she sighed after gently backing from his embrace and reluctantly allowing their eyes to part.

"Now hurry and go to the bathroom before the new girl starts making eyes at me again," he said, swatting her on the rear end.

Her arm shot out, finding his nipple with practiced ease and giving it a sharp twist.

"Ouch!"

"You had that coming," she said playfully, prying her hand away and heading toward the building. She swung the right glass door open to the tune of an electronic bell, propped the door on her rear end, and stuck her tongue out at him.

Ray smiled and rubbed at the sharp ache on his chest. Perhaps his mind had finally deserted him, as he was getting a kick out of watching Tina trying to tiptoe around the bodies in the aisle with a cute, pursed-lipped look of disgust on her face. By the time she reached the bathroom, he was laughing.

She stopped in front of the door and looked across the empty booth in front of the window, over the line of syrups and sweetener packets, and right into her boyfriend's eyes.

Ray stopped laughing and just smiled.

I'm going to marry that girl someday, he thought.

Their eyes lingered a moment longer, then she stuck out her tongue and threw her rear end into the swinging door. She hadn't even started to turn around to enter before the door was ripped all the way open and she was jerked into the darkness.

"Tina!" Ray screamed, sprinting to the front door. He hurtled the bodies at full tilt, reaching the door to the women's room before it could fall back into place. "Tina!"

He shouldered the door, slamming it into something forgiving, which let out a loud hiss as it was pounded into the wall behind the door.

"Ray!" Tina screamed from the shadows off to the left from one of the stalls. "Help me! Ra—!"

There was an abrupt tearing sound, followed by a gurgle. He threw himself toward the sound of her voice, sprinting toward the first stall. Closing his eyes, he lowered his shoulder and prepared to strike, but his feet slid out from beneath him. He slammed into the door with his arms flailing for balance, his momentum following his feet beneath the closed stall door. Firecrackers exploded in his vision as his head hammered the tiled floor.

"Ray!" Darren called, his voice muffled by the closing bathroom door.

Ray slapped his palms down to either side and tried to push himself up, but both hands slipped in something slick, depositing him again onto his back. It was warm, soaking through his shirt and jeans and into his skin.

Darren burst through the door.

This time, whatever had been behind it was quick enough to leap out of the way and scurry up the white-tiled wall to the ceiling by the broken overhead lights.

"Ray!" Darren shouted, grabbing his friend beneath the armpits and sliding him backward toward the door.

"What about Tina?" Ray wailed. "Tina!"

Her headless form flew from the darkened stall and struck the wall beside him, crumpling into a heap of flesh that poured more warmth in a rapidly expanding puddle. Ray tried to grab for her, desperately attempting to snag hold of anything he could get a grip on to pull her toward him, but he couldn't reach her... couldn't reach her...

"Tina!" he screamed as Darren slammed the door into the wall once again and dragged him out into the diner, the lights flickering with the blue glow of dying fluorescents.

"We have to get out of here!" Darren shouted, fighting against Ray's efforts to get back through the slowly closing door even as he still slipped in his girlfriend's blood, making crimson snow angels on the tile.

"Not without Tina!"

Darren looked back over his shoulder for help. April was standing in the doorway with both hands clapped over her open mouth, eyes as wide as golf balls.

"Help us!" he shouted at her, spurring her to action.

A bright light bloomed behind April through the closing glass door as she rushed to Darren's aid and grabbed hold of Ray's left arm so Darren could handle his right.

"Tina!" Ray railed, still trying to fight to his feet as they dragged him through the mess of corpses. "We can't leave her here!"

The bathroom door opened and something black appeared in the middle of the doorway, though staying back just far enough that the triangular stretch of light couldn't reach it. Yellow eyes with seething black spots focused on him. The thing let out a hiss like a roar, extending a pale yellow flap of skin from under its chin, shaking it furiously. Its open jaws revealed twin rows of teeth like serrated blades and a sharp, triangular purple tongue.

Another dropped from the ceiling behind it, landing in a crouch and staring through the other thing's black legs with its amber dewlap slapping the floor.

"Hurry!" Jill screamed, yanking the front door outward. Evelyn had pulled the truck right up onto the curb, the bumper nearly against the front window of the diner.

"Give us a hand!" Darren shouted, dragging Ray to the doorway where Jill propped the door on her hip and grabbed hold wherever she could and gave a solid tug.

Ray watched the first thing stick a black claw through the doorway into the strobing electric glow. It jerked it back with a scream like a ruptured steam valve. The other creature behind it shoved it aside and hurled the hand dryer from the wall at the overhead stretch of twin bulbs over the counter. The plastic lenses shattered and there was a flash of light. Glass rained from the ceiling onto the corpses as darkness descended in a blink, marred by the twin rays of light from the truck's headlights directed toward the kitchen.

The front of the pickup passed between Ray and the diner. There was pressure around his chest, and the next thing he knew he was being heaved from the ground, his legs hanging uselessly, heels dragging on the ground.

"Tina!" he screamed.

He felt the corrugated metal floor of the truck bed against his back and then Darren's weight was atop him. Thrashing, he tried everything in his power to get his friend off of him.

With a squeal and a bang, Jill threw the gate closed and sprinted around to the passenger door, leaping in beside April and slamming the door.

"They're in!" she yelled.

Evelyn jerked the truck into reverse and pinned the gas. The tires screamed off the cement walk before catching and launching them backward. Evelyn stomped the brake, threw the gear into drive, and stabbed the gas again. The truck raced forward, narrowly missing another truck stalled at the gas pump, and sped across the dirt parking lot before bounding over the curb and up onto the highway.

"No!" Ray screamed. "We can't leave her here!"

Darren absorbed every blow his friend threw, crying as he wrapped his arms around Ray's chest and hugged him tight.

"Let me go!" he screamed, landing a flurry of blows against Darren's ribs. "Tina's still in there! We have to go back!"

Darren held him as the wind intensified with the truck's increasing speed.

"Stop it!" Ray screamed, his words trailing into the throngs of sobbing.

He brought both fists to Darren's back and buried his face in his friend's shoulder, shuddering against Darren, overcome by the tears.

V

**SOMEWHERE NEAR
SPRINGFIELD,
MISSOURI**

Phoenix whooped with joy. After spending his entire life in one room, here he was seeing the whole world from the back of a flying stallion. Treetops flew past mere inches beneath his feet, close enough that he could have stepped right off onto them. The mane of spikes curled in his fists, he leaned back and stared up into the storm, the lower reaches of the black clouds touching his face while the lightning flared all around him. The cool air was perfect, its touch on his skin sublime. Every sensation from the bulging muscles between his legs to the tickle of the air between his toes was new and exciting, and he wished for it never to end.

Those leathery wings rose and fell so slowly that Adam wondered how it was even possible they stayed aloft, the time between exaggerated flapping so long it was excruciating. He watched the boy flying ahead of him on the back of that largest stallion, its front legs tucked up against its chest, the rear legs pointed straight back with spiked cleats for hooves, the tail unfurling awkwardly, and couldn't help being amazed. The child was embracing all of the changes in the world while the rest of them were struggling to rationalize them. The landscape passing beneath was foreign as forests grew so tightly together that the strangely colored foliage and the treetops looked like the Andes from a great height, jagged, foreboding. Falling from atop his steed's back onto them would be suicide. Fields where once crops had grown were now overrun with tangles of thorny and snarled feral species that more closely resembled nightmare patches of bud-less roses. There were no longer well-hoed rows, but never-ending interlaced vines, dead-looking like a briar patch. The streams and rivers flowed as black as tar, reflecting the lightning from above as though it were instead flashing deep under the current.

Adam clenched the jagged spines, pinching his knees as tightly against the flexing sides of the mare as he possibly could, and dared another infrequent glance back over his shoulder. Norman hugged the back of another steed with a ragged row of spines that branched like antlers, his head cocked just to the right so he could see around the beast's head without having to relinquish the chokehold. His clothes flapped on the wind, his face bright red as though he were holding his breath. The horse swerved off to the right, banking gently to absorb the gusting wind beneath its nearly transparent wings before allowing the breeze to carry it back into formation.

Peckham was a good fifty yards back, though all Adam could see were the man's black boots pressed against either flank as the soldier had his face buried in the stallion's rugged neck, not even daring to raise his head. Of them all, he was taking the changes the worst, somehow unable to accept the reality of the situation while the others were beginning to succumb to it. Norman was quite sure that he had died in the plane crash, though he was reluctant to admit it to anyone. Adam had resigned to being a passenger inside of his own flesh, reserving judgment for the point when it made something resembling sense, while to Phoenix, this was the world, as he had never seen it before. The cloud-choked sky was the most beautiful thing he'd ever imagined, the lightning as precious as diamonds. He hated to even blink, for fear he might miss something.

When Adam turned around, Phoenix's horse had its wings set, arched out to either side like a goose dropping from the sky, its legs churning in anticipation of hitting the ground. The spiked mane stood erect like a Mohawk, the tail pointing straight to the heavens.

The trees fell away beneath them to reveal a widening meadow with wavering grasses. A lake as clear as a mirror showed them the sky as if it were a hole straight through to the other side of the globe. Other animals the colors of flame milled around its bank, grazing in the tall weeds and drinking from the motionless water amidst the tall reeds. Birds as colorful as tropical parrots flapped from the back of one of the large creatures to the next, flocking in concentric circles around them like a mirage of rainbows.

The lead stallion dropped right through the cloud of birds, filling the sky with loosed feathers as they panicked. Adam's steed floated downward through the path created by the first, allowing him to clearly see the avian things. Some had bills like toucans on stumpy bodies with long tail feathers that appeared like there was a prehensile tail beneath the way it wavered in the air; others had short blood-red beaks as though they'd been freshly pecking carrion and feathers that were so tiny they looked more like scales; still others had long flattened heads with the horns of a toad, mottled pond-scum green and sunlight yellow with long black legs like a stork.

The boy's horse hit the ground at a gallop, slowing gracefully before shaking its head with a neigh and circling a small patch of grass in the middle of a herd of beasts that looked to be a cross between lions and bison, painted with brushes dipped in the sunset.

Adam prepared for a rough landing as the ground rose to meet them way too quickly, but at the last second, the equine's wings inflated and it alighted every bit as smoothly as if the whole flight had been nothing more than a dream. It trotted between a pair of the orange-bearded bovines and sidled up to the other horse, which was already ripping mouthfuls of knee-high grass that smelled of marigolds.

"Did you see that?" Phoenix hollered, running up to Adam's steed and tugging on his pant leg. "We were so high I could have touched the clouds!"

Adam smiled as he dismounted, his trembling legs making the ground feel as though he was still atop the thundering animal.

"I know," Adam said, marveling at the light in the boy's eyes. "It was pretty amazing."

Phoenix's smile was so wide it threatened to tear his cheeks back to his ears. He looked like he was about to say something, but then just turned and dashed toward the tall reeds separating the field from the lake. They looked like bamboo blooming out of so many cornstalks with furry appendages atop them like lazily wagging tails.

"That was... There are no words for it," Norman said, dropping down to the ground. He raised his right hand and gently stroked the broad side of his ride, flinching at first as though he had expected it to not really be there when he tried to touch it.

Peckham dismounted last, and without a word. He simply stumbled away from the thing, which clopped over to share the patch of grass with its brethren. When he looked at Adam and Norman, his eyes were glassy as though he was looking right through them.

"Where's the kid?" Norman asked, slinging his backpack off and dropping it on the ground. He arched his back and stretched out the kinks.

"Over there," Adam said, nodding to the wall of reeds behind him.

The weeds were a good foot taller than Phoenix and there wasn't the slightest trace of a path, but he didn't care as he stumbled blindly forward, crashing through the coarse foliage like an elephant. The tips of the broad leaves were sharp, but they didn't cut him, instead making him itch, but even that was a miraculous sensation in a life all but devoid of it. He could hear all sorts of tweeting and cawing all around him, but he couldn't see anything shy of his hands swatting away the thick vegetation from his face. Slowly, he began to see the faint twinkling of the shimmering lake through the tiny gaps in the brush, taunting him like flecks of gold in a streambed. Those gaps grew larger, the flashing blue surface of the lake brighter until he was sure that with the next sweep of his arms he would burst through the cover and emerge onto the bank, but he stopped suddenly and tilted his head to the lake.

"What are we supposed to do from here?" a voice whispered.

Phoenix held his breath so as not to betray his presence.

"We find our way to Salt Lake," a beautiful, soft voice responded. To Phoenix, the voice was more familiar than his own, and his heart jumped in his chest.

"That's great, but how do you propose doing that?"

"I don't know. I didn't expect to get this far riding whatever those things were."

Phoenix inched closer, carefully drawing his hands apart to create a gap in the reeds.

The lake stretched out ahead of him, all the way to the end of the horizon. The lightning flashed from the surface in an awe-inspiring display of pyrotechnics. They were sitting on the bank with their backs to him, their bare feet dangling in perfectly transparent water.

He didn't recognize the one on the left with the shorter hair, trying to skip the round stones off of the smooth water only to have them sploosh into the depths, but the one on the right... he'd memorized her shape the first time he saw her in his dreams.

"I'm scared," the figure on the left said quietly.

"Me too," the girl said and draped her arm over the boy's shoulder.

Phoenix took a step back in surprise, the reeds crunching underfoot.

The girl turned to face him, jerking her arm back to her side.

"Who's there?" she nearly shrieked.

There was a moment of hesitation where Phoenix wasn't sure if he should turn and sprint back in the direction he had come from or not, but he knew there had to be higher forces at work if he were to find the girl of his dreams in the middle of nowhere.

"I'm sorry," Phoenix said, his voice cracking. He cleared his throat as he stepped out into the open. Both the boy and the girl retreated from him, splashing into the lake up to their knees. "I didn't mean to startle you."

"Where did you come from?" the boy asked, stretching his left arm in front of the girl and dragging her back behind his body.

Phoenix stepped to the right to see around the guy, who took another step so that he was directly in the way.

"I came from over there," he said, unable to mask the tremor. Was it fear? Excitement? "The horses needed a break. I think the others did too."

"The others?"

Phoenix saw a pair of piercing blue eyes peer over the boy's shoulder from behind, her blonde hair shimmering against the electric flaring. He wanted nothing more than to see her face.

"The men who rescued me from The Swarm."

"There are other people with you?" the girl asked. "I... we... we didn't think that anyone else had survived."

"They're soldiers. They let me wear some of their clothes."

The other boy sniggered and clapped his hand over his mouth.

"Sorry," he said. "It's just that, you know, they don't fit. What happened to your clothes?"

"I didn't have any," Phoenix said. There was a part of him that wanted to cry. Who was this boy keeping him from the girl from his dreams and why was he laughing at him?

"Never mind him," the girl said, stepping out from behind the boy and shoving his arm back down to his side when he tried to bar her passage. "I'm Melissa Stringer. My friends call me Missy. This is my brother Mare. That's his real name."

"I'm Phoenix," he said, unable to hide the sigh of relief.

He couldn't take his eyes from her face for fear it would disappear like so many times before. If he could have drawn features on a star worthy of its beauty, hers would have been the face he used. When she offered a smile, it seemed as though the entire world lit up.

"Phoenix," she said. He never imagined he would have heard his name spoken by her tongue. "That's a pretty name. I'll bet your parents were hippies, weren't they?"

"I never knew my parents."

"Oh," she said, stepping out of the lake and back onto the bank. She turned back to her brother. "Are you coming or what?"

"Do you think it's safe? I mean... can we trust this guy?"

"He doesn't appear to be one of those black lizard men—"

"The Swarm," Phoenix interrupted.

"Okay. He doesn't look like one of The Swarm." She looked to Phoenix for his approval, which he gave with a smile and a nod. "And he hasn't tried to kill us yet... I think that's a pretty good start, don't you?"

Mare looked angrily at her, sloshing through the lake and onto the bank.

"You think this is funny, huh? I don't see anything remotely amusing about this entire situation. We're standing on the bank of a lake in God knows where after having ridden here on the backs of some freakishly mutated cows. Our father turned into a monster and tried to kill us. We have nowhere to go. No family. No nothing. What in the world could possibly be funny?"

Tears glistened on her eyes, forcing her to turn away, swiping at them with the backs of her hands.

"Would you rather we were dead like everyone else?" she whispered.

"No," he said. The last thing in the world he had wanted to do was hurt her feelings. "God, no. I just don't understand any of this. I don't know what we're supposed to do."

He set his right hand gently on her shoulder and she turned into it to embrace him.

"I know, little brother, but if we give up hope we've got nothing."

Phoenix felt as though he were intruding on something private. He'd never seen anything like this. The genuine feelings and love between these two people hurt his chest to even ponder.

"Phoenix," a distant voice called.

The two broke their embrace, startled, and then turned again to him.

"Come with me," Phoenix said, tears pouring down his own cheeks. And with that he whirled and disappeared into the reeds. He felt her hand grab onto the back of his shirt so that he wouldn't lose her; her flesh even that close to his skin was electric. Pushing on, he followed the path he had forged through the foliage until he walked right out into the field.

"There you are," Adam said. "I was starting to think that you got lost or some—"

The words died as another shape emerged like an apparition behind Phoenix. His gaze shot to his backpack and his gun, but they were fifteen feet away—

A slender girl, surely no older than Phoenix, stepped into the golden grass behind him, followed by another boy who looked roughly the same age.

"These are the men who saved me," Phoenix said, gesturing to them. The boy and girl stepped around to Phoenix's left and stared at them.

"Hi," was all Adam could think to say.

The newcomers looked from one soldier to the next, their eyes skittish as though they were about to bolt, before the boy finally spoke.

"Did we win?" he asked.

Adam looked back over his shoulder to Norman, who simply shrugged.

"What do you mean?" Adam asked, puzzled.

"The war. Did we win the war?"

Adam dropped his stare to his feet, kicking free of a tangle of grass that felt as though it had grown over the top of his boot.

"No," he said. He couldn't even bring himself to look the kid in the face. "No one won."

"No!" Peckham shouted, leaping to his feet. He pointed straight at the girl in the middle.

"It's okay," Norman said, jogging over to his commanding officer. "They're just kids, Peck."

"No!" Peckham shouted again, locking eyes with the medic. His irises flamed with his returned faculties. "Look!"

Peckham grabbed Norman by either side of the face and turned him to face just to the left of the lake in time to see a flock of birds rise as one from the field with a screech. Lines tore through the weeds like water behind a shark's fin, tatters of ripped grass and clods of dirt thrown behind. There had to be twenty parallel tracks ripping straight through the field toward them.

"They found us!" Phoenix screamed.

One of the cattle bleated and then belched through its torn air bladder, a spray of blood flying into the air as the enormous thing's body was jerked down into the grass. The warm blood landed like steaming rain on the golden grass. More cattle brayed and stampeded away from their fallen kin, moving at an unnaturally fast pace given their size.

"Go!" Norman shouted, shoving Peckham toward the horses, now standing motionless with their sharp ears pointed straight up, mouths frozen in the midst of chewing.

"Come with me," Phoenix said, taking Missy by the hand and leading her through the tall grass. As soon as his steed saw his intent, the stallion knelt before Phoenix and allowed him to clamber right up onto its back. Straddling the beast, Phoenix reached back for Missy.

"What about Mare?" she wailed.

Phoenix looked past her and nodded.

Missy spun and saw her brother tugging himself onto the back of one of the other horses behind a soldier. He wrapped his arms around the man's midsection and looked right at her. His mouth opened and his face grew red as he shouted something, but she couldn't hear a word over the frightened whinnies of the horses and the awful frenzied mooing.

She turned back to Phoenix and snatched his hand, letting him pull her as she threw her right leg up over the horse's back and tried to balance herself, reaching around Phoenix and clasping her hands against his stomach.

The horse's wings extended from beneath her legs and arose in two great arches. She screamed at the prospect of what was coming next and buried her face in the boy's back.

Bolting upright, the stallion galloped forward, raising its wings straight up in the air, and then brought them quickly with a whoosh of air that nearly bucked them from its back. The next thing she knew her stomach was falling and she could feel the rapid climb in altitude.

"Where are we going?" she screamed, unable to bring herself to open her eyes.

Phoenix turned as well as he could, his cheek resting against her forehead.

"More man tears," he said.

Missy opened her eyes and looked at him, stunned.

"It was your voice," she said, trying to see his face. Until that moment she realized that she hadn't truly looked at the boy who had just saved her life.

The clouds settled about their ears, the horse's belly reflecting back up at them from the lake below. Behind, the other equines fell into formation in a flying diamond design.

None of them looked back down to see the black shapes converge on the spot where they had been only a heartbeat prior.

VI

EAST OF ELKO,
NEVADA

Jill drained the last of a can of Diet Pepsi while she turned the dial slowly through the static listening for even the faintest voice. It was all dead air. No matter how loud she cranked the volume, she couldn't discern anything from the roaring crackle of nothingness.

"It's an old truck," Evelyn said. "Not the most modern stereo either, I'm afraid."

Her weary red eyes scanned the length of the headlights, watching for the first hint of a car stalled in their way. Thus far the traffic on I-80 eastbound had been fortuitously light, allowing her to keep the speed right around forty miles an hour with sufficient notice to slalom through the dead cars in the lanes or crashed onto the shoulders. It would be much more difficult the closer they got to the next major city, which she assumed would be Salt Lake City, so they needed to take advantage of the open road while they had it.

It was all she could do to keep from looking in the rear view mirror. Ray stared blankly off to the north side of the road. Every now and then his back would hitch with the throngs of a new wave of tears, but he was otherwise devoid of affectation. He was simply a shadow against the darkness. Darren tried every so often to place a consolatory hand on his friend's shoulder only to have it shrugged off, leaving him to back up against the cab with his head resting against the window, staring at the road as it fell away in the red glare from the taillights.

April leaned against Jill's left shoulder from the middle seat, mewling occasionally as the real world permeated her defenses. She could only watch the road in front of them, letting the candy bars melt in her mouth without even tasting them. She thought for a moment that she'd heard her mother calling to her from the static only to have it dissipate into the grumbling noise.

"How did you survive?" Jill asked, turning down the sound as she'd repeatedly combed slowly through both AM and FM without the slightest audible sound to distinguish stations.

"I was preparing to replant my kelp when I saw the first of the mosquitoes coming under the door. I hid in the aquarium I was about to fill. My dad... My dad died in his sleep."

"I'm sorry," Jill whispered.

"So am I," Evelyn sniffed, wiping the blooming tears from her eyes and trying to force the thought from her mind. "How about you? How did you guys manage to survive?"

"Jill's psychic," April said, tucking her right arm beneath Jill's left. "She knew what was going to happen."

Evelyn turned from the road and looked at Jill, who rolled down her window a crack to get some air.

"I have... dreams," Jill said, her eyes growing distant as the met with the horizon. They were winding through foothills, the road cut straight through so that the trench walls beside them rose and fell while the highway stayed relatively flat. "Only I'm not sleeping. Premonitions."

"What did you see?"

The headlights flickered once as though counteracting a surge of power. Evelyn looked quickly to the road, relaxing only slightly as the lights stayed on.

"I saw... so much death. My sorority sisters... they were dead and bleeding and there were all sorts of insects crawling all over them." Her voice deteriorated to a whimper. "I didn't know exactly what was going to happen, but somehow I knew... I just knew that we had to hide somewhere where we could be sealed inside. They had a hot tub. We hid in there, but Rick..."

Her voice trailed off to silence.

"There was nothing you could have done," Evelyn whispered. "I've gone over it a million times and there isn't a thing I could have done differently... shy of not climbing under the tank."

The silence spoke what they were all thinking.

"What's that?" April whispered, sitting up and pointing straight through the windshield.

There was a flash of light from the distant horizon glowing brighter and brighter before fading back into the darkness.

Another, closer, this time from the opposite side of the road. The headlights of one of the wrecked vehicles on the shoulder glowed brighter and brighter, pointing off into the sage, while those of the other car in the tangle focused on them. The headlights intensified until they were like twin suns, before suddenly snapping off.

"I don't know..." Evelyn said, her voice trailing off. Her truck's headlights grew brighter and brighter, turning night to day around them. The lights in the dashboard became much more intense and the radio screeched static, raising the volume of its own accord. With a pop, all of the lights snapped off and the radio died, leaving them barreling through complete blackness, marred only by the occasional flare of purple flame across the sky.

Grinding her teeth, Evelyn stomped her foot on the brake. She heard the boys in back slam up against the cab behind her as the rear tires fishtailed for traction. April screamed and Jill brought her feet up against the dashboard, pulling the seatbelt tightly across her chest.

They sat there in the middle of the pink highway, miles from nowhere, in the pitch black.

"You've got to be kidding me," Evelyn said, pounding her fist on the wheel. "Come on!"

She revved the engine, hoping by some slim chance that would bring back the lights, but there was still nothing.

There was a knock from the window behind her. She reached back, her hand trembling, and slid the window open.

"What's going on?" Darren asked. "Is everyone all right?"

Evelyn sighed in frustration.

"I think so," Jill said, giving April's hand a squeeze. "How 'bout back there?"

"A little warning would have been nice."

"Sorry," Evelyn said, burying her face in her hands. "You aren't hurt, are you?"

Darren checked Ray, who'd managed to sit up again to stare out across the nothingness.

"No," he finally said. "What happened?"

"All of the lights got really bright, and then they just shut off," April said. "We watched it like it was coming toward us in a wave, hitting the other cars ahead of us first."

"But the engine's still running," Darren said.

"I just can't see to drive," Evelyn said, shaking her head.

"Then we go slowly," Darren said calmly, feeling the tension in the car like gunpowder awaiting the touch of a flame. "Line up the outside tires with the grooves in the shoulder, you know, those things that buzz if you drift onto the shoulder to keep the truckers awake? So long as you can hear that buzzing, you'll know you're on the road."

"But how am I supposed to see well enough to keep from hitting any of the cars stalled out here?"

"Watch the lightning and keep your speed down. Hopefully, since this highway appears to be so straight, you ought to be able to see something in your way miles in advance. If not, so long as you aren't going too fast, the collision shouldn't be too bad."

"You're willing to take that chance?"

"Versus sitting out here in the dark doing nothing? Oh yeah."

Evelyn ripped her eyes from the rear view mirror where she'd been watching Darren in time to see a dark shape knife across the road in front of them, followed by another. All she'd been able to discern was two bodies moving fast, mere shades darker than the night.

April let out a small shriek, cutting it off as she slapped her hand over her mouth.

"Okay," Evelyn said, easing her foot off the brake. The car began rolling forward. She gave it just a touch of gas and moved to the right until she heard the first grinding sound beneath the right tires. She looked up at the speedometer, but the needle was useless. Going this slowly, the grooves on the shoulder sounded more like knuckles running down a washboard.

The window closed behind her and Darren and Ray bedded down for the ride.

"How fast do you think a man can run?" Evelyn asked.

"I don't know, maybe fifteen miles an hour at a sprint?" Jill said, keeping her knees braced against the dash.

"Then we'll do twenty."

Evelyn pressed on the gas, gauging the speed by feel, and leaned forward over the wheel to give her just that much more advance warning if she needed to stomp on the brake.

CHAPTER 10

I

FORT COLLINS,
COLORADO

They'd flown over mountains, but until
the Rocky Mountains rose into view on
the western horizon, he hadn't known the
meaning of the word. The enormous peaks
had appeared from the plains like giant teeth,
as though some great thing had tried to take
a monstrous bite out of the earth itself only
to have them snapped free from its oversized
mouth. In time the enamel had rotted from
within to expose every shade of blue from the
faintest powder to the deepest hue this side
of purple. They were magnificent, though
not nearly as much as the fact that the girl
from his dreams was pressed up against him
from behind without enough room for a fly
to pass between them. Something prevented
him from thoroughly enjoying it, however. All
at once he wanted to heave up the contents
of his gut as if getting everything out of his
system would be enough to cure him of the
illness, but he knew there was more to it than
that.

Somewhere, not so far away, he was sure,
something was growing on the earth like a
cancer, eating away at the very life force of
the planet, killing it slowly. He could feel it

simultaneously calling to him and repelling him.

He looked over his left shoulder to the south, surveying the distant remains of Denver. Overpasses had fallen, standing from the piles of smashed cars like nails driven from the sky. Deep black smoke churned up into the sky as the northern suburbs burned, obscuring the vague outline of the downtown buildings toppled against one another like dominoes. A black ring of scorched earth encircled the entire city. A haze of dust hung over the front range from the Rockies to the west all the way across the city to where the airport burned with flames stories high, consuming a seemingly limitless supply of fuel to the east.

Somewhere in there... somewhere beneath that cloud of ash and settling debris was the source of his turmoil, and he knew with complete certainly that his destiny also lay somewhere beneath in the shadows.

Phoenix shivered, the cold having snuck up on him and draped itself over him, and turned his attention back to the west, straight ahead, as they passed over a small town. He kept his eyes on the majestic mountains for fear of rationalizing the sights that were cruising by beneath. Houses burned at random. Cars were mangled in collision at every intersection. They passed over a college campus with so many corpses scattered across every available inch of land that they were like mites on a bird's skin.

He kept his sights on the snowcapped peaks that stabbed into the bellies of the clouds, which roiled angrily and struck back with forks of lightning, trying to wrench free. A lake appeared ahead, surrounded by pine trees now more reminiscent of the cones they once held aloft, sharpened spires that looked about as plush as broken glass, and stretches of meadows where the grass had been blown flat. With snapping sounds like flags on a stiff wind, the horse's wings expanded, billowing to slow their advance. It dropped from the sky, descending gracefully until it hit the ground in stride, trotting right up to the edge of the lake and thrusting its muzzle down into the water. A skein of gray ash floated in the middle where a flock of ducks with peach heads and orange streaks around their eyes slept with green bills tucked beneath auburn wings.

"I've never seen anything so beautiful," Missy said, swinging her legs over the side of the equine, unable to steal her eyes from where the Rockies held them entranced. Phoenix offered his hand to allow her leverage to hop down into the grass, which crackled beneath her weight.

"I have," Phoenix whispered as he grasped a spine and swung from the stallion's back.

Missy planted her fists on her hips and rolled her torso in circles with audible grinding. To Phoenix, it appeared as though there was a glow about her, shining even in the dark.

There was more clomping of hooves behind him, and the next thing he knew, the other three animals were trotting past him to the bank to drink alongside their leader.

"This was home once upon a time," Adam said, his voice hollow. "I grew up not far to the south of here... Always figured one day I'd come back to raise my family here."

"I'm sorry," Norman said, clapping Adam on the shoulder.

"Look at it now. Everything's gone."

Phoenix looked into the man's eyes, which shimmered with tears.

"Everything is not gone," the boy said, walking up to Adam and kneeling at his feet. He ripped a handful of the dead grass from the dirt, roots and all. "It is merely in a state of rebirth."

He cupped his left palm and set the ball of roots into the center, closing his eyes with an uncomfortable look on his face as though he was trying to pass a stone. As they watched, the dried and crumpled straw stood up like hair on an electrical current. Roots struck like tiny serpents, lancing right into his palm. The color darkened from a bland gray-yellow to a shade of gold to shame the sun. The blades grew longer and longer, until they stood nearly a foot tall, wavering on an unseen wind. From the middle arose a small globe atop a thin stalk. It was a sickly brown color with black thorns protruding from it like a mace.

Phoenix pinched his eyes shut tightly, his face turning turnip red, his hand trembling. The sphere split like a baked potato, but rather than a pale colored filling, what looked like feathers redder than the richest arterial blood poked out, folding outward until they tucked that unattractive husk beneath the long, leathery petals. From the center rose four long stamens like horns trumpeting its creation. The petals were shaped like those of a snapdragon, appearing to be animate and merely waiting for someone to try to sniff it before nipping their nose.

Phoenix opened his eyes and brought his free hand to the upper portion of the petals, stroking it like a pet. The plant's mouth yawned wide, exposing a crimson buildup of fluid.

He pried the roots from beneath his skin and gently set the whole plant back on the ground. Carefully, he broke off the bloom, pouring the fluid onto the wound in his hand, which sucked it up like a floor drain.

"Here," he said, turning and offering the flower to Missy.

She took the stem from between his fingers, conscious of the black thorns that now poked downward beneath the guise of the petals. Bringing it right beneath her nose, she looked up to Phoenix, who simply smiled, and then drew in a deep breath.

"It smells like cinnamon," she said. "How did you do that?"

"One day this field will be in full bloom as the earth heals itself... provided she's given the chance."

"What does that mean?" Mare asked, leaning over to sniff his sister's flower.

"Before the spring can cleanse the planet's wounds and bring about the process of healing, there must first be winter."

They all watched Phoenix, waiting for him to elaborate. A sadness clouded his eyes. Winter would soon be upon them, the season when everything living must prepare to die.

"He will dwell in the parched places of the desert, in a salt land where no one lives," Phoenix whispered, barely audible over the sloshing of the horses replenishing their spent reserves. "He will be a like a tree planted by the water that sends out its roots by the stream. It does not fear when heat comes; its leaves are always green. It has no worries in a year of drought and never fails to bear fruit."

"What is that supposed to mean?" Mare asked.

"It is a verse The Woman read to me," Phoenix said, a wan smile tracing his lips. "It means that we all must weather four seasons. This dead grass will live again. As shall we."

Snowflakes began to fall all around them, though rather than pristine white, they alighted the color of ash.

"I've never seen snow before," Missy said, twirling in a slow circle with her head cocked back to the sky and her arms out to her side. Neither had Phoenix, yet still it was nothing compared to this beautiful girl and her sense of child-like wonder.

"That's our cue to keep moving," Peckham said, the only words he'd uttered in hours. "None of us are equipped to face a winter storm."

Adam looked to the snowcapped mountains. On the other side lie their goal, though Lord only knew what they would find when they arrived.

Missy held the flower back out to Phoenix, blood oozing from the pinched stem.

"It's for you," he said, and though there were a million thoughts racing through his mind, he had no idea how to even begin expressing them.

"Thank you," she said, giving his hand a gentle squeeze before turning back to the horses.

Phoenix stared down at that hand, still feeling the warmth of their union.

"Aren't you coming?" she called, already astride his stallion.

He smiled and jogged over beside the steed, carefully laying a hand on the horse's neck. It whinnied and shook its head, but allowed Phoenix to grip the spines on its flank. With a tug and a leap he was straddling the animal's back. Her arms wrapped immediately around him.

The horse galloped back toward the field, taking to flight and banking around a stand of pines before rising into the mountains.

II

Utah

The night had come and gone, though with the cloud cover, the world took on a dreary grayness. Granted, she could see well enough to push the car up past what she assumed to be thirty-five and still have enough time to swerve before ramming into anything, but the road had become more difficult. She missed the straight shot through the desert where she could see every detail of the highway until it terminated against the foothills, which they now wound through. They'd barely started up the increasing slope into the mountains when the sun had arisen behind the claustrophobic ceiling of clouds, but it had been enough light for her to be able to come up over hills and around bends without having to slow to five miles an hour. There were more cars through this section of the highway, though the majority of them were off the road, crashed into embankments at the start of the graceful curves as though they'd been headed straight and just kept on going, one hitting another until there was a small snarl just around every curve.

The traffic through Wendover, just across the state line into Utah, had been the worst they'd encountered since having to circumnavigate the cities on the western border of Nevada, but was easily enough avoided via a detour down side streets through residential neighborhoods and a small business district. There were many bodies where they had fallen along the sidewalks and in the park, black piles of humanity waiting for their eventual reclamation by the earth. It was as they were finally merging back onto the highway that they saw the most unsettling thing of all. A young man dangled from a noose strapped to a streetlight, twirling gently on the breeze, the words "MORE MAN TEARS" painted onto the asphalt beneath him.

That had been enough to kill the conversation and force each of them to deal with their own inner demons. The thought in and of itself was not so unappealing, but the manner in which the boy had taken his own life was distressing, as though he'd gone out of his way to make sure that any survivors to pass through would see his body when he could have just climbed into his own bed and taken enough sleeping pills to pass into a dream. They'd been fortunate to find one another. Jill could only imagine the despair he must have felt. No one else left around him. No hope but a cryptic string of nonsense words. Had their roles been reversed, she could easily imagine tying a rope beneath the front awning of the sorority house and kicking away a stool.

All of the unavoidable death was indeed tragic, but to take one's own life after surviving the holocaust was more than she could bear. She couldn't close her eyes for fear that the image of that poor boy would be there, waiting for her just behind her closed lids, so she alternated energy drinks with Pepsis until she felt as though her bladder would explode.

"Would you mind pulling over?" she whispered so as not to wake April, who had fallen asleep against her shoulder.

Evelyn looked over at her with weary eyes, the sclera now more red than white. Her lip bled from where she'd been nipping it to keep herself awake, her own caffeine-induced jitters playing out on her white knuckles atop the wheel. She could only nod, her eyes scanning to either side of the road until she came to a reasonably wide shoulder on the other side of the highway between two large rock formations that looked like two children facing each other on their knees, resting their chins on hands clasped in prayer.

She didn't dare kill the engine for fear that it wouldn't start again. The lights never had returned, though April had been able to check in the fuse box without them having to stop and give up any more driving time. All of the fuses had been popped, which explained why about the only thing the car would do was drive. The gas gauge wasn't working, nor was the heat gauge. There was no radio. No nothing. She could only imagine how much trouble they would have been in if they'd been driving one of those newer cars with all of the computerized gizmos. They would still be sitting in the middle of nowhere waiting for either someone to come along and pick them up or for the desert heat to slowly bake them.

Gravel crunched under the tires, the suddenly uneven road rousing the boys in the back, who'd been huddled together for warmth.

"What're… we d-doing?" Darren asked after drawing back the window with a shivering hand. "Are we h-here?"

Now that the car was no longer moving, it felt as though the warmth was finally catching up with him. The absence of the wind of passage left only the blessedly warm still air to permeate through his goosebump-prickled skin.

"Bathroom break," Evelyn said, dropping the gear into park and throwing open the door. She hopped down onto the gravel. The ground felt somehow harder than it had before, or maybe it was just because she'd been sitting there in that truck for the last ten hours.

Jill scurried past Evelyn, who raised her arms to the sky and stretched out a yawn. She went just past the stone tower to the left and squatted, staring out toward the northeast as she felt the pressure stream away. The foothills leveled off to desert, interspersed with rock formations that rose from nothing but sand and small clusters thorny briars. Even farther, just before the amber sands met with a jagged horizon formed by distant mountains, it looked as though the sand became snow.

Her eyelids gently closed, and for one wonderful moment, with the warmth on her skin and the discomfort abating, she almost felt normal again. When she opened her eyes again, there were car tracks through the desert as though someone had driven straight between the twin stands of rock on the side of the road like some kind of gateway. It wasn't just a single set of tracks, but many sets atop one another. There were wide tire tracks and thin tire tracks like a bike would leave. How could she not have noticed them before? Surely no matter how badly she had to go to the bathroom she couldn't have been so preoccupied as to miss all of the tracks.

She followed them with her stare, the lines wending away to the spot where the sand changed to white. Beyond, a ridge of mountains stood like an iguana's back against the gray sky. There was a point where the mountains fell flat with the ground before rising again. Through that small opening, the faintest hint of deep blue water glimmered as though the sun had looked upon it just for her. A tower of smoke drifted from behind the ridge to the left, obscuring the lake momentarily, and then was gone.

As were the tracks.

The desert was as smooth as the wind had left it.

Jill closed her eyes and counted to three before opening them again. Still nothing but uninterrupted desert.

"We're here," she said, the corners of her lips curling into a smile. She stood and tugged her pants back up. She dashed back around the rock to where the others were milling about the car. Evelyn was rolling out a kink in her neck with a freshly opened can of pop in one hand and a Snickers in the other. April and Darren embraced on the other side of the car as she attempted to warm his chest against hers, his cheeks with her breath. Ray still sat in the bed of the truck staring off into space. "We're here!"

"We're where?" Evelyn asked, leaning up against the side of the truck so she could feel the idling engine.

"Here!" Jill called excitedly. She hurried around Evelyn and hopped into the truck, bounding across the seat until she saw what she was looking for on the floorboard. Grabbing it, she backed from the cab and ran over to the stone formation to the left and shook the can noisily. She pressed the button and sprayed a runny red stream onto the flattest surface in the largest letters she could manage: MORMON. Rushing to the right tower of rock, she spray-painted the word TEARS in big, bold letters. "This is the gateway," she said, looking from one face to the next as though it should have been obvious to them as well by now.

"Salt Lake City's still sixty miles to the east," Evelyn said.

"We're not going to Salt Lake City."

"I thought we were all agreed that we were."

"No. Don't you see? It was never Salt Lake City. We just assumed it was. We're supposed to go to the lake itself. Mormon tears. The Great Salt Lake! The others will find us there."

"How is anyone else supposed to know to go out there in the middle of nowhere?"

Jill gestured to the drying paint on the rocks.

"The sign, of course. And they'll follow the tracks."

"What tracks?"

Evelyn looked exasperated.

"Our tracks," Jill said, walking back around to the passenger side door and climbing in. She sat in the middle, staring straight ahead, waiting for them.

"Is she for real?" Evelyn asked April over the hood.

"All I know is we're still alive," April said.

Darren stepped out of her embrace, parting with a tender kiss on the lips. Their eyes lingered long after they drew apart, until Darren reluctantly climbed back up into the bed of the truck beside Ray, who still seemed oblivious even to his presence.

April clambered in next to Jill and slammed the door at nearly the exact same time as Evelyn, who jerked the gearshift into drive and sat silently a moment with her foot on the brake.

"Are you sure about this?" she finally asked, looking at Jill beside her, who simply nodded, all the while wearing a dreamy expression.

"'Cause if you're wrong, we're going to run out of gas out there…"

"I'm not wrong."

"Oh-kay," Evelyn sighed, taking her foot off the brake and allowing the truck to coast forward. "You'd better be right."

Jill smiled as Evelyn cranked the wheel to the left and guided them right between the two columns of stone.

"Head toward that small gap between the mountains," Jill said, pointing toward the distant horizon.

Dust was torn from their tread, swirling all around them. Jill turned and stared through the window between Darren and Ray, back in the direction of the highway. The cloud thrown from their wheels parted momentarily, allowing her to see the twin lines of their progress stretching back, all the way to the gateway.

She smiled.

Whether it was white sand or salt, Jill couldn't be sure. The last thing she wanted to do was to stop even long enough to find out. She'd know soon enough regardless as it stretched as far as she could see to either side, interrupted only by fallen sections of old split-rail fencing. It looked as though at one point this entire area had been part of the lake, evaporating to leave its salty memory.

What she had erroneously believed to be mountains were formations of rock in their semblance. There were only spotted patches of what looked like pines growing out of the fissures in the otherwise smooth stone. As they approached, she began to think of the water-molded stone monoliths as castles rather than hills, for they stood almost as if in guard of the lake beyond, which they could see in the distance through the gap that was growing closer with each passing mile. No, not castles… a fortress.

The cliffs to either side slanted steeply several hundred feet above them as though they were driving through a trench; gray stone that almost looked polished. With one long last look at the salt desert behind, they passed through the ridge and onto the long bank leading to the edge of a lake so large it appeared to be an ocean, the white earth like the most amazing tropical beach. Long-legged birds as red as flame waded through the shallows, stabbing long black bills down into the water to reappear with golden fish flopping around before tilting their heads all the way back and bobbing up and down as they choked their dinner into their gullets. Snow white birds glided in circles overhead, calling like gulls, though when they banked the sky blue feathers covering their backs stood out momentarily against the roiling gray sky.

While once the sky around them had been filled with lightning, it now seemed to be retreating from them, flashing at the furthest reaches of their vision in the black hearts of the thunderheads. The oppressive clouds allowed just a hint of sunlight through to glimmer from the white caps rolling in toward the shore.

"It's perfect," Jill whispered.

Evelyn nodded, unable to form words. She didn't know what she expected to find, but certainly nothing this beautiful.

"What are we supposed to do now?" she asked, driving the car across the remaining hundred yards of sand until they were nearly to the water.

"I wish I knew," Jill said, mesmerized by the inland sea, so blue it was almost black.

"This is where we're supposed to be, though?"

"I think so."

"I thought you were sure. Back there you said you were positive, and I can only imagine we're already running on fumes. There's no way we could even make it back to the highway, let alone to—"

"Shh," Jill whispered. "Back there."

She pointed back toward the rock wall that was now behind them. Through the eons as the oceans had retreated to the coasts, miraculously leaving this one saline testament to its mainland existence, and the lake had dwindled to its current size, the water had eroded the base of the cliffs. There were enormous mouths of shadow hiding the caverns behind.

"This is where we're supposed to be," she said.

Darren tapped fervently on the glass behind them.

"Look!" he shouted loud enough to be heard over the engine.

"What's going on?" Evelyn gasped, throwing the truck into park and leaping out her door.

"Check this out!" Darren cheered. "You won't believe it!"

He was standing on the bed of the truck, his right hand across his brow to shield his eyes, staring back in the direction they had come.

"What is it?" Evelyn asked, climbing up onto the left rear tire and straddling the sidewall. She similarly covered her eyes to block out the glare.

There were several flashes of light, reflections as though cast by small mirrors many miles away.

The others were already following their tracks.

III

UTAH

◉

Ebony water raced past beneath them as Phoenix's heart began to beat faster and faster. They were so close now and he knew it. He could feel it resonating within his bones as though they'd been struck by so many tuning forks, though until now it had been difficult to discern one sensation from the other as the butterflies panicked in his stomach, causing a warm feeling to settle over his body, despite the fact that his skin was poky with gooseflesh. The latter was entirely new to him, but he'd felt it when Missy first climbed astride the steed and wrapped her arms around him. It was as though together they formed a circuit that caused electricity to course through his body. He'd never felt so tortured and yet so alive.

He wanted to at once scream his delight up into the clouds with the wind riffling through his hair and turn and embrace her with the warmth of her breath mingling with his. Both were extremes he had never in his lifetime imagined. It was as though he had fallen asleep in that basement and had awoken in this glorious dream. He could barely remember anything before the prior morning as it felt like he'd lived an entire lifetime since.

The horses had needed several breaks during the night to lap from a convenient source of water and graze from the banks. Each time the stallion had begun to drop from the sky, he felt his heart tearing in half, for he was certain that once they were on the ground that Missy would want to change the riding arrangements so that she could be with her brother, but she never so much as asked, instead climbing right up behind him each and every time that their rides were suitably sated and ready again for flight. He loved the pressure of her arms across his abdomen and her chest against his back, the tickle of her breath against the side of his neck, against his ear when she spoke.

Rugged mounds of stone arose from the water randomly like icebergs in the arctic, though rounded and capped with a crust of salt that reminded Missy of the mountain peaks they had breezed through during the night. Though they had flattened themselves against the stallion's back and huddled together for warmth, the darkness had brought a wicked chill that they all feared might be their undoing before reaching their destination. One of the rest stops had brought them to a cabin, where while the horses were recuperating, they had pillaged the shack for more clothing. Even stuffing themselves into layer after layer of sweatshirts and pants, light jackets and awkwardly-sized winter jackets had barely taken the sting from the icy wind, though now that they had finally descended in altitude and were feverishly-anticipated moments from their end goal, they were starting to sweat beneath all of the layers. They would need them in the months to come, they were certain, so tossing them off into the lake wasn't an option any more than standing up on the steed's back to take them off. None of them wanted to stop now. It had been such a remarkably long journey that the sooner they reached the payoff the better. Granted, they had no idea what to expect when they arrived, but there had to be something grand awaiting them. There just had to be.

Just when Phoenix was certain that the lake extended infinitely ahead, Missy leaned against his shoulder and spoke directly into his ear.

"There!"

Phoenix's eyes scanned the horizon. Short rocky ridges lined the end of the world from this vantage, though several objects shimmered in front of them like the most beautiful jewels. His breath stalled in his chest and his heart fluttered. She was right. He could feel that it was their destination as clearly as he had felt the opposite sensation when they had been near Denver.

"Adam!" he whooped back over his shoulder, waving his arm. As soon as he was sure that he had the doctor's attention, he pointed toward the edge of the lake.

Adam perked up behind the horse's bobbing head and Mare leaned around to his right to try to get a better look.

Phoenix had to turn around and look again; he couldn't bear for such a glorious vision to be out of his sight another instant. As they closed at a maddeningly slow speed, details began to come into focus. The beach was every bit as white as it had been in his dreams, the water crashing against it just as dark. Thick black smoke poured out of the mouth of the mountain. There was an old pickup parked at the edge of the sand, the lake lapping at its front tires. A good half-dozen bicycles lie on their sides in the sand, their tracks trailing them back to the eternal skyline.

Several animals wearing collars, roughly the size of dogs, tussled out in the open, their blue eyes shining like amethyst, long downy fur reflecting what little sunlight permeated the clouds.

The stallion started its descent, legs churning, and Phoenix felt his stomach dropping with it, his heart accelerating so quickly he feared his chest might be no longer able to contain it. Several shadows appeared in front of the cave's mouth against flames that licked at the roof, as inviting as anything he'd seen in his life. One of the shadows hailed them with a waving arm as the horse stamped into the sand, kicking up clouds of salt.

Phoenix leapt from the equine before it even stopped moving, using the wing to lunge down into the sand. He tumbled to his knees but quickly found his feet and raced up to the figures as they approached.

Arms extended to his sides, he tried to hug them all at once.

"Welcome home," a pretty girl with short blonde hair said. "We've been expecting you."

CHAPTER 11

I

DENVER,
COLORADO

Death stood atop what had once been a thirty-story building made of glass. The heat generated by the explosion had fused it into a construct that rose to the heavens like a black crystal. Lightning flashed circles around his head, the clouds boiling. His cloak of flesh snapped out in front of him on the gale, crackling with suffering as he surveyed all that lie below. The ground encircling the tower was black and crawling as though covered by ants. His forces were swarming. Soon they would all be drawn here to create the most fearsome army to ever set foot on the planet, and when it was complete, they would march through the mountains and lay siege to what remained of the formerly dominant species. Man's time had now come and gone. As they had turned their backs on Him, now so had He turned away from them.

The world needed to be cleansed of this breed cast in His image, yet reflecting the darkness of His soul that He had held eternally at bay. They could have been gods, but they chose instead to be murderers.

The flaps of his cloak fell to either side as he reached his clawed hands from within, holding out the final clay disk over the world trembling hundreds of feet beneath. With a flick of his wrists, he snapped it in two, the remaining fragments falling around his feet.

A loud hiss like a stadium full of cheering spectators assaulted him from beneath, every yellow eye trained upon him at the top of the spire, the ground now looking as though covered in smoldering embers.

He raised his arms out to his sides and held them there. The hissing built to a palpable fevered pitch, the noise escalating until it sounded like an avalanche. He dropped his arms to his sides. Sparks turned to towers of flame in a ring about the buildings. The flames climbed several stories, and black smoke gushed into the sky.

The seventh seal had been broken.

Death turned away from his minions. Pestilence and Famine parted to allow him passage to the rooftop doorway. War stood in his path, towering over the much smaller man and exuding an aura of powder eclipsed only by that surrounding Death.

Their eyes locked.

With a single nod, Death took a step toward War, who moved out of his way, allowing his master to slither into the darkness and down to the throne chambers beneath.

He strode over to the edge of the building without even looking at his weaker siblings and pulled back the cowl shielding his head. Bright red eyes flared through those ragged slashes in his faceplate.

All sound fell silent beneath him, save for the wind screaming from the face of the monolithic structure, though even such a force could not knock him from his feet as his studied the armada he would soon lead.

The last of the clay pieces were ground to dust beneath his heels.

Let heaven and hell alike quake beneath their advance.

The winter would soon be upon them.

TURN THE PAGE FOR AN EXCLUSIVE
EXTRACT FROM

GOD'S END

BLIZZARD OF SOULS

CHAPTER 1

I

MORMON TEARS

Phoenix stood on the white sand, staring out across the Great Salt Lake, Mormon tears, as the sun rose somewhere behind the black clouds. Though it appeared as only a muted stain of gray against the distant horizon, he could feel its radiating warmth on his face. Closing his eyes, he reveled in the sensation, its gentle caress on the soft skin of his eyelids, chasing away the bitter cold that sliced into him like hooks of ice. He sighed and the wind stole the cloud of exhaust from his lips, carrying it back over his shoulder. Deep inside he could feel a sense of contentment, of peace, for the first time in his entire life. The theater of the sky stretched infinitely in all directions, though a lone spotlight of sunshine permeated the ceaseless nuclear stormheads to shine upon him on his stage of sand, the foamy ivory brine lapping at his chafed red toes. He knew he needed to enjoy moments like these, for they would be fleeting. The dark power was building beyond where the sky met with the seemingly eternal black water and the spotted islands of smooth stone rising from it. Even from such a great distance, he could feel the enemy's swelling ranks gathering their awesome strength for the battle to come. His adversary's evil power emanated across the hundreds of miles separating them like an earthquake, issuing aftershocks of impending bloodshed that caused the earth itself to shiver.

In his mind, the ebony waters continued rolling toward the shore, the waves bringing with them a thickening slush of ice. Lightning crashed from roiling thunderclouds, an ultraviolet blue against their black hearts, turning the waves crashing into the beach to a deep crimson.

They were coming.

The time had come to begin preparations.

"It's beautiful, isn't it?" Missy said from behind him, causing him to open his eyes.

Phoenix turned to face her, a smile forming on his lips as it always did when he saw her. After living so long in the darkness, unable to see her face even in his mind, he tried to commit every expression to memory, the sound of her voice more comforting even than the beat of his own heart.

"Yeah," Phoenix whispered, though he'd already forgotten all about the lake behind him.

Missy blushed, but didn't appear self-conscious in the least. She had a quiet confidence about her that belied a hidden strength she had only begun to tap into. He worried that she didn't see him as he saw her, but it didn't matter. The only thing that was truly important was being close to her.

She walked past him to the edge of the water and imagined the sunrise.

"We aren't safe here, are we?" she asked without turning to face him. She didn't have to try to read his expression as she knew that he would tell her the truth.

"We're safer here than anywhere else."

"That wasn't my question."

"No," he whispered. "They will find us here."

"What are we supposed to do then? Where can we possibly go?"

"They'll find us wherever we go. This is where we are supposed to be. This is where we will make our stand."

"And will we win?"

Phoenix remained silent.

"That's what I thought," she said, turning back to him with a wan smile.

"I didn't say we wouldn't."

"You didn't say anything at all."

"The truth is that I just don't know."

"How much time do we have?"

"I'm not sure. All I know is that the time is at hand to ready ourselves for war."

"Against whom? Those black lizard men?"

"Against God," he whispered.

A shiver crept up her spine, erupting as goosebumps from the backs of her arms.

"Come on," she said, forging a weak grin and trying to force the implications of his words from her mind. "The others are making breakfast. I'm sure we could both use something to eat."

Phoenix matched her smile and turned his back to the inland sea. More people had arrived during the night, their vehicles parked at odd angles all across the beach, the sounds of life only now beginning to filter out of the system of caves in the stone hillside. There was an old pickup with a camper shell in the bed off to the left, shades drawn tightly over the windows. A ring of motorized dirt bikes surrounded a canvas tent, the tarp covering it flapping on the breeze. Mountain bikes and ten-speeds leaned against the rock fortress, which they had only begun to explore. There were a half dozen cars parked off to the side as a windbreak, all of them older models from a dirty white Ford truck with California plates to an ancient Buick now more rust than metal. Nothing with integrated computer components survived the blackout trailing on the heels of the atomic wind. Phoenix had heard someone speculate in the darkness about an electromagnetic pulse created by the nuclear detonations, but that meant nothing to him.

The mutated equines that he and his friends had ridden in upon appeared as comfortable in the water as they did in the air, their crested seahorse heads rising from the lake behind him as they splashed toward the shore from wherever they had gone during the night, summoned by the smell following the thick black smoke out of the mouth of the widest cave. Phoenix didn't recognize the scent, but his mouth was already beginning to water.

"What is that?" he asked, his voice dripping with wonder.

"Baked beans," she said with a chuckle.

"They smell wonderful."

"Are you telling me you've never had baked beans?"

He grinned, his eyes alight. There was something charming about his naïveté.

Faces he only vaguely recognized from during the night began to emerge from where they'd bedded down at a comfortable distance from one another, drawn by the intoxicating scent. Soon they would have to reach out to one another or they would be butchered like so many sheep.

They needed to steel themselves against the coming winter.

ABOUT THE
AUTHOR

Michael McBride lives with his wife and four children in the shadow of the Rocky Mountains, where he shoots people for money. He thanks you for joining him on this journey through the apocalypse and invites you to return to "More Man Tears" in God's End: The Blizzard of Souls. To explore the author's other novels and short fiction or to contact him directly, please visit

www.mcbridehorror.com.

SPECIAL THANKS

Anna Torborg, Emma Barnes, and Snowbooks; Shane Staley; Dennis Duncan; Greg Gifune; Leigh Haig; Brian Keene; Troy Knutson; Don Koish; David Marty; Dallas Mayr; Elizabeth and Tom Monteleone, and the BBC grunts; Matt Schwartz; Tom Tessier; and my wife and family.